MW00605472

OIL
CAPITAL

The History of American Oil,
Wildcatters, Independents
and Their Bankers

BERNARD F. CLARK, JR.

Library of Congress Control Number:
2016903602

ISBN: 978-0-692-70943-6

This book is dedicated to my father, Bernard F. Clark, who spent his career wrestling with the independent producer's constant demand for capital as Executive Vice President and Chief Financial Officer of Mitchell Energy & Development Corp. from 1956 until 2001.

Style is adapted, primarily from
The Associated Press Stylebook and Briefing on Media Law
and *The Chicago Manual of Style*.

CONTENTS

INTRODUCTION

"The oil and gas business is always out of money.
It just inhales capital."
Joe Bridges

The history of oilmen and the energy bankers who loan them capital is inextricably bound together. Energy bankers have reacted, adjusted and evolved alongside the same business cycles, regulatory changes and commodity-price gyrations that have challenged the generations of oilmen they banked. In many respects, however, it is remarkable how little has changed during the past 100 years in the fundamentals of lending against collateral that has been hidden underground for millions of years. Nor has there been much change in the relationship between the early wildcatters willing to risk their—and their banker's—last dime and the bankers who cautiously evaluate the oilmen and their collateral.

While the fundamentals have remained unchanged, bankers' analyses, tools and documentation of oil and gas lending have evolved in step with wildcatters' tools for finding, drilling and producing the very oil and gas that serve as the bankers' collateral and wildcatters' salvation.

The early connection between banks and independent explorers—known as wildcatters—is, perhaps, closer than is commonly known. In the oil industry, "wildcat" refers to a well drilled in an area with little or no production. A wildcatter is the optimistic, daring or just plain desperate enough individual who drills these wells. But historical references suggest the earliest use of the term *wildcat* was to describe less-reputable banks that, before 1863, were set up in out-of-the-way locations—thought of as haunts of wildcats—to restrict the number of holders who could, only by presenting them in person, redeem these banks' notes.[1]

A Detroit company wrote to one of its customers in 1838, according to a letter published by a Vermont newspaper, "We have had nearly *sixty new Banks* start into operation within about the last three months. They are called the 'Wild Cat Banks' — the notes they issue are called "Wild Cat Money" — our state is full of it; if you take Five dollars to-day, perhaps to-morrow, four of the five may be good for nothing — a dollar in specie is almost as rare as a swallow in mid-winter."[2]

More than 40 years later, "wildcat" was used to describe oil and gas prospectors. "When an operator goes into an undeveloped field, and puts down a test well, he naturally desires to have the profit of his risk," New York's *The Sun* reported in 1883. "It costs him something like $6,000 to put down that wildcat well, for which in most cases, he gets no return, for the majority of wildcat wells produce nothing."[3]

The oft-colorful history of oil and gas exploration and production has been widely documented in books, articles and films in which wildcatters and oilmen have been either lionized or criticized but always "super-sized." The less romanticized history is not as well known. But, for those involved in the industry, many lessons can be learned—and relearned—from a review of the historical relationships of wildcatters and bankers and the evolution of the loan documentation that has bound these parties.

Very few oilmen started with sufficient wealth to personally finance their operations. Along with manpower, rigs and drill pipe, capital has always been a critical tool in the exploration for and development of oil and gas. From the earliest days of the industry, producers have required more start-up capital for acquisition, drilling and development of oil fields than can be generated out of cash flow from ex-

---

[1] Michael Quinion, "Wild Strike," *World Wide Words, Investigating the English Language Across the Globe*, accessed October 18, 2014, (quoting the *Rutland Herald*, March 20, 1838).
[2] *Rutland Herald*, March 20, 1838, quoted in Quinion, "Wild Strike."
[3] Quinion, "Wild Strike."

isting production. The accomplishments of oil companies were and are as dependent upon access to capital as access to the hydrocarbons they seek to exploit.

An independent oilman, Joe Bridges grew up in West Texas' Permian Basin. A University of Texas engineering graduate, Bridges has worked in oil and gas fields as an energy banker at First City in Houston, as a chief financial officer for a public oil and gas company and as the founder of his own oil and gas companies. He said in a 2012 interview of the role that access to capital has played and continues to play in the American industry, "The oil and gas business is always out of money. It just inhales capital."[4]

This book tells the story of this enduring relationship in the context of the evolution of the two industries. Because changes in lending against oil and gas property have closely followed the milestones of the oil and gas industry, this evolution is best discussed chronologically in the context of U.S. and global events in the industry.

---

[4] Joe Bridges (President, Bridges Family Petroleum, Inc.), interview by the author, October 2, 2012.

CHAPTER 1

Private Ownership—
The Foundation of the
U.S. Oil and Gas Industry

"Whosoever the soil belongs, he owns also the sky and to the depths."
Accursius

To fully appreciate the relationship between the oil and gas industry and its bankers, one must step back and better understand the American history of oil and gas and its legal foundations. It is a history that dates back to the 16th century. Compared with almost every other oil-producing country in the world, ownership of oil and gas in the U.S. by private parties, often landowners, is an anomaly. And, it is no coincidence that nowhere else is oil and gas technology and infrastructure better developed than in the U.S.

The synergy of a capitalist economy and the private ownership of minerals propelled the U.S. to become the world's leader in exploration and exploitation of oil and gas and ushered in the Hydrocarbon Age: the birth of combustion engines that transformed the ground- and marine-transportation industry, made air travel possible, increased industrial productivity and continues to make goods and services increasingly affordable. "The Allied cause had floated to victory upon a wave of oil," Britain's Lord Earl Curzon declared, days after the end of World War I.[5] Two decades later, the U.S. provided the fuel again that, literally, resulted in the Allied Powers' victory in World War II.

Much of the oil supporting the Allies' efforts during the First World War came from newly discovered oil fields in U.S. boomtowns on the Gulf Coast and in Texas, Oklahoma and California.[6] After the war, oil and gas companies continued to improve their operations and tools, explored offshore California and in the Gulf of Mexico, and went abroad to discover and develop oil resources in Southeast Asia, the Middle East, West Africa and South America.

U.S. universities and colleges taught not only Americans to become petroleum engineers and geologists; they also educated citizens of foreign countries who, with American know-how and technology, developed their countries' reserves. Yet, after decades of exploration and development abroad, no country enjoys the U.S.' level of development, infrastructure, technology and innovation. And, certainly, no country can claim as many successful, independent oil and gas companies.

While there are many reasons for the American petroleum industry's success, most essential has been its entrepreneurial spirit, combined with the ability to negotiate directly with private mineral owners to explore for and produce oil and gas resources.[7] Much of the devel-

---

[5] Daniel Yergin, *The Prize: The Epic Quest for Oil, Money & Power* (Simon & Schuster, January 15, 1991), 167.

[6] U.S. production accounted for 67% of world production in 1917, with a quarter of production exported to foreign markets, the bulk of which was headed for the European war effort. The U.S. satisfied 80% of the Allies' wartime petroleum requirements. Yergin, *The Prize*, 162. A British Admiralty forecast for petroleum supplies estimated the Allies' needs as of December 31, 1918, in case the war lasted that long: "Their requirements were set down to be 7,790,000 tons. The expected sources were Persia, 750,000 tons; Mexico, 600,000 tons; Trinidad, 180,000 tons; creosote, 180,000 tons; shale, 100,000 tons; and Borneo, 75,000. The Unites States was allocated 5,905,000 tons." Isaac F. Marcosson, *Black Golconda, Romance of Petroleum* (Harper & Brothers, 1924), 288.

[7] "Why do Asian and European customers pay so much for energy in the first place? For that matter, why [does Mexico] … ? To a large extent, it is because their domestic industries and home governments have not fostered robust energy sector competition squeezing out both indigenous and foreign direct investment in energy supply, infrastructure and services. Bottom line, this could be the most important lesson the U.S. experience has to offer the world at large." Michelle Michot Foss et al., "Sharp Cycles Ahead," *Oil and Gas Investor*, September 1, 2013.

opment of the U.S.' natural resources is a direct result of the country's legal regime, which recognizes the right to private ownership of minerals in the ground. Other than the U.S., private ownership of minerals is recognized today only in a small percentage of land in Canada's provinces and on the former British Crown islands of Trinidad and Tobago.[8, 9]

In most of the world, the sovereign or government owns the minerals in the ground, including petroleum. In many of these countries, the national oil company controls extraction of the resources as well, resulting in little to no outside participation in their development. In 2007, national oil companies controlled more than 80% of the world's reserves.[10] Yet, during the past eight years, U.S. daily production has increased more than 40%, while non-U.S. production has grown by only 3.2%.[11] The main reason for this disparity has been the U.S. "shale revolution," brought about by technological advancements in drilling, completion and reservoir understanding. Those advances

---

[8] Terence Daintith, a Fellow at University of London's Institute of Advances Legal Studies, provides an extensive review of the private vs. public ownership of natural resources among the world's oil-producing countries in his book, *Finders Keepers? How the Law of Capture Shaped the World Oil Industry* (Routledge, August 31, 2010). Much of the discussion in this chapter on mineral ownership is taken from Daintith's book.

[9] Lou-Ann Baptiste and Gerald Lewis, *Mineral Rights in Trinidad and Tobago: Issues, Challenges and Recommendations*, Land Conference 2011 Conference Theme, The University of The West Indies at St. Augustine, Trinidad and Tobago (2011).

[10] As Robert Pirog explained: "Every firm in the top ten reserve holders, with the exception of Lukoil, in both 2006 and 2000 was state owned. Among the major international oil companies, ExxonMobil is ranked fourteenth, BP seventeenth, Chevron nineteenth, ConocoPhillips, twenty-third, and Shell is ranked twenty-fifth in 2006. These five firms hold only 3.8% of world liquid reserves, and their major holdings are in the United States and Canada ... In 2006, seven of the top ten producing companies were state owned, including the five largest producers. Although the three largest international oil companies were among the top ten producers, and two of them BP and ExxonMobil, even managed to increase their total output, their production was from relatively small reserve bases, shortening the time they can remain in the market as producer without major new discoveries." Robert Pirog, *The Role of National Oil Companies in the International Oil Market*, CRS Report for Congress (August 21, 2007) (citing Energy Intelligence Research, *The Energy Intelligence Top 100: Ranking the World's Oil Companies* (2007 and 2001 editions), 3 and 5)).

[11] U.S. production 2007, 8,409 mbbl/d and 2014, 14,021 mbbl/d. Non-US World Production 2007, 76,721 mbbl/d and 2014, 79,180 mbbl/d. U.S. Energy Information Administration, Independent Statistics & Analysis. "International Energy Statistics (Petroleum)." Accessed March 16, 2016.

have been homegrown by the incentive for private gain, supported by the economic and legal environment in the U.S.[12]

National oil companies can't compete; structurally, they are not designed to compete. "Because of their close ties to the national government, in many cases their objectives might include wealth redistribution, jobs creation, general economic development, economic and energy security, and vertical integration," Robert Pirog, a specialist in energy economics and policy with the Congressional Research Service, reported in 2007.

"Many of these companies have been found to be inefficient, with relatively low investment rates. They tend to exploit oil reserves for short-term gain, possibly damaging oil fields, reducing the longer-term production potential. Some also have limited access to international capital markets because of poor business practices and a lack of transparency in their business deals," he added.[13]

U.S. oil and gas exploration has been a story of private enterprise from its beginning. Standard Oil Co. was the country's first integrated oil company. Today, the super-majors, such as Exxon Mobil Corp., Chevron Corp. and others, are well known in the U.S. and abroad. But the history of U.S. oil discoveries has been the story of the independent and often-unheralded wildcatter, beginning with the country's first oil well.

"Since the earliest days of the industry, independents have done most of America's wildcatting and have found vast amounts of domestic petroleum," Roger M. Olien and Diana Davids Hinton wrote in *Wildcatters: Texas Independent Oilmen*. "Of particular importance to the domestic petroleum industry, for example, are the amounts and sources of capital independents have used to carry out their specific industry functions."[14]

---

[12] "Reversing the Trend," *The Wall Street Journal*, May 19, 2014.
[13] Pirog, *The Role of National Oil Companies.*
[14] Roger M. Olien and Diana Davids Hinton, *Wildcatters: Texas Independent Oilmen* (Texas A&M University Press, May 24, 2007), 3. (Original, 1984 edition identifies Hinton as Diana Davids Olien.)

Chapter 1: Private Ownership

The ratio of independents to major oil companies was reported in the 1940s and, again, in the early 1980s as 1,000 to 1. In the 1940s, there were more than 20,000 independents versus 20 majors. In 1982, *The Dallas Morning News* reported that there were more than 18,000 independents and 20 majors and super-independents.[15] In 2015, the Independent Petroleum Association of America estimated there were between 6,000 and 8,000 oil and gas producers and, among them, fewer than a dozen majors.[16]

Although the first commercial wells were developed in Pennsylvania, beginning in Titusville in 1859, most of the history of the American wildcatters and of the growth of lending to finance them has occurred in Texas and Oklahoma and, to a lesser extent, California. Early investment in Appalachian oil and gas fields in Pennsylvania, West Virginia and Tennessee and in fields in Ohio and Indiana in the Civil War era was almost exclusively by private parties, such as by Carnegie, Mellon and Pew and other East Coast financiers.

The cost to drill a well in the 1860s was reportedly between $5,000 and $15,000.[17] Because the risk of not finding a market for the oil, if found, was almost as great as the risk of drilling a dry hole, early wildcatters quickly learned to sell down some of their risk to willing investors. The "oil capitalists"—those wealthy enough to invest in this new industry—invested individually at first, but they soon diversified their risk by sharing it with others via informal associations. These investors later began to incorporate to be able to make public calls for capital, which required the investors to seek special charters from states due to the lack of comprehensive laws on incorporation.[18]

---

[15] U.S. Senate, Seventy-Ninth Congress, Second Session, *Hearings before a Special Committee Investigating Petroleum Resources* (Washington D.C.; U.S. Government Printing Office, 1946), 27, 53; Jim Landers, "Economy Drains Small Texas Oil Firms," *Dallas Morning News*, March 31, 1982, quoted in Olien and Hinton, *Wildcatters*, 5.

[16] Frederick Lawrence (Independent Petroleum Association of America), interview by the author, August 27, 2015.

[17] Daintith, *Finders Keepers*, 59-60.

[18] Daintith, *Finders Keepers*, 60-61: "The next step was for such groups to incorporate as companies, thus enabling them to make public calls for capital. This required the intervention of the legislature in each case, as Pennsylvania did not acquire a truly comprehensive incorporation law until 1874; earlier laws covered such areas as manufacturing (1840),

Another method of quickly raising capital was the subdivision of the original base lease into discrete, smaller tracts. Once a successful well was drilled, the wildcatter could often make more money by subdividing the lease, selling a percentage to subsequent investors and drillers, rather than continuing to drill the balance of the tract with his own money.

"Subleasing became the industry norm in a remarkably short space of time," Terence Daintith, a British law professor, wrote in *Finders Keepers*. "Subleasing was also a money machine. ... Far more money could be made this way than by actual production. While some of the earliest subdivisions of leaseholds retained quite large lots, subleases of an acre, a half-acre and even less quickly became the norm in promising territory."

Subleases, he added, "provided the vehicles for a massive flow of capital into the industry from people of speculative spirit who had the means to operate, or to invest, only on a small scale. The presence of this vigorous class of small investors was a major reason why development in the United States so far outstripped that in the European oil fields of Romania and Galicia, where this class of persons hardly existed and the technological advance necessary for effective development had to be funded by foreign capital."[19]

In the U.S., by the turn of the 19th century, the fields of Appalachia were being eclipsed by discoveries elsewhere, principally in Texas, Oklahoma and California. This is where oil banking was born and where it matured. As the industry's exploration and production technology evolved, local laws and regulations evolved, making it easier to assess the financial risks of underwriting this new industry. The energy banker was born in the boomtowns of Tulsa, Oklahoma City, Fort Worth, Dallas, Houston and Midland, near where gushers were being discovered by the bankers' capital-starved oilmen.

---

and coal and metal mining (1853) but did not extend to the oil business. Special charters were accordingly sought by oil promoters and were granted in large numbers. The same was true of West Virginia, where the legislature incorporated 174 oil companies between 1863 and 1867."

[19] Daintith, *Finders Keepers*, 62-64.

Chapter 1: Private Ownership

While it took a particular mindset to be willing to throw the dice and explore in the early days of the industry, the costs of entry were low compared with the cost today. In Texas, political sentiment led to protection of the homegrown, independent oilmen and intentionally thwarted the efforts of large, integrated oil companies, which had developed back East.

This mindset that incubated a nascent and successful industry was the same political climate that spawned the growth of local, independent bankers to the exclusion of national banks. But, as will be seen, this home-spun "anti-Eastern-establishment," agrarian sentiment ultimately prevented Texas bankers from being able to compete with the larger, East Coast banks and, by the 1980s, contributed to the downfall of the Texas-grown energy bank.

But before discussing the turmoil of the 1980s, it is necessary to understand how the fundamental differences unique to U.S. oil and gas law affected the industry's growth and how U.S. regulation of production created the environment that benefited both the oilman and his banker—a profitable relationship that continues to this day.

History of Mineral Ownership

Throughout the history of civilization, the ownership of minerals, including petroleum, has been erratic. In spite of the patchwork provenance of lands that came to form the U.S., the private landowner has owned both the surface and all minerals beneath his land in every state in the union. How did the U.S. end up with this unique law, particularly since U.S. law is derived from the laws and customs of different sovereigns that once owned the land that is now the U.S.?

Is this difference the catalyst that propelled the U.S. to be the inventor, innovator and leader of the industry? And is this distinction also what nurtured the development of readily available capital that is so critical to the industry?

Mining and control of mineral production has been important to civilized nations since the Iron Age. Very little is known of the business of mining prior to the Greeks. A mining industry flourished in ancient Greece from 700 B.C. to 200 B.C. where minerals were considered to be the property of the state, regardless of who owned the overlying surface. Mining rights were granted to private individuals for periods of between three and 10 years. A royalty of 1/24th of the net profits was due the state; the surface owner received nothing.[20]

The Greek city states had a sophisticated mining administration—for the times. "A director of the mines considered applications from individuals seeking mining rights and determined where such individuals might prospect for ore," Northcutt Ely and Robert F. Pietrowski reported in a 1975 paper to the International Bar Association. "Matters such as location with reference to the direction and extent of veins and the proper distance between different claims in the same area were governed by regulations."[21]

Scholarly research into Roman law concerning mineral ownership is unclear, but it appears that the private owner of land (*res in patrimonium*) also owned any minerals located on and under the land.[22] However, because most of the Roman Republic—and, later, the Roman Empire—was acquired through conquest, what the State acquired, the State owned, including a great majority of mines and known mineral deposits. "Due to [Rome's] extensive state ownership of mines, the underlying theory became accepted that the State held the primary control over all mineral resources," Ely and Pietrowski reported.[23]

As the administration of Roman law melted away, Europe was governed by hundreds of feudal lords who generally claimed ownership of the minerals within their respective areas of authority. Warfare

---

[20] Northcutt Ely and Robert F. Pietrowski, Jr., "Changing Concepts in the World's Mineral Development Laws," (paper presented at the IBA Seminar on World Energy Laws Held in Stavanger Norway, May 1975 London: International Bar Association), 7.

[21] Ely and Pietrowski, "Changing Concepts," 10-11.

[22] Daintith, *Finders Keepers*, 33. Under Roman law, property that was not owned by any one individual (*res extra patrimonium*) was either owned by the state (such as roads, ports, public buildings (*res publicae*)), or owned in common (such as the air, flowing waters, the sea (*res communes*)) or was the property of no one (enemy property, wild animals (*res nullius*)).

[23] Ely and Pietrowski, "Changing Concepts," 7.

among these feudal lords was common and was often caused by disputes over mines.[24]

The Age of Discovery following the Middle Ages became possible only as control in Europe became concentrated among a handful of powerful rulers. These sovereigns were rich enough to be able to finance exploration of the New World in hopes of finding great mineral wealth. The roots of American mineral ownership are derived primarily from two of the country's original colonialists—England and Spain.

Spain's imprint on mineral ownership in its territories is apparent in the oil-producing states of Texas, California and New Mexico, in particular.[25] The 13 English colonies and the territory subsequently acquired by the U.S. generally adopted English law regarding ownership of land and minerals. Although both England and Spain were monarchies carved out of territories once under Roman control and Roman law, the laws of England and Spain developed differing concepts as to the ownership of minerals and the severability of mineral ownership from the surface owner.

Another colonialist, France, laid claim to the land that was the Louisiana Territory and acquired by the Jefferson administration in 1803. However, except for the state of Louisiana, French civil law was not adopted by the 15 states that were carved from the Louisiana Purchase.

Mineral Laws of England

In England, a grant of land by the Crown reserved to the monarchy title only to any gold, silver and other precious metals.[26] What was not

---

[24] *Moore v. Smaw*, 17 Cal. 199, 222 (Cal. 1861): "Upon the breaking up of the Roman Empire, the Princes and States which declared themselves independent, appropriated to themselves those tracts of ground in which nature has dispensed her most valuable products with more than ordinary liberality...."

[25] The influence of Spain's colonization of the New World can also be seen in the law of community property over the marital estate that is a result of the Spanish heritage over lands that became the states of Arizona, California, Idaho, Nevada, New Mexico, Texas and Washington as well as Louisiana with its civil-law origins.

[26] *Queen v. The Earl of Northumberland*, 1 Plowden 310, 336-7, 75 Eng. Rep. 472, 510-11 (1567).

reserved by the Crown was the property of the landowner. As such, the owner of the soil was also presumed to be the owner of minerals as per English common law as adopted from the Latin maxim *cujus est solum, ejus est usque ad coelum et ad inferos*—i.e., to whosoever the soil belongs, he owns also the sky and to the depths.

The maxim is attributed to Accursius, a 13th-century Roman law scholar from Bologna, but it is not found in classical Roman law. It may have been brought to England with Edward I on his return from the Crusades. This concept was cited by English Judge Lord Edward Coke in 1587[27] and appears later in William Blackstone's *Commentaries on the Laws of England*: "... [T]he word 'land' includes not only the face of the earth, but every thing under it, or over it."[28]

However, even in England, the laws were not uniformly applied. Two regions of England—Cornwall and Devonshire, where tin and lead had been mined by the Celts for hundreds of years predating the Roman invasions of the Isles—were granted special exemption from the law regarding property rights. The monarchy recognized separate ownership of the ancient tin mines and the local law was controlled and enforced by chartered tin-mining companies called "stannaries" from the Latin word for tin, *stannum.*

The first royal charter was formally granted in 1201 by John I, 14 years before he signed the Magna Carta, which confirmed the "ancient right" of tin-miners to the free right of entry on unoccupied lands provided payment of a royalty to the Crown equal to 1/8th or 1/9th

---

[27] *Bury v. Pope*, 1 Cro. Eliz. 118, 78 Eng. Rep. 375 (Ex. 1586).

[28] "Land hath also, in its legal signification, an indefinite extent, upwards as well as downwards. *Cujus est solum, ejus est usque ad coelum*, is the maxim of the law, upwards; therefore no man may erect any building, or the like, to overhang another's land: and, downwards, whatever is in a direct line between the surface of any land, and the center of the earth, belongs to the owner of the surface; as is every day's experience in the mining countries. So that the word "land" includes not only the face of the earth, but every thing under it, or over it. And therefore if a man grants all his lands, he grants thereby all his mines of metal and other fossils, his woods, his waters, and his houses, as well as his fields and meadows." William Blackstone, *Commentaries on the Laws of England*, vol. 2 (Oxford 1766), 18.

of the tin produced.[29] Stannary laws formalized customs exclusive to the Celts of Cornwall dating to pre-Roman times where, essentially, the miners were self-governed and self-regulated through their own "Stannary Parliament" and "Stannary Courts."

The Stannary laws were subsequently incorporated into the English legal system and their separate courts continued to be recognized until the end of the 19th century. The influence of the self-governing customs and practices of Cornwall's ancient tin-miners would be embodied hundreds of years later in the early mineral-ownership laws created by mining communities in the 1840s' California Gold Rush.

Prior to World War I, some private ownership of minerals was permitted in a few other regions in the world, such as Russia (Baku fields), Romania and Galicia, which is land that is presently along the Polish-Ukrainian border. But, except for a very few fields prior to the turn of the century, the growth of a local oil industry outside of the U.S. was sporadic. Not only did American landowners enjoy private mineral ownership, they also enjoyed the benefits and security of an established body of laws that protected their rights to private ownership.

In contrast to the U.S. farmer, the Galician peasant was never able to enjoy the benefits of a successful oil and gas industry. Galacia was part of the Austro-Hungarian Empire. Following emancipation in 1848, the peasant farmer was granted a small plot of land and ownership of any minerals therein. But, unlike ownership of farmland in the U.S., peasant-owned land was not normally included in public land-title registers, which made a secure title all but impossible to obtain and gave rise to much litigation.

As a consequence, it wasn't possible to attract the magnitude of capital necessary to finance a transition from the primitive bucket-and-spade methods of mining to the mechanized techniques of oil extraction that were developing in the U.S. Daintith wrote, "Local and foreign capitalists found it impossible to assemble the landholdings

---

[29] George R. Lewis, *The stannaries: a Study of the Medieval Tin Miners of Cornwall and Devon* (D. Bradford Barton Ltd. 1965, reprint of 1908 publication), 239-40.

they needed to justify substantial investments enjoying reasonable protection against risks of drainage of the oil they had found by innumerable small-scale operations on their perimeters."[30]

By the end of World War I, the strategic and economic potential of oil was recognized and nations that permitted private mineral ownership nationalized their hydrocarbon resources. As a result, the success of Pennsylvania's wildcatters was not to be repeated in European fields.[31]

Countries that nationalized oil and gas resources incited little public protest because there was no protection of private property rights like that enshrined in the U.S. Constitution and—perhaps more importantly—virtually no petroleum exploration or production activity at the time in most of these countries.[32]

Mineral Ownership in the 13 Colonies

In its colonies, England could have applied the Roman practice of reserving minerals for the Crown. But its claims to minerals in its colonies varied from time to time and place to place. In 1670, the King granted approximately 1 billion acres of land in the Hudson Bay drainage basin in Canada to the governor and Hudson's Bay Company. This land grant, which comprised roughly half of what is now Canada, included everything from the surface to the center of the earth except for "gold, silver, gems and precious stones to be found or discovered."[33]

In the colonies that formed the U.S., however, minerals generally passed along with Crown grants. For example, Charles II's 1681 grant to William Penn expressly included all minerals, including gold, silver and precious stones—although with a 20% royalty on gold and sil-

---

[30] Daintith, *Finders Keepers*, 143-4.
[31] England's nationalization of its oil and gas resources was preceded by Queensland, Australia, in 1915; the Dutch, French and Romanians in the 1920s; and Mexico's constitutional change in 1917 and subsequent expropriation of foreign oil companies' assets in 1938. Daintith, *Finders Keepers*, 143-4.
[32] Daintith, *Finders Keepers*, 429-30.
[33] Daintith, *Finders Keepers*, 318.

ver.[34] That colonial grants expressly included minerals and the land suggests that a reservation in favor of the Crown was a possibility.

Following the American Revolution, early legislation by the Continental Congress indicated an interest in reserving federal ownership of mineral rights on land that was being conveyed to encourage settlement. But this early legislation was not incorporated into the Constitution and early land transfers included any minerals located above and below the surface.[35] Other federal action was taken during the 1800s, but, generally speaking, the nation's goal of settling new lands won out over efforts to save and exploit mineral wealth for the new nation.[36]

Surveyors under homesteading statutes were charged with classifying public lands as either "mineral" or "non-mineral" in character. Mineral lands were to be withheld from homesteading, but surveyors could only judge mineral characteristics from outcrops, affidavits of homesteaders and other interested parties. The surveyors had little incentive to abide by their charge and the system was subject to abuse

---

[34] Daintith, *Finders Keepers*, 318. Under the Charter for the Province of Pennsylvania, granted to William Penn, Charles II granted to Penn: "And all the Soyle, lands, fields, woods, underwoods, mountaines, hills, fenns, Isles, Lakes, Rivers, waters, Rivuletts, Bays, and Inletts, scituate or being within, or belonging unto the Limitts and Bounds aforesaid, togeather with the fishing of all sortes of fish, whales, Sturgeons, and all Royall and other Fishes, in the Sea, Bayes, Inletts, waters, or Rivers within the premisses, and the Fish therein taken; And also all Veines, Mines, and Quarries as well discovered as not discovered, of Gold, Silver, Gemms, and Pretious Stones, and all other whatsoever, be it Stones, Mettals, or of any other thing or matter whatsoever, found or to bee found within the Countrey, Isles, or Limitts aforesaid." The Avalon Project, Documents in Law, History and Diplomacy. "The First Charter of Virginia; April 10, 1610." Yale Law School, Lillian Goldman Law Library, Avalon.law.yale.edu.

[35] The Land Ordinance of 1875 reserved to the congress one-third of all gold, silver, copper and lead minerals within lands acquired from Indians of ceded to the United States from the original states. J.C. Fitzpatrick, "Land Ordinance of 1785, May 20, 1785," *Journals of Continental Congress*, vol. 28, 375 (Fitzpatrick ed. 1933); Sylvia L. Harrison, "Disposition of the Mineral Estate on United States Public Lands: A Historical Perspective," 10 *Pub. Land L. Rev.* 131 (1989): 137-138.

[36] *Act of March 3, 1807*, Ch. 46, Sections 2-4, 2 Stat. 445 (1807) (authorizing the sale of the Northwest Territory and reserves all discovered lead mines); *General Preemption Act of 1841*, Ch. 16, Section 1, 5 Stat. 453 (1841) (authorizing the survey of public lands excluding from sale known mines, coal lands and salt deposits); *Homestead Act of 1862*, 43 U.S.C. Sections 161 et seq. (repealed 1976) (permitting homesteading on unappropriated, surveyed public lands).

and fraud.[37] Finally, the Stock Raising Homestead Act of 1916 did away with the necessity of classification of lands and reserved any coal and other minerals to the U.S. together with "the right to prospect for, mine, and remove the same."[38]

During the early history of America, the emphasis was more on encouraging settlement and agriculture than on concern over potential mineral wealth that might lie below the new frontiers. In addition, there may have been lingering hesitation emanating from the English common law concept as to whether the subsurface minerals could be owned separate and apart from the surface. This is evidenced by the 1807 act that not only intended to reserve for the federal government known lead mines but also the surrounding lands.[39]

Whatever the reasons up through the 1800s, American sentiment among the populous and legislators was that governmental leasing of minerals was impracticable and "un-American."[40] It was not until the Mineral Leasing Act of 1920 that the U.S. government introduced the concept of leasing federal land while it retained its mineral rights.[41]

Previously, the General Mining Act of 1872 authorized "all public lands containing petroleum or other mineral oils, and chiefly valuable therefor" to be "free and open to occupation, exploration, and purchase by citizens of the United States."[42] The act allowed a prospector to stake claim to both minerals and surrounding lands for development.

By the turn of the century, in order to protect the U.S. Navy's growing dependence on oil, President Taft withdrew more than 3 million acres of federal lands in California and Wyoming from private mineral-exploration claims. The federal action was challenged and Supreme Court Justice Joseph Rucker Lamar delivered the court's opinion in *United States v. Midwest Oil Co.* in 1915:

---

[37] Harrison, "Disposition of the Mineral Estate," 143.
[38] *Stock Raising Homestead Act*, 43 U.S.C. Sections 291-301 (repealed 1976).
[39] *Act of March 3, 1807*, Ch. 46, Sections 2-4, 2 Stat. 445 (1807).
[40] Daintith, *Finders Keepers*, 210.
[41] *Mineral Leasing Act*, Ch. 85, 41 Stat. 437 (1920) (codified and amended in 30 U.S.C. Sections 181-287 (1982)).
[42] Harrison, "Disposition of the Mineral Estate," 143.

As these regulations permitted exploration and location without the payment of any sum, and as title could be obtained for a merely nominal amount, many persons availed themselves of the provisions of the statute. Large areas in California were explored; and petroleum having been found, locations were made, not only by the discoverer, but by others on adjoining land.

And, as the flow through the well on one lot might exhaust the oil under the adjacent land, the interest of each operator was to extract the oil as soon as possible, so as to share what would otherwise be taken by the owners of nearby wells. The result was that oil was so rapidly extracted that on September 17, 1909, the Director of the Geological Survey made a report to the Secretary of the Interior which, ... called attention to the fact that ... at the rate at which oil lands in California were being patented by private parties, it would "be impossible for the people of the United States to continue ownership of oil lands for more than a few months.

After that, the government will be obliged to repurchase the very oil that it has practically given away. ... In view of the increasing use of fuel by the American Navy there would appear to be an immediate necessity for assuring the conservation of a proper supply of petroleum for the government's own use ... .[43]

Ultimately, Congress enacted the Mineral Leasing Act of 1920, which codified the system for leasing and development of federally owned lands.

Mineral Laws of Spain

Unlike England, Spain claimed all minerals for the monarchy. In 1348, more than 140 years before Columbus discovered the New World,

---

[43] *U.S. v. Midwest Oil Co.*, 236 U.S. 459 (1915).

Spain's King Alfonso the Just (Alfonso XI) and, under a subsequent decree, Juan I of Aragon, in 1387, declared that all silver, gold and lead mines—along with any other metal and salt springs—belonged to the monarchy.[44, 45]

Four centuries later, in 1783, Spain's King Charles III signed an ordinance to correct abuses reported in New Spain—i.e., Mexico and Texas—and declared, "The mines are the property of my Royal Crown."[46] But he provided that, without separating minerals from his royal patrimony, he could conditionally grant minerals to his subjects. The Ordinance of 1783 specifically provided that a landowner could mine gold, silver, rock salt or other fossils, expressly including bitumen or other production of the earth, provided a royalty was paid to the royal treasury. Failure to either pay the royalty or continuously operate the mines resulted in a forfeiture of the grant and the mine or mines could then be granted to another.

Unlike in English law, Spanish law considered minerals in the ground separate and apart from ownership of the surface.[47] "The Spanish Mining Ordinance of 1783 appears to have contained the essentials of the modern oil and gas lease," wrote Carlos B. Masterson in the *Texas Law Review*, "The subjects of the Crown were granted the

---

[44] Merrill Rippy, *Oil and the Mexican Revolution* (Leiden, Netherlands, E. J. Brill, 1972), 1.

[45] "Alfonso XI's declaration that: "All mines of silver, and gold, and lead, and of any metal whatever or whatsoever kind it might be, in our royal Seigniory, shall belong to us; therefore, no one shall presume to work them without our special license and command; and also the salt springs, basins, and wells, which are for the making of salt, shall belong to us." Charles H. Shamel, "Mining, Mineral and Geological Law," *The Making of the Modern Law: Legal Treatises* (Gale, Making of Modern Law, December 17, 2010), 21 (quoting 1383 Law of Don Alonzo XI).

[46] *Reales Ordenanzas para la Direccion, Regimen i Gobierno del Importante Cuerpo de la Mineria de Nueva-Espana, i de su Real Tribunal General*, De Orden De Su Magestad (1783), tit. 5 art. 2.

[47] The Ordinance of 1783 stated, "Any one may discover and denounce [claim] a vein, not only on common land, but also on the property of any individual, provided he pays for the extent of the surface above the same and the damage which immediately ensues therefrom, and also waters for moving the machines employed for the reduction of ores, provided in each case, that no more of the water be used, than is necessary of such purposes." Royal Ordinances May 22, 1783 for the Direction, Regulation, and Government of the Important Body of Mining of New Spain, promulgated by Carlos III, King of Spain.

minerals, provided they mined them under the terms expressed and paid a royalty.

"So long as they complied with the terms of the grant, their title to the mines was in fee," meaning the mine could be sold or passed onto the mine-owner's heirs and assigns. "Abandonment or failure of the miner to comply with the conditions of the grant worked a forfeiture."[48]

Spain imposed its systems of governance and laws upon its colonies in the Americas. This is the reason that most Latin American countries regard hydrocarbon resources as forming a part of the inalienable riches of the nation. This, over time, led to severe constitutional restrictions on the private capitalization of exploration and development, especially foreign capital, to finance the search for oil and gas.[49]

Following Mexico's revolution and independence from Spain in 1821, the Spanish Mining Ordinance of 1783 was adopted as the law of Mexico, which, at the time, included present-day Texas, New Mexico, Arizona, Utah, Nevada and California and part of Colorado and Wyoming.

Mineral Law in Texas
Following Texas' independence from Mexico in 1836, the new republic's constitution continued to enforce all laws inherited from Spain and Mexico to the extent "not inconsistent with this constitution." This led the Republic of Texas' second president, Mirabeau Lamar, to complain that Texans were the only people "to have adopted a system of laws of which the great body of the people are entirely ignorant [and which] are written in a foreign tongue."[50]

Although not all of Texas' newly minted citizens were from U.S. states or territories, most of the Anglos who wrested control of the territory formerly known as the Mexican states of Coahuila and Tejas

---

[48] Carlos B. Masterson, "Severance of the Mineral Estate by Grant of Land and by the Sovereign and Adverse Possession," 30 *Tex. L. Rev.* 323 (1952).
[49] Daintith, *Finders Keepers*, 210.
[50] Wallace Hawkins, *El Sal del Rey* (Texas State Historical Association, 1947), 12.

were more familiar with the English law of the 13 colonies. Soon after independence, Texas lawmakers rejected the Spanish Civil Code under the Act of 1840, adopting, instead, the common law of England, except that the legislature and courts continued to honor the land grants inherited from Spain and Mexico—other than a number of last-minute, fraudulent and excessively large grants made by Mexico just before Texas' independence.[51] Specifically, the act declared that Texas retained all mineral rights to its lands.[52]

Just as Mexico had confirmed land titles granted previously by Spain, consistent with Spanish law, Texas reserved all minerals to all public and unappropriated lands, which, at the time of its independence, covered more than 216 million acres.[53] Under the Act of 1840, Texas repealed most of Mexico's codified civil laws, but, importantly, expressly retained "such Laws as relate to the preservation of Islands and Lands, and also of Salt-Lakes, Licks and Salt-Springs, Mines and Minerals of every descriptions; made by the General and State Governments."[54]

Five years later, when Texas joined the U.S., it retained title to public lands, rivers, tidelands and minerals thereunder. If a parsimonious U.S. Senate had, instead, adopted a proposal the prior year that the U.S. gain Texas' public lands—and minerals—in consideration for assumption of Texas' $10 million of debt, the U.S. would have gained the 216 million acres for 4.6 cents an acre.[55] The acquisition would have ranked as one of the best real estate deals in the history of the country along with Seward's Folly—the purchase of Alaska from Russia in 1867 for some 2 cents an acre—and the Louisiana Purchase in 1803 for some 3 cents an acre.

Ironically, under the Compromise of 1850, the U.S. assumed Texas' debt after all. The Act resolved the status of the Western terri-

[51] Thomas Lloyd Miller, *The Public Lands of Texas, 1519-1970* (Norman: University of Oklahoma Press, 1972), xi.
[52] Masterson, *Severance of the Mineral Estate*.
[53] Miller, *The Public Lands of Texas*, 159.
[54] *Act of 1840 January 20, 1840*, Republic of Texas.
[55] Miller, *The Public Lands of Texas*, 25.

tories acquired in the Mexican-American War. In exchange for assuming Texas' debt, the federal government received Texas' 67 million acres in what are now parts of New Mexico, Oklahoma, Kansas, Colorado and Wyoming.

The subsequent real estate deal was some 15 cents an acre—more than three times what Texas would have received five years earlier and this deal didn't include Texas' public lands, which would later yield the oil-rich fields of East Texas, the Permian Basin, South Texas, the Gulf Coast and the Texas Panhandle. Notwithstanding its luck of delayed admission to the U.S. under terms that included retaining ownership of all its public lands, Texas' sovereignty over its vast resources would be, nevertheless, significantly reduced by legislative action soon after the Civil War.

Just as legend has it that Abraham Lincoln attributed the start of the Civil War singularly to Harriet Beecher Stowe's novel, *Uncle Tom's Cabin*,[56] private ownership of oil and gas in Texas can be singularly attributed to a dispute over a salt lake known as El Sal del Rey, located just north of the Rio Grande in what would become Hidalgo County. El Sal del Rey was prized for its inexhaustible supply and purity of its salt. More than a mile long, the lakebed consists of crystal salt composed of 99.0897% sodium chloride.[57]

Indigenous people, including the Aztecs and Huastecans, had known about this lake.[58] Following the war for independence from Mexico, the Republic of Texas granted this land in 1838 to H.M. Lewis' predecessor-in-title, which title was later confirmed by a land patent

---

[56] Upon meeting Ms. Stowe at the start of the Civil War, sources quoted Lincoln as saying "So this is the little lady who started this great war." Given that the quote did not first appear until 1896, much doubt has been cast upon the authenticity of the quotation. Daniel Vollaro, "Lincoln, Stowe, and the 'Little Woman/Great War' Story: the Making and Breaking, of a Great American Anecdote," *Journal of the Abraham Lincoln Association* (2009), vol. 30: 1.

[57] La Sale Del Rey, as it is currently known, was acquired by the state of Texas in 1992 as a part of the Lower Rio Grande Valley National Wildlife Refuge. Handbook of Texas Online, Eloise Campbell, "La Sal Del Rey," accessed November 29, 2015, Texas State Historical Association, Tshaonline.org.

[58] Hawkins, *El Sal del Rey*.

issued in 1847, and affirmed in 1850 by the legislature, releasing all claims to the land.[59]

During the Civil War, however, the importance of salt became paramount and, in 1862, the Texas legislature attempted to void the patent in order that the state could take over the salt lake for the war effort.[60] In the same year, the Texas Supreme Court in *Cowan v. Hardeman* upheld the 1837 act that had prohibited any grant of land by the Republic that included salt, gold, silver or other minerals or islands. The court held that any grant by the Republic—and, later, by the state—that included lands upon which salt springs were located transferred only the land, not the minerals, even when minerals were not expressly excepted in the patents to private landowners.[61]

Following the Civil War, one of the issues Texas' 1866 constitutional convention took up was competing claims to El Sal del Rey[62] to settle the private claims to the lake that the state had attempted to usurp for the war effort. Subsequent cases reviewing the history of the 1866 constitutional congress found that the recommendation of the convention was for enactment of an "ordinance," clearing title to the lake. Yet, in the state's subsequent publication of the convention proceedings, the "ordinance" was mistakenly included as an "article" of the constitution itself, which affected all lands granted by the state prior to the date of the 1866 constitution.[63]

---

[59] The land containing the salt lake was originally granted by Spain in 1787, but that grant was not recorded until 1851 and, therefore, not effective when the Republic of Texas granted to Maria de los Santos Manchacha one league and one labor of land (4,600 acres), including the lake in 1838. Manchacha subsequently sold the land to H.M. Lewis. Lewis received a patent from the State in 1847, which was affirmed in 1850 by the legislature. Miller, *The Public Lands of Texas*, 159-160.

[60] *Cox v. Robison*, 105 Tex. 426 (Tex. 1912).

[61] *Cowan v Hardeman*, 26 Tex. 217, 222 (Tex. 1862) (holding that the purpose of the 1837 act was a doctrine as old as common law (even though ancient Spanish laws would have been the controlling precedent at the time), under which royal mines belonged to the sovereign and there was no need for expressing reservation)).

[62] "In the face of its patent and express relinquishment, had theretofore disputed the title, and the exigencies of war, that doubtless prompted it to such action, had now passed, it is fair to assume that its purpose was to provide for the validation of that particular title [to El Sal Del Rey]." *Cox v. Robinson*, 435-36.

[63] *Cox v. Robinson* (Tex. 1912).

Chapter 1: Private Ownership

The Texas constitution was, thus, rewritten to provide that "all mines and mineral substances were released to the current surface owners" and not just the salt deposits of El Sal del Rey; it included minerals under all lands that had been granted by the sovereign to private owners prior to such date. Thus, an argument over a salt lake and a printing error caused Texas to lose control over oil, gas and other minerals that the Texas General Land Office estimated in 1944 to be worth billions of dollars.[64] Today's value would be multiples of billions.

Personal preferences and rivalries may have played some part in this action that would have momentous consequences for the Texas oil industry. The chair of the constitutional committee reviewing the dispute had also been the attorney for the losing party whose mineral claim was defeated in *Cowan v. Hardeman*.[65] This abdication of mineral ownership in lands previously granted by the state was repeated in the constitution of 1876.[66]

In 1884, Texas' Commission Appeals Court interpreted the 1866 and 1876 constitutions as releasing all minerals on private lands granted prior to 1876, but not prospectively as to any future grants.[67] After the 1876 constitution through 1919, the Texas legislature passed a number of laws governing the sale and ownership of minerals on lands sold by the state after 1876. Principally, the laws provided for the reservation to the state of minerals on all lands sold by the state, provided the lands were classified as "mineral lands" at the time of the grant.

Although salt was easily the most recognized mineral in the early history of Texas, other minerals, including petroleum, had been known and prized by generations of Native Americans. Petroleum was collected at the surface from local watering holes at places with

---

[64] Miller, *The Public Lands of Texas*, 32 (citing the Report of the Commissioner of the General Land Office of Texas, 1944).
[65] Daintith, *Finders Keepers*, 219.
[66] Constitution of 1876, Article XIV, Section 7: "The State of Texas hereby releases to the owner or owners of the soil all mines and minerals that may be on the same, subject to taxation as other property."
[67] *State v. Parker*, 61 Tex. 265 (Tex. Civ. App. 1884).

names that came to be translated as Sour Lake, Oil Spring and Tar Spring.[68]

Prior to the arrival of Europeans, tribes were aware of oil seeps. They travelled from far and wide to gather oil to heal battle wounds and skin diseases, to soften and preserve leather, and to repel insects. Later, after the Civil War, locals continued to make use of oil-soaked soil for illumination. W.C. Gilbert, a wildcatter, said in a 1953 interview about oil pioneers:

> My grandmother often told me about 'em going down to the edge of the lake, and they'd take a shovel or two and cut out blocks of dirt and bring it up and put it on benches in front of the Sour Lake Hotel at night. They had several croquet sets out there, and that was [in] the day before electricity, of course. And they'd set these blocks of dirt on fire, and that way it'd illuminate the yard, so they could play croquet out there. Oil in the mud and dirt. Yes, it was very apparent. And I know that's one of the indications that probably my grandfather saw there when he bought this tract of land.[69]

The earliest European written report of oil in the lands that became Texas was told by the survivors of the ill-fated De Soto expedition.[70] In 1539, the early Spanish explorer and conquistador De Soto set out from Cuba and landed in Florida in search of gold, silver and passage to China. After he died along the western bank of the Mississippi River somewhere near what is now the Arkansas-Louisiana border, his men tried to continue his quest. Crossing the Sabine River into territory now known as Texas, his men found the land and people too inhospitable and retreated to the Mississippi River.

---

[68] C.A. Warner, "Texas and the Oil Industry," *The Southwestern Historical Quarterly*, 50, no. 1 (July 1946): 2.
[69] W.C. Gilbert, interview by W.A. Owens, "Pioneers In Texas Oil," *Dolph Briscoe Center for American History, The University of Texas at Austin* (Austin, Texas, July 22, 1953), T114:8-9.
[70] Miller, *The Public Lands of Texas*, 166.

Chapter 1: Private Ownership

By 1543, his men built boats to float down the Mississippi with plans to sail to Mexico, which was known as New Spain at the time. These survivors reported using oil from seeps near Sabine Pass, which is at the present-day border of Texas and Louisiana on the Gulf Coast, to make their boats watertight as they journeyed to Panuco in the modern Mexican state of Veracruz that Hernan Cortes founded in 1522.[71] It would be almost another 400 years before anyone would realize that De Soto and his expedition were on the right track for gold—black gold.

Even a casual passerby, Fredrick Law Olmsted, noted on his 1854 visit to Texas "a slight odor of sulpherreted hydrogen" at Sour Lake.[72] However, the bulk of Texas' true oil wealth was hidden deep underground. Even if its infernal location had been known in the days of the Texas Republic and the state's constitutional conventions following the Civil War, other than medicinal uses and a substitute for whale oil as a source for artificial light, petroleum was of little commercial value at the time.

Following its 1876 constitution and to protect Texas' mineral ownership on lands it subsequently conveyed to private landowners, it was important for the state to designate "mineral lands" as those tracts that were potentially mineral-bearing. Notwithstanding the awareness of the presence of oil in Texas, the state's mineral surveys were incomplete and left much to be desired even into the late 1800s.

Much of the acreage conveyed after 1876 was sold without any mineral designation, thereby passing out of the state's hands to the patentee the ownership of both the surface and minerals. By 1901, Texas General Land Commissioner Charles Rogan—fed up with the state's failure to retain its mineral rights for the benefit of future gen-

---

[71] Miller, *The Public Lands of Texas*. It was reported from the journey "Finding a scum the sea casts up, called copee, which is like pitch, and used instead on shipping, where that is not to be had, they payed the bottom of their vessels with it." Miller, *The Public Lands of Texas*, 23 (citing Edward G. Bourne, *Narratives of the Career of Hernando De Soto I*. Translated by Buckingham Smith. Bradford Club, 1866, 209).

[72] Handbook of Texas Online, Roger M. Olien, "Oil and Gas Industry," accessed March 13, 2016, Tshaonline.org.

erations of Texans' education—began to classify all lands sold after 1901 as "mineral."

However, solving for one solution created another problem for Texas lawmakers. Private, surface owners of "mineral lands," on which the state had retained the mineral rights, received no compensation from the state's lessees that used the surface to explore for minerals. These aggrieved constituents appealed to their state legislators and their pleas were answered. In 1919, to promote development of Texas' reserved mineral interests, the legislature passed the Relinquishment Act that appeared to give the surface owners title to 15/16ths of the minerals under their "mineral lands." [73]

Texas' constitution had set aside such lands for the permanent school fund and the act to give away interests in such lands was challenged in the courts as unconstitutional. To arrive at the legislators' goal within the confines of the constitution, the Texas Supreme Court had to waltz around the language of the statute. The court construed that, instead of an outright gift, the act designated the surface owner as the state's agent for leasing its oil and gas interests and entitled the surface owner to share equally in the bonus, rentals and royalties, provided that the state earned at least a 1/16th royalty on oil and gas. [74]

Subsequently, in 1931, the legislature passed the Sales Act; in this, the surface-owner of land sold after enactment became entitled to all rentals and bonuses, while the state continued to receive a minimum of a 1/16th royalty from any production. [75]

This early history of transferring sovereign ownership of mineral rights to Texas' private citizens—either as outright mineral owners or as the primary beneficiaries of leasing minerals retained by the state—set the stage. With this, every wildcatter with access to enough money was enabled to punch holes across the state in search of the New World conquistadors' undiscovered *El Dorado*.

---

[73] *Relinquishment Act*, (Act of July 31, 1919, Laws 36th Leg., 2nd Called Session, ch. 81, p. 249) Rev. Stats., arts. 5367-5382.
[74] *Relinquishment Act*, (Act of July 31, 1919, Laws 36th Leg., 2nd Called Session, ch. 81, p. 249) Rev. Stats., arts. 5367-5382.
[75] *Sales and Leasing Act of 1931*, House Bill 358. Acts 42nd Leg., Reg.Ses., ch. 271.

Chapter 1: Private Ownership

Private Oil and Gas Ownership in California

Following Santa Anna's defeat by Sam Houston at the Battle of San Jacinto, Mexican officials in Mexico City rejected the Treaties of Velasco that had been signed by their general. Further, they refused to recognize the Rio Grande as the Republic of Texas' southern border, claiming Texas' border was the Nueces River, instead.[76]

Anticipating the U.S.' need to defend its new border upon Texas' statehood in a few months, President Polk dispatched General Zachary Taylor in July of 1845 to Corpus Christi where the Nueces empties into the Gulf of Mexico.[77] Polk wanted to protect the Texas border, but he also had designs to acquire—by purchase or conquest—Mexico's northern territories of Alta California and Santa Fe de Nuevo Mexico. Under the guise of an expedition to map the new Oregon Territory, Polk sent U.S. Army Captain John Fremont with 60 men west. Fremont entered Alta California in December of 1845 and slowly made his way north.

Mexico continued to dispute Texas' annexation by the U.S. and the border and refused to accept U.S. offers to buy Mexico's claims to Texas and California. Taylor moved his forces in Corpus Christi south to the mouth of the Rio Grande just north of Matamoros, ostensibly to keep an eye on Mexico's cavalry. In full view of the local Mexican general and on lands still claimed by Mexico, each morning the American camp raised and each evening lowered the Stars and Stripes to the sounds of the fife and drum.

Eventually, the Mexican cavalry took the bait and struck. In April of 1846, Taylor reported to Polk that open hostilities had been initiated by Mexico. This gave Polk the political cover he needed to go to

---

[76] Miller, *The Public Lands of Texas*, 9. Records of Spanish and Mexican land grants to this region were maintained by Mexico until after the Mexican War and the Treaty of Guadalupe Hidalgo in 1848. Copies of these grants prior to the Republic were subsequently acquired by the Texas General Land Office and, with few exceptions, such grants have been upheld by Texas' court and are valid today.

[77] T.R. Fehrenbach, *Lone Star: A History of Texas and the Texans* (Open Road Media: April 1, 2014), 270.

Congress on May 11, 1846, for a declaration of war, which he received on May 13, beginning the Mexican-American War.[78]

By June, in Sonoma, California, Anglo settlers staged the Bear Flag Revolt. Within days, they were joined by the U.S. Army, led by Fremont who *happened* to be in the neighborhood. Fremont and other American army forces that were led by Brigadier General Stephen Kearny, along with naval forces led by Commodore Robert Stockton, quickly secured the California territory. By January of 1847, the Mexican forces signed the Treaty of Cahuenga, ceasing hostilities in Alta California, which was declared a U.S. territory.

Commodore Stockton appointed Fremont as the new territory's military governor. But, with orders from Polk, Brigadier General Kearny assumed the role. Fremont was forced to give up the governorship a few months later, after the arrival of fresh troops from the 1st Regiment of New York Volunteers. For his insubordination, Fremont was escorted to Fort Leavenworth by Kearny (through a gruesome pass in the Sierra Madres that Fremont mapped for settlers a year earlier) and court-martialed for disobedience and assumption of powers.[79] His sentence however, was quickly commuted by Polk for his services to the country. Not inconsequentially, Fremont was married to the daughter of the powerful U.S. Senator Thomas Hart Benton.

Fremont resigned his commission and settled in California in 1847 on a 10-league ranch called Ranchos Las Mariposas the he had acquired from a Mexican citizen for $3,000 and was located near the foothills of the Sierra Nevada. Gold was soon discovered on the ranch and Fremont would play an important role a dozen years later

---

[78] Fehrenbach, *Lone Star*, 271.

[79] Ironically, Fremont's military escort back to Fort Leavenworth for court martial passed through Hasting's Cutoff in June, following the winter during which the Donner Party set out too late in the season and took the ill-fated "short cut" through the Sierra Madres that had been mapped by Fremont a year earlier. As the first party to arrive at the scene following the disastrous winter, the troops buried the remains of the 31 pioneers that perished in the heavy snows during the prior winter. Hasting's Cutoff later became known as "Donner Pass."

in establishing California law regarding the ownership of minerals and, thereby, oil.

In Mexico City, Mexico's army was outmaneuvered and out-gunned by American troops, which eventually occupied the capital; Mexico capitulated. Its loss was not only the disputed Texas territory between the Nueces and Rio Grande, but also its claims over the terri-tories of Alta California and Santa Fe de Nuevo Mexico. Ultimately, Mexico gave up more than 55% of its territory.

Under the terms of the 1848 Treaty of Guadalupe Hidalgo, then-existing Mexican law—to the extent not in conflict with the U.S. Con-stitution—was maintained in the newly acquired Western territory, including Mexican laws related to land titles. This provided the U.S. with the "golden" opportunity to continue the Spanish and Mexican tradition of state ownership of all minerals. However, within 10 days of the treaty, California's military governor—Richard Mason by this time—abolished by proclamation all Mexican laws and customs relat-ed to mining rights on public lands.[80]

While Mason abolished Mexican mining law, the general laws of the U.S. did not take effect officially in California until two years later, creating a legal vacuum for the first two years of the California Gold Rush.[81] A few months later, after having abolished established legal precedent, Mason was more explicit, stating, "Gold may be dug on government land, without charge or hindrance."

Discretion being the better part of valor, perhaps his edict was more a recognition of the reality of the times; his troops were insuffi-cient to impose the government's will on more than 4,000 miners, who had been in the first wave of the rush. "[C]onsidering the large extent of country, the character of the people engaged, and the small scattered force at my command, I resolved not to interfere, but permit

---

[80] John C. Lacy, "The Historic Origins of the U.S. Mining Laws and Proposals for Change," 10 *Nat. Resources & Env't* 13, 13 (Summer 1995).
[81] On February 12, 1848, Colonel Mason declared: "From and after this date, the Mexican laws and customs now prevailing in California, relative to the denouncement [i.e., making a formal clam] of mines, are hereby abolished." Gregory Yale, *Legal Titles to Mining Claims & Water Rights in California under the Mining Law of Congress of July, 1866* (1867), 17; *see also,* Daintith, *Finders Keepers,* 212.

all to work freely, unless crimes and broils should call for interference," Mason reported in August of 1848.[82] Not that the prospectors and camp followers needed any encouragement, Mason literally gave every gold-digger the license to steal—at least on public lands. In a short period of four years, California's population swelled to more than 200,000.[83]

Similar to the customs of the ancient Celtic miners formalized under England's Stannary laws, the regulatory void in California—and, later, in Nevada—was filled by the development of mining-camp rules by the miners themselves, such as a system for recording mineral claims and restrictions on the number of claims that might be held. Daintith wrote, "Key features of such rules were the establishment of a general legal jurisdiction over the area occupied by the camp; provision of a system for recording claims; the determination of the size and defining features of each claim … ; restrictions on the number of claims that might be held; and fixing of the work obligations required to preserve the claim—if these were not respected, the claim would be forfeited."[84]

As with the Stannary laws, such rules became codified under the California Civil Practice Act and could be admitted as evidence in mining litigation when not in conflict with the U.S. Constitution and state laws. By 1866, there were at least 500 separate mining districts and another 500 mining communities that governed the Western mining industry.[85]

Notwithstanding the legacy and legitimacy of its claim to all minerals, including recently discovered gold, the U.S. and, subsequently, the state of California abdicated any mineral ownership on private lands located in California's boundaries.

After an unsuccessful run against James Buchanan in 1856 as the U.S.' first Republican Party candidate for president, Fremont returned to Ranchos Las Mariposas to protect his claim to his gold mines. Cali-

---

82 Daintith, *Finders Keepers*, 212.
83 Harrison, "Disposition of the Mineral Estate," 146.
84 Daintith, *Finders Keepers*, 213.
85 Harrison, "Disposition of the Mineral Estate," 146.

fornia historian W.W. Robinson described, "Creek beds were so rich that Fremont's Mexicans scooped up flakes in cups and pans, and with their knives dug gold out of the crevices in the bedrock.

"The news of the strike spread and soon throngs of miners were all over the ranch. For several years prospectors mined at will and Fremont was without power to evict these trespassers, for his title had not yet been confirmed [by the state of California]. Several valuable mines were developed on Las Mariposas by men who thought they had the same right there they had elsewhere in the Mother Lode country."[86]

To establish his claim to the minerals found on his land, Fremont brought suit against a miner, who, in 1860, extracted five pounds of gold worth $2,000.[87] Upon refusing Fremont's demand that he return the gold, Fremont sued the prospector in a case brought before the California Supreme Court. The question in the case was whether the original land grant in 1844 by Mexico's governor of California to the preceding landowner—and that was confirmed by the California Supreme Court in 1854—passed title to the minerals to Fremont. The miner countered that the gold did not belong to Fremont because the original grant did not include title to the minerals, which were claimed by and belonged to the sovereign.

The California Supreme Court recognized that minerals were claimed as a part of the Spanish and Mexican patrimony. Curiously, notwithstanding that the claim was based on precedent of the Spanish law, the court based its holding on precedent of English regalian rights. The court acknowledged that, under ancient English law, all mines of gold and silver belonged to the sovereign; however, the king

---

[86] "Creek beds were so rich that Fremont's Mexicans scooped up flakes in cups and pans, and with their knives dug gold out of the crevices in the bedrock. The news of the strike spread and soon throngs of miners were all over the ranch. For several years prospectors mined at will and Fremont was without power to evict these trespassers, for his title had not yet been confirmed [by the state of California]. Several valuable mines were developed on Las Mariposas by men who thought they had the same right there they had elsewhere in the Mother Lode country." William Wilcox Robinson, *Land In California: The Story of Mission Lands, Ranchos, Squatters, Mining Claims, Railroad Grants, Land Scrip, Homesteads* (University of California Press, 1979), 144.

[87] *Moore v. Smaw and Fremont v. Flower*, 17 Cal. 199 (Cal. 1861).

or queen could elect to grant such minerals to their subjects. Accordingly, the court held that mineral ownership could pass to landowners by grant:

> [W]e are clear that the doctrine there advanced [by the defendant] cannot be sustained. It is undoubtedly true that the United States held certain rights of sovereignty over the territory which is now embraced within the limits of California, and that such rights vested in the new State upon her admission into the Union. But the ownership of the precious metals found in public or private lands was not one of those rights. ... Sovereignty is a term used to express the supreme political authority of an independent State, or nation. Whatever rights are essential to the existence of this authority are rights of sovereignty. ... To the existence of this political authority of the State – this qualified sovereignty, or to any part of it – the ownership of the minerals of gold and silver found within her limits is in no way essential.[88]

The court ruled in favor of Fremont. Therefore, the U.S. Army captain who helped secure California for the U.S. also played a pivotal role in severing for its citizens a bounty that was measured in sacks of gold. A few years later, upon the discovery of the Ventura oil field in 1865, it would be further measured in barrels of oil.[89]

Fremont, in 1863, sold his ranch and mines to a New York City banker, who hired Fredrick Law Olmsted, noted landscape architect of New York's Central Park and a former visitor to Texas, to be superintendent of the gold mines. Within two years, the owner was bankrupt and the ranch and mines were sold at a sheriff's sale.

---

[88] *Moore v. Smaw and Fremont v. Flower*, 217-218.
[89] In June, 1865, a wildcatter, Thomas R. Bard, drilled several wells on Ranch Ojai near Ventura. Soon after, California had its first oil boom with 65 oil companies operating from Humboldt County south to Ventura. William Rintoul (Department of Conservation, Division of Oil and Gas, California), *Drilling Through Time, 75 years with California's Division of Oil and Gas* (California Division of Oil and Gas, 1990), 5.

Meanwhile, miners took hundreds of millions of dollars of gold and, later, silver as well from public lands, never paying for the privilege. A weak effort by California's General Land Office to collect even a small fee, via a license and royalty, "was denounced by the secretary of the treasury as impracticable, un-American, and unconstitutional."[90] There was an underlying sentiment of the still-nascent nation that the government and its laws should protect those who undertake the risk and labor of discovering and producing something of value—whether by lease or trespass.

Oil and Gas Law in Louisiana

On September 21, 1901, in a rice field near Jennings, Louisiana's first oil well was brought in nine months after the Spindletop discovery near Beaumont, Texas. Louisiana had been a part of the U.S. for almost 100 years by then; however, laws had not yet been established on oil and gas ownership in the state.[91]

The North American heartland drained by the Mississippi River and its tributaries was originally claimed by De Soto for Spain in 1541. France held claim to it from 1682 until 1762, when it ceded the territory to Spain to induce Spain's support in France's Seven Year War against England.

However, the following year, France and Spain lost to England. Under the Treaty of Paris that ended hostilities, England took nearly all of the Louisiana Territory east of the Mississippi and Spain kept the larger western part, along with the Isle of Orleans, the area around New Orleans.

Under Napoleon in 1801, France took back the western half of the territory and New Orleans from Spain with the hope of building an empire in North America. A slave revolt in Haiti and the need to finance an imminent war with Britain, however, led Napoleon to

---

[90] Daintith, *Finders Keepers*, 217.
[91] Patrick Ottinger, "From the Courts to the Code: the Origin and Development of the Law of Louisiana on Mineral Rights," 1 *LSU J. of Energy L. & Resources* 6 (2012).

abandon these plans and sell the entire territory to the U.S. two years later.

President Jefferson had instructed his representative, Robert Livingston, to purchase New Orleans and its adjacent land for $10 million. Instead, in France, Livingston was offered all of the Louisiana territory for $15 million, which exceeded his authority. Like any good landman seeking acreage, he agreed, certain that the U.S. would accept the offer, even though the boundaries of the territory were unclear.

During negotiations, Livingston asked his French counterpart, Talleyrand, "What are the western bounds of Louisiana?"

Talleyrand replied: "I do not know. You must take it as we received it."

"But what did you mean to *take*?" urged Livingston.

"I do not know," Talleyrand replied.

"Then you mean that we shall construe it our own way?" Livingston asked.

Talleyrand replied, "I can give you no direction. You have made a noble bargain for yourselves and I suppose you will make the most of it."[92]

At the time of the Louisiana Purchase, the territory consisted of all or part of 15 present-day states and portions of two Canadian provinces. Congress divided the land into the Territory of Orleans— land south of the 33rd parallel that is, mostly, present-day Louisiana— and all parts north as the District of Louisiana. With the boundaries of France's claim to the territory still ill-defined, the U.S. and Spain disputed whether its western border was the Sabine River or the Calcasieu River. To the east, they disputed territory north of New Orleans and Lake Pontchartrain known as West Florida.[93]

---

[92] United States Dept. of State, *State Papers and Correspondence Bearing upon the Purchase of the Territory of Louisiana* (Washington, Govt. Print Office, 1903) quoted in Oliver Stockwell, "The Boundaries of the State of Louisiana," 42 *La. L. Rev.* 1043 (Spring 1982): 1046.
[93] England had ceded the land east of the Mississippi back to Spain in 1783.

Chapter 1: Private Ownership

In 1821, these claims were resolved by treaty.[94] The Sabine River formed the western boundary; the U.S. owned the rest of the Floridas, taking in East Florida.

Unlike the other U.S. states and territories, which adopted English common law, Louisiana retained the civil law used by Spain and France.[95] Prior to the French Revolution, landowners were considered owners of the minerals below. During the revolution, the state asserted the right to regulate mineral ownership and production.

Under the law of July 28, 1791, the republic required its citizens to renounce their rights to minerals beneath their lands. This right was reaffirmed in the mining law of 1810 and incorporated in the Napoleonic Code. Under the French system, ownership of the mineral deposit did not vest in the surface owner; rather, the deposit is *res nullius*—that is, owned by no one—until discovered and reduced to effective possession.[96]

The Louisiana Civil Code was first adopted in 1808 and was based, in part, on Spanish law, but much of it was taken from Napoleonic Code. It was written in French and it was not until 1870, long after Louisiana's admission as a state, that the code was first written in English.

Although the Napoleonic Code provided for limitations on mineral ownership under regulations related to mines and quarries, these provisions were not carried over into the Louisiana Civil Code, a meaningless omission given that there were no mines in the state.[97] Built upon the 18th- and early 19th-century civil codes of Spain and France, which had no oil or gas exploration, Louisiana's civil code provided little instruction to the state's early oil-industry pioneers or

---

[94] The Adams-Onis Treaty of 1819, signed by John Quincy Adams, U.S. Secretary of State, and Luis de Onis, Spanish Minister, was ratified in 1821, but not after Henry Clay and other senators demanded (unsuccessfully) that negotiations be re-opened for Spain to give up claims to Texas as well.

[95] There is lively scholarly debate as to which system, French or Spanish, Louisiana most borrowed. Patrick Martin and J. Lanier Yeates, "Louisiana and Texas Oil & Gas Law: An Overview of the Differences," 52 *La. L. Rev.* 769 (March 1992): 722 n.11.

[96] Ely and Pietrowski, "Changing Concepts," 14.

[97] Harry S. Sachse, "A Comparison of the Landowner's Rights to Petroleum in France and Louisiana," 23 *La. L. Rev.* 722 (1963): 723.

the judiciary for establishing rules over title to oil and gas in the ground at the beginning of the 20th century upon the discovery near Jennings.[98]

The words "oil," "gas" or "minerals" did not even appear in the early editions of the code. "[O]il and gas were products unknown to the redactors [draftsmen] of the Civil Code, and in the absence of other legislation on the subject matter of oil and gas, it became the task of the courts to 'hammer out' the 'ground rules' by a process of analogy to the disparate provisions in the Civil Code," Patrick Ottinger, an LSU adjunct law professor, wrote.[99]

The only guide readily available was the development of oil and gas jurisprudence in the common-law states, but common-law property rights were alien and confusing to the Louisiana jurist. "The decisions of other states were of small value [to the process of developing the mineral law of Louisiana] because Louisiana is a civil-law state with an old civil code," LSU law professor Harriet Spiller Daggett wrote in *Mineral Rights in Louisiana*.[100]

Consistent with common-law-state judiciaries, the Louisiana courts accepted that the landowner has paramount rights to the petroleum and other minerals under his surface.[101] But the Louisiana Supreme Court did not accept the surface-owner's right to convey the subsurface estate separate from the surface. Similar to other producing states, Louisiana courts held that only the landowner has the right

---

[98] Martin and Yeates, "Louisiana and Texas Oil & Gas Law," 775.

[99] Ottinger, "From the Courts to the Code," 16.

[100] Harriet Spiller Daggett, *Mineral rights in Louisiana* (Louisiana State University Press, 1949), xxiv.

[101] In 1808, the earliest digest of the new territory's laws compiled after the Louisiana Purchase provided, similar to the *ad coelum* maxim, "The ownership of the soil carries with it the ownership of that which is above it and under it. The owner may make upon it all the plantations and constructions which he thinks proper, save the exceptions established under the title of servitudes and real services. He may construct below the soil all manner of works and pits which he thinks proper and draw from them all the profits that they can produce subject to the modifications resulting from the regulations of police." Article 9, Chapter I, Title II, Digest of the Civil Law Now in Force in the Territory of Orleans (the "Digest"). The Digest was a compilation of preexisting law but not as a replacement for such prior laws. The Civil Code of Louisiana, first adopted in 1825, replaced such prior laws. Martin and Yeates, "Louisiana and Texas Oil & Gas Law," 769-860.

to explore and produce petroleum from under the ground—a right that the landowner could lease to third parties.[102]

Louisiana courts held that the lease to explore for oil and gas was subject to forfeiture if the lessee failed to produce within 10 years.[103] The courts' decisions were policy-driven to encourage the development of the state's natural resources, prohibit land speculation, simplify land titles and provide a structure that incented and benefited local landowners.[104]

Such was the mineral law known by Louisiana judges at the time of the discovery of petroleum in the state. Although the legislature adopted a joint resolution in 1936 that authorized drafting a code to govern oil and gas, it was not until 1975 that Louisiana finally enacted a mineral code.[105]

Oil and Gas Ownership in Alaska

In contrast to the mineral laws of the early producing states, the development of mineral law in Alaska is instructive and illustrative of the thesis that private ownership of minerals in the Lower 48 has been instrumental in the fulsome development of the U.S.' mineral resources.[106] Unlike other states, where most of the mineral develop-

---

[102] Louisiana is not alone in adopting the non-ownership theory of petroleum. Other states also follow this theory, such as California, Kansas and Oklahoma, which is contrary to the ownership-in-place states, such as Texas. Martin and Yeates, "Louisiana and Texas Oil & Gas Law," 805.

[103] *Frost-Johnson Lumber Co. v. Salling's Heirs*, 150 La. 756, 836, 91, So. 207, 235 (1920); Article 753 of the Louisiana Civil Code of 1870.

[104] Ottinger, "From the Courts to the Code," 23-25; Martin and Yeates, "Louisiana and Texas Oil & Gas Law," 806. "A recognition that the prolonged divorce of the ownership of the land from the undeveloped mineral interest thereunder is detrimental to the welfare of the State, both as tending to inhibit development of our mineral resources (without the spur of a time limit and of a financially interested landowner), and as tending to divert in the event of production the royalty rentals therefrom away from the local landowner and the local community often into the hands of such absentee financial interests as for long range investment acquire mineral interests at a time with virtually valueless on the open market." *Reagan v. Murphy*, 235 La. 529, 105 So.2d 210, 217 (La. 1958) (Tate, J. Dissenting).

[105] 1974 La. Acts No. 50; La.R.S. 31:1 et seq.

[106] As discussed below, the unfettered private ownership was the catalyst of petroleum development but was also, without question, the cause for historical (and current) physical and economic waste.

ment is predominantly between private owners and lessees, mineral development in Alaska rarely occurs on private lands. There are three reasons: The federal government retained title to 60% of the land; under Alaska's Statehood Act, the state was required to retain ownership of the mineral estate, even where it conveys the surface to private citizens; and the bulk of the remaining land is owned by Native Alaskans.

Purchased from Russia in 1867, Alaska did not achieve statehood until 1959. Congress continued to have doubts about the territory's ability to support a state government. To aid in this, the U.S. gave the state more than 165 million acres, expressly including minerals, so any revenue derived from this would help fund the new government.[107]

Regarding the land that was retained by the federal government, the state continues to challenge federal reluctance to authorize mineral development of the Alaskan National Wildlife Refuge (ANWR) and the National Petroleum Reserve-Alaska (NPR-A).[108] Since 1977, the Trans-Alaska Pipeline System has transported oil from Alaska's North Slope, most of which is state land. Production peaked at 722,000 barrels a day in 1988 and declined to about 170,000 in 2015.[109]

Despite 40 years of production, the Slope remains relatively unexplored. For comparison, Alaska had less than 1% as many producing wells as Texas in 2009.[110] And unlike Texas, which had approxi-

---

[107] *Trustees for Alaska v. Alaska*, 736 P.2d 324, 335-6 (Alaska 1987).

[108] In October, 2014, the state claimed that 20,000 acres in ANWR and near Exxon Mobil Corp.'s Point Thomson gas development were improperly mapped, challenging federal title to it. "Alaskans have suffered from many roadblocks to resource development on federal lands. Our hope is that the BLM [U.S. Bureau of Land Management] will move quickly to convey lands that we can offer for oil and gas leasing and development." Joe Balash, Natural Resources Commissioner, State of Alaska, quoted in Margaret Kriz Hobson, "Alaska Moves to Reclaim Part of ANWR from Federal Government," *E&E Energy Wire Newsletter*, October 20, 2014.

[109] U.S. EIA, Independent Statistics & Analysis. "Alaska North Slope Crude Oil Production," accessed April 2, 2016, Eia.gov.

[110] The U.S. EIA reported that, in 2009, Texas had more than 262,300 producing wells compared with 2,350 wells in Alaska. U.S. EIA, Independent Statistics & Analysis. "Alaska North Slope Crude Oil Production," accessed March 6, 2016, Eia.gov.

mately 4,148 registered operators with producing wells in 2014,[111] fewer than 100 companies held leases in Alaska.[112] The Alaska Oil and Gas Association had a 2015 membership comprised of 11 producers, mostly major oil companies.[113]

The cost of operating in a remote and harsh environment like northern Alaska requires a major capital undertaking, which most independent operators can't afford to fund from cash flow nor will the typical energy banker underwrite. Yet even along the southern coast in and around Cook Inlet, where conditions are less harsh and comparatively less costly, there is a disparity in the pace of exploration with that of other states. This can be attributed, in part, to the lack of private mineral ownership, the lack of capital sources that grow up around private exploration and the bureaucratic—versus private capital—mindset, which does not lead to the same incentives for resource development.

The American Legacy

During the 90 years between the Alaska Purchase and its statehood, the U.S. recovered from a civil war and won two world wars. It had become an economic powerhouse and world leader, fueled in no small part by the oil and gas industry that was homegrown and controlled most of the world's hydrocarbon production, refining and distribution. The Cold War was under way and the Alaska territory was within 60 miles of Russia.

While reluctant to let Alaska become a state, the U.S. dictated and enforced the terms of admission to statehood, including the retention of Alaska's mineral wealth for the public good. Times had changed from when commercial production of petroleum first began in America. Harry S. Sachse, a lawyer and scholar, wrote:

---

[111] "Drilling Location and Oil Wells Across Texas." Accessed March 6, 2016, Texas-drilling.com.

[112] Chargeable Acreage by Lessee Summary, Department of Oil and Gas, State of Alaska. Accessed January 4, 2015.

[113] Alaska Oil and Gas Association. "Member Companies." Accessed March 6, 2016, Aoga.org.

> Petroleum was discovered in the United States during
> a period of economic laissez-faire and governmental
> weakness. The federal government lacked the political
> power to claim ownership of petroleum under private
> property. The states, on the other hand, without in-
> ternational obligations and before the period of social
> welfare legislation and of federal income tax, having
> sufficient powers of taxation, had no reason to claim
> the ownership of minerals which at that time in any
> event would have been politically impossible.[114]

Would history have been different if, instead of private mineral
ownership, the U.S. had insisted on retaining ownership and control
of the young nation's mineral wealth as it was able to do with the
Alaskan Territory? One needs only to compare the relative development of Alaska's mineral wealth to that of the Lower 48 for the answer.

The historical development of the laws pertaining to ownership
of minerals in the U.S. serves as the very foundation for the story of
independent producers and the evolution of their relationship with
energy bankers. Without access to private mineral ownership and, as
discussed below, access to capital, there would have been no opportunity for the early wildcatter to survive and, ultimately, evolve into
today's independent producer with access to bank capital, public markets and private equity.

Further, Alaska's oil and gas industry, like much of the world, has
benefited from innovations in oil and gas production that were nurtured in the Lower 48 states by an environment of private enterprise
built upon the foundation of private mineral ownership. Current development of the Lower 48's unconventional oil and gas resources is a
further example of innovation.

"Although other places, such as China and Europe, have substantial shale resources, they don't have the entrepreneur-friendly sys-

---

[114] Sachse, "A Comparison of the Landowner's Rights," 725.

tem needed to develop those resources quickly and productively," *Foreign Affairs* reported in 2014. "As much as other countries may envy this catalyst for domestic growth, they will not be able to replicate it, because only the United States possesses the unique ingredients necessary to fully develop shale resources.

"A legal system that enshrines the private ownership of land and the resources below it, along with open capital markets and a reasonable regulatory system, has led to the growth of thousands of independent oil and gas companies all of which are in intense competition with one another. As a result, nearly four million oil and gas wells have been drilled in the United States, versus 1.5 million in the rest of the world. The bustle of drilling activity in the United States has also led to increases in innovation within the industry on an order of magnitude that other countries can only dream of."[115]

---

[115] Robert A. Hefner III, "The United States of Gas, Why the Shale Revolution Could Have Happened Only in America," *Foreign Affairs* 93(3) (May/June 2014).

CHAPTER 2

The Early Years:
1900-1930s

"You may all go to Hell, and I will go to Texas."
Davy Crockett

C entral to the opportunities and success of the independent oilman was the independent streak of the Texas people and its politicians, as evidenced most succinctly by Davy Crockett in the above remark made on his way to join the men of the Alamo.[116] The Republic of Texas was born from a distrust of leaders in distant lands trying to control her destiny.

Upon statehood and following the Civil War, Texas' independent mindset was directed against control by the East, including control by East Coast banks. Beginning with the early days of the republic, Texas had only a few banks. Further, its 1845 constitution prohibited the

---

[116] "A gentleman from Nacogdoches, in Texas, informs us, that, whilst there, he dined in public with col. Crockett, who had just arrived from Tennessee. The old bear-hunter, on being toasted, made a speech to the Texians, replete with his usual dry humor. He began nearly in this style: 'I am told, gentlemen, that, when a stranger, like myself, arrives among you, the first inquiry is - what brought you here? To satisfy your curiosity at once to my-self, I will tell you all about it. I was, for some years, a member of congress. In my last canvass, I told the people of my district, that, if they saw fit to re-elect me, I would serve them as faithfully as I had done; but, if not, *they might go to h__, and I would go to Texas.* I was beaten, gentlemen, and here I am.' The roar of applause was like a thunder-burst." Hezekiah Niles, et al., *Niles Weekly Register, Volume 50* (The University of Chicago Librar-ies, April 9, 1836), 99.

incorporation of state banks; this prohibition lasted until 1904, except for a brief period during Reconstruction between 1869 and 1876.[117]

The first bank wasn't even formed in the state until 1861 and it was done only though the use of a loophole in the law and an 1835 State of Texas-Coahuila charter issued under Mexican rule. The utter lack of banks and banking facilities had a deadening effect on financial and industrial growth, which was the intention of the agrarian-controlled legislature. Businessmen and merchants exchanged promissory notes like cash. When hard money was required for transactions, the major currency was old silver Spanish and Mexican coins. Precious little coinage from the U.S. had penetrated Texas.[118]

In 1876, the state's populist constitution was amended to discourage non-Texas banks from operating in the state in an effort to return to local control the power that had been usurped by the U.S. government during Reconstruction. More specifically, the amendment targeted East Coast banks and monopolies, principally railroad magnates.

The banking code further inhibited the growth of Texas banking institutions by preventing the establishment of branch banks as well as the fact that, in Texas, "no horse or homestead could be attached for private debt, nor any wage or salary garnisheed," T.H. Fehrenbach wrote in *Lone Star: A History of Texas and the Texans*.[119] The capital requirements of federally chartered banks proved a high hurdle during Texas' early statehood. Only 13 national banks existed in the state through 1880. The number of national and private banks began to expand more rapidly in the last two decades of the 1800s. By 1905,

---

[117] Handbook of Texas Online, Lawrence L. Crum, "Banks and Banking," accessed March 13, 2016, Tsha.org.

[118] Fehrenbach, *Lone Star*, 321.

[119] "This rule, together with the fact that in Texas no horse or homestead could be attached for private debt, nor any wage or salary garnisheed, gave farmers immense protections. But it made the rise of any really significant financial institutions impossible." Fehrenbach, *Lone Star*, 437.

there were 440 national banks supported by growing agricultural, commercial, industrial and mining activities.[120]

As the 19th century came to an end, populist sentiment was directed, in particular, against large anti-competitive entities, including railroads and integrated companies like John D. Rockefeller's Standard Oil Co. Local politicians, eager to get elected, campaigned on voters' distrust of big business. The promotion of antitrust laws and attacks on monopolies were useful tools by Texas politicians to garner public support.[121]

They resisted control by any single, tight-knit faction or interests, especially when that interest could be stigmatized as "foreign," meaning non-Texan.[122] Texas was an agrarian state with little to no manufacturing industry. Before the political bull's-eye was painted on Standard Oil, the robber barons of the railroads were the popular target of the state's farmers, ranchers and merchants. Everyone counted on the railroads to get their produce and livestock to the larger markets of the East.

In the 1890s, Texas Attorney General Jim Hogg, who had won a court challenge against railroad magnate Jay Gould, successfully campaigned for governor on a platform that promised regulation of the railroads' high freight rates. Once elected, Hogg formed the Texas Railroad Commission, as promised, to regulate railroads and protect local ranchers and farmers. The commission's mandate was expanded soon after the turn of the century and it would play a critical role in the development of the oil industry, exerting influence far beyond railroads and even Texas' borders.

---

[120] Handbook of Texas Online, Lawrence L. Crum, "Banks and Banking," accessed March 13, 2016, Tshaonline.org.
[121] "After memory of the Lost Cause, most successfully manipulated by the bourbon Democrats and their successors, the most useful symbolic issue in Texas politics was monopoly." Diana D. Hinton and Roger M. Olien, *Oil in Texas: The Gusher Age, 1895-1945* (Clifton and Shirley Caldwell Texas Heritage, March 15, 2002), 21.
[122] Hinton and Olien, *Oil in Texas*, 15-23.

Chapter 2: The Early Years

Early Capital Sources

Antitrust sentiment successfully protected and nurtured the nascent Texas oil industry from the control of Rockefeller's Standard Oil. However, Texas' popular independence streak also supported an "open range" mentality in the oil patch that both helped and hurt the early independents.

In the decades prior to the discovery of the East Texas Field in the 1930s, independent oilmen across the country encountered landowners, suppliers, rig hands and the major oil companies as they tried to explore, drill and produce. By and large, they had relatively minor interaction with bankers, lawyers or accountants.[123] Few, if any, bankers were willing to risk their depositors' life savings on loans secured by collateral that could neither be measured nor seen.

A typical independent's "business plan" in the early days was to follow the geological trends, talk a farmer or two into leasing a small parcel and finagle or cobble together a second-hand rig, steam boiler and drilling crew that he paid with food when short of cash—thus known as "bean wages"—to drill a well with the hope of hitting oil before his money ran out.[124] If oil was found, the plan was to produce it as quickly as possible, so a neighboring oilman's well didn't drain the reservoir first.

These shallow wells typically cost less than $10,000 each.[125] A few, better-heeled independents could arrange a bank loan. But, even then, these loans were more likely secured by hard assets—equipment,

---

[123] "Whether or not most business deals were, as folklore has it, sealed with a handshake, the independent of 1920 did not design his business deals to fit a jungle of legal tangles, regulatory red tape, and complex tax laws. State regulation of oil was in its infancy in such places as Texas and Oklahoma; most states did not regulate the industry at all." Roger M. Olien and Diana D. Hinton, *Wildcatters*, 14.

[124] "The reason they were called bean jobs, literally beans was what they lived on. I know one fellow, he was getting ready to start a well, and he told me "Well, I have a hundred – pound sack of beans." ... In those days you'd get them for 3 or 4 cents a pound, so $3 or $4 would buy a whole sack of beans. Then they'd put up tents, ... or shacks of some kind." Ford Chapman, Midland independent recorded recollections, November 8, 1978, tape in the Abel Hanger Collection, Permian Basin Museum, Library, and Hall of Fame, Midland, Texas, quoted by Olien and Hinton, *Wildcatters*, 70.

[125] Olien and Hinton, *Wildcatters*, 57.

rigs and produced-oil inventory—rather than by prospective or even by producing properties.

Less well-heeled wildcatters had to use whatever hard collateral they could find. R.R. Penn, a young newspaper reporter covering the latest play in Corsicana Field, decided to get into the business in 1921 and called his wife back in Dallas, telling her to borrow on "everything but her wedding ring" and bring him the funds for a promising deal. [126]

Perhaps the most improbable grubstake tale was almost a real-life Jed Clampett story. Instead of shooting the ground and discovering oil, Harry Sinclair got his start when he shot off his big toe. E.P. "Matt" Matteson, an old oilfield hand who worked for White-Sinclair Oil Co., predecessor to the Sinclair Oil Corp., retold the story in 1953:

> The history of Harry Sinclair is that he was a drug clerk in a small town in Kansas. And this White, who later became his partner, was a small-time shallow well promoter. ... White got in a pinch for money [and] Harry had collected $750 from an insurance company from shooting his big toe off while getting through a barbed wire fence hunting rabbits. He got Harry interested – of course, you look for money where there is money. He got Harry interested in putting in that $750 to help him out to get casing and things he needed in order to finish this well. ... But that is the story, and I guess it is authentic, that the $750 he got for his big toe was really the start of the Sinclair Corporation.[127]

---

[126] Olien and Hinton, *Wildcatters*, 14.
[127] Mody C. Boatright, "E.P. Matteson, Pioneers in Texas Oil, An Oral History," *Dolph Briscoe Center for American History, The University of Texas at Austin* (Austin, Texas, July 22, 1953), T-90:7-8. An alternate version of the story had Sinclair collecting $5,000 insurance money, and reporting that some critics implied "that the discharge might not have been accidental." Doug Hicks, *Nearly Forgotten, The Amazing Story of the Glenn Pool, Oklahoma's First World-Class Oil Field* (Schnake Turnbo Frank, Inc., 2005), 121.

Harry Sinclair and his partner, P.J. White, would discover Cushing Field and, by the time of Sinclair's retirement in 1954, Sinclair Oil was a billion-dollar empire.[128]

Other would-be oil entrepreneurs used different capital-raising techniques—some fairly; others, dishonestly. The Roaring Twenties was not without unscrupulous promoters, who played on inexperienced investors' post-war, get-rich-quick mentality and popular "black gold" magazine articles. From *Wildcatters*:

> Promoters approached all varieties of potential investors, but wealthy persons ignorant of oil – doctors and lawyers and their widows – were favorite clients. Legitimate and less than legitimate companies alike took names calculated to appeal to the gambling instinct. Thus when the oil and gas fields of the Texas Panhandle opened up, among the 110 corporations doing business in Hutchinson County were the Double Five Company, the Straight Eight Oil Company, the Lucky Ten Oil Company, and the Magic Eighty Oil Company.[129]

Isaac Marcosson, in his 1924 chronicle of the American oil industry, *The Black Golconda*, described how unscrupulous stock promoters fleeced unsuspecting oil investors who were swept up by the enthusiasm of the latest oil booms. Marcosson credits Fort Worth as the capital of the most elaborate efforts to part honest, hard-working citizens from their meager dollars. Marcosson profiles a "Dr. F.A. Cook," a self-claimed conqueror of Mount McKinley, which is now known as Denali, and the North Pole.

Cook's solicitations were slick. He wrote to a widow in Alabama, when soliciting her to increase her investment, "After wandering … as far as the Arctic on the cold, bleak hills around the North Pole, I learned a lesson that all men and women were made up of humanity.

---

[128] Internal bank-communication materials compiled by Bank of Oklahoma and provided by Mickey Coats.
[129] Olien and Hinton, *Wildcatters*, 15.

Appreciating that our sojourn in this world is but of a short duration, … [i]n my declining years, my desire is to bring about, or cause to bring, happiness, pleasure, luxuries, and the things [people] love best. … [T]he confidence you have exhibited, brings upon my shoulders the responsibility of securing real results for you, and with your cooperation, I will."

In 1923, Henry Zweifel, a federal prosecutor, secured indictments against Cook and 104 other defendants. All were sentenced; Cook received 14 years and a $12,000 fine. One of the defendants asked to be sent to Leavenworth instead of the Atlanta penitentiary. Apparently this stock promoter had sold a block of fake stock to one of the wardens in Atlanta.[130]

Early promoters and drillers weren't shy either about invoking the powers of saints and rhabdomancy—the science of divination by rods or wands. Typically, these were no more than a forked twig called a "doodlebug," which was said to react in a certain way when held in both hands of the "expert" sometimes known as a "dowser," walking over the premises.[131]

As late as the 1950s, unscrupulous promoters continued to claim to possess the "magic sauce" to find oil. In one securities-fraud criminal case, defendant Ben H. Frank claimed to be able to locate oil with a device he promoted as a "magnetic logger," which the court described in common parlance as a "doodlebug."[132] Frank was found guilty of violating securities laws and of mail fraud. Perhaps it was his attorney who had the magic sauce: The conviction was reversed on appeal due to erroneous jury instructions.[133]

---

[130] Isaac F. Marcosson, *The Black Golconda* (New York Harper & Brothers, 1924), 297-329.

[131] Howard R. Williams and Charles J. Meyers, et al., *Williams and Meyers, Manual of Oil and Gas Terms, Fourth (4th) Edition* (Matthew Bender, 1976), 160.

[132] The prospectus prepared by Frank stated, "After ten years of work, and thousands and tens of thousands of experiments, Ben H. Frank has perfected what he calls a Magnetic Logger. A machine or device by means of which he can locate an oil pool, tell approximately the depth of the producing saturated Oil Sands to within 25 to 150 feet, and roughly gauge the size of the well when fully and properly completed, all before the well is drilled or even started." *Frank v. United States*, 220 F. 2d 559, 562 (10th Cir. 1955).

[133] Frank was found to have violated Section 17(a) of the 1933 Securities Act. *Frank v. United States*, 220 F. 2d 559, 564.

Chapter 2: The Early Years

On the other hand, the University of Texas may have been the most successful beneficiary of divine intervention when the Santa Rita No. 1 well came in in 1923. In 1919, Rupert Ricker, a University of Texas law-school graduate newly discharged from the U.S. Army, returned to his West Texas hometown of Big Lake to open a practice. He was taken by oil fever, however, and applied for leases on university land based on the geological theory of University of Texas professor J.A. Udden.

Udden suggested that an underground fold of rock might run from the area around Marathon, Texas, through Pecos County and into Upton and Reagan counties, which would make "excellent cover" for an oil pool. Ricker went to Fort Worth to promote enough of his leases to an oil company or two and raise the $43,000 filing fee due the General Land Office for 674 sections—that is, 431,160 acres—of university land spanning three counties.

Ricker was unsuccessful in generating the experienced oilmen's interest in the unproven scrub land of West Texas. As the 30-day filing fee deadline neared, he sold his ideas, maps and preliminary leases for $2,500 to Frank Pickrell, a war buddy from El Paso he ran into by chance on the street.[134]

Pickrell and his partner, Haymon Krupp, a dry-goods merchant from El Paso, had no better luck at flipping the prospect and decided to develop the acreage themselves. They formed Texon Oil & Land Co., but shares of the company were selling too slowly to fund drilling. To speed the fund-raising, Pickrell sold "certificates of interests" for $200, representing a 5/10,240th (0.048828%) undivided interest in an area dubbed "Group I," a 16-square-mile block.

Among the investors were some ladies in a Catholic fellowship in New York. As Pickrell explained years later, it was their investment that gave the name—and, perhaps, divine intervention—for the success of the test well, Santa Rita No. 1. "These women became a little worried about the wisdom of their investment and consulted with their priest. He apparently was also somewhat skeptical and suggested

---

[134] Olien and Hinton, *Wildcatters*, 18-19.

that the women invoke the aid of Santa Rita, who was the patron saint of the impossible. ...

"[T]wo of these women handed me a sealed envelope and told me that the envelope contained a red rose that had been blessed by the priest in the name of the saint. The women asked me to take the rose back to Texas with me – to climb to the top of the derrick and scatter the rose petals, which by then were dry, over the rig and to say 'I hereby christen thee Santa Rita.'"[135]

Texon raised more than $100,000 from the sale of interests and used the funds to make rental payments and buy used drilling equipment. Although they had hired a geologist to select a site for their test well, Texon staked its location nearer the railroad line to save on transportation costs.

On August 23, 1921, just four hours before the lease would expire, if drilling operations were not commenced, the well was spud. After drilling for 646 days with a cable-tool rig at rates averaging fewer than five feet a day, the driller shut down operations just above the 3,050-foot level when he saw evidence of gas escaping from the casinghead.

Convinced they had an oil well, the driller and his tool dresser left the site to lease surrounding mineral acreage—while the discovery was still unknown. The next day, May 28, 1923, and with no further drilling, Santa Rita No.1 roared to life, gushing oil over the top of the derrick.[136]

Pickrell and his novice investors, with the help of the patron saint of the impossible, discovered what became known as Big Lake oil field. Santa Rita No. 1—the first successful well drilled on Texas' University Lands—proved an auspicious beginning for the University

---

[135] "Santa Rita No. 1," Board for Lease of University Lands, University of Texas System, accessed October 12, 2013, Utsystem.edu.
[136] Handbook of Texas Online, Julia Cauble Smith, "Santa Rita Oil Well," accessed March 13, 2016, Tshaonline.org.

48

of Texas and other mineral owners in what became the Permian Basin.[137]

Royalties from Santa Rita No. 1 and subsequent West Texas wells were a legacy that originated with Republic of Texas President Lamar's plea in 1838 that land be set aside for "the establishment of a university where the highest branches of science may be taught."[138] But it took decades, state constitutions in 1866 and 1869, and legislative and regulatory actions before Lamar's wish was met. The state formally set aside 50 leagues (221,420 acres) of rich farmland in upper East Texas to be sold at public auction with proceeds dedicated to establish a permanent fund.

Even then, the state's path to establishing The University of Texas was hijacked under the 1876 constitution when the 50 leagues of fertile East Texas land was substituted with 1 million arid acres in West Texas. Supporters of the university complained that the switch was nowhere equitable and the legislature subsequently increased the western land dedication to 2 million acres that would later comprise a significant portion of Big Lake and other, prolific, Permian Basin fields.

But because this land in the late 1800s was considered poor for farming or grazing, there was little demand for it in public auction. By the time of the Santa Rita No. 1 discovery, most of the 2 million acres remained in the hands of the state.[139, 140]

---

[137] In 1940, the Santa Rita rig was moved from its original site to the University of Texas campus in Austin. Its presence commemorates a time of transformation for both the University of Texas and Texas A&M University, which shared in the university's land royalties. In 1990, after nearly 70 years of production, the Santa Rita No. 1 was finally plugged.

[138] Katherine Elliot and Charles A. Gullick, et al., ed., *The papers of Mirabeau Buonaparte Lamar*, vol. II (Austin, Tex., A.C. Baldwin, printers 1921-27), 349.

[139] Miller, *The Public Lands of Texas*, 120-125.

[140] Much of the state's untapped oil bounty, therefore, remained under state control for the benefit of generations of Texans as envisioned by President Lamar. With oil and gas royalties dedicated to the University of Texas and, in 1876, also to Texas A&M University, these public schools have been and continue as world-class institutions—including in research and training future petroleum-industry leaders of the U.S. and world. In May, 2016, for example, a new Saudi energy minister was named: Khalid al-Falih, a 1982 engineering graduate of Texas A&M.

Independents' Relationship with Majors

Assuming a lease could be secured and sufficient grubstake raised to fund drilling, even if the wildcatter made a discovery, he was, then, at the mercy of the majors, who made the market for crude and shipped it to their refineries for sale to the burgeoning gasoline market.[141] Majors were not required by any law to purchase third-party production; consequently, until an independent could sell his oil, it had to be stored onsite.

The nature of the times was the undoing of many a wildcatter. For example, as told by Olien and Hinton in *Wildcatters*, one Texas independent, Ed Landreth, exploiting an error in Crane County's early land survey, found an unleased strip of land—known in law as a "vacancy"—that he was able to lease in 1927 from the state. The lease was no more than 1,000 feet at its widest, but it ran more than four miles down the middle of the Gulf-McElroy oil field.

To undo Landreth, Gulf Oil Corp. quickly commenced drilling offset wells with six rigs along the property line. Landreth responded in-kind and his wells were even more prolific than Gulf's. Following more than a year of litigation over the vacancy and title, Landreth won the suit, but he was left with 800,000 barrels of oil in storage and no market.

A major, Gulf was the natural buyer, but there was no doubt that it would refuse to help this interloping profiteer. Undeterred, Landreth held onto the stored production for more than a year as he made big bets in other plays in the emerging Permian Basin.

Eventually, his luck took a turn for the worse and he was forced to liquidate much of his oil property. He sold his Crane County production—unfortunately after posted prices had halved—to Magnolia Oil Co., which was later amalgamated into what was Mobil Oil Corp. and is now part of Exxon Mobil Corp. He sold his producing lease to The Texas Co., which became Texaco Inc. and is now a part of Chevron Corp. as is Gulf Oil.[142]

---

[141] Olien and Hinton, *Wildcatters*, 27.
[142] Olien and Hinton, *Wildcatters*, 29-31.

However, not all independents viewed the majors as adversaries. For the most part, major oil companies and independents enjoyed a symbiotic relationship, with majors being the source of most of the capital independents used to lease, drill and explore for oil. Easy money for producers from stock promoters and a willing public was harder to come by after the 1929 stock-market crash. With the effects of the Depression becoming felt in oil boomtowns, independents increased their reliance on the majors as a source of capital.

This capital was in the form of contractual agreements, such as farmouts, dry-hole or bottom-hole contributions and investments in drilling ventures. The independents would attempt to monetize their successful efforts by selling their oil or their wells to the majors.[143] The majors, however, weren't always doing so well either, as petroleum-product demand had declined as the Depression deepened and they were faced with large acreage positions of their own that had to be drilled or, else, forfeited when the leases expired.

In the Permian Basin, for example, most leases had a primary term of 10 years, during which the lessee had to produce oil on the acreage or the lease would expire. During the 1930s, majors and some large independents farmed out much of their undeveloped acreage to smaller independents. In this arrangement, the major contributed the land and, sometimes, a portion of the drilling costs; the wildcatter drilled the well with sweat equity and was responsible for the balance of the cost.

In 1942, E.E. Reigle, a veteran Permian Basin wildcatter, explained how the majors, who might own thousands of acres in an area, would approach independents to do a deal: "They'd say, 'We'll give you this 160 [acres], and you drill a well on it. ...' This was your well, your acreage, see, but it was proving up a whole bunch of their stuff."[144]

---

[143] Olien and Hinton, *Wildcatters*, 25.

[144] E.E. Reigle, a veteran Permian Basin wildcatter, explained, "We drilled a lot of wildcat wells, but we didn't try to sell you an interest or the druggist an interest, or anyone like that. We went in there and maybe someone promoted us, selling us a lease or something in the area. ... Anyway, we would drill the well, and then maybe sell off acreage to Shell

With farmouts and cash from majors, the independents of the 1930s could take on ventures without much up-front capital, thus without extensive promotion outside the industry. The majors could count on the independents to risk everything to prove up a field and, if the production held up, sell their leasehold to the majors, who had more capital access and, therefore, more time to develop the field in a more deliberate, scientific fashion. The independents' advantage was that they could enter a play early—even before there was a play—for a fraction of what it would cost to enter later, after the leasehold was proven to be oil-bearing.

But having less capital than the majors meant that independents were in no position to lock up all of the prospective acreage around the well they drilled. Often, they had only enough money to spare for a small portion of the promising acreage, making early field discoveries a balkanized patchwork of independents, each one looking out only for himself.

Spindletop—Idle Dreams and Insane Notions

Discovered in January of 1901, Spindletop was an early example of this phenomenon. The early connection with banking and Spindletop's discovery highlights the rather-tenuous relationship of the two industries. Patillo Higgins, Spindletop's original promoter, did not try to get a loan from the local bank in Beaumont to drill his idea; no bank would consider lending to such a speculative venture. As it turned out, very few Beaumont citizens had any interest in it either.

Higgins finally convinced a few local businessmen to participate, forming the Gladys City Oil, Gas, and Manufacturing Co. But, after much delay and three failed attempts—all above 400 feet in depth—

---

or Atlantic. Or where we couldn't sell them anything, we'd probably go in there and drill a well offsetting them, and then Atlantic would give us $10,000 dry-hole money, Shell would give us $5000 dry-hole money. You know, that was enough to meet bare expenses. We could drill the well ... once in a while you'd make something. But that's the way we did it ... We didn't sell interests in the well, we didn't do any promoting, things like that." E.E. Reigle interview, *Petroleum: Industry Hearings Before the Temporary National Economic Committee* (New York: American Petroleum Institute, 1942), 456, quoted by Olien and Hinton, *Wildcatters*, 71.

his investors quit. He sought the opinion of an "expert" to bolster his efforts to raise more capital and arranged for a geologist from the Texas State Geological Survey to visit the property.

But, instead of seeing Higgins' vision, the geologist was concerned that the mounds like Spindletop, rising above Gulf Coast prairies, did not resemble oil-bearing structures back East. The state's geologist not only disagreed with Higgins, he wrote an open letter that was published by the Beaumont newspaper, warning local citizens to not be taken in by any get-rich schemes peddled by Higgins. He added that ventures to explore for oil in the area are "idle dreams or insane notions of irresponsible parties."[145]

Not surprisingly, Higgins began to look for interest beyond Beaumont, placing an ad in a trade journal. It was answered by Captain Anthony Lucas, who had been making a living drilling salt wells in South Louisiana. Higgins leased Lucas' 663 acres at $50 an acre. Lucas paid Higgins $11,500 in cash and the balance with a 7% note payable in two equal, annual installments.

Lucas had little better luck, reaching the top of the oil-bearing target and having collected less than a barrel of oil before the uncased wellbore sanded up and the well was lost. Lucille Silvey Beard, a graduate-school student, recounted in her master's program thesis a few years later, "At this point Lucas had exhausted his funds, his wife having sold their furniture piece by piece to enable him to carry on operations as long as possible. They used packing boxes in improvising necessary household furniture to take its place, while Lucas sought outside financial assistance so vital to his purpose."[146]

Lucas travelled east for investors. He was rebuffed by Standard Oil, but found a more receptive ear from the country's most successful drillers, the firm of Guffey and Galey, which was backed by the Mellon family in Pittsburgh.[147] Guffey and Galey agreed to drill up to

---

[145] Hinton and Olien, *Oil in Texas*, 27.
[146] Lucile Silvey Beard, "The History of the East Texas Oil Field" (Master of Arts Thesis, Faculty of the Graduate School of Hardin-Simmons University, June, 1938), 11, accessed March 6, 2016, Texasranger.org/E-Books.
[147] The Mellons turned that investment into what became Gulf Oil Corp.

three test wells in exchange for 7/8ths of Lucas' interest in the prospect.

The well was spud on October 27, 1900, and reached 1,020 feet in depth by January 10, 1901; the well came in, shooting a column of oil 100 feet above the top of the derrick. The rate was estimated to be 100,000 barrels a day. A few days later, a reporter first used the term "gusher" to describe it; Spindletop made news around the world.[148]

Initially, local papers were reporting that Spindletop confirmed the existence of a subterranean river of oil that flowed from Corsicana through Beaumont and emptied into an oil lake under the Gulf of Mexico.[149] Like many early geological theories about oil, this was just another fanciful explanation for the prodigious flood of Spindletop's production. In fact, as more wells were drilled, oilmen understood a new kind of geological trap was discovered—one in which the oil is trapped against the impermeable salt dome that penetrates the hydrocarbon-bearing sedimentary basin—of which there are many along the Gulf Coast.

Spindletop was uniquely situated to be the training ground for many successful independents, primarily because of the highly fractured nature of the oil-bearing reservoirs called fault blocks associated with the intrusive salt-dome structure. Wells were closely spaced and many a dry hole was drilled only tens of feet from commercial wells, while other producers could drill successful wells between previous dry holes.[150]

Importantly, the surface ownership was equally fractured, providing ample opportunity for many oilmen to try their luck. Even the former Texas governor, Jim Hogg, got into the act. The Hogg-Swayne Syndicate—consisting of Hogg, seven attorneys, a banker and a newspaperman—acquired a 15-acre lease from the partnership of Guffey, Galey and Lucas at a price of $180,000, plus $105,000 to J.M. Page for

---

[148] Yergin, *The Prize*, 69.
[149] Hinton and Olien, *Oil in Texas*, 35 (citing *The Houston Press*).
[150] James A. Clark and Michel T. Halbouty, *Spindletop* (Random House, 1952).

the surface tract, which Page had purchased for a $150 down payment and a $300 two-year note a few years prior to the Lucas gusher.[151]

In all, upfront costs were $310,000. The syndicate's members contributed $40,000 of their own money combined and, to come up with the $270,000 balance due, Hogg sold parcels as small as 1/20th and 1/24th of an acre to raise the rest. Hogg-Swayne sold one 1/20th-acre tract to the Texas Oil and Development Co. for $50,000—equivalent to a per-acre price of $1 million. Some of their purchasers formed companies and, subsequently, further divided their already-infinitesimal holdings to sell to additional prospectors.[152]

More than 300 wells were drilled on the 15-acre tract as there was no regulation that set minimum-acreage requirements. Many a derrick went up on lots no larger than 50 by 50 feet called "door mats" by the *Oil Investor's Journal*. "In some places, the legs of derricks touched others; derrick men were said to have placed planking from the top of one derrick to another as a catwalk escape route in the event of a blowout."[153]

The rush to drill on every square foot was the cause of much waste, but it also gave hundreds of men the opportunity to learn the oil business from scratch—an opportunity that renowned wildcatter Michel Halbouty, who carried ice water to the drillers at Spindletop as a boy, called the "Spindletop University of Roughnecks and Roustabouts."[154]

Without Rules; Capture and Waste

Not only was there no law regarding minimum spacing between wells, there was no regulation of the amount of oil any one well could produce on a monthly basis. Private ownership of minerals drew entre-

---

[151] Hinton and Olien, *Oil in Texas*, 33.
[152] "The syndicate members made tremendous profits in the next few weeks selling parcels of land in quarters, eighths, sixteenths, and thirty-seconds of an acre for small cash payments and the remainder out of oil." Clark and Halbouty, *Spindletop*, 108.
[153] Hinton and Olien, *Oil in Texas*, 34.
[154] Clark and Halbouty, *Spindletop*, 110; Douglas Martin, "Michel Halbouty, Oilman of Legend, Dies at 95," *The New York Times*, November 14, 2004, Nytimes.com.

preneurs to the oil industry, but, by the 1920s, it was being undermined by the flawed legal principle called the "rule of capture."

Prior to the 1920s—and, at times, later—American courts' rulings reflected the scientific community's lack of understanding of oil and gas development. Court decisions of the time likened the physical properties of subterranean oil and gas to underground rivers of water and ownership principles akin to early common-law-based ownership theories of wild birds and animals (*ferae naturaei*), passing from field to field. Under ancient common-law theory, such property (wild game) could only be owned when reduced to possession (caught or killed).[155]

Louisiana courts looked to provisions of their civil code for direction on the rights to ownership of fish and bees,[156] accepting early geologic theory that oil moves over extended subsurface areas without human intervention. But this reference was not without criticism and dissent. In a decision by the state's supreme court in 1922, dissenting Justice Provosky wrote, "Will it seriously be said that the system of laws which recognizes ownership in things so light of wing as birds and bees, and so fleet of movement as fish, and of so trifling value, denies ownership to a substance so infinitely less mobile as oil, and so

---

[155] *People's Gas Co. v. Tyner*, 131 Ind. 277, 31 N.E. 59 (1892) (underground water); *Westmoreland & Cambria Nat. Gas Co. v. DeWitt*, 130 Pa. 235, 18 Atl.724, 725 (1889) (wild animals); "because of their fugitive nature, since they are supposed to percolate restlessly about under the surface of the earth, even as the birds fly from field to field and the beasts roam from forest to forest ... Their 'fugitive and wandering existence within the limits of a particular tract was uncertain' ... They belong to the owner of the land, and are part of it, so long as they are on or in it, and are subject to his control; but when they escape, and go into other land, or come under another's control, the title of the former owner is gone. Possession of the land, therefore, is not necessarily possession of the gas. If an adjoining, or even a distant, owner, drills his own land, and taps your gas, so that it comes into his well and under his control, it is no longer yours, but his." *Pierson v. Post*, 3 Cai. R. 175, 2 Am. Dec. 264 (N.Y. 1805) is the seminal American jurisprudence wild-animal decision. The case involved a dispute between Post, who was in hot pursuit of a fox, and Pierson, who seeing the fox flee and cornered in an abandoned well, shot the fox and kept it for himself. New York's supreme court overruled the trial court, and held that Pierson, who captured the fox, was the rightful owner, notwithstanding Post's efforts and pursuit.

[156] "[P]igeon, bees, and fish, which go from one pigeon house, hive or fish pond, into another pigeon house, hive or fish pond, belong to the owners of those things; provided, such pigeons, bees or fish have not been attracted thither by fraud or artifice." Article 519 of the Civil Code, see La. Civ. Code Ann.art. 3415 (West 2011).

valuable that its possession is not threatening to become the apple of discord between the nations of the earth."[157]

By the late 1920s, petroleum's economic importance had been well demonstrated; however, development of this resource was still stymied by the question of ownership. During the latter half of the 1800s, courts—principally in Pennsylvania, Ohio and West Virginia, which were the country's earliest oil producers—wrestled with it. The question was reduced to whether oil and gas in the ground was unconditionally owned by the property owner, like coal and other hard minerals,[158] or whether ownership was determined only at the time it was produced to the surface, like the law pertaining to underground water.[159]

The courts had to find a way to allow two or more landowners to enjoy petroleum-property rights that would encourage investment without infringing on the non-participating neighbors' rights. The fugacious nature of oil and gas and the permeable nature of the oil-bearing formation underground allow oil to flow without regard to surface-property boundaries, resulting in that a property owner can be producing his neighbor's oil and gas as well as his own.

Late 19th-century judges had to reconcile the historical primacy of private-property rights in Anglo-American jurisprudence with the widespread desire to develop this new energy source to fuel the ever-expanding American economy.[160] For the most part, courts in oil-producing states recognized the ownership or qualified ownership to such underground minerals prior to production to be held by the owner of the property. However, given the assumed mobility of oil—and, more so, gas—courts also held that such ownership could be lost

---

[157] *Frost-Johnson Lumber Co. v. Salling's Heirs*, 150 La. 756, 803, 91 So. 207, 224 (1922); Sachse, "A Comparison of the Landowner's Rights," 735 n. 4.

[158] *Kier v. Peterson*, 41 Pa. 357 (1862) (Woodward, J., concurring) (stating that petroleum "is part of the land. It is land.").

[159] *Wood County Petroleum Co. v. West Virginia Transportation Co.*, 28 W. Va. 210 (1886).

[160] "Generally, [early courts] did not trouble themselves to explain how this result could come about: thus the Ohio Supreme Court, in *Kelley v. Ohio Oil Co.*, was content to affirm that '[p]etroleum oil is a mineral, and while in the earth it is part of the realty, and should it move from place to place by percolation or otherwise, it forms part of that tract in which it tarries for the time being.'" Daintith, *Finders Keepers*, 32.

if production by an adjacent landowner's well caused oil or gas to drain across property lines and be produced by the neighbor.

It is not without coincidence that courts' opinions include references to petroleum as if it were alive: "In which it tarries,"[161] "the power and the tendency to escape without the volition of the owner"[162] and "to percolate restlessly about under the surface of the earth, even as the birds fly from field to field and the beasts roam from forest to forest."[163]

A 1925 ruling characterized oil as "restlessly and ceaselessly moving about in the bowels of the earth in response to natural forces and influences which have never been fathomed or mastered by human science."[164] In 1907, a Pennsylvania court observed, "What can the neighbor do? Nothing, only go and do likewise, He must protect his own oil and gas. He knows it is wild and will run away if it finds an opening and it is his business to keep it at home."[165]

Daintith, in his analysis of the history of the rule of capture, argues that early jurists were not swayed by analogies to English law related to wild animals. In fact, early on, American courts rejected English law related to wild animals; in early American life, wild animals were, at best, a source of sustenance and, more often, a nuisance. This pioneering spirit was reflected in the nation's laws, allowing access for hunting even to private land that was not enclosed, Daintith noted. "By the middle of that century, there was a general presumption that landowners who did not post notices of exclusion welcomed hunters to come onto their undeveloped land."[166]

---

[161] *Kelly v. Ohio Oil Co.*, 57 Ohio St. 317, 49 N.E. 399 (1897).

[162] *Westmoreland & Cambria Natural Gas Co. v. De Witt*, 130 Pa. 235, 18 A. 724, 725 (Pa 1889).

[163] *Medina Oil Development Co. v. Murphy*, 233 S.W. 333, 335 (Tex. Civ. App. 1921).

[164] *Texas Pacific Coal and Oil Co. v. Comanche Duke Oil Co.*, 274 S.W. 193, 194 (Tex. Civ. App. 1925) (rev'd).

[165] *Barnard v. Monongahela Natural Gas Company*, 216 Pa. 362, 365, 63 A. 801, 802 (1907).

[166] Daintith, *Finders Keepers*, 34. This early American right is the basis for the "Posted: No Trespassing" signs still seen in country settings, notwithstanding that the early American-pioneering open-range mentality has been fenced in under current state statutes. Brian Sawers, "The Right to Exclude From Unimproved Land," 83 *Temple Law Review* 665 (2011): 677.

Chapter 2: The Early Years

In a *Temple Law Review* article, Brian Sawers noted, "English law restricted hunting by landownership and class; both limitations were rejected in the colonies. In Illinois, an English traveler was told by locals that a system that limited hunting to landowners would not be tolerated. The right to hunt, without property qualifications or other restrictions, was protected by state constitution, statute, and case law."[167]

Later critics of the early Appalachian court opinions ridiculed the jurists' lack of understanding of reservoir mechanics. Hydrocarbons do lie (largely) static like hard minerals; however, when pressure is unnaturally changed by a wellbore piercing the formation, the hydrocarbons naturally flow—that is, migrate—toward where the pressure is lower, which is at the surface. Wells drilled near a neighbor's land would likely capture the neighbor's oil and gas as well if the neighbor did not, likewise, have a producing well.

The rationale to harmonize these inconsistent positions was explained by the Texas Supreme Court in 1923 in *Stephens County v. Mid-Kansas Oil & Gas Co.*: "If the owners of adjacent lands have the right to appropriate, without liability, the gas and oil underlying their neighbor's land, then their neighbor has the correlative right to appropriate, through like methods of drainage, the gas and oil underlying the tracts adjacent to his own."[168]

Essentially, the drained landowner's recourse was not to be found in the courts, but through self-help.[169] The rule of capture, as interpreted by oilmen, was that "you own it, unless someone takes it away from you first." This rule made sense in England when applied to plentiful game and fish, but, when applied to scarce and significantly more valuable petroleum resources, the rule was lost in translation

---

[167] Sawers, "The Right to Exclude From Unimproved Land," 677.

[168] *Stephens Co. v Mid-Kansas Oil & Gas Co.*, 113 Tex. 160, 254 S.W. 290 (1923).

[169] *Michalson v Nutting*, 275 Mass. 232, 175 N.E. 490, 77 A.L.R. 1109 (1931) (holding, "His remedy is in his own hands. The common sense of the common law has recognized that it is wiser to leave the individual to protect himself, if harm results to him from this exercise of another's right to use his property in a reasonable way, than to subject that other to the annoyance, and the public to the burden, of actions at law, which would be likely to be innumerable and, in many instances, purely vexatious.")

in American courts. The capture theory created an incentive to exploit petroleum resources as quickly as possible, which caused wasteful drilling and wasteful production.[170]

The rule of capture was not so much a "right to capture," but more of an absolute defense to liability for draining the adjoining owners' reserves. The consequence of this legal license to "capture what you can" permitted—even encouraged—oilmen to produce every well flat out lest their neighbors helped themselves to it first.

As the technological knowledge of the industry progressed by the latter part of the 1920s, the simplistic view of underground rivers of oil was replaced with the knowledge that untapped oil and gas is relatively *in situ* and not fugitive.[171] Not only did the technology highlight the flawed legal theory of ownership, it also confirmed that drilling too many wells too close together and producing every well unchoked would prematurely diminish the reservoir's ability to produce, resulting in less overall, ultimate recovery.[172]

W.L. Summers, an early scholar of oil and gas law, characterized the rule—even before it became known as the "rule of capture"—as "a relic of barbarism."[173] But, before the judicial decisions could catch up with technological knowledge of the day, it would take the courts, legislatures and producers (and their lawyers) almost a decade to rein in these wasteful and self-destructive legal principles. Only then could bankers gain comfort to make loans to early oil pioneers.

Through the middle of the 1930s, the common practice in the oil field was to let the well flow at maximum capacity for as long as the well would produce. Shutting in a well to wait for proper construction of surface storage or a pipeline connection could spell doom for the

---

[170] Howard R. Williams and Charles J. Meyers, *Oil and Gas Law*, 1 Sections 203.1 and 204.4 (1988).

[171] A.W. Walker, "Fee Simple Ownership of Oil and Gas in Texas," 6 *Tex. L. Rev.* 125 (1928).

[172] In 1917, the U.S. Bureau of Mines established an experimental station at Bartlesville, Oklahoma, to study new ways of improving production methods. In 1919, the Bureau of Mines estimated that 80% of the recoverable underground petroleum was being lost under flush production methods. Nicholas Malavis, *Bless the Pure & Humble: Texas Lawyers and Oil Regulation, 1919-1936* (Texas A&M University Press; 1st edition, 1996), 18.

[173] W.L. Summers, "Property in Oil and Gas," 29 *Yale Law Journal* 174 (1919): 179.

well as the uncased wellbore would likely sand up and, when reopened, produce at diminished rates, if at all.

Given the independents' lack of capital or credit, this was just as well. The quicker and greater volume a well could produce, the quicker the producer could pay off his creditors and recover his investment. Moreover, it would have been economic suicide for any one producer to restrict his well's production if all of the surrounding producers were producing fullbore, thereby draining his acreage. In fact, courts implied an obligation on the producer as the lessee to develop the property as quickly as reasonably possible.[174]

This lack of restraint created many a boom-and-bust cycle for the independents as each major discovery was made and played out during more than 30 years after Spindletop. As exploration technology improved, so did the frequency and size of wildcatters' discoveries. Early, localized booms in Texas and Oklahoma expanded to the Rockies, California and Louisiana and market problems became national. "Ever-larger new discoveries vastly increased reserves of crude oil," Olien and Hinton wrote in *Wildcatters*. This led to a decline in prices, "undermining the financial position of an increasing number of independents across the country."[175]

By the late 1920s, there was a glut of oil on the market. Oil in storage is estimated to have been more than 500 million barrels.[176] "It was obvious that changing the situation would not be easy and, under existing law, might be impossible."[177]

Oil-price fluctuation caused by the booms and busts discouraged banks during the 1920s from enthusiastically lending to explorers. In 1920, the posted price for 36-degree API, Midcontinent crude oil was $3.50 a barrel; in 1921, it fell to $1; and, during the balance of that

---

[174] *Leonard v. Prater*, 18 SW2d 681 (Tex.Civ.App. 1929).
[175] Olien and Hinton, *Wildcatters*, 43-45.
[176] U.S. EIA, Independent Statistics & Analysis. "U.S. Ending Stocks excluding SPR of Crude Oil." Accessed March 6, 2016. Eia.gov.
[177] Olien and Hinton, *Wildcatters*, 43-45.

decade, it varied from $1 to $2.29. In all, there were 23 increases and 27 decreases in the posted price during the 10-year period.[178]

The stock market crash of 1929 and the Great Depression that followed converted a number of oilmen to conservation—not so much to save oil, but to save the industry from the ruinous overproduction that had violently shaken oil prices. Oilmen's options had narrowed to three possibilities: self-help, state regulation or federal control. Whichever path they finally settled upon would surely be challenged in the courts.[179]

East Texas: The Discovery that Changed the World

For stock-market investors, the Great Depression came on October 29, 1929. For oil producers—majors and independents alike—their "Great Depression" would come one year later. On October 3, 1930, Columbus Marion "Dad" Joiner's Daisy Bradford No. 3 discovered the East Texas Field—the largest U.S. oil field by that time, exceeding those of California and Oklahoma. The field would prove to be between five and 12 miles wide and 43 miles long underneath five East Texas counties.

The city of Kilgore was smack in the middle and was transformed overnight. "People poured into Kilgore, leaping 'like fleas off a dead dog' from the train station," the *Houston Chronicle* reported in an article about the era. "The town's population exploded—from 600 to more than 8,000. The town threw itself into the frenzy of drilling.

"They ripped stores in half along the town's main street, in one instance erecting 24 derricks on half a city block. They tore down the First National Bank and drilled right through its terrazzo floor. They even sliced the sacristy off the Presbyterian Church, throwing up three more derricks in its place."[180]

---

[178] Wallace Wilson, Continental Illinois National Bank and Trust Company of Chicago, "Bank Financing of Oil and Gas Production Payments" (paper presented to the Faculty of the Southwestern Graduate School of Banking, Dallas, Texas July 1962), 16.
[179] Malavis, *Bless the Pure & Humble*, 25.
[180] Alan Bernstein et al., "Houston & Oil: The Feast, The Famine, The Future," *Houston Chronicle*, June 2, 1985.

At its peak by the middle of 1931, the East Texas Field was producing 750,000 barrels a day. The output was 60% of Texas oil, 37% of U.S. oil and 22% of world oil.[181] The productivity, coupled with a decline in domestic consumption as a result of the Depression, resulted in an oil glut: The price was $1.10 a barrel before Daisy Bradford No. 3, but soon declined to 15 cents and, even, two cents.[182]

It spawned new law and regulation. Olien and Hinton wrote, "As a tidal wave of East Texas production swamped the national crude oil market, prices fell to levels at which production was often unprofitable. East Texas brought oilmen to abandon the hope of the late twenties that the industry could resolve its own problems and regulate itself without outside interference. In a painful, five-year struggle punctuated by violence, oilmen adapted to government regulation. The passage from freewheeling flush production to proration and regulation was rocky and turbulent."[183]

Prior to the enactment of conservation laws that controlled how much could be pumped from each well, only a few banks in the country made secured loans to oil producers located in the producing states of Oklahoma and Texas. Typical of the day, Dad Joiner's capital did not come from the local bank. He bartered, finagled and promoted interests in the well.

"The money came in very slowly and there were times when the well was shut down for days waiting for funds to buy much needed equipment," Beard recounted. "Sometimes there was no money for paying wages, or for settling with the grocer in Overton for foodstuff furnished in running a cook tent for the crew.

"Mr. Walter D. Tucker, an Overton banker, who had obtained a block of leases prior to Joiner's entry in East Texas, turned over his lease holdings to Joiner, enabling Joiner to acquire many valuable leases that he could not otherwise have had. Not only this, Mr. Tucker and his associates worked indefatigably in behalf of the Joiner drilling

---

[181] Wilson, "Bank Financing of Oil," 16.
[182] Yergin, *The Prize*, 244-259. Bryan Burrough, *The Big Rich: The Rise and Fall of the Greatest Texas Oil Fortunes* (Penguin Books, 2009).
[183] Olien and Hinton, *Wildcatters*, 43.

activity, straining their resources to the limit in order to keep the well going. During the drilling of the first two wells, in order to help Joiner in keeping expenses at a minimum, Mr. Tucker himself worked on the well with the drilling crew, while his wife superintended the cooking for them."[184]

Where hard cash was required, Joiner raised money for the Daisy Bradford by selling certificates of fractional interests in the well. Unfortunately, Joiner oversubscribed the well and he and his investors spent a lot of time with lawyers in more than 200 lawsuits. Bryan Burrough wrote in *The Big Rich* that, for example, one lease was sold 11 times.[185] In this case, Joiner would have been better off had the third well been a dry hole; investors would never have been the wiser. But the well came in.

Not all oil promoters intended to actually drill the wells. A defendant in a stock-promotion scheme a few years earlier "advertised a drilling campaign so incessantly that to save his face he had to put down a well. To his great surprise he got oil," Marcosson wrote. He saw no income from the venture, as he had fully sold every share in the well; however, he used his "success" in subsequent stock promotions.[186]

Within a year of the Daisy Bradford No. 3, the area of the East Texas Field was a reincarnation of the Wild West. The mistakes at Spindletop and every major discovery thereafter were repeated. And, because of the field's massive reserves, the ramifications of repeating these mistakes were multiplied many times over.

By the middle of 1931, it was said a man could leap from derrick to derrick and never touch the ground for six miles. Wells were being drilled at a rate of eight a day. In one year, more than 3,600 wells were

---

[184] Beard, "The History of the East Texas Oil Field," 27.
[185] "To raise money for his third well on the Daisy Bradford land, [Joiner] had sold three rounds of investment certificates to dozens of local people. In return for a hundred dollars, each of the certificates entitled the buyer to 4 of the 320 acres Joiner had set aside for investors. This meant only the first eighty certificates were valid." Bryan Burrough, *The Big Rich: The Rise and Fall of the Greatest Texas Oil Fortunes* (Penguin Books, 2009), 67.
[186] Marcosson, *The Black Golconda*, 328. The defendant, Henry H. Hoffman was found guilty of stock fraud and received two years in prison and was fined $5,000.

drilled—and everyone seemed to find oil.[187] To protect claims and sabotage neighbors' claims, pipelines were dynamited, derricks and bridges bombed, and creeks set on fire with burning oil.[188]

Without any restrictions on rates of production for any well, adjoining lease-owners raced to produce the maximum they could sell—even at depressed market prices—to produce more than their neighbors. The price posted for oil across the country fluctuated with the seasons and with the announcement of each new discovery. Production records were rarely preserved or reliable.

For bankers accustomed to calculable and limited risk in the more established markets for land, cotton and cattle, the early days of oil banking were not for the faint of heart. Joiner sold most of his holdings to H.L. Hunt for $24,000 in cash and four, laddered payments totaling $45,000, plus a $910,000 payment to be made out of future production.[189]

Hunt was rebuffed by banks in Shreveport, Louisiana, when seeking an early loan of $50,000 against his interest in 4,000 acres that included the Daisy Bradford. Burrough wrote that Louisiana bankers, "like their brethren across the country, had yet to appreciate the intricacies of the oil business; if they couldn't physically see their collateral, their vaults stayed shut." [190]

The early days of the oil business were speculative and too hazardous to attract traditional, commercial-bank credit. Unable to predict future production rates and prices necessary to pay back the loan, few producers were able to get more than a cup of coffee from his local banker.[191] Bank credit, if available at all, was only extended to

---

[187] Burrough, *The Big Rich*, 75.
[188] "The Oil Wars," Texas State Library Archives, accessed March 7, 2016, Tsl.state.tx.us.
[189] Hinton and Olien, *Oil in Texas*, 174.
[190] Burrough, *The Big Rich*, 75-81.
[191] "For an oilman to get money from a banker in the twenties was no small achievement. Few banks customarily made loans for oil ventures, whose risky nature was fully appreciated by prudent bank directors. Those few that did lend money to oilmen would not accept their major asset, oil-producing properties, as collateral; bankers knew that there was no reliable way to determine a property's future production level, that production could decline precipitously in a short time, and that crude oil prices were notoriously unstable." Olien and Hinton, *Wildcatters*, 28.

producers with access to the records of other, reputable operators of properties in the same area and only for an amount that could be repaid in a very short period of time.[192]

Unusual for the times, as Hunt did not have substantial resources prior to developing his East Texas stake, he was able to get a loan in Dallas from First National Bank for $50,000, unsecured because the bank's president, Nathan Adams, was so confident of the field's potential. This failure to secure the loan upfront almost caused Hunt to lose his entire fortune two years later after Dad Joiner, who sold his acreage to Hunt, had seller's remorse and threatened to sue Hunt for fraud.

Sensing that Joiner was preparing to file a *lis pendens* on the acreage, Hunt had his attorney, J.B. McEntire, and an army of stenographers prepare mortgages overnight, granting liens in favor of First National Bank and Hunt's major supplier, Continental Supply Co. The mortgages were recorded in the Henderson County courthouse the next morning as soon as it opened, which was not a moment too soon: An hour later, Joiner's attorney filed suit.[193]

In a 1954 report, Eugene McElvaney, senior vice president of Dallas' First National Bank, echoed that it was foolhardy for any banker in those early days to loan money against "a fugitive asset hidden deep in the bowels of the earth beyond the sight or touch of man, and which a few scant years ago would have been rank speculation."[194] But as the magnitude of the East Texas Field became better appreciated, McElvaney wrote, and bankers recognized the need for ready capital to finance the new bonanza, the unrestrained rule of capture for the most part kept them on the sidelines:

[192] R. Elmo Thompson (President, The First National Bank & Trust Co., Tulsa, Oklahoma), "Legal And Other Aspects of Financing The Oil Industry," 3 *Rocky Mt. Min. L. Inst.* (1957).

[193] Burrough, *The Big Rich*, 75-81

[194] Eugene McElvaney (Senior Vice President, First National Bank in Dallas, Dallas, Texas), "Some Aspects of Financing Oil and Gas Transactions," *Fifth Annual Institute on Oil and Gas Law and Taxation as it Affects the Oil and Gas Industry, Southwestern Legal Foundation* (1954), 309.

When Nature placed its greatest single wealth producing asset fortuitously on the virtual doorstep of the financial center of the Southwest, a critical and constructive examination of the needs for developing that
asset was imperative if banking was to keep attuned to
both its responsibilities and its opportunities. Shun-
ning still, as it always had and I'm sure always will, the
risk of the pure wildcatter in his search for oil, bankers soon recognized that here had been discovered a
natural warehouse with billions of dollars of measura-
ble collateral if the owners could but find ways and
means of producing it and appropriating not only for
their own enrichment but for the benefit of our overall economy.

Feeling their way cautiously, and I might add
courageously, deserting well entrenched banking policy, what are now the leading oil banks of the country
actually experimented in new and unproven territory.
And yet, despite the abundance of known reserves
which engineering soon proved to the entire satisfac-
tion of borrower and lender, the ruthless pursuit of
the old law of capture, every man for himself and the
devil take the hindmost, quickly rendered East Texas
a chaotic ocean of oil, glutting the market in an orgy
of waste and profligate overproduction which threatened the very economic foundation of the industry
and destroyed the value to which those pioneering
banks were looking for the safety of their loans on
discovered but unproduced oil.[195]

Efforts in Reining in Overproduction

Not only were bankers aghast; the politics of oil were also going
through growing pains at both the federal and state levels. During the
1920s, a campaign for regulation was led by Cities Service Co. president Henry L. Doherty. He warned that the industry was operating in
a way that undermined its own future, criticizing the rule of capture as

---

[195] Eugene McElvaney, "Some Aspects of Financing Oil," 316.

"extremely crude and ridiculous," prematurely exhausting reservoir pressure, leaving oil underground that was otherwise recoverable.

Doherty personally lobbied presidents of other oil companies, regulators and even corresponded with President Coolidge.[196] Finding states unable to address national supply issues, he advocated federally sanctioned cooperative development or unitization. As an alternative, Doherty suggested application similar to state laws patterned after irrigation and drainage districts that regulated water access in Western states. He advocated requiring unit development of oil fields under the supervision of oil districts staffed by landowners.

Studies commissioned at the federal level as well as technical studies by geologists supported Doherty's position. But he was opposed by most of the major oil companies, particularly Sun Oil Co. president J. Howard Pew and Gulf Oil Corp. president G.S. Davidson, who preferred self-regulation without governmental interference. In addition, Amos L. Beaty, president of The Texas Co., said that compulsory unitization violated the U.S. Constitution's due-process and contract clauses.

Coolidge shared the oilmen's distaste for governmental regulation of business and preferred that the industry self-regulate through trade associations. As science progressed, more oilmen agreed with Doherty's premise that regulated production would mean higher recovery at less cost. But they continued to object to Doherty's solution, preferring *laissez faire* capitalism over interference from regulators who neither understood the science nor the business of the oil industry.[197]

In 1924, the Louisiana legislature passed its first modern oil and gas conservation law. It prohibited wells from being drilled within a certain distance of each other, established a common market for petroleum in the state and provided for governmental determination of the amount of petroleum that could be taken from each well. The al-

---

[196] Malavis, *Bless the Pure & Humble*, 19.
[197] Malavis, *Bless the Pure & Humble*, 17-29.

lowable amount depended upon the market for petroleum and, at least in principle, the perimeter area the well could drain.[198]

With such a radical departure from the rule of capture, it isn't surprising that the constitutionality of the statute was attacked. But it was upheld by the state's courts on the ground that, under Louisiana's property laws, oil and gas are not susceptible to private ownership until extracted; therefore, no one has the right to complain if he is not allowed to extract it.[199] Moreover, constitutional challenges filed in federal courts upheld the act, consistent with a nascent conservation movement gaining momentum in other federal decisions that petroleum was an important natural resource and it was within the police power of the state to regulate its production.[200]

Other states were also attempting to limit well production—described as "allowables"—on a field-by-field basis under their conservation laws before the East Texas discovery. The Oklahoma Corporation Commission was empowered in 1915 to regulate production to match market demand, but its efforts were challenged in the courts and many of Oklahoma's operators did not feel bound by law to comply.[201]

By the time of the East Texas discovery, the price of oil in Oklahoma had fallen to as low as 10 cents per barrel. Established in 1907 by Oklahoma's first constitution, the Corporation Commission had oversight of the oil industry. But it had been allocated meager field personnel and resources to enforce its duties and was enmeshed in legal tangles with independent producers.

---

[198] Sachse, "A Comparison of the Landowner's Rights," 735 n.4.

[199] *State v. Thrift Oil & Gas Co.*, 162 La. 165, 110 So. 188 (La. 1926).

[200] *Lilly v. Conservation Commissioner of Louisiana*, 29 F. Supp. 892 (E.D. La. 1939). "The effect of the federal case, which relied on certain language of *Ohio Oil Co. v. Indiana*, … ruled that the state should have the right to insure the orderly production of one of its most valuable resources—whether that resource is susceptible of private ownership or not." Sachse, "A Comparison of the Landowner's Rights," 735.

[201] Olien and Hinton, *Wildcatters*, 52. Under the Act of 1915 the Oklahoma legislature defined waste as including "economic waste, underground waste, surface waste, and waste incident to the production of crude oil or petroleum in excess of transportation or marketing facilities or reasonable market demands." Okla. Laws 1915, c. 197; Okla. Stat. tit. 52, c.3.

After the Oklahoma City Field was discovered in 1928, production from wells drilled on individual town lots extended to the grounds of the state capitol. According to a 1938 report, "it is said that the noise was so great that the windows of the legislative halls had to be closed so that deliberations on amendments to oil and gas laws could be heard."[202]

In 1931, the commission was further hamstrung by an injunction Champlin Refining Co. obtained against state enforcement of proration laws. In August, Oklahoma Governor William H.D. "Alfalfa Bill" Murray declared martial law around wells in 27 oil fields to be enforced until oil reached $1 a barrel.[203]

The National Guardsmen were met with resistance. Rifle butts and tear gas were used to quell more unruly workers and daily production declined by 300,000 barrels. But the field hands in Oklahoma City were savvier than the guardsmen. By reversing gauges, so they would appear to be closed, producers continued pumping into pipelines that flowed to the warehouse district on the eastern side of downtown and into storage tanks that were trucked out under cover of night.[204]

California attempted to rein in chaos and wastefulness as well. For example, in the Los Angeles City Field, which was discovered in 1890, an eight-block area downtown had more than 500 producing

---

[202] William R. Richards, Thomas A. Mitchell and Michael S. Johnson, *"Oil and Gas Conservation in Utah After Cowling: The Law of Capture Receives a New Lease on Life,"* 14 J. Energy Nat. Resources & Envtl. L. 1, 1994, 5 (quoting Symposium, *"Legal History of Conservation of Oil and Gas,"* Min. L. Section of the A.B.A. 233 (1938))).

[203] In the declaration, Murray cited the need to protect the state's oil reserves and noted an alleged attempt by one of the state's leading independents, Harry Sinclair, to bribe state legislators. Murray accused Sinclair Oil officials of "holding numerous secret meetings with seditious intent and intrigue, against the State Government." [sic]. "One of these secret meetings was held in the city of Tulsa last March ... to consider the possibility of bribing forty members of the Legislature and impeaching the Governor." Murray alleged that Sinclair's "intrigues" were specifically designed to drive the price of oil through the floor "against the best interests of the school children of the State." Page S. Foshee, "'Someone get the Governor an Aspirin:' Ross Sterling and Martial Law in East Texas," *East Texas Historical Journal*, Vol. 41, Issue 2 Article 5 October 2003, Scholarworks.sfasu.edu.

[204] Kenny A. Franks, "Hot Oil Controversy," *Encyclopedia of Oklahoma History and Culture*, Okhistory.org (accessed April 3, 2016).

wells by 1897.[205] In 1903, with the 1899 discovery of Kern River Field, California was the nation's No. 1 oil-producing state, accounting for almost 25% of total U.S. production.[206]

In 1929, the state passed a conservation law, encouraging voluntary agreements to prevent "unreasonable waste of natural gas" and stated that "the blowing of natural gas into the air shall be *prima facie* evidence of unreasonable waste."[207] As elsewhere, the small producers who were affected the most refused to comply with voluntary restrictions.[208]

California further adopted a minimum-spacing rule in 1931; however, the statute was ineffective to prevent wasteful offset drilling in that it proscribed the minimum spacing of one well per acre.[209] This one-acre spacing remained the rule until 1977, following discovery of Cal Canal Field by Occidental Petroleum Corp. It had petitioned for field-wide, 40-acre spacing after a small leaseholder, J.C. Thompson, filed an application to drill three wells on tracts no greater than 1.25 to 2.5 acres adjacent to its leasehold. The state approved Occidental's application and the order was the first time spacing greater than one acre had been established.[210]

The Texas Road to Proration

Beginning in 1917 and expanding upon Texas' authority created in 1891 by Governor Hogg to assert control over the railroads, Texas set

---

[205] The 500 wells were in a four-mile swath stretching westward from what is now the site of Dodgers Stadium.

[206] Rintoul, *Drilling Through Time*, 8 and 13. Cities Service group suffered from the flush production from the Signal Hill and Huntington Beach fields, near Los Angeles in the early 1920s. Daintith notes that this experience may have influenced Henry Doherty's support for fieldwide unitization laws that would better control the rate and ultimate recovery of production. Daintith, *Finders Keepers*, at 9.

[207] Rintoul, *Drilling Through Time*, 53.

[208] Olien and Hinton, *Wildcatters*, 52-53.

[209] *Town Lot Drilling Act*, Cal. Stat. 1931, c.586, discussed in Section of Mineral Law, American Bar Association, *Conservation of Oil & Gas: A Legal History, 1948*, ed. by Blakely M. Murphy (American Bar Association, 1948), 50-52.

[210] Paul E. Land, "Cal Canal Gas Field," *California Department of Conservation, Division of Oil & Gas, Publication no. T26S* (Division of Oil & Gas 1983), accessed March 6, 2016, ftp.consrv.ca.gov at 2-3; Rintoul, *Drilling Through Time*, 62.

out on a tortuous quest to right the oil and gas industry from its self-destructive path of waste and economic ruin. But efforts by progressive legislators and oil companies—typically the majors—were frustrated at every turn by scofflaw independents, known as "hot oilers," who fought back in the courts and in the field, flouting the early efforts to regulate order out of chaos.

As a result of the state's early antitrust sentiment, no company could engage in more than one phase of the petroleum business; it could only work in producing, transporting, refining or retail sales.[211] This greatly benefited the independents by making it difficult for the better-financed majors, principally Standard Oil, to compete with them. Nevertheless, Standard, which didn't participate in Lucas' Spindletop because of Texas' antitrust law, was surreptitiously doing business in the state through a labyrinth of companies it controlled.[212]

Standard was an easy target for politicians and prosecutors and, in 1907, its Texas refining affiliate was fined $1 million.[213] The following year, one of its refineries was confiscated and sold to John Sealy, a prominent Galveston businessman, at a sheriff's sale for $85,000. Sealy owned the refinery only briefly before exchanging it for a large position in Magnolia Oil Co. in 1911 in part with a loan from a New York bank associated with Socony—that is, Standard Oil Co. of New York. Thereafter, Sealy was Standard's Texas connection.[214]

Other majors, such as Gulf Oil and The Texas Co., had better political and investor connections in the state and were, for the most part, able to operate in the background without prosecution. In 1915, independents organized as the Texas Oil Producers and Landowners Association to defeat The Texas Co.'s attempts to have state law

---

[211] David F. Prindle, *Petroleum Politics and the Texas Railroad Commission* (University of Texas Press, Austin, 1981), 20.
[212] Hinton and Olien, *Oil in Texas*, 53-54.
[213] Hinton and Olien, *Oil in Texas*, 54.
[214] Hinton and Olien, *Oil in Texas*, 54.

amended to dissolve the antitrust rule and legalize its pre-existing involvement in more than one aspect of the oil business.[215]

In 1917, a compromise was reached, allowing companies to work in all phases of the business—except for pipelines, which would be regulated as common carriers.[216] Political and industrial leaders, despite their determination to control the influence of outside capital—i.e., the Easterners—in the Texas oil industry, realized that full development of the state's resources *required* outside capital. It was better for the state's economy that its oil was refined locally, allowing the state to better profit from the sale of the oil, rather than sending it to the East Coast where those refiners would profit instead.

The Rise of the Texas Railroad Commission

Since the Texas Railroad Commission was already regulating rates charged for rail transportation, it was delegated the responsibility in 1917 to regulate pipeline rates as well.[217] This was the beginning for the commission's soon-expanding role in this young and wild industry. Following the repeated booms and busts and recognition of the strategic importance of oil amidst World War I, Texans amended the state's constitution in 1917 to permit laws promoting the conservation of natural resources.[218] In 1919, the Railroad Commission was made responsible for implementing new laws regarding physical waste, such as gas-venting and water incursion in reservoirs.[219]

Based on this mandate, the commission issued 38 regulations, the most controversial being Rule 37, which barred wells from being drilled closer than 300 feet of one another and closer than 150 feet of

---

[215] Hinton and Olien, *Oil in Texas*, 55. The organization's formation was led by Ross Sterling, a Texas governor and a co-founder of Humble Oil Co., which is now part of supermajor Exxon Mobil Corp.

[216] Hinton and Olien, *Oil in Texas*, 55-56.

[217] Prindle, *Petroleum Politics*, 20.

[218] Tex. Nat. Res. Code Ann. Section 111.013 (Vernon 1978) (original version at 1917 Tex. Gen. Laws, ch. 30, Tex. Rev. Civ. Stat. art. 6019 (Vernon 1962)). February 20, 1917. This law declared pipelines to be common carriers, subject to the jurisdiction of the Railroad Commission.

[219] Tex. Nat. Res. Code Ann. Section 81.051 (Vernon 1978) (original version at 1919 Tex. Gen. Laws, ch. 155, Tex. Gen. Civ. Stat. art. 6023 (Vernon 1962)).

a property line. Rule 37 was promulgated primarily to reduce fire hazards and to minimize wells from watering out.[220] But the commission was woefully understaffed; thus, it was unable to significantly affect field operations in the 1920s.[221]

Meanwhile, the regulations were endorsed—if not drafted—by the majors, whose scientists understood the long-term benefits of controlled production and whose balance sheets could weather restrictions. Compliance was more successful in fields that were primarily held by the majors and largest independents.

Conservationists in Texas and elsewhere were also concerned about economic waste as a result of collapsed oil prices. Oil was so cheap that no one thought twice about using it for any sort of fuel need. To protect such a valuable national resource, conservationists argued that prices should be high enough to both reflect the value of the oil and to discourage indiscriminate use.

The majors, represented by the American Petroleum Institute (API), urged producers in 1929 to limit their production to the total volume each produced in the last nine months of the previous year. The API formed regional committees to study unitization of oil fields to better control production.

In June, President Hoover called on governors of oil-producing states, trade-association representatives and the majors to a meeting at the Broadmoor Hotel in Colorado Springs to discuss uniform state oil regulation. Independents were leery of national efforts to control production, fearing that the majors would gain the upper hand. Speaking on behalf of the Southern Oklahoma Oil and Gas Association, Wirt Franklin worried "that in the name of conservation a compact may

---

[220] Olien and Hinton, *Wildcatters*, 91-93, Rule 37. Adopted November 26, 1919, Rule 37 was the first Statewide Rule regulating the oil and gas industry and made *Railroad Commission v. Bass*, 10 S.W.2d 586 (Tex. Civ App.- Austin 1928) writ dism'd, 51 S.W.2d 1113 (Tex. Comm'n App. 1932). Today, Rule 37 prohibits wells within 1,200 feet of one another or within 467 feet of any property line.

[221] The commission had between nine and 17 deputy supervisors during this period to enforce compliance across Texas. "To say that the [RRC] made much difference in field operations during the 1920s, ... would be hard to defend." Hinton and Olien, *Oil in Texas*, 93-94.

[vest] absolute authority in a commission, which might fall under the domination of the major[s],"[222] Nicholas Malavis wrote in *Bless the Pure & Humble: Texas Lawyers and Oil Regulation, 1919-1936.*

Independents further feared that a commission under the control of the majors, which had production abroad as well as in the U.S., "could restrict domestic production to any extent it might desire, and allow domestic demand to be filled by the importation of foreign oil,"[223] according to an account. Malavis wrote, "Disunity and ill-will among majors and independents broke up the conference, leaving nothing accomplished except the creation of the Independent Petroleum Association of America (IPAA), under Franklin's leadership. The IPAA soon became a leading voice for independent oilmen."[224]

But any discussion of controlling prices raised the specter of Standard Oil, stoking monopoly fears. Thus politicians, particularly in Texas, eschewed price legislation.[225] Even efforts to minimize physical waste were opposed by independents as a disguised effort to control prices.

Science was catching up with the industry and most acknowledged that open hole, tightly spaced wells would lead to the premature decline of any reservoir. In Yates Field, which was discovered in West Texas in 1926, leaseholds were large, thus the number of operators was manageable. There, voluntary proration and spacing were accepted and submitted to the Texas Railroad Commission to oversee.[226] Unitization efforts were led by Humble Oil Co. president Will Farrish's cynical assessment that "no one in the industry today ... has

---

[222] The independents' answer to the oversupply of oil was to promote a $1.00 tariff per barrel of imported oil, a proposal that was aimed directly at the majors. Malavis, *Bless the Pure & Humble*, 40, 46.

[223] "History of IPAA," IPAA, accessed December 15, 2015, Ipaa.org.

[224] Malavis, *Bless the Pure & Humble*, 40. The IPAA continues to hold its annual mid-year meeting at the Broadmoor each even-numbered year in commemoration of its heritage.

[225] Hinton and Olien, *Oil in Texas*, 181.

[226] The field was mainly owned by Roxana (Shell), Humble, the California Company, Simms Oil Co. and McMann Oil & Gas Co. Hinton and Olien, *Oil in Texas*, 155.

sense enough or knows enough" to solve the problem of over-production.[227]

In September of 1927, Yates Field was producing 192,000 barrels a day. Humble had a large quantity of oil in storage; the value would decline if field over-production drove down prices. Humble had the only pipeline near the new field. Farrish promised to extend his pipeline to the field if the Yates producers agreed to unitize their operations with a daily capacity not to exceed 30,000 barrels a day.[228]

Some producers were concerned that such an agreement would violate federal antitrust law and refused to participate. But a sufficient number agreed to semi-monthly nominations under a plan that could be renewed for successive 90-day periods.[229] The Yates agreement was the working model the following year for the Railroad Commission's first effort to regulate oil production.[230]

Until then, where the lease positions were small and producers were starved for capital, voluntary compliance was non-existent. Flush oil production would overwhelm pipelines and storage capacity; it would prompt refineries to reduce the posted prices they would pay for the production; and, with uncontrolled venting of associated gas, it would deplete reservoir energy, causing saltwater to encroach and wells to lose value, prompting the independents to pack up in search of the next *El Dorado*.

Neither the 1917 nor 1919 law authorized the Railroad Commission to control the rate of production. Early, tentative efforts by the commission were rebuffed by politically active, vocal producers. In the Texas Panhandle, most producers routinely enhanced output by shooting hundreds of quarts of nitroglycerin down their wells, fracturing the rock formation and greatly increasing production beyond the capacity of pipelines, storage tanks and railroads.

---

[227] Daniel Yergin, *The Quest: Energy, Security, and the Remaking of the Modern World* (Penguin Books: September 20, 2011), 206.

[228] Malavis, *Bless the Pure & Humble*, 30-31.

[229] Malavis, *Bless the Pure & Humble*, 31-32.

[230] "The regulation of oil production in the Yates field, initially through operators' voluntary cooperation and later by the Railroad Commission's proration orders, marked a watershed in the legal history of petroleum." Malavis, *Bless the Pure & Humble*, 30-32, 39.

Chapter 2: The Early Years

In the 1920s, the commission tried to slow production by banning this "shooting" of wells. It backed down, however, when producers protested that their neighbors would drain their oil from their leases if they were not similarly allowed to shoot their wells.[231]

Lacking regulatory oversight, the market in Panhandle Field began regulating itself. "Humble [Oil] … and others began to cut back takes in selected areas, leaving producers without a market," Hinton and Olien wrote in *Oil in Texas*. "In business terms, the cutbacks were only common sense; why should Humble pay for more oil when it already had as much production and oil in storage as it could use?"[232]

The majors were often in the same fields as the independents. When production exceeded take-away capacity, which the majors usually controlled, they took their own oil to the refineries, leaving the independents without a market. All the while, their wells were being drained by the majors' wells that continued to produce.

The independents sought relief from the state, claiming antitrust. In March of 1930, the legislature passed the Common Purchaser Act, which required oil purchasers that were common carriers to purchase oil ratably, without discrimination between producers or fields. The Railroad Commission was charged with implementing the law, apportioning production among all fields in Texas and prorating production among wells within each field. It was totally unprepared for the task.[233]

The act was promptly challenged by larger producers, having access to refineries, as violating their rights to due process and constituting restraint of trade and overreach by the Railroad Commission. At the time, the commission's constitutional charge was to prevent only physical waste—not economic waste. The commission, therefore, attempted to control economic waste under the guise of preventing physical waste.

---

[231] Hinton and Olien, *Oil in Texas*, 142.
[232] Hinton and Olien, *Oil in Texas*, 182.
[233] Hinton and Olien, *Oil in Texas*, 182-183.

Courts upheld challenges to the commission's field-proration orders in the Panhandle[234] and East Texas fields.[235] The commission found itself frequently second-guessed by judges regarding whether it had the power to regulate, whether it had followed due process and even whether it had its facts right.

U.S. Judge Joseph C. Hutcheson, sitting in federal court in Tyler, was a particularly dismissive and staunch skeptic of the commission, frequently frustrating the commission's efforts to control the rate of production. In a decision enjoining the commission's rule in 1931, Hutcheson wrote:

> Certainly when a subordinate body like the railroad commission of Texas undertakes as here to deal in a broadly restrictive way with the right of a citizen to produce the oil which under the law of this state he owns, it must be prepared to answer this imperious query, "is it not lawful for me to do what I will with mine own," by pointing to a clear delegation of legislative power.
>
> This must be found, not in the recitative portions of its orders, for the commission may not more than any other agent, lifting itself by its bootstraps, supply, by claiming, the power it does not have, but in the statutes themselves, which have created, which control, and which are the source of the commission's power.
>
> Especially must this be so when, as here, under the thinly veiled pretense of going about to prevent physical waste the commission has, in co-operation with persons interested in raising and maintaining

---

[234] *Danciger Oil & Refining Co. of Texas et al. v. Smith et al.*, 4 F. Supp. 236 (N.D. Tex. 1933). The court originally granted Danciger's original motion for an injunction to restrain the Railroad Commission from enforcing its field wide prorationing rules. Following trial, however, the court found reluctantly, that the Commission's field-wide rule for the Panhandle Field, "whether in our opinion wise or unwise" was not arbitrary, excessive or irrational.

[235] *MacMillan et al. v. Railroad Commission of Texas et al.*, 51 F.2d 400, 404-405 (W.D. Tex. 1931).

prices of oil and its refined products, set on foot a
plan which, seated in a desire to bring supply within
the compass of demand, derives its impulse and
spring from, and finds its scope and its extent in the
attempt to control the delicate adjustment of market
supply and demand, in order to bring and keep oil
prices up.[236]

The resulting impact of courts enjoining prorationing was predictable, but, by 1931, the magnitude caught even some of the most
vociferous independents off guard. "As East Texas oil wells gushed,
crude prices tumbled," Hinton and Olien wrote.[237] Unlike prior, localized, boom-bust cycles, the East Texas Field was so huge and prolific
that the price collapse affected West Texas producers.

Witness the city of Odessa in West Texas, which saw its population swell dramatically as a result of the 1920s Permian Basin discoveries. "But once the East Texas field came in, oil people packed their
bags and moved out," Hinton and Olien wrote. "Odessa's bank failed
in April 1931. So many taxpayers were delinquent that the city had
trouble paying on its bonded debt, and it had to cut off the new hotel's water for nonpayment of water bills."[238]

Oil from Texas was even underselling Russian petroleum in Europe. Market prices in Texas and elsewhere in the U.S. were so far
below production costs, which averaged around 80 cents a barrel, that
they portended ruin for most of the state's and country's producers.[239]
At these prices, a producer's only hope was that the East Texas Field
would rapidly decline. But its prodigious output went beyond inde-

---

[236] *MacMillan et al. v. Railroad Commission of Texas*, 404-405. Prindle, *Petroleum Politics*, 30.
[237] "As early as March, the field's producers were selling crude at distress prices of thirty-
five to forty cents a barrel, a price less than half that required by producers in Oklahoma
and North Texas to break even. On July 8, Humble Oil, one of the field's largest buyers,
dropped prices to a dime a barrel; the following day several other majors cut their posted
price to six or seven cents. On July 10, the *Oil Weekly* reported that an East Texas operator had sold 40,000 barrels at two cents a barrel. East Texas crude was so cheap, it had
begun to displace imported crude in American markets; no one could produce and ship
crude from Venezuela for two cents a barrel." Hinton and Olien, *Oil in Texas*, 183.
[238] Hinton and Olien, *Oil in Texas*, 194.
[239] Yergin, *The Prize*, 233.

pendents' wildest dreams, turning into a nightmare, as supply continued to mount like a tsunami from which there was no escape.

In the summer of 1931, Ross Sterling, the co-founder of Humble Oil and now Texas' governor, ordered a special legislative session to find a resolution to the crisis, but, still, there was no consensus among the legislators or the producers.[240] While the legislators were deliberating, Hutcheson and his fellow federal judges ruled against the commission's exercise of power beyond anything more than physical waste.[241]

In response to the ruling, the legislature passed the Anti-Market Demand Act, barring the commission from trying to match oil supply with demand, and annulled the commission's statewide proration rules. Without the force of the legislature or regulation by the commission, East Texas producers who favored production limits attempted to enforce voluntary restrictions through self-help. Producers who didn't see the need for conservation and continued to produce all-out found their wells sabotaged and their pipelines dynamited. Some 1,200 producers met in Tyler and asked Governor Sterling to declare martial law to save them from themselves.

Texas was not alone in attempts to control production. Oklahoma's Governor Murray declared martial law around the Oklahoma City and Seminole fields. One week later, on August 17, 1931, Texas' Sterling declared that East Texas was in a "state of insurrection" and "open rebellion" and called out 1,300 National Guardsmen to shut down the field.

His orders were carried out by Brigadier General Jacob Wolters who rode in on horseback as recent rains had made roads impassable by vehicle. Production was shut down within a matter of days, but not for long.[242] Lawsuits were filed and, by October 13, 1931, Judge Hutcheson enjoined the commission from further actions in controlling the field's production.

---

[240] Humble Oil and others favored controls; independent Danciger and Gulf Oil were opposed to any regulation on East Texas production. Olien and Hinton, *Wildcatters*, 59.
[241] *MacMillan et. al. v. Railroad Commission of Texas, et al.*, 51 F.2d 400 (W.D. Tex.1931).
[242] Yergin, *The Prize*, 244-259.

Tempers in the field were at the point that, without state-imposed restrictions, local oilmen were prepared to take matters into their own hands. "The feeling is very strong, Governor," Wolters wrote to Sterling from Kilgore on October 14, 1931. "All day men have openly said that if the Governor could not hold the field down, they were going to take charge of it themselves, hang a few *S.Bs.* and if necessary dynamite pipelines and save this field from destruction and save the oil industry."[243]

If the commission was prohibited by the courts from taking action, the governor was determined to personally assume responsibility for production in the field. He responded by lowering the allowable amount of production from each well, without consulting the commission.

In November, in response, the producer-plaintiffs amended a suit they had filed against the commission's action, adding both the governor and Wolters, claiming a price-fixing conspiracy. They alleged that the governor, as a founder and former director of Humble Oil Co., and Wolters, as a lawyer and lobbyist who often represented The Texas Co., should be disqualified from taking any action related to controlling oil production.[244]

In February of 1932, Judge Hutcheson ruled in favor of the plaintiffs, ending the governor's martial-law order and making the commission, again, responsible for policing only for the purpose of preventing physical waste.[245] The inability of Texas to regulate production made efforts by other states futile. Faced with the prospect of shut-in Oklahoma crude being replaced by Texas' unregulated production, Oklahoma's governor had relented in the fall of 1931 and allowed production from the state's fields to resume.

---

[243] General Brigadier Jacob F. Wolters to Governor R.S. Sterling, 14 October, 1931, Headquarters Military District of Upshur, Rusk, Gregg and Smith Counties, Records of Ross S. Sterling Texas Office of the Governor, Archives and Information Services Division, Texas State Library and Archives.

[244] *The Pittsburgh Press*, November 21, 1931.

[245] *Constantin et al. v. Lon Smith et al.*, 57 F.2d 227 (E.D.Tex. 1932).

The Texas governor called another special session of the legislature and rammed through the Market Demand Act, allowing market rationing and giving the commission the power to prevent economic waste.[246] The tide had turned in favor of state regulatory agencies with several federal court decisions that affirmed the Railroad Commission's proration rules in a Permian case and upheld Oklahoma's conservation statutes.[247]

But as the judiciary was coming around to state control of production, political threats to the Railroad Commission's existence added confusion to the markets. That the commission survived these threats was more the result of political ineptitude than legislative foresight. On the eve of the deciding vote, anti-commission independents roughed up a key pro-commission legislator in the lobby of the Driskill Hotel, blocks from the capitol. News of the altercation quickly outraged public opinion, leading to a Texas senate vote of 20 to 10 that the commission had the power to regulate production, while the injured state representative watched the vote from a wheelchair in the chamber.[248]

Efforts to engage President Franklin Roosevelt's administration to take on a more active role in regulating production at the federal level were complicated in part by political maneuvering by Texas' most powerful congressman, Sam Rayburn. The death nail was delivered by ill-timed, ham-fisted comments by Interior Secretary Harold Ickes to American Petroleum Institute members in Dallas. At the time, Congress was debating a bill to grant federal control of state production. Ickes accused the states—Texas, in particular—of being lackadaisical in preventing waste, implying that the time had come to think of the oil industry as a public utility and regulate it accordingly.

Although independents and majors disagreed on proration laws, they could agree against a federal, utility-regulatory scheme. The fed-

---

[246] Olien and Hinton, *Wildcatters*, 64.

[247] *Danciger Oil & Refining Co. of Texas v. Smith*, 4 F. Supp. 236 (N.D. Tex. 1933); *Champlin Refining Company v. Corporation Commission of Oklahoma*, 286 U.S. 210 (1932).

[248] Prindle, *Petroleum Politics*, 37.

eral bill perished and state control over regulation of oil and gas production, such as it was, survived.[249]

Meanwhile, conservationists were developing greater scientific justification for restrictions on production to protect not only the reservoir energy, but the surface waste. Even Judge Hutcheson was finally convinced by the evidence of reservoir mechanics. He agreed that, in East Texas, restricting open-flow production was not a disguised, price-fixing scheme; instead, it served to reduce waste and promote ultimate recovery of hydrocarbons.[250]

On the state level, the Texas Supreme Court ruled in 1935 that the rule of capture could be properly restrained through regulation that protected landowners from unfair drainage by their neighbors. The ruling affirmed the Railroad Commission's authority to enforce the state's conservation laws.[251]

Still, hundreds of thousands of barrels known as "hot oil" were being produced above the daily quotas set by the commission during 1932 and 1933.[252] Surreptitious nighttime shipments of cross-border bootlegged oil were frustrating Texas' conservation efforts.[253] The term "hot oil" was coined in East Texas.

Daniel Yergin wrote in *The Prize*, "It was said that, one chilly night, a state militiaman was talking to an operator suspected of producing above the allowable limit. The militiaman was obviously shivering, and the thoughtful operator suggested that he lean against a tank containing some of the suspect oil. 'It's hot enough,' said the operator, 'to keep you warm.'"[254]

---

[249] Prindle, *Petroleum Politics*, 36-39.

[250] Hinton and Olien, *Oil in Texas*, 189, citing *Amazon Petroleum Corporation v. Railroad Commission of Texas et al.* 5 F. Supp. 633. 634-637 (E.D. Tex. 1934); see also, Malavis, *Bless the Pure & Humble*, 164-166.

[251] *Brown v. Humble Oil & Refining Company*, 126 Tex. 296, 83 S.W.2d 935, on rehearing 87 S.W. 2d 1069 (Tex. 1935).

[252] Prindle, *Petroleum Politics*, 34.

[253] Yergin, *The Prize*, 234.

[254] Yergin, *The Prize*, 237. The oil would have been some 150 degrees Fahrenheit—more than warm enough to take the chill off the East Texas night, according to F.B. Plummer and E.C. Sargent, "Underground Waters and Subsurface Temperatures of the Woodbine Sand in Northeast Texas," The University of Texas Bulletin, No. 3138, October 8, 1931.

In 1933, the federal government finally stepped in. President Roosevelt appointed Interior Secretary Ickes to be "Oil Administrator" under the National Recovery Administration to bring order to the "utter demoralization" of the oil industry as prices in East Texas fell as low as four cents. Governor Sterling had contacted Ickes via telegram in May of 1933, seeking federal action, explaining that "the situation is beyond the control of the state authorities."[255] Ickes concurred and warned President Roosevelt, "The oil business has about broken down and ... to continue to do nothing ... will result in the utter collapse of the industry," with a huge loss in terms of the nation's oil reserves.[256]

Acting under the authority of the Oil Code of the National Industrial Recovery Act, Ickes exercised the federal government's new, extraordinary power to set monthly production quotas for each state. He sent telegrams to the governors of the oil-producing states, telling them what each state's quota would be.

This brought price support, again, to U.S. producers. But the National Industrial Recovery Act was overturned by the U.S. Supreme Court in January of 1935 as an impermissible grant of authority to the executive branch to set state production quotas without sufficient checks and balances.[257]

Without control over hot oil, the whole system of price stability would collapse. Addressing constitutional objections, Congress quickly passed new legislation, which became known as the Connally Hot Oil Act[258] for its sponsor, U.S. Senator Tom Connally of Texas. The act removed the constitutionally objectionable federally imposed production controls, but specifically empowered the federal government to enforce state-set production allowables and prohibited interstate sales in violation of state-production laws. The act was upheld by the courts in a number of decisions, the first of which was in 1936.[259]

---

[255] Yergin, *The Prize*, 237.
[256] Yergin, *The Prize*, 237.
[257] Malavis, *Bless the Pure & Humble*, 183.
[258] 15 U.S.C. § 715 (2000).
[259] *Griswold v. The President of the United States*, 82 F. 2d 922 (5ᵗʰ Cir. 1936).

Chapter 2: The Early Years

Whether quotas could be enforced figured into the risks that early energy bankers weighed in their loan decisions. A letter from First National Bank in Dallas, in reply to an August 20, 1935, letter from a First City banker from Houston, highlights the issues of the day:

> Referring to your letter of August 20th, there are a few rather disturbing uncertainties with respect to the oil industry at the moment, with particular reference to East Texas. Probably the most important of these is the possibility of the promulgation of new regulations which would involve the matter of acreage in arriving at well allowables. This of course might have a serious effect on wells located on small tracts. ...
> [W]hereas we might have figured the possible income from a well on a one-acre tract at, say, $600 per month, we are giving careful consideration to the possible position of our loan should the income be just half that amount by reason of a reduction in the allowable; a circumstance which of course would also affect the actual value of the property.
>
> The hot oil situation continues to give us some concern. If it isn't corrected or relieved to some appreciable extent, we believe a cut in the price of crude is almost inevitable. While such a cut might be more or less temporary, nevertheless we are trying to make our loans on such a basis as might in any event carry them through on a materially reduced income should we suffer a cut.[260]

To forestall additional federal legislation, representatives of nine of the major oil-producing states gathered in Dallas in 1935, drafting the Interstate Oil Compact (IOC) to form an interstate commission exclusive of the federal government, providing for voluntary state participation in establishment of state allowables.[261] States ratifying the

---

[260] Eugene McElvaney, Vice President, First National Bank Dallas, Letter to W.A. Kirkland, Vice President, First National Bank in Houston, August 22, 1935.
[261] Malavis, *Bless the Pure & Humble*, 188-189. Prindle, *Petroleum Politics*, 73.

IOC included Texas, Oklahoma, New Mexico, Kansas, Illinois and Colorado. Michigan joined in 1939; Arkansas, Louisiana, New York and Pennsylvania in 1941; Kentucky, 1942; Georgia, 1946; Indiana and Tennessee, 1947; Mississippi, 1948; Arizona, 1951; Nevada, Nebraska, North Dakota, Washington and Alaska, 1953; Oregon, 1954; South Dakota and Wyoming, 1955; and Utah, 1957. California never joined.[262]

The IOC and the Connally Hot Oil Act survived judicial review and became the framework for present-day oil regulation, in which the federal government plays a minimal role. This legislation gave teeth to states' conservation laws by preventing the transportation of illegally produced oil across states' boundaries.[263] After 1935, state-based control under the aegis of the IOC—and, later, demand for greater supply during World War II—proved sufficient to check serious instability in the oil industry.[264]

While the Railroad Commission had the imprimatur of the courts and legislature, the commission still faced the problem of getting its constituents—primarily, the independents—to comply. Prorationing was a necessity, but it had to be done in a way that would reassure the independents and royalty owners that they would not be exploited by the majors.

Prorationing might be imposed by force, but, until it acquired the assent of the independents, the Texas oil industry would remain in an internal war. The commission had to win over its constituents by prorating production from each of Texas' fields based on well-spacing and production-allocation formulae skewed in favor of producers with wells located on smaller tracts. This provided independents with

---

[262] Theoretically, California, which did not prorate to market demand, could have destroyed the IOC states' production control by drowning the market in unprorated oil. But California, though a major producing state, was in a geographically isolated market, unable to affect the rest of the nation's demand for production.

[263] Thompson, "Legal And Other Aspects of Financing The Oil Industry," *Rocky Mountain Mineral Law Institute*, 1957, Chapter 2, page 1.

[264] Malavis, *Bless the Pure & Humble*, 191.

equal, if not better, footing, compared with that of the majors, which typically controlled larger tracts in more prolific areas in any field.[265]

The commissioners were elected officials and, therefore, their regulations to prevent physical and economic waste were not based on a pure application of engineering science. By the mid-1930s, the science of petroleum engineering had concluded that field-wide unitization—as happened with the voluntary cooperation in Yates Field in the 1920s—was the best way to maximize ultimate recovery, rather than a patchwork of smaller tracts producing all-out.

The majors' and large independents' greater access to capital was reflected by their control of the largest and most-prolific leases within Texas. By 1935 in East Texas, the 29 largest operators owned 10,410 wells, while more than 1,000 small independents owned more than 12,000, approximately 65% of which were drilled on small tracts known as Rule 37 exception wells.[266]

The API estimated in 1937 that more than $200 million had been spent in the East Texas Field to drill protection wells—that is, wells to protect against drainage caused by neighbors' wells.[267] In addition to sparing that cost, if the state were to order field-wide unitization, reservoir pressure would have been conserved and greater ultimate recovery of the resource achieved.

But field-wide unitization would have benefitted the larger lease-owners at the expense—and, perhaps, the demise—of the hardscrabble independents. It would have been political suicide for the commissioners and incited further civil disobedience. Promotion of well-spacing rules favoring smaller tracts and proration rules favoring stripper-well production had the intended effect of protecting the small producer and penalizing the majors.

---

[265] Because every tract no matter how small was entitled to at least one well to "prevent confiscation" if not drilled, producers with larger tracts were restricted in the total number of wells per acre they could drill. Prindle, *Petroleum Politics*, 39, 47.
[266] Prindle, *Petroleum Politics*, 49-50.
[267] Robert E. Hardwicke, "Legal History of Conservation of Oil in Texas," *Legal History of Conservation of Oil and Gas: A Symposium* (Chicago: American Bar Association, 1938), 256.

The commissioners were not bashful about their efforts to spread the wealth inside Texas. "The major companies, even those that had been born at Spindletop, were controlled by out-of-state capital," David Prindle wrote in *Petroleum Politics and the Texas Railroad Commission*. "As the most important goal was to keep oil money in Texas, the Commissioners felt it was legitimate to support inefficient production."[268]

East Texas illustrated the bias. By 1939, the commission had granted so many Rule 37 exceptions to the one-well-per-10-acre spacing rule that there were more than 25,000 wells in the field—the equivalent of an average density of about one well per four acres. There were many examples of one-acre tracts with five to 10 wells; in particular, one acre in Kilgore hosted 27 wells.

The commission allowed just under 500,000 barrels a day from the entire field, giving each well a maximum of less than 20 barrels. Thus, in the most prolific field in the world, wells capable of producing 10,000 barrels a day were restricted to 1/5th of 1% of their open-flow potential, while offset wells were constantly being drilled around them.[269] The method was considerably less than perfect, but, in the end, politically expedient.

Proration of Gas?
Up through the 1940s, producers, regulators and bankers were focused on oil—not natural gas. "From the earliest days of oil production, the industry had problems with natural gas," Prindle wrote.[270] Unlike oil, gas could not be stored in open pits or trucked to markets. In 1930, when oil was selling for $1 a barrel, the price of natural gas, where it could be sold, was three cents per thousand cubic feet (Mcf).

When a gas-bearing zone in Panhandle Field, which eventually covered some 5 million acres across Texas, Oklahoma and Kansas, was discovered in Texas in 1918, the city of Amarillo offered five

---

[268] Prindle, *Petroleum Politics*, 49-50.
[269] Prindle, *Petroleum Politics*, 50.
[270] Prindle, *Petroleum Politics*, 55.

years of free gas to any industry willing to locate in the city and employ 50 or more people. There was not a single taker.[271]

After the discovery, wildcatters followed the common practice of letting the gas vent into the atmosphere with the hope that oil would eventually follow up the wellbore. But, after a year and more than 60 wells had been drilled, not one produced oil, like the wells in nearby Wheeler County that were brought in eight years earlier.[272]

It was not until 10 years later, having proven the magnitude of the field as a purely gas field, that gas pipelines were finally constructed to Wichita Falls, Dallas, Fort Worth and, later, to Oklahoma and Kansas. By and large, however, for the first 80 years of the petroleum industry, natural gas was, at best, a nuisance in the wildcatters' search for oil.[273]

Finding markets for the gas and constructing pipelines to transport it were encouraged by Texas conservation law. In 1899, the state passed a law, following the 1894 discovery of Corsicana Field as the city was drilling for water.[274] The new law required gas wells to be shut in within 10 days of completion until the gas could be used for light, fuel or power.[275]

Almost as soon as the law was passed, it was ignored or evaded by most producers. Precious few markets for gas existed except for where it was found; initially, it was used to fuel street lamps.[276] For the Texas producer unlucky enough to hit dry gas, which was the case in approximately 70% of the fields in Texas, it was a nuisance. In the

---

[271] Ernest O. Thompson, "Flare Gas Wastage in Texas: Steps Taken to Utilize," speech to the American Gas Association, May 1, 1947, Texas State Archives, Railroad Commission Collection, box 4-3/318, cited in Prindle, *Petroleum Politics*, 55.

[272] *Handbook of Texas Online*, Julia Cauble Smith, "Panhandle Field," accessed March 13, 2016, Tshaonline.org.

[273] Prindle, *Petroleum Politics*, 55.

[274] Drilling for water at Corsicana, Navarro County, in 1895, the American Well and Prospecting Co. encountered an oil showing at 1,033 feet. Oil was an unwelcomed intruder and promptly cased off; drilling resumed to 2,580 feet where an artesian water flow was found. There, it was completed as a water well." Beard, "The History of the East Texas Oil Field," 8.

[275] Acts 26th Lg. Reg. Session, 1899, Ch. 49, p.8.

[276] Nissa Darbonne, *The American Shales* (CreateSpace, April 30, 2014), 5 (citing Natural-gas.org).

early days of the industry, dry-gas wells were often capped and forgotten.[277]

Other than for heating and illumination of city streets near the few pipelines that were built by the early 1930s and as feedstock for carbon-black plants, the major use was in manufacturing "condensate gasoline."[278] Wet gas consists of both methane—i.e., "dry gas"—and heavier hydrocarbons (butane, propane, ethane, etc.), which fall out of the well stream naturally through gravity or via mechanical processes.

The process of "stripping gas" was the only available source of income for stranded gas fields that were too far or too small to be connected to markets by pipelines and that happened to produce wet gas. Companies that produced wet gas could make a profit from stripping the liquefiable hydrocarbons, then venting the remaining dry gas—about 90% of the total well flow.

As the gas stream was flowed from the reservoir with higher temperatures and expanded at the surface, its temperature dropped and the heavier hydrocarbons would drop out of the stream as condensate. By one estimate, roughly 1 billion cubic feet (Bcf) of gas was stripped and flared daily in Panhandle Field in 1934 alone.[279]

Associated gas—i.e., casinghead gas produced in association with crude oil—was similarly wasted; it too was flared at the wellhead. By 1925, producers had persuaded the Texas legislature to exempt casinghead gas from the 1899 conservation law that prohibited the flaring of produced gas. Pipeline operators that were slow to construct lines out of known gas fields were even less inclined to invest in construction of gas pipelines out of oil fields. Casinghead gas was produced only as a result of oil production; therefore, it was an unpre-

---

[277] Prindle, *Petroleum Politics*, 56.

[278] "According to evidence presented by the State, in July, 1935, before the prohibitions of House Bill 266 became effective against uses therein declared wasteful, there were in the West Panhandle field 41 stripping plants producing natural gasoline, consuming daily 1,847,339 M.C.F. sweet gas, from which the gasoline production saved only 3 percent of the fuel value of the gas in its original state. Between February 1, 1933, and August 1, 1935, 709 billion cubic feet of gas were said to have been blown into the air after the natural gasoline content had been extracted." *Thompson v. Consolidated Gas Utilities Corp.*, 300 U.S. 55 (1937).

[279] Prindle, *Petroleum Politics*, 57.

dictable supply, since it depended on sufficient market demand for the oil and, after successful proration regulations were imposed, a well's allowable volume.

With no transportation for the casinghead gas, producers chose to flare it rather than invest in laying a pipeline or invest in re-injecting it into the formation. In the early 1940s, a special committee appointed by the Railroad Commission estimated that more than half of the state's casinghead gas was being flared. It was calculated to be an amount equal to 1.5 Bcf a day from the state's larger fields.[280] The best estimate was that gas flared from Texas was about 900 Bcf annually.[281]

The commission only made halfhearted efforts to enforce gas-production proration in the early 1930s, while it was attempting to enforce oil proration, and it met with similar pushback from courts. Lawsuits over the Panhandle Field proration orders were appealed up to the U.S. Supreme Court. In a 1937 case, the plaintiffs' complaint was that the regulatory restrictions on their ability to produce were below their obligations to deliver to the buyer—less even than the wells' productive capacity and less than the capacity of transportation and marketing facilities.

The plaintiffs, who owned both gas wells and pipelines sufficient to transport their production, argued that the orders were not to prevent waste or to protect co-owners of the common reservoir. Instead, they argued, it was solely to compel the plaintiffs and others with means to purchase gas from producers who had not provided themselves with a market and marketing facilities.

Supreme Court Justice Louis Brandeis, who authored the opinion that the Texas rule was unconstitutional, declared in February of 1937 that the commission's order presented "no more glaring instance of the taking of one man's property and giving it to another."[282] Under the Texas rule, Brandeis wrote, "the pipeline owner, a private person,

---

[280] Prindle, *Petroleum Politics*, 64.
[281] Prindle, *Petroleum Politics*, 58.
[282] *Thompson v. Consolidated Gas Utilities Corp.*, 79.

is, in effect, ordered to pay money to another private well owner for the purchase of oil [gas] which there is no wish to buy."[283]

A resolution to end wasteful oilfield practices was achieved among courts and within industry. However, proration of natural gas languished. Three systemic reasons worked against gas regulation that differed from oil regulation, Prindle noted. First, there was limited ability to coordinate gas production among fields. It could only be transported by pipelines, which were limited in number and rarely interconnected.

Second, gas producers contracted with specific pipelines under fixed-price, long-term contracts, while oil was usually sold at that day's price. Oil was simply more fungible than gas. Third, over time, the lack of enforceable gas regulation created a vacuum in which industry developed its own traditions of operation, creating inertia against subsequent regulatory efforts.[284]

But, by the end of the World War II and because of further national recognition of petroleum's importance in national defense, federal attention became focused on the wasteful practice of gas-flaring. In addition, large interstate oil and oil-products pipelines built during the war effort were sold to private enterprises that converted them to transport Texas' and other natural gas to new, developing markets on the East Coast. With the build-out of the Gulf Coast petrochemical industry during the war effort, gas as a feedstock was becoming more important and more valuable. Increased demand led to increases in its price, albeit modest from a 21st-century perspective, from 1.8 cents per Mcf in 1940 to 3.7 cents by 1947.

When the Railroad Commission renewed regulation efforts in the 1940s, it attempted to target gas on a field-by-field basis and make pipelines take proportionately from every producer in the field. Prindle wrote, "Gas prorationing, therefore, became a matter to be constructed afresh for each field, depending on the physical circumstances of that field, the established economic relationships, the expressed

---

[283] *Thompson v. Consolidated Gas Utilities Corp.*, 78.
[284] Prindle, *Petroleum Politics*, 98-99.

wishes of the operators, and the Commission's own notions of fairness. The result was chaos."[285]

Although the commission was stymied in its efforts in effective gas prorationing, it was effective at prohibiting glaringly wasteful practices. Perhaps the most persuasive argument for increased state control over gas-flaring—as with the argument to rein in oilfield wastefulness—was the specter of federal regulation. In 1946, the Federal Power Commission held a series of hearings on the matter.[286] Within a year, the Railroad Commission issued an order to shut-in oil wells in the Seeligson Field in South Texas until reinjection of casinghead gas was a field-wide practice and flaring eliminated.[287] With subsequent support of Texas courts, it issued orders that shut down 17 more fields for flaring. [288]

But, by this time, everyone with a seat at the table—independents, majors, state regulators—understood that re-injection of casinghead gas increased overall recovery of the reservoir's oil by maintaining the needed level of reservoir pressure. In spite of the visceral opposition to regulations, improved gas-cycling technology, along with higher gas prices, actually paid back the investment in capture-and-reinjection equipment within two years. The net result of the court's affirmation of the commission's authority to regulate gas production made both oil and unassociated-gas properties a better collateral bet for energy lenders.

The Legacy of East Texas

The East Texas discovery was a landmark not just because of its size; it forged regulatory order out of the industry-wide chaos created from the flood of production. State regulation won out over federal intervention and the Texas Railroad Commission emerged from six years

---

[285] Prindle, *Petroleum Politics*, 98-99.
[286] Prindle, *Petroleum Politics*, 65.
[287] Prindle, *Petroleum Politics*, 66.
[288] *Railroad Commission v. Shell Oil Co.*, 206 S.W. 2d 235 (1947); *Railroad Commission v. Flour Bluff Oil Co.*, 219 S.W. 2d 506 (Tex. Civ. App. 1949) error ref'd.; and *Railroad Commission v. Rowan Oil Co.*, 259 S.W. 2d 173 (1953).

of challenge and struggle with greatly enhanced stature, able to control production in the largest oil-producing state and thereby gain influence over petroleum prices across the country.[289]

The cause of all the turmoil—the rule of capture—was finally tamed by regulators and courts. The rule had certainly been the root of waste, unnecessary drilling and destructive boom-and-bust cycles, but it was also the catalyst that created the U.S. energy industry, vibrant industrial activity and capital to fund the independents' growth.

"The rule has been perceived as essentially, one might say quintessentially, American: a rule that places a high value on vigor, on getting there first, on winning one's wealth through free competition," Daintith wrote in *Finders Keepers*. "The consistent concern of those courts was to protect the party who had undertaken the costly work of drilling for oil against an opponent—whether lessor or trespasser—who had not, and to insist on possession was the key to such protection."[290]

The rule of capture was not an American invention, but, he added, many historians cite its "crucial importance to the early development of the U.S. oil industry." He cited Yergin, who wrote in *The Prize* that the rule was "the most important in shaping the legal context of American oil production and the very structure of the industry from its earliest days."[291]

In a speech before the House of Commons in 1947, Winston Churchill said, "Democracy is the worst form of government, except for all others that have been tried."[292] Perhaps, the rule of capture was the least-worst rule of property ownership[293] to bring about accelerated growth of a nascent industry by fueling the proration wars that, in

---

[289] "The Railroad Commission's power to control production in the largest oil-producing state and to limit it to market demand also gave the commission a profound influence over petroleum prices and industry economics throughout the whole United States. In Texas, the Commission shaped the business economics of producers large and small and the economic prosperity of large producing regions throughout its power over field and well allowables. East Texas brought all of this about." Hinton and Olien, *Oil in Texas*, 190.
[290] Daintith, *Finders Keepers*, 7 and 36.
[291] Daintith, *Finders Keepers*, 7, citing Yergin, *The Prize*, 32.
[292] Winston Churchill, in speech before the House of Commons, November 11, 1947.
[293] Daintith, *Finders Keepers*, 424.

turn, triggered increases in the average price of oil in the U.S. Paul Frankel, a leading petroleum economist, wrote in 1946, "These somewhat primitive methods were exactly what was needed to make the young industry, in the first instance, aggressive and, in due course, great."[294]

Yergin summarized the impact of the proration wars: "Despite its haphazard growth, the regulatory system as it finally evolved did indeed possess a powerful underlying logic. It rewrote the book on production and even, to some degree, on what constituted 'ownership' of oil reserves. It brought a whole new approach to production, technically as well as legally and economically.

"… The system worked. The flood was stayed. And, in the process, both the management of petroleum surplus and the relationship between oil companies and the government had been forever changed."[295]

Establishing a floor on prices came at a time when producers' costs were rising. The early days of low-budget, shallow wells drilled with borrowed equipment and crews paid bean wages were over. Having picked over the easy formations, new fields were being discovered at greater depths possessing more-challenging geology and requiring more technology and engineering.

"Drilling became more time-consuming and expensive," Olien and Hinton wrote in *Wildcatters*. "In 1932, for example, the average cost of a well was $12,000; by 1938, that figure had reached $25,000. A half-dozen years later, the cost of drilling to 4,000 to 5,000 feet averaged $35,000."[296]

Greatly enhanced by the proration wars was the relationship of oil companies and their financiers. As production stabilized, following successful enforcement of conservation laws in several of the princi-

[294] P. Frankel, *Essentials of Petroleum: A Key to Oil Economics* (Cass, 1969), quoted in Daintith, *Finders Keepers*, 11.
[295] Yergin, *The Prize*, 241-242.
[296] Olien and Hinton, *Wildcatters*, 82.

pal producing states, a number of the banks in the Southwest and Midwest were more willing to extend credit to the producer.[297]

Without the introduction and subsequent court enforcement of conservation laws, the stability of the economic factors necessary for successful financing of oil may never have been achieved.[298] Proration rules slowed the initial rate of well production and had the side effect of slowing the pace at which the producer was able to recover his investment. This created demand for longer-term credit. Fortunately, slower production also led to more disciplined commodity markets, which, in turn, created the crucial element: a predictable cash flow that bankers needed to lend with confidence.[299]

Thus, proration, with all of its intended consequences, was also the unintended, but proximate, cause of the birth of commercial oil and gas financing, which helped prepare the fertile ground in which small, independent operators were able to compete effectively with the large integrated oil companies in the development of their exploration successes.[300] McElvaney wrote:

> In addition to providing an essential safety factor for all oil credits it has of course created demand for the credit itself. As contrasted to a relatively short and unpredictable return of invested capital, as characterized by the old practice of unrestricted and wasteful production, proration in preserving the maximum inherent reservoir energies has, of course, retarded income to an extended but fairly predeterminable basis of future income.

---

[297] John R. Scott (Vice President, Republic National Bank of Dallas), "Some Aspects of Oil and Gas Financing," *Fifth Annual Institute on Oil and Gas Law and Taxation as it Affects the Oil and Gas Industry, Southwestern Legal Foundation* (1954), 325.

[298] McElvaney, "Some Aspects of Financing Oil and Gas Transactions," 317.

[299] "The development of improved engineering techniques, notably during the late 1930's and early 1940's, and gradual improvement in conservation laws made it possible for banks to make oil loans safely for periods of three to five years." Wilson, "Bank Financing of Oil," 17.

[300] A.G. Gueymard (Senior Vice President and Manager, Petroleum & Minerals Department, First City National Bank of Houston), "The Seventies-An Era of Transition For Petroleum & Minerals Financing," 17 *Rocky Mt. Min L. Inst.* 557 (1972): 558.

Such necessary postponement of capital return has of course created an inevitable need for a greatly expanded volume of credit on extended terms both for development and other purposes. Thus proration, through all of its legal ramifications, including particularly its essential market demand feature, has been the greatest single contributing factor to the stability of the industry and to the successful financing of oil in the ground as an integral function of commercial banking.[301]

The East Texas discovery was initially ignored by the major oil companies; instead, more than 400 companies got their start in the field. McElvaney wrote that it "found its immediate destiny in the hands of hundreds of small independent operators as well as many complete neophytes in the industry. It brought about the greatest economic waste in overdevelopment in the history of the industry.

"But at the same time it distributed its benefits in so many different directions, it created such vast and varied needs [for the uses of hydrocarbons], it precipitated so many crises that the first three years of East Texas became in a sense the birthplace of our economic dependence on oil, of conservation as we know it today, of scientific discoveries leading to more accurate determination of reserves, and as a result of these, financing of oil in the ground."[302]

---

[301] McElvaney, "Some Aspects of Financing Oil and Gas Transactions," 317.
[302] McElvaney, "Some Aspects of Financing Oil and Gas Transactions," 315.

CHAPTER 3

Energy Lending
Following Proration

"When asked how much he wanted, Murchison, replied, 'All I can get.'"
Bryan Burrough

Prior to market stability, energy bankers were few and far between. Some of the earliest oil-banking occurred in Oklahoma by producers themselves. Perhaps the oldest energy bank—and almost certainly the only one run by oilmen—was Exchange National Bank of Tulsa, which was formed after the Glen Pool, Cushing and Osage fields' discoveries near Tulsa.[303]

In 1910, oilmen Harry Sinclair and P.J. White, owners of the White-Sinclair Co., and a half dozen other oilmen took over the failing Farmers National following a local crisis in the oil business that threatened a financial catastrophe for Tulsa.[304] It was said that, before Sinclair took over Farmers National, "bankers in the early Glenn Pool years, attuned to the needs of farmers, ranchers and merchants, were as comfortable with the oil business as a drunk in church."[305] Sinclair was later quoted as saying, "All of us thought the future of Tulsa and the future of oil cried out for an oil bank. And it became what we

---

[303] The bank is now known as Bank of Oklahoma.
[304] Personal correspondence from Mickey Coats, Bank of Oklahoma, copy of internal publication, *The Oil Bank for Oil Men*, at 9, contained in a notebook circa 1990 located at Bank of Oklahoma (hereinafter referred to as "The Oil Bank for Oil Men").
[305] Hicks, *Nearly Forgotten, The Amazing Story of the Glenn Pool*, 123-124.

hoped it would—the biggest and best known oil bank in America."[306] They recapitalized it with $400,000 as Exchange National Bank of Tulsa and financed local independents.

According to an internal history of the bank, "The Exchange was to be primarily an oil bank. Every official and director was personally interested in or familiar with almost every oil well, lease or prospect in the state. One or more of them usually knew what was behind every security offered by borrowers.

"If the security was sound, the loan was made promptly. This service to oilmen probably did more than any other thing to convince Tulsans that their city could be the national center of the oil business."[307]

One of the earliest loans secured by reserves in the ground—i.e., a "reserve-based loan"—reportedly was made by The Exchange Bank in 1928.[308] After the 1929 stock-market crash, Sinclair and the other founders were again called upon to recapitalize the bank, reorganizing it as the National Bank of Tulsa. At the time, it was the largest capitalized bank in the Southwest and known locally as "The Oil Bank of America."[309]

In the earliest days of oil lending, the most that banks were willing to provide were short-term loans, typically with three- to 12-month terms and usually underwritten on the basis of the net worth of the borrower or secured by crude oil in storage or in transit. Since most wells were drilled at shallow depths of between 1,000 and 2,500 feet, drilling costs on a footage basis were such that, coupled with

---

[306] Banknotes, "The Trailblazer," *BOK Financial Employee Weekly*, Editor Russ Florence, undated internal bank communication materials compiled by Bank of Oklahoma and provided by Mickey Coats, September 28, 2015.

[307] Wilson, "Bank Financing of Oil," 11.

[308] Wilson, "Bank Financing of Oil," 16, based on personal communication with W.L. Kendall. The loan security consisted of a recorded mortgage on the property and a direct assignment to the bank of the proceeds of production.

[309] Mickey Coats (EVP, Bank of Oklahoma) in discussion with the author, June 20, 2013. It succumbed to the oil-patch bank collapses of the 1980s, taken over by the FDIC and recapitalized in 1990 by another Oklahoma oilman, George Kaiser, chairman of Kaiser-Francis Oil Co. Kaiser wanted to preserve the existence of a local energy lender, as so many had been taken over by large, money-center banks.

open-flow production, successful wells could reach payout in a very short period—often a few hours or days. Funding the next well from cash flow resulted in very low demand for bank capital.[310]

During the early years of reserve-based lending, only the most reputable borrower need apply and even they were limited to a maximum loan equal to net cash from 12 months of production from the mortgaged properties. Often, the loan required repayment in six months because there was no enforceable restriction on allowables among competing field producers.[311]

Prior to successful enforcement of prorationing, McElvaney wrote, "lending on oil in the ground was practically unheard of and considered beyond the pale of prudent banking practice. Without inauguration and ultimately successful administration of regulatory measures having to do with maximum efficient production and prevention of waste, the stability of the economic factors involved in the financing of oil could never have been achieved."[312]

In the years following successful prorationing, additional banks entered the scene and more loans became available, including in larger amounts and with longer repayment periods.[313] Early on, those banks intrepid enough to make reserve-based loans relied upon their customers, who were larger oil producers, to vet the reserves of smaller producers seeking credit.

By the mid-1930s, Houston's First National Bank was considering getting into the business of making oil loans and queried established oil lenders in Tulsa and Dallas about their underwriting policies and procedures for establishing the value of the pledged oil and gas collateral. In response, Elmo Thompson, vice president of National

---

[310] Wilson, "Bank Financing of Oil," 16.

[311] Thompson, "Legal And Other Aspects of Financing The Oil Industry," 34-35; 1st NB Dallas letter 8/14/34.

[312] McElvaney, "Some Aspects of Financing Oil and Gas Transactions," 316-317. See also, Lyon F. Terry, "Bankers Like to Do Business with Oil Men," *The Oil and Gas Journal* (November 21, 1955): 168. "Under such conditions development and expansion by the independents had to be financed, if possible, by equity money; there were few bank loans possible, and those had to be short maturity. Even prior to the depression, the violent fluctuations in crude-oil prices did not inspire confidence in producing property."

[313] Thompson, "Legal And Other Aspects of Financing The Oil Industry," 35.

Bank of Tulsa, offered in 1934, "It is my thought you could without difficulty refer production leases offered for collateral to the Land and Engineering Departments of one of the three substantial oil companies located in Houston and obtain a most accurate appraisal of the value of the lease, the prospective life of the production, and its desirability for collateral purposes.

"… As a matter of fact, Houston and Tulsa are probably the only two cities in the United States where this valuable information is readily available to the banks. Of course a volume of this type of loans would justify the employment of a full-time or part-time man to make personal inspections and make personal appraisals, which man, of course, should be backed with experience in actual oil production."[314]

Energy Lending Expands to Money-Center Banks
Prior to proration Sid Richardson, one of the many colorful, early wildcatters, followed the traditional driller-promoter model. Richardson used cash flow from current production, second-hand equipment and supplies and labor he bartered for—often on credit, paying his workers once a month and sometimes in groceries. With proration, this became less necessary.

"Because proration was strictly followed in the pipeline-short Permian Basin, Richardson was able to obtain loans from First National Bank in Dallas on his production," Olien and Hinton wrote. "As the scale of his operations grew and Richardson moved into the intermediate rank of independents, he found that his financial needs took him to banks in Chicago, Boston, and New York. Like their smaller Texas counterparts, these banks viewed oil as less speculative after statewide control of production was assured by the Texas Railroad Commission."[315]

More banks began to look into energy lending as a new area to put their depositors' money to work. In the late 1930s, oil-patch and

---

[314] Elmo Thompson, Vice President, National Bank of Tulsa, to W.A. Kirkland, Vice President, First National Bank, Houston, dated August 25, 1934.
[315] Olien and Hinton, *Wildcatters*, 75.

Chicago banks began adding technical staff capable of analyzing reserve values. After World War II, most of the larger East Coast money-center banks added these experts to their staffs as well, making possible the adoption of appropriate and realistic credit policies in the banking fraternity.[316]

Bankers accepting of production for loan collateral in Texas, Oklahoma and other states where proration regulations helped to control local markets[317] were wary of advancing their depositors' money to oilmen with production from states where the regulatory regime was not as well developed.[318] Into the 1950s, most lending to oil and gas producers continued to be by oil-patch banks.

It was natural that the local bankers would respond to local market demand and, over time, develop the technical expertise, greater knowledge of producing fields and a network among producers. John Scott, a vice president of Republic National Bank of Dallas, wrote, "In my opinion, the banks located in the producing area of the country, provided they are equipped with the proper talent, personnel and capital, are in a better position to handle this type of business, since they talk the language of the producer, understand him, can follow his activities and usually are aware of the conditions surrounding the oil and gas producing business."[319]

However, as early as the 1930s, some producers, if turned down by their local bankers, could find an easier mark from the big New

---

[316] Gueymard, "The Seventies-An Era of Transition," 558. "It took a long time for bankers to forget the old price gyrations and the overproduction of the early thirties and to learn to appreciate oil and natural gas reserves and production as security for loans. But, as the authority and effect of the state-commission orders slowly became recognized, the stability of production property became more and more respected." Terry, "Bankers Like to Do Business with Oil Men," 169.

[317] "[Oil loans] are not available today to properties in states without or with unenforced conservation laws, nor are they available for long periods of time to secondary production because they [secondary production] are not presently included in proration regulations." Thompson, "Legal And Other Aspects of Financing The Oil Industry."

[318] States without proration regulations include California, Colorado, Illinois, Kentucky, Mississippi, Montana, Ohio, Utah and Wyoming. Lowe, John and Owen Anderson, Ernest Smith and Christopher Kulander, Cases and Material on Oil and Gas Law, 6th Ed. (West, 2013), 694.

[319] Scott, "Some Aspects of Oil and Gas Financing," 325-26.

York lenders. Among these was Clint Murchison, Sr., an early partner of Sid Richardson and an equally colorful, early, Texas wildcatter. Burrough wrote:

> All through the hot oil wars Murchison's mind thrummed with ideas for new pipelines and refineries and oil fields, all limited only by his chronic shortage of cash. His genius, though, was not so much finding oil as finding money. In 1933, he heard of a young loan officer at the Bank of Manhattan [one of many predecessor banks to today's JPMorgan Bank] named Ruston Ardrey, a native Texan who had opened the bank's first energy department.
>
> In those days the big New York banks steered clear of anything but the shortest-term loans to wildcatters, deeming them too risky. But Ardrey had made a five-year-loan to an Oklahoma independent, and when Murchison heard about it, he flew to New York. When Ardrey asked how much he wanted, Murchison, replied, "All I can get."
>
> He left with a one-million-dollar loan, the promise of more to come, and a crucial new ally; he called Ardrey "the Big A." In time Murchison would introduce him to dozens of other oilmen ... .[320, 321]

Post-War Lending Through the 1950s

During World War II, all available steel was dedicated for use in the war effort; after the war, drill pipe became readily available again to drillers. At the same time, demand for oil was growing as well as drilling costs, resulting in a substantial step-up in exploration costs. In 1956, explorers drilled 58,160 wells in the U.S. at a cost of $3 billion; at the time, it was forecasted that $3.6 billion would be spent in 1957.[322]

---

[320] Burrough, *The Big Rich*, 85.
[321] In 1957, Richardson was judged the richest man in America by the *Ladies' Home Journal*. Burrough, *The Big Rich*, 251.
[322] Thompson, "Legal And Other Aspects of Financing The Oil Industry," 33-34.

The boom peaked around that time as most of the post-war growth in demand had been satiated.[323] Also, rising oil prices in the era resulted in competition from other fuels, such as coal and natural gas in power generation and heating.

Ironically, growth in the use of natural gas along the East Coast was helped by the need to get oil there to fuel the war effort. To circumvent German attacks on East Coast-bound oil and oil-product tankers sailing from the Gulf Coast,[324] the federal government commissioned a 24-inch-diameter pipeline known as the "Big Inch." Construction commenced in 1942. It was completed in less than a year, stretching 1,476 miles from Longview, Texas, in the East Texas Field, to refiners in Norris City, Illinois, with additional 20-inch-diameter pipe connecting to refiners in Pennsylvania and New Jersey.

The first 1,254 miles were completed in about four months. The Big Inch was capable of carrying more than 300,000 barrels of crude oil a day.[325] It was followed in 1943 by the 20-inch-diameter Little Big Inch from Houston to New Jersey, carrying approximately 200,000 barrels a day of refined products.[326]

After the war, the pipelines were declared surplus war inventory and privatized in 1947.[327] Texas Eastern Transmission Corp., now owned by Duke Energy Corp., purchased the lines and converted them to carry natural gas to Illinois and the East Coast.[328] In just four years, from 1946 to 1950, annual transportation of natural gas increased 250% to 2.5 trillion cubic feet (Tcf). The gas supply displaced

---

[323] Gueymard, "The Seventies-An Era of Transition," 559.
[324] Between January and April, 1942, 46 oil tankers were sunk and 16 damaged by German U-boat attacks. Daily crude shipments from the Gulf to the eastern seaboard were reduced from 1.4 million barrels in the spring of 1941 down to 100,000 barrels per day by January, 1943. Texas Eastern Transmission Corporation (Tetco), *The Big Inch and the Little Inch Pipelines, The Most Amazing Government-Industry Cooperation Ever Achieved* (May 2000), 9, Historicmonroe.org.
[325] Tetco, *The Big Inch and the Little Inch Pipelines*, 30 and 40.
[326] Tetco, *The Big Inch and the Little Inch Pipelines*, 40.
[327] *Handbook of Texas Online*, Jerrell Dean Palmer and John G. Johnson, "Big Inch and Little Big Inch," accessed March 13, 2016, Tshaonline.org.
[328] "History of 'Big Inch' and 'Little Big Inch' Pipelines Now on Display," accessed March 1, 2016, Duke-energy.com.

existing oil-fueled power generation and boilers and absorbed most of the post-war increases in domestic energy demand.[329]

Reduced demand for oil for powering boilers and the growth in post-war development of the Middle East's vast reserves led to lower prices. In response, the Texas Railroad Commission constricted field-wide proration in the late 1950s and maintained the cutback into the early 1960s. Prices continued to remain depressed. At one point, what was allowed was one third of wells' estimated potential deliverability. By 1962, the number of days of allowable production per month stood at just seven.[330]

This was not a problem for the major oil companies, which were able to simultaneously import cheaper oil from the Middle East. However, smaller producers were hit hard. "[A] low market demand threatened the domestic independents with extinction," Prindle wrote. "If they could not run their wells, they could not make a living. In the latter half of the 1950s, therefore, independents began to hurt, and by the early years of the next decade they were desperate."[331]

The Railroad Commission had no ability to control production outside Texas' boundaries. Complex global market forces were crowding the state to the margins of world production. By 1965, only half of the wells in Texas that had been pumping a decade earlier were still in service. Faced with competition from the majors' import of foreign oil, many of the independents found it hard to maintain the margins of the 1940s and early 1950s. As costs rose for domestic exploration and production, a number of smaller producers elected to sell out.[332]

In addition, World War II also brought about greatly increased income-tax rates, making it essential for oil companies to consider the tax-related cost of their operations. Tax rates in excess of 50% of net income hampered internal generation of capital for oil companies, which needed to continuously re-invest to find new reserves.

---

[329] Yergin, *The Prize*, 412.
[330] Prindle, *Petroleum Politics*, 75.
[331] Prindle, *Petroleum Politics*, 75.
[332] Gueymard, "The Seventies-An Era of Transition," 559.

In 1962, Wallace Wilson, an energy banker with Continental Illinois, wrote, "A company either expands or it contracts; seemingly there is no middle ground. When capital for exploration and development is adequate, the deductions for intangible drilling expenses, depletion, and depreciation reduce income taxes to a minimum. If adequate capital is not available, drilling must be curtailed and a large part of the cash flow of the company is paid out in taxes, a process which usually is irreversible."[333]

Producers were facing not only the cost of higher taxes, but postwar inflation for labor and materials. Wilson continued, "Studies made by individual companies and trade associations showed that the average cost of replacing producing capacity was approaching, or in some cases, exceeding the average realization at posted prices ... .

"[Some of these] companies and individuals decided that their holdings would yield a greater return by liquidation for cash than with continued operation. Other companies, typically larger independents and majors concluded that growth could be achieved more economically through property acquisition than by conventional exploration and development. Thus the stage was set for the 'sellout trend.'"[334]

The demand for desirable oil-producing properties exceeded supply, causing their values to increase. The buyers looked to the banks to provide the maximum amount of financing leverage for their acquisitions. The only additional ingredient needed was a financing structure that would not further complicate the tax problems of either the seller or the buyer.

Capital providers answered the demand with a new type of loan structure—the production-payment loan, a type of non-recourse financing that relied entirely upon delivery of future volumes of oil from the properties sold. Production payments, *per se*, were not a new invention. Production payments have been used since the early days of the industry—originally reserved by the lessor in addition to a roy-

---

[333] Wilson, "Bank Financing of Oil," 18.
[334] Wilson, "Bank Financing of Oil," 18; *see also* Gueymard, "The Seventies-An Era of Transition," 559.

alty reservation as a form of deferred bonus for granting of the lease. In the heyday of the East Texas Field's development, many operators financed their wells with production payments sold to investors at substantial discounts.[335] These early transactions did not involve bank financing; however, in some instances, production payments were used to collateralize loans after 1935.[336]

In the post-war years, commercial banks were eager to expand their share of the market for capital flowing into the energy industry. With improvements in reservoir engineering, bankers had greater confidence in reserve estimates and improved forecasts of future cash flow from production upon which to underwrite the production-payment loan.

As the market for oil properties heated and competition among banks grew, this new form of financing caused bankers to stretch their underwriting criteria. Wilson wrote, "This has created some problems for banks who wish to preserve valued customer relationships while staying within the limits of safe lending. Some of these problems include longer term loans, the advisability of including undeveloped reserves as acceptable collateral, and the need for new criteria to define safe loan limits."[337] The 1950s would not be the only time conservative underwriting of reserve-based loans would lose out to bankers' desire for market share—a tension that continues to this day.

ABCs of Production-Payment Lending

A production payment is simply an obligation to pay a fixed amount of money to the production-payment owner from the sale of future production from identified wells. The purchaser of the production payment assumes the risk that the wells will produce sufficient volumes that, when sold, will repay the production payment. However, if

---

[335] Perhaps the best example from the early days is the trade H.L. Hunt negotiated for the Daisy Bradford well. In addition to a minimal upfront cash payment, the consideration for Hunt's purchase of Dad Joiner's East Texas holdings included a $910,000 production payment. Hinton and Olien, *Oil in Texas*, 174.
[336] Wilson, "Bank Financing of Oil," 18.
[337] Wilson, "Bank Financing of Oil," 2.

the burdened wells fail to produce the necessary volume, the producer is not personally liable to the party that purchased the production payment. In other words, the producer does not guarantee that sufficient reserves will be produced nor that the price of those reserves, when sold, would be sufficient to repay the value of the production payment. A production payment is, thus, a "non-recourse" obligation for the producer and the purchaser of the production payment has an "economic risk" as to whether the property will ultimately pay the full amount.

The structure also had a favorable federal-tax treatment.[338] The seller (A) would advertise to sell its producing properties on a certain date, typically at year-end. The interested purchaser (B), usually a major oil company, with an intermediary (C), usually a limited partnership or corporation with nominal net worth and often affiliated with a recognized charitable or non-profit institution that specialized in buying oil payments, would contact banks, insurance companies, pension funds or a combination to determine the maximum amortizing loan that could be placed against A's producing properties.[339]

The amount of the financed oil payment purchased by C, the holder, was designed so that the net income for B, the operator, would be quite small—only enough to cover operating costs—and result in insignificant annual federal income taxes until the oil payment was paid off and the production payment released, at which time the operator would receive the full proceeds from future production. The B party, when its bid was combined with a production payment to C, could afford to pay a higher price to A because it was able to defer the income stream of the properties out into the future until the production payment was paid in full.[340]

---

[338] Internal Revenue Code § 337.

[339] *Comm'r v. Fleming*, 82 F.2d 324 (5th Cir. 1936); Edward E. Monteith, Jr. (Executive Vice President, Republic National Bank of Dallas, Dallas, Texas), "Financial Criteria Of Oil And Gas Lending, Institute," *Oil and Gas Law* (1966), 295; Wilson, "Bank Financing of Oil," 6.

[340] The ABC production-payment structure would typically add a 20% premium to the purchase price. Frank Dartez, retired Guaranty Bank reservoir engineer whose career began in 1960 with Cities Service Co., interview by the author, March 23, 2015.

Chapter 3: Energy Lending Following Proration

The production payment was typically financed based on the collateral loan amount equal to between 60% and 75% of expected oil production over a fixed term—usually one to five years. Seller A would sell its working interest to B, subject to a reserved production payment equal to the "collateral loan amount," plus an interest rate of between 0.0625% and 0.5% above the bank rate of interest. Seller A would, then, sell the reserved production payment to C, which obtained 100% bank financing while pledging the production payment as collateral.

The production-payment-holder C party would skim the difference in interest rate from the monthly amortization payments on its loan. It paid taxes only on the differential in the interest rate between that reserved and borne by the oil payment and the rate charged by the lending institution. The balance of C's receipts was construed to be the return of his capital investment on which he was allowed cost depletion.[341]

Since C was, usually, a very nominal corporation compared with the amount of the loan, the loan was based on the projected value of the properties dedicated to the oil payment. B acquired the working interest in the properties burdened by the oil payment and was not taxed on income from the property's production attributable to C's production payment, thereby deferring tax obligations until the payment terminated. Because the income taxes involved were greatly reduced until the oil payment was paid, properties transferred under this structure would be worth more than straight-up sales for cash.[342]

Chase bankers, in a paper presented to the American Institute of Mining and Metallurgical Engineers in 1953, provided an example of a bank underwriting a production-payment loan at a 5.5% to 6% discount rate compounded semi-annually. In this case, the oil payment

---

[341] Monteith, "Financial Criteria of Oil and Gas Lending," 296; *see also* Lyon F. Terry and Kenneth E. Hill, Vice Presidents, Petroleum Department, The Chase National Bank "Valuation of Oil and Gas Producing Properties for Loan Purposes," (paper presented at Annual Meeting of Petroleum Branch, American Institute of Mining and Metallurgical Engineers, 1953), 5.
[342] Terry and Hill, "Valuation of Oil and Gas Producing Properties," 5.

was valued as the sum of 60% of the present value of the property's proved developed producing reserves (PDP), between 45% and 60% of its proved undeveloped (PUD) and, depending upon the nature of the reserves, up to between 10% and 20% for probable (2P) reserves.[343] In this example, value is assigned to non-producing reserves, whereas earlier production-payment loans were based on only current production.

Impact on Sales of Oil and Gas Properties

The popularity of this form of financing had caught on by 1954 among most of the energy-lending banks,[344] although it was reported that, in parts of the country outside of Texas, some financial institutions were reticent to join in.[345] By at least 1965, it was reported that ABC loans constituted more than 65% of the outstanding oil loans.[346] Oil-payment financing became the most important criteria in determining the total sales price to be received by the seller.[347]

Until the 1960s, insurance-underwriting regulations prohibited these companies from giving value to more than 25% of a borrower's PUD reserves and prohibited consideration for 2P reserves.[348] This more conservative approach promulgated by the National Association of Insurance Commissioners may explain why, early on, commercial banks were the preferred lenders in ABC transactions.

The economics of oil-payment loans could be adversely affected if the state constrained production allowables, thus reducing operating cash flow. Lenders had no recourse to the producer (B), but required under its loan to C, its borrower, that C require that B continue operations until the loan was paid.

---

[343] Monteith, "Financial Criteria of Oil and Gas Lending," 296; Wilson, "Bank Financing of Oil," 28-30.

[344] At least 10 banks were actively engaged in production-payment financing in 1949. Grover Ellis, Jr., "Production Payments and Other Trends in Petroleum Financing," Graduate School of Banking, Rutgers University, New Brunswick, N.J., June, 1955.

[345] Scott, "Some Aspects of Oil and Gas Financing," 335.

[346] Monteith, "Financial Criteria of Oil and Gas Lending," 295.

[347] Monteith, "Financial Criteria of Oil and Gas Lending," 295-96.

[348] Monteith, "Financial Criteria of Oil and Gas Lending," 300.

Chapter 3: Energy Lending Following Proration

The most active purchasers of oil properties under this structure were major oil companies, which could withstand the impact of prorationing rules and, thereby, provide indirect credit support for the production-payment loan. Small independents, meanwhile, were not as favored as purchasers in ABC transactions and, thus, were more often the seller.[349] The ABC loan became the conduit through which the majors acquired production for their integrated enterprises and independents gained capital to continue to make new oil discoveries.

"By the 1960s, a significant oversupply of oil had developed in the U.S. and both majors and large independents cut back dramatically on exploration and turned to acquisitions," Frank Dartez, an energy banker for Citibank at the time, said in an interview in 2015. "Acquisitions would add to the company's reserves without contributing to the oversupply."

This created a huge demand for acquisitions and acquisition departments were established by most companies. Independents, both large and small, were being financially squeezed by low allowables, while every major and large independent sought to increase its reserves. "Competition was fierce," Dartez said.

"When a company or set of producing properties came on the market, multiple bids were received, sometimes within a few days. Since the ABC-production-payment structure offered significant tax advantages, it was the preferred method of financing." This created numerous opportunities for the energy banks, which also competed for the financing.

Due to the size of the large property acquisitions in the 1960s, the money-center banks in New York were the only ones with loan capacity and expertise to structure and manage the financing. They would lead with the largest share of the financing and participated out the remainder to energy banks in Texas, Oklahoma, Louisiana, Illinois and California.

---

[349] Monteith, "Financial Criteria of Oil and Gas Lending," 296; *see also* Terry, "Bankers Like to Do Business with Oil Men," 8.

Up until the mid-1960s, virtually every large ABC financing had been by Chase Manhattan Bank. Dartez recalled how his bank was able to compete with it. "Chase had a certain mystique due to extensive field files that had been accumulated over the years, established by lending relationships with the major oil companies that went back to 1936. Citibank, on the other hand, did not establish a formal energy department until the late 1950s, although it had long-standing relationships with most major oil companies as well."

To underwrite the financing for each transaction, banks required a detailed engineering report of the proposed acquisition properties. Dartez said an opening for Citibank to compete with Chase occurred because "the Chase engineers stayed in the bank and relied on their field-file information and phone calls. Citibank engineers, on the other hand, immediately set up appointments with both the consultant and the company to review the engineering data on the principal properties and get up to date on current activity and plans."

In several cases, Citibank's approach proved to be an advantage. "In about 1965, a huge opportunity became available for Citibank to finally break the monopoly that Chase had had on agenting large transactions. Seagrams Distillers, a good customer of Citibank with offices just across the street, decided to enter the oil business by acquiring Texas Pacific Coal & Oil Co."

The oil company had extensive holdings in several states. "But its crown jewels were interests in most of the largest and most prolific fields in the Permian Basin of West Texas. The challenge was that most of these large fields were either undergoing operations for, or there were plans for, waterflooding in the near future," he said.

Most banks were not willing to include future waterflood reserves in their evaluations. "However, Citibank's independent consultant felt that including waterflood reserves was justified and TPCO was not going to sell, if it couldn't get some value for the waterflood reserves. Citibank's engineers felt that, because the waterflood reserves were spread over a large number of fields, some waterflood reserves could be included on a conservative basis."

It was able to convince other lenders of this and was able to close the transaction. Dartez said, "Chase's monopoly was finally broken and Citibank went on to be the agent bank on a number of other large acquisitions."[350]

Variations on a Theme

Over time, variations of the ABC structure were documented, including a "carved-out" production payment, in which A sold a production payment that was carved out of A's current production to a special-purpose corporation (B) with A retaining its interest in the property subject to B's production payment. B would obtain purchase-financing from its bank by pledging the carved-out production payment as collateral.

The desired tax effect for A under this year-end sale was to recognize current income from the sale proceeds to offset losses carried forward or incurred in the current year or to avoid loss of part of statutory depletion with respect to the particular property in the year that the sale was made.[351] Depletion deductions were typically taken on a percentage basis, calculated at 27.5% of revenue, but subject to a statutory depletion limit of no more than 50% of net income on a lease-by-lease basis.

Joe Bridges, the oil and gas producer who was an energy banker at First City Houston in the 1970s, said in an interview in 2012 that, in addition to being a tax-efficient mechanism for acquiring production, "the ABC-financed production sales were used by producers, principally the majors, to manage the producer's federal income-tax exposure, selling just enough production at year-end to bring 50% of lease net income to be equal to 27.5% of lease revenue to take maximum advantage of the percentage depletion allowance."[352]

---

[350] Dartez, author's interview.
[351] Gueymard, "The Seventies-An Era of Transition," 566. "The majors would sell just enough production to maximize percentage depletion, based on annual revenue capped by net profits."
[352] Bridges, author's interview.

Another variation was called the "equipment production payment" in which A carved a production payment out of a part of his working interest for the express purpose of equipping wells to be drilled on the property. In such cases, a third party, B, would purchase the production payment from A, but would pay the sales proceeds directly to the equipment supplier. Alternatively, A could convey the production payment directly to the equipment supplier as payment for services or materials provided in drilling or equipping the wells on the property, in which case the equipment supplier would take on the risk of whether or not the production payment would be repaid out of future production.[353]

Through the 1960s, the ABC structure became more sophisticated and tailored to address operational issues as well as modifications triggered by changes in the federal tax code.[354] After 1961, commercial banks were faced with competition from life-insurance companies, which, following a change in insurance-underwriting regulations, were permitted to make direct purchases of production payments, thus avoiding the need to "finance" C and would acquire the production payment for its own account.[355] However, as subsequent investment opportunities—such as money-market investments and corporate bonds—became more attractive to insurance companies by the latter part of the '60s, insurance companies had less interest in production payments, unless producers were willing to meet the competitive yield of between 6% and 7.5%.[356]

By 1966, a few years before the Tax Reform Act of 1969 wrote the final chapter on the tax-advantaged ABC structure, lawyers in most producing states and money centers were devising intricate formulae by which the simple, flat-percentage production payment was

---

[353] Hubert Dee Johnson (Carrington, Gowan, Johnson, Bromberg & Leeds), "Legal Aspects of Oil and Gas Financing," *Institute on Oil and Gas Law* (1958): 148-49.

[354] John R.A. Beatty (Partner, Shearman & Sterling), "Selected Problems in Oil and Gas Financing," 11 *Rocky Mt. Min. L. Inst.* (1966).

[355] Beatty, "Selected Problems in Oil and Gas Financing."

[356] Fagin, K. Marshall, Manager, and W.T. Drummond, Assistant Manager, "Life Insurance Company Loans on Oil & Gas Properties," 1 *Journal of the Society of Petroleum Evaluation Engineers* (1968-69): 22.

sliced and diced, front-end loaded, subjected to contingencies and cal-culated on a property-by-property basis.[357] For example, in addition to production payments, "proceeds production payments" were used in part to avoid the "real property" characterization of the term-limited, overriding-royalty treatment of the production payment and the sev-erance-tax and federal documentary-stamp-tax obligations that would otherwise result.[358]

In some of the longer-tenured production payments, banks and insurance companies would bifurcate the income stream. In this, the bank held the early repayments of principal, leaving the insurance company to look to future production for maturities of between 10 and 15 years.[359]

Oil Payments Only—Not Natural Gas

The literature of this period of ABC loans referred to "oil bankers" and "oil payments" and not natural gas. One explanation may have been the uncertainty over the ultimate recoverable price for gas sold into interstate commerce. In addition to reservoir, proration and commodity-price risks, the U.S. Supreme Court in 1954 added a regu-lated-price risk to underwritten gas production.[360]

The *Phillips Petroleum Co. v. Wisconsin* decision resulted in the price of interstate gas sales being subject to area-wide "just and reasonable" rate-base hearings before the Federal Power Commission under the Natural Gas Act of 1938.[361] Subject to administrative review, a pro-ducer—and its banker—could find that the prices under which it had

---

[357] Beatty, "Selected Problems in Oil and Gas Financing," 108.

[358] Beatty, "Selected Problems in Oil and Gas Financing," 105.

[359] Fagin, "Life Insurance Company Loans," 23.

[360] *Phillips Petroleum Co. v. Wisconsin*, 347 U.S. 672 (1954).

[361] 15 U.S.C.§§717-717w, The Federal Power Commission originally had ruled that it did not have jurisdiction over Phillips Petroleum as a natural gas company under the Natural Gas Act of 1938, but the Supreme Court disagreed. "Justice William O. Douglas wrote that this was a 'question the Court has never decided' and 'involves considerations of which we know little and with which we are not competent to deal.' He contended that the FPC's original decision was 'made by men intimately familiar with the background and history' of the Natural Gas Act, and should have been sustained." Phillip L. Zweig, *Belly Up: The Collapse of the Penn Square Bank* (Ballantine Books, August 12, 1986), 18.

contracted to sell its gas production to an interstate pipeline were above the FPC's price ceiling and subject to refund or rollback.[362]

The regulatory experience for independent George Mitchell following *Phillips* was typical for gas producers. Beginning in the early 1950s, Mitchell's company, Christie, Mitchell and Mitchell, was producing a lot of gas from Boonsville Field in North Texas. Seeking a market, the company cut a long-term, interstate-sales contract with Natural Gas Pipeline Company of America in 1953 for delivery to the Chicago market. After *Phillips*, the FPC reviewed the contract and determined the rate was too high, requiring Mitchell to renegotiate the contract. Due to the depressed gas prices of the time, it was reduced by only a penny—from 14 cents to 13 cents—but this amounted to nearly a 10% reduction.[363]

As of 1960, at least, it was unclear what a producer was required to show to support the FPC deeming its price "just and reasonable." The FPC's "cost of service" rate-making determination, which had been applied to pipelines since the 1930s, relied on the cost of providing the service rather than the market value of that service. The FPC's staff was substantially increased to determine prices that would allow producers to cover their costs plus a "fair" profit.

This regulatory analysis was possible to apply to just a few interstate gas pipelines, but expanding the FPC's mandate to include all gas producers meant that regulating prices on a well-by-well basis was an extreme administrative burden for it. Until a final decision by the FPC, the producer and its lender had no assurance of what the authorized price would be.[364]

In 1959, 1,265 applications for rate increases or reviews were made. In that year, the FPC was only able to act on 240 cases. As a

---

[362] Monteith, "Financial Criteria of Oil and Gas Lending," 301.

[363] B.F. "Budd" Clark, Vice Chairman, interview by Joseph Kutchin in Joseph W. Kutchin, *How Mitchell Energy & Development Corp. Got its Start and How it Grew: An Oral History and Narrative Overview* (Universal Publishers, 1998), 70. Mitchell lowered its sales price, but negotiated for Natural Gas Pipeline to pay for gathering costs and processing through Mitchell's processing plant.

[364] John T. Maginnis, "Financing Oil and Gas Development," 15, *The Business Lawyer* 693 (April 1960): 694-695.

result of the uncertainty, gas dedicated to interstate pipes was sold at artificially low price ceilings. By the end of the 1970s, the difference between the price of interstate gas (lower) and intrastate gas (higher) created an interstate-supply scarcity amid a surplus of what could truly be produced. The FPC continued to struggle and, confronted with insufficient winter gas supply in the U.S. Northeast, Congress replaced the price-regulation regime in 1978 by passing the Natural Gas Policy Act.[365]

Until then, however, extra due diligence for loans secured by gas production required the lender and its lawyers to examine the sales contracts of the borrower and associated certificates.[366] Entering into a long-term, gas-payment loan, therefore, bore an additional risk for the lender and the producer that did not affect oil-payment loans and may have provided a chilling effect upon financing development of natural gas.

Closing the ABC Loophole

The end of the ABC loan structure came with the Tax Reform Act of 1969. In addition to a further reduction in the oil and gas depletion allowance from 27.5% to 22%, the new law treated the ABC carved-out production payment not as a sale of real-property interests, but as a loan. Therefore, income that had been tax-free would now be treated as income subject to depletion.

The bankers who had grown sizable books of ABC loans in the late '50s and early '60s lamented the loss of this vehicle that had been a driver of business.[367] The ABC and retained-production-payment structure had been used in thousands of transactions and accounted for the acquisition of nearly all the major producing-property purchases.[368]

---

[365] "The History of Regulation," Natural Gas Supply Association, accessed March 1, 2016, Naturalgas.org/regulation/history.
[366] Maginnis, "Financing Oil and Gas Development," 695.
[367] Thomas G. Stevens, "Current Developments in Petroleum Financing," 23 *Journal of Petroleum Technology* 202, (1971).
[368] Gueymard, "The Seventies-An Era of Transition," 559.

These included Humble Oil's purchases of Monterey Oil Co. and Honolulu Oil Co. along with Getty Oil Co.'s purchase of Tidewater Oil Co.[369] Additional deals included Continental Oil Co.'s and Tenneco Oil Co.'s purchase of Delhi Taylor Oil Co. and many others.

Dartez credited the acquisition by Continental (Conoco) of Consolidation Coal Co. in 1966 as the catalyst for the tax change. "A Pennsylvania newspaper wrote an op-ed piece about the great tax ploy to deduct mortgage principal and interest from income," Dartez said. "This took hold and the tax reform was passed."[370]

While the impact of the 1969 tax reform was material—eliminating the tax benefits of the carved-out production payment and the retained production payment—the act did not negate—and, in fact, specifically provided for—financing under the "development production payment" to encourage new oil and gas development. Proceeds derived from this financing structure had to be dedicated to development costs—both tangible and intangible—on the property from which the production payment was carved. Under this, monies loaned for this purpose had to be kept separate and used to pay actual costs as they were incurred.[371]

Nevertheless, as the 1960s came to a close, energy bankers were ready to pronounce the end of the era of development financing. Tom Stevens, an energy lender in Houston, wrote in 1971, "This type of lending is what really got oil banking off to a running start during the 30's and 40's and was done extensively until only a few years ago.

" … The principal reasons for the decline in this type of lending are the demise of the independent operator, who was the principal customer for this type of credit, and the lack of success in finding new oil and gas fields of the magnitude that would require development financing."[372]

However, like Mark Twain's remarks about reports of his demise, speculation on the death of energy lending was greatly exaggerated.

---

[369] Stevens, "Current Developments in Petroleum Financing," 695.
[370] Dartez, author's interview.
[371] Gueymard, "The Seventies-An Era of Transition," 566.
[372] Stevens, "Current Developments in Petroleum Financing," 203.

Chapter 3: Energy Lending Following Proration

While the structure and pace of the original days of energy lending may have come to an end, the next couple of decades would bring about transformational changes in global geopolitical and energy markets, creating new opportunities for independent producers, which, in turn, created huge demand for capital, thus opportunities for bankers and other capital providers.

Notwithstanding these changes to come, many of the basic principles of energy lending have remained remarkably consistent during the past 100 years. This can be easily seen by a look at the early discussions of bankers and their lawyers on loan underwriting and documentation.

CHAPTER 4

Elements of Energy Lending

*"It's people who sign the note, it's people who promise to pay,
it's people who pay or fail to pay; and the banker's ultimate judgment
above the ground in the matter of oil loans
is no less important than the engineer."*
Eugene McElvaney

Essential parameters valid today were equally critical in underwriting the risks associated with early production-secured loans and were factored into the decision of whether or not to lend to an oil company. In a presentation in the Fifth Annual Southwestern Legal Foundation program in 1954, McElvaney observed:

> The necessity of basic credit decisions in all these areas of human and economic consideration is at once apparent. The banker's judgment and discernment must both supplement and complement the function of the engineer's judgment [on the value of reserves] below. As a matter of fact, aside from the purely technical aspects of financing oil in the ground, and I don't for a moment discount their essential importance, it should be kept everlastingly in mind that it's still credit. Credit in its simplest terms is the creation of obligations of people to repay money. It's people who sign the note, it's people who promise to pay, it's people who pay or fail to pay; and the bank-

er's ultimate judgment above the ground in the matter
of oil loans is no less important than the engineer.[373]

He outlined factors used in evaluating oil and gas loans at the
time, which are quite similar to the metrics energy lenders consider
today: Is the operator qualified and financially capable of producing
the oil? How long is it going to take to produce it, considering the
projected decline curve? How much is it going to cost to produce the
recoverable oil—not based on today's cost, but that of the subsequent
months, the next year and in the years after that? What will be the
price of oil over the life of the property? What will be the cost of
money over the life of the property? What will be the effect of any
adverse legislation or regulation, including rules regarding taxes?[374]

Improved engineering technology to more accurately estimate reserves—the banker's collateral—and forecast production rates—the
borrower's ability to meet debt service—substantially increased the
reliability of valuations used for loan security and amortization. As
noted previously, pioneering energy lenders relied upon advice from
their larger producer customers to provide an indication of the value
of a prospective borrower's collateral. Through the late 1930s and into
the 1950s, energy banks added technical staff members capable of
analyzing reserve values, which made possible the rapid adoption of
appropriate and realistic credit policies for borrowers.[375]

The importance of the reservoir engineer to the successful underwriting of a loan against collateral that could not be seen or readily
identified could not be over-emphasized by early energy lenders. The
most essential element to banking loans "is the engineering progress
that now enables a fairly accurate determination of producible underground reserves," McElvaney wrote. "Here in essence is the ultimate
safety factor that is of prime necessity to the successful lending of
money on oil in Nature's own warehouse."[376]

---

[373] McElvaney, "Some Aspects of Financing Oil and Gas Transactions," 321-24.
[374] McElvaney, "Some Aspects of Financing Oil and Gas Transactions," 321-24.
[375] Gueymard, "The Seventies-An Era of Transition," 557-58.
[376] McElvaney, "Some Aspects of Financing Oil and Gas Transactions," 318.

In the 1950s and '60s, not surprisingly, most of the bank officers extolling the importance of engineering expertise were, for the most part, engineers themselves who both evaluated the collateral and banked the loan. McElvaney wrote:

> As we recognized at the outset, the petroleum engineer in the broader concept of his function has made possible the financing of petroleum properties. Particularly in the technical aspects of his determination he assumes a position of vast responsibility, he can be the hero or the villain. Underground he is the Alpha and the Omega.
>
> Underground he is the interpreter—he is the judge and the jury. He pits himself and his finite judgment against Nature herself in all her majesty and her mystery. He uncloaks the profound secrets of countless ages, untouched or unaffected by human elements, and translates his knowledge and his experience for the guidance of those who will make innumerable uses of his findings. Specifically on his basic conclusions rest the intrinsic safety of both risk and borrowed capital.[377]

In spite of the mythical pedestal upon which some bankers placed engineers, reservoir engineering in its infancy was more art than science. John Scott, the Republic National Bank officer, wrote in 1954, "We so frequently see wide variations of values in appraisal reports on the same oil property. Just as often we find substantial differences in the findings of reputable engineers as compared with those of our own staff. Petroleum engineering is still not such an exact sci-

---

[377] McElvaney, "Some Aspects of Financing Oil and Gas Transactions," 319-20. *See also* Scott, "Some Aspects of Oil and Gas Financing," 326, and Frederic L. Kirgis, "Financing an Oil Venture," 1959 *U. Ill. F.* 459 (1959), 503. That most energy bankers were engineers based on interview of Robert Wagner, former energy banker, First City Bank, N.A., by the author, March 15, 2012.

ence as to permit complete unanimity in the interpretation of all various data on the part of two or more engineers."[378]

Recognizing the margin of error, the bias of the bank engineer's perspective was cynically assessed by one law commentator at the end of the '50s: "If the [lender's] valuation engineer has had much experience in this type of work or expects to stay in this line of work long, the owner can count on the estimate being conservative," Hubert Dee Johnson wrote in 1958.[379]

Still, by the 1950s, the art of estimating ultimate recovery of future reserves had progressed beyond the early, informal process of asking large operators in the field what their estimate of future production would be.[380] Russell F. Hunt, a vice president of First National Bank & Trust Co. in Tulsa, wrote an article in 1953 on what producers should bring when seeking a bank loan. The list included basic information—logs, initial production, completion techniques, bottom-hole pressure, casing size, total depth, any available core data and electric logs, whether the well was flowing or on pump, the amount of production allowed, full capacity, lease-operating costs and "many other facts, and factors as there are many types of production with each type having its own individualities."[381]

Much of this information was private; therefore, the bank was reliant upon the trustworthiness of the producer. With some degree of understatement, Hunt observed, "Instances have been known where an owner, knowing the truth and consequence of basic fact, has colored in his favor, or withheld vital data relating to his properties. In such a circumstance a capable and experienced appraiser can be misled into conclusions that are later disappointing to him and perhaps to others."[382]

---

[378] Scott, "Some Aspects of Oil and Gas Financing," 321.
[379] Johnson, "Legal Aspects of Oil and Gas Financing," 145.
[380] Thompson letter to Kirkland.
[381] Russell F. Hunt, Vice President, First National Bank and Trust Co., Tulsa, "A Banker's Viewpoint on … Oil Loans," *The Independents' I.P.A. of A. Monthly*, January, 1953, 20.
[382] Hunt, "A Banker's Viewpoint on … Oil Loans," 20.

Not all banks wanted their engineers to be both salesmen and underwriters. First National Bank in Dallas, which was one of the top Texas energy banks in its day, limited its technical people to evaluating collateral, rather than working also as loan officers."[383] Actually, having the bank's engineers responsible for only the engineering evaluation made a great deal of sense. Regulatory bank examiners and bank credit managers were uncomfortable with someone making business-development decisions based on their own evaluation.

In addition, the evaluation of the oil and gas properties could be time-consuming and there was competitive pressure to make a timely decision. If the engineer was also the account officer, there was the temptation to skip or shortcut some of the credit analyses.

But most banks' loan officers were comprised exclusively of engineers well into the 1970s. Bob Wagner who joined First City Bank's energy group in Houston in 1974 was, at the time, a bit of an odd duck, having a liberal-arts academic background. Wagner was not a member of the bank's "engineers club"—a fact he was reminded of each day as the engineer-bankers would go out for lunch without him.[384]

Before the end of the 1970s, the energy business was booming and so was energy banking; engineers were being replaced by managers with marketing and business-development skills. It became more common to separate the engineering function from the credit function.

However, each bank used its engineers somewhat differently. At some, the engineers simply developed an engineering evaluation that met the bank's guidelines on pricing and risking. The loan officers would then take the evaluation and, based on certain industry yard-

---

[383] "The purpose of the engineer is to keep you from overselling yourself. If the engineer is in the position to be influenced by marketing goals, his judgment might not be totally objective." Robert Shockney, Senior Vice President, Energy Division, First National Bank in Dallas, quoted by Geoffrey Leavenworth, "Big Texas Banks Vie for Energy Loans," *Texas Business*, December, 1979.
[384] Wagner, author's interview.

sticks and guidelines along with financial analysis, determine the appropriate loan value.

At other banks, the engineers determined an engineered loan value based on their evaluation of the properties. This value was then subject to further financial analysis. In all cases, the account officer made the final recommendation since, in theory, he understood factors regarding the borrower's finances beyond the engineering of its collateral.

Both approaches worked very well because most banks had checks and balances in their systems and the final recommendation was rarely an individual decision. However, Dartez recalled a situation where he had just joined Bank of the Southwest and it had been offered a participation in a credit to a medium-size independent in Shreveport, La.[385] The agent was a New York bank with a business-development office in Houston.

In addition to Bank of the Southwest, participations had been offered to First National Bank in Dallas and First City Bank in Houston. Bank of the Southwest was a bank where the engineer made loan recommendations and Dartez personally did this particular evaluation. His calculated loan value was significantly below the requested loan, but the other participating banks had approved the credit.

This was 1980—when competition was high and the guidelines used by some banks were more aggressive than others. Dartez decided to visit the engineer with First City to see if he would share the guidelines he used, so he could explain to his bank why he recommended *against* participation.

The First City engineer was very cooperative and readily shared the criteria he had used. In many cases, the criteria were *more* conservative than Bank of the Southwest's. When asked how he could possibly support the requested credit, he said the engineers at First City did not calculate loan values—that was up to the account officers. In Dartez's opinion, this would be atypical of decisions made to-

---

[385] Dartez, author's interview.

day, but it was not unusual in the heady days of the energy boom in the early 1980s.

Valuing Collateral

Today's credit underwriting of reserve-based loans has not changed materially from the standards employed upon successful enforcement of proration rules in the mid-1930s. Bankers would analyze the loan value of the producing-property collateral based on projected net cash flow over a fixed period, discounted back to present value (PV). In an example, Lyon Terry and Kenneth Hill, officers of Chase National, utilized an 8% discount rate in 1953 to arrive at a PV of future reserves.[386]

According to a paper they presented that year, the purchase price for oil and gas properties was, typically, equal to one-half of future net revenue discounted at 4%. "It is rather surprising more often than not the latter method, i.e., one-half of a four percent discount of future net revenues is very close to the future net revenue discounted at 10½ percent," they wrote.

Based on known geological and geophysical information, reservoir engineers can estimate the amount of producible oil from a given reservoir. But whether it would be a good use of the oil company's capital—and that of its investors—to drill and produce such reserves depends on myriad factors. Not the least of these is whether the expected profit from producing the reserves is a better use of funds than the potential return on other investments the company could make.

Another factor in determining the producer's rate of return on an investment is its weighted-average cost of all capital sources—both debt and equity. To compute this percentage, the average of the cost of each source of financing is weighted by the fraction of the total financing that source represents.

Debt has an explicit interest rate associated with it and equity has an implicit cost associated with attracting and retaining investors. A producer's cost of capital must be included in the investment-decision

---

[386] Terry and Hill, "Valuation of Oil and Gas Producing Properties," 2.

process. The appropriate discount factor to evaluate any property acquisition or drilling program must be customized based on the capital cost and the nature of the reserves, expected rate of production and estimated sale price.

While individual companies may use a bespoke discount rate for evaluation of their investments and future drilling operations, bankers tended to take a more industry-wide-average approach. Discounting the future value of reserves that are likely to be produced by the operator through future drilling operations is, in effect, an "educated guess" by the banker of whether his collateral will one day be turned into production. The appropriate PV discount that lenders used depended on how much confidence they had in whether they could accurately predict future value.

Terry and Hill wrote, "For properties that are fully developed, long-lived, and whose reservoir conditions are well known, estimates of reserves and operating conditions can be made with considerable certainty so that the discount factor should be correspondingly low. And conversely where the opposite is true, the factor should be relatively high."[387]

Notwithstanding this early, customized approach to valuing the PV of different producing reservoirs by well-decline characteristics, most energy bankers settled in on a "standardized" discount rate of 10% per annum (PV10). In the 1970s, the U.S. Securities and Exchange Commission promulgated regulations for public companies' reserve reporting. Ron Harrell, chairman emeritus of reserves-analysis firm Ryder Scott Co. LP, wrote in 2014:

> Richard Adkerson, currently vice chairman, president and CEO of Freeport-McMoRan Inc., was employed by (or worked closely with) the U.S. Securities and Exchange Commission (SEC) in the mid-late 1970s. A few years ago, he told me the SEC "agonized" over the proper PV "discount rate" to be made a part of the oil and gas reserves information to be required of

---

[387] Terry and Hill, "Valuation of Oil and Gas Producing Properties," 2.

industry. During the Carter administration years, prime rates ranged from, say, 8 – 12 % (sometimes higher, occasionally lower). Richard remembers a hallway conversation where he and another individual decided "Let's use 10%." And it stuck.[388]

This PV10 discount rate has been used by the SEC to this day and was used in energy banks' reserve analyses at least throughout the 1970s until after 2000. Because it was a general rule, generally applied, the discount rate was not particularly tied to the cost of capital, future expected rates of interest or even to the current interest rate. Even when the banks' prime rate was at a high of 20% in the early 1980s, the discount rate for determining reserve values held steady at 10%.

Simply, an apples-to-apples application of applying the same discount rate across the board to all reserves and all producers made the underwriting effort easier. Additionally, a lower discount rate of 10% per year would, on balance, favor longer-lived reserves, than a field with shorter-lived reserves. On balance, a banker prefers that his collateral produce over a longer period of time after stated maturity of the loan—just in case if, at maturity, the loan had not fully amortized. Additional production life would provide some cushion for ultimate repayment of the loan.

There were reports, however, that not all banks adhered to a flat PV10, especially as the energy-lending market showed initial signs of distress in the early 1980s. *American Banker* reported, "But before the oil glut really took hold [in 1982], many banks were discounting cash flows at about 12% and escalating [oil] prices about 8% per year on a base of $32 per barrel.

"A survey taken by Fidelity Bank of major energy lenders indicated that many were revising these assumptions to reflect lower prices and higher cost of funds. Penn Square says that for the last two months it has figured on oil prices holding at $30 a barrel for two

---

[388] Ron Harrell, Chairman Emeritus, Ryder Scott Petroleum Consultants, personal correspondence with the author, August 1, 2014.

years, then rising at 8% per year. It is now discounting reserves at 15%."[389]

In 2004, as oil prices were rising and competition among lenders heated up, more banks began to use a discount rate of 9% to increase customers' borrowing bases.[390] Of course, given the multiple variables in determining the borrowing base, a bank can use a lower PV discount rate, but be more conservative in its advance rate against total proved, producing reserves, for example. In this, it would still arrive at a lower borrowing base than a bank that uses a higher PV discount rate.

But if all other variables are held constant, the lower the discount rate the greater the loan-collateral's value. For example, consider a set of producing properties with a long reserve life and an undiscounted value of $100 million at Year 10. Its current PV discounted at 10% per year is equal to $3.855 million.

This reserve value would increase if discounted at a lower PV discount rate. For example, at PV9, its value is equal to $4.244 million; at PV8, $4.632 million. The value of the reserves discounted at PV8 is almost 20% more than at PV10.

Of course, if every bank uses the same, lower discount rate, there is no competitive advantage to any one lender. On the other hand, if the lower discount rate gives a boost to the amount that all banks were willing to lend, bankers may take on greater risk without any reward—i.e., greater market share—on their dollars loaned.

By mid-2014, a Macquarie Tristone survey of 39 energy banks showed only one bank using a 10% discount rate for forecasting future net income from oil and gas properties. Four were using 8%; one, 7%; one, 6%; and the balance, 9%.[391]

---

[389] "Penn Square Bank, Maverick Oil Lender," *American Banker*, April 26, 1982. Americanbanker.com.

[390] "We use PV-10 generally, whereas some banks have gone to using PV-9 values." John David, Union Bank Oklahoma City, Oklahoma, quoted in Leslie Haines, "Banker Up," *Oil and Gas Investor*, April 29, 2004. The oil-price reference is from U.S. EIA, Independent Statistics & Analysis. "Petroleum & Other Liquids." Accessed March 6, 2016. Eia.gov.

[391] Macquarie Tristone Energy Lender Price Survey, Q3, 2014.

By 2014, there were more than 70 years of energy-banking history on chickens coming home to roost after relaxing credit standards. During the early energy-banking period through the 1960s, various formulae were utilized to determine maximum loan value for a set of producing properties. Some of the guidelines were based on the percentage of present worth determined by the bank's discount value; the estimates of total volume of production over the half-life of the estimated reserves or a fixed period of time, usually one to three years; a percentage of fair market value; or a percentage of reserves or net income remaining at a calculated loan payout.

Many bankers related loan value in the 1960s to a percentage, e.g., 75%, of the "market value" of a property. Theoretically, if worse came to worst, a loan could always be repaid by selling the property, provided the loan balance was always at or below the desired percentage of market value.

Unfortunately, over time, bankers found there were several difficulties with the use of fair-market valuations—primarily because, when worse did come to worst, this was usually when the market for oil and gas properties had become reduced by depressed oil or gas prices and, therefore, a glut of distressed properties and newly upside-down loans would appear. The market valuation at the time the loan was made would prove impossible to realize in a fire sale or upon foreclosure.

Even though a percentage of "market value" was not the best metric, neither was blind reliance upon the estimated value of reserves. Wallace Wilson penned an in-house bank manual on energy lending for Continental Illinois in the 1960s. He cautioned, "Engineers estimate reserves by use of equations; sometime complex, frequently simple. In most cases the problem is in determining the values used in the equation rather than in solving the equation.

"All of the factors used in the volumetric equation are averages, none are ever determined precisely. ... Most engineers agree that reserve estimates, even when properly made with adequate data, are subject to inaccuracy in order of 10 to 25%."[392]

Given this margin for error, not surprisingly, most bankers recommended that the that the total estimated production from the property should be at least twice as great as the production required to pay off the loan.[393] This cushion would need to be increased for loans with maturities longer than four years, where the field was mature with high operating costs that might be subject to escalation or when there was a concentration of value in a small number of wells that made up the collateral.[394]

In addition to having an ample cushion at projected maturity, a maximum ratio of loan-to-collateral value was recommended. Terry and Hill, in their 1953 paper, recommended the ratio of maximum loan amount not exceed between 60% and 70% of the estimated value of the collateral, depending upon other factors considered.[395]

Other banks were more conservative in their advance rate. For example, at about the same time, Russell Hunt with First National Bank & Trust in Tulsa reported, "Generally speaking, we have found that most banks making oil production loans required an appraised value to loan ratio of at least 3 to 1, or in other words, loan not more than one-third of the net valuation figure after giving effect to estimated operating costs."[396]

Both parameters typically reached the same loan amount because the present worth of net cash income from the first half of future production with a typical decline curve in total production over the life of the reserves generally approximates to about two thirds of the total value.[397]

---

[392] Wallace Wilson, "Determination of Loan Value," Internal Bank Memoranda, Continental Illinois Bank and Trust, June 1967, at 4, 5 and 9.
[393] Terry and Hill, "Valuation of Oil and Gas Producing Properties," 7.
[394] Wilson, "Determining Loan Value," 9.
[395] Terry and Hill, "Valuation of Oil and Gas Producing Properties," 7.
[396] Hunt, "A Banker's Viewpoint on … Oil Loans," 20.
[397] Hunt, "A Banker's Viewpoint," 20. In ABC-structured financings, the loan ratio could be higher, reflecting the improved net cash flow on an after-tax basis attributable to the ABC structure.

While this was true in the 1950s when most properties were generally declining, it was not true in the 1960s when conditions changed dramatically. Dartez recalled that, when he began his banking career in 1963 with what is now Citibank, the guideline for determining loan value was based on the half-life of the undiscounted cash flow. In other words, the loan value was what could be repaid, principal plus interest, from the first 50% of projected cash flow.[398]

Allowables in Texas had reached an all-time low in the mid-1960s, resulting in extremely long-life properties where the half-life was eight to 10 years or more. Some transactions were structured where insurance companies took the longer maturities. Independent engineering reports always included a present-worth calculation, but the money-center banks essentially ignored this value. At this point in time, this was understandable since the forecast was that allowables would increase in the future, resulting in escalating cash-flow forecasts. If one rolled the forecast forward to Year 3, for example, the present value was higher than in Year 1.

When Citibank sought to participate the Texas Pacific Coal and Oil financing to the banks in Texas, significant resistance was encountered. According to Dartez, the most common yardstick used by the local banks was a loan value equal to 50% of present worth. It was a yardstick that was probably appropriate for smaller independents, whose producing properties were somewhat concentrated.

Dartez recalls that a senior executive of Texas Commerce Bank in Houston felt that the TPCO loan was risky and would never pay out. However, history proved that the loan performed pretty much as expected. Dartez attributed this to the fact that the reserves were spread over hundreds of high-quality properties, with no major concentration of risk in any one property.

The 1970s brought about major changes in Texas energy banking. Oil allowables had increased to 100%, which meant that present value was again an important factor. The money-center banks were slow to recognize and adapt. A number of large out-of-state banks as

---

[398] Dartez, author's interview.

well as international banks opened business-development offices in Houston and Dallas.

However, the Texas banks had grown to become regional banks and were better able to compete where the difference in loan values came into play. At one point, First City Bank had dual standards: On large credits, the bank used half-life to calculate loan values, but continued to use 50% of present worth on smaller credits. After a while, this became too confusing and the bank moved to a middle-ground guideline set at 57% of present worth.

Dartez had developed a sophisticated risk-analysis approach at Bank of the Southwest to determine loan value, producing a customized advance ratio that ranged between 40% and 65%. The average advance ratio for the bank's entire portfolio was about 56%, which fit well with industry practice. In fact, although the various energy banks used different yardsticks and approaches to determine loan value, experienced loan officers and engineers tended to coalesce around a similar conclusion. Today, the upper limit of the advance ratio set by most energy banks is 65%, although all will say that the final determination is based on rigorous engineering and financial analysis.

It was not until the 1960s that there was even a general consensus of what "proven reserves" actually meant. In 1962, the Society of Petroleum Engineers (SPE) formed a 12-man Special Committee on Definitions of Proved Reserves for Property Evaluation. The committee's goal was to find common ground among industry participants on the very basic definition of "Proved Reserves" in property evaluations. Business would be easier if everyone used the same yardstick in buying, selling and lending against oil and gas properties.

Two-thirds of the committee consisted of producers and pipeline operators, reservoir-evaluation consultants and a university professor; the remaining third, capital providers, evidencing both the importance of the matter and the lenders' desire to be able to compare apples to apples. The capital providers included two insurance companies and two bank lenders—Wallace Wilson with Continental Illinois and C.R. Dodson with United California Bank.

After three years of discussion, the committee submitted a one-page proposal for the definition of "proved petroleum reserves." In this, to be classified as proved, the engineer must be able to certify the existence and likelihood that such reserves could be produced with a standard of high confidence—or what later became known as "reasonable certainty."

At the time, the concept of "probable" and "possible" reserves was used by some producers, but largely ignored by lenders and investors. The proposal passed without one dissenting vote or abstention.[399] The SPE's definitions of reserve classifications have been modified over time, but the adoption by the industry of the first committee's efforts facilitated both access to capital as well as transfers of producing properties.

Early Loan Documentation

A banker's goal in the earliest days of the energy-lending business was—unsurprisingly—to keep it simple. Oil loans were generally term loans with fixed amortization from proceeds of production paid directly to the bank by the producer's oil purchaser. These loans were fully funded at closing—not lines of credit or revolving loans that the borrower could access at some future date.

Amortization of the loan began immediately out of production-sales proceeds from the pledged wells. Loans were made against and secured by existing production and not by undeveloped reserves. Providing advice to a Houston banker that was looking to enter energy lending, Elmo Thompson of National Bank of Tulsa wrote in 1934, "We never make loans upon anything but producing leases or producing royalties and then with a mortgage upon the property or a deed of trust in the case of Texas properties, to secure the debt, as well as an assignment to our bank of the proceeds of the pipe line runs.

---

[399] Ron Harrell, Chairman Emeritus, Ryder Scott Petroleum Consultants, "Reserve Estimations for Business Decisions – Almost a Century of Progress in Creating Reserve Definitions" (paper presented in Muscat, Oman, March 26-28, 2007).

"Even though the agreed repayment plan calls for a stated sum of money each month, we usually have the entire proceeds from the sale of oil paid to our bank, deducting the amount to be paid upon the loan and placing the balance in the account of the borrower. This is an added precaution against decline in production or decline in price, as it enforces such declines to come from that portion of the runs going to the borrower."[400]

Also in 1934, Dallas-based McElvaney responded to the same inquiry, recommending that, in the economic climate of the time, loan maturities be kept very short. "We have attempted to keep our oil loans within a relatively short pay-out period, say 9 to 12 months as a maximum," he wrote, "so that in the event of any reduction in the price structure or allowable, which, of course, would have the effect of lengthening the pay-out, we would still have a satisfactory loan.

"We have in some instances taken loans on a pay-out basis of 15 to 20 months, but these have been governed by outside circumstances such as the unquestioned responsibility of the borrower outside of the interest pledged, etc."[401]

Generally, in the early days of oil lending, the loan documents consisted of a promissory note for a fixed term to evidence the repayment obligation, the mortgage or deed of trust covering the oil and gas leases and production to secure the loan, and a letter to the producer's oil purchaser, directing sales proceeds from the mortgaged wells be mailed directly to the bank. The "keep it simple" mantra continued through the 1950s.[402]

The legal distinction between real versus personal property affects many aspects of the producer's rights and, accordingly, the bank's rights to its collateral. Oil and gas reserves in the ground are considered "real property," as is the oil and gas lease covering such

---

[400] Thompson letter to Kirkland.

[401] Eugene McElvaney, Vice President, First National Bank, Dallas, Texas, Letter to W.A. Kirkland, Vice President, First National Bank in Houston, August 14, 1934.

[402] "Personally, I prefer to have the deed of trust or mortgage and the promissory note contain sufficient provisions to set forth the conditions and agreements, believing these instruments alone should speak for themselves and the transaction." Scott, "Some Aspects of Oil and Gas Financing," 329.

reserves, and the lien securing such hydrocarbons is created under a mortgage—or in states where permitted, a deed of trust. Rights to hydrocarbons that have been produced, whether stored on location or sold to the purchaser, are considered "personal property" and the lien covering such collateral is created under separate rules for perfecting liens on personal property.

Historically, in addition to a mortgage on the oil and gas lease covering the reserves in the ground, banks almost always "take an assignment of the oil produced from the interest pledged, the assignment being taken in the form of a separate instrument from the deed of trust," McElvaney wrote. "Ordinarily we file a certified copy of the assignment with the company purchasing the oil and instruct that they furnish necessary transfer orders to accomplish payment direct to the bank each month."[403]

Documentation of early producing loans was simpler than present-day credit facilities. There were few loan agreements. Commitment letters and term sheets did not play an important part in production loans. In these earlier loans, commitment letters were only used in instances in which a borrower had entered an agreement to purchase a property or was making a purchase offer and wanted to first obtain a definite commitment from a bank for the financing. For example, in an ABC loan, Seller A would ask for a letter from Purchaser C's bank, committing to finance the purchase.[404]

The Bank's Lawyers

The role of the bank's counsel by the end of the 1950s was similar to its current duties. After the application for bank credit had been approved by the lending officer's credit committee, with the aid of the appraisal report of the petroleum engineer, the lender's attorney would prepare the legal documents, including preparation or review of title opinions and preparation of the promissory note, lien instruments and other loan documents.

---

[403] McElvaney letter.
[404] Scott, "Some Aspects of Oil and Gas Financing," 330.

In addition, it was the role of the bank's counsel to prepare or approve the transfer orders for payment of production revenues after verifying the accuracy of the legal descriptions and the ownership of the interest described under the mortgage.[405] Bank lawyer Hubert Dee Johnson reported in 1957:

> Usually the lender's attorney obtains his first information about a proposed oil and gas loan after quite a number of previous conferences have taken place between the lending officer and the borrower, and at this time the attorney has to gather quite a bit of information in a fairly short period of time. This explains the usual remarks of the borrower and the lending officer to the effect that the lawyer is slowing down the closing.[406]

The bank lawyer's role, along with the appreciation (or lack thereof) for the role, has changed very little over the years.

Up through the 1980s, the relationship between energy banks and their lawyers—in Texas, at least—depended upon where the bank was located. In Dallas, bankers at the main energy lenders—First National, Republic and Mercantile—traditionally parceled out their legal business among the leading law firms in the community, often playing one firm off another as sources for leads for new corporate customers. *Texas Monthly* reported in 1976, "Big Corporate Power in Dallas revolves primarily around the big banks, First International [formerly First National] and Republic of Texas [Republic Bank], the state's first and second largest holding companies.

"These Dallas banks formed the cornerstones of the local business community. Nate Adams of First National, Fred Florence of Republic, and R.L. 'Bob' Thornton, Sr., of the Mercantile not only built their own banking empires, they also guided the development of the

---

[405] Thompson, "Legal And Other Aspects of Financing The Oil Industry," 38.
[406] Johnson, "Legal Aspects of Oil and Gas Financing," 143.

surrounding oil fields, the growth of local corporations, and the overall destiny of the city."[407]

In contrast, Houston banks directed legal work and clients to their allied law firms. "Houston law practice is rife with tales of heavy-handed banking tactics," the magazine reported. "In effect the firms can use the banks to promote their own business."[408]

In the mid-1970s, Dallas had five firms with 30 or more lawyers, but none with more than 45. *Texas Monthly* characterized the market as having an "amoeba complex," which caused Dallas firms to split into factions just as they were approaching the 50 mark. Houston was a different story; the reason was the banks.[409]

In Houston, prominent lawyers started banks in the early 1900s and became leaders in the city's power centers. These lawyers-cum-bankers led both their banks and law firms, nurturing a symbiotic relationship. The bank would lend money—documented by the bank's lawyers—to growing businesses and recommend its lawyers to its borrowers as company counsel. The law firm, in turn, would recommend the bank to its clients.

As such, a handful of Houston's largest firms had a steady, dependable source of business upon which to build institutional clients. By the 1970s, this structure helped to sustain and grow the law firms, which became dominant power-brokers in their own right.

By the mid-1970s, the three big firms in Houston were Baker & Botts (160 lawyers), Vinson, Elkins, Searls, Connally & Smith (186) and Fulbright, Crooker & Jaworski (185). At the time, there were only two firms in all of the country that were larger, both located in New York: Sherman & Sterling (226) and Dewey, Ballantine, Bushby, Palmer & Wood (197). "No one outside New York is any longer even close [to it and Houston]: there is nothing in Chicago, Los Angeles,

---

[407] Harry Hurt III, "The Most Powerful Texans," *Texas Monthly*, April 1976, Texasmonthly.com.
[408] Hurt III, "The Most Powerful Texans."
[409] Griffin Smith, Jr., "Empires of Paper," *Texas Monthly*, November 1973, Texasmonthly.com.

Philadelphia, Boston, or Washington to match them," the magazine added.[410]

Three years later, another *Texas Monthly* article put the lawyer count at each of the big three firms around 200 and added that three other "Houston firms—Andrews, Kurth, Campbell & Jones; Butler, Binion, Rice, Cook & Knapp; and Bracewell & Patterson—also ranked among the largest in the country. Neither Dallas nor any other city, except New York, had such a formidable legal armada. However, the greatest source of power for some of the big Houston firms—and a real key to their role in the overall structure of Big Corporate Power—is their relationship with banks. In Houston, unlike in other cities, law firms dominate banks."[411]

Claiming the oldest pedigree, Baker & Botts, which is now known simply as Baker Botts, was formed in 1865 and was seen more as representing Eastern establishment interests, such as railroads, major oil companies and insurance companies.[412] It had ties to local banks, including Commercial National, which was chaired for many years by the founding Baker's son, Capt. James A. Baker, Sr., and later merged with South Texas National Bank.

Baker Botts also represented its successor banks, including Houston National Bank of Commerce and Texas National Bank, which had been two of the oldest banks in the state and, upon their merger, became Texas Commerce Bank.[413]

Fulbright, formed in 1919, also had ties to local banks, principally Second National Bank, which became Bank of the Southwest. Officing in the bank's downtown headquarters in the 1970s, Fulbright's contacts with the bank extended to the highest levels. Partners Hugh Buck and Leon Jaworski were bank board members and Jaworski was

---

[410] Smith, Jr., "Empires of Paper."
[411] Hurt III, "The Most Powerful Texans."
[412] Malavis, *Bless the Pure & Humble*, 5: "Preoccupied with major oil company clients, Baker & Botts had no time to represent those young, unestablished and unrespectable pioneers of the Texas oil industry known as wildcatters. These rugged individualists who gambled their future in pursuit of black gold turned to smaller local law firms, such as Vinson & Elkins in Houston."
[413] "History: 175 Years," Baker Botts, accessed May 1, 2016, Bakerbotts.com.

chair of the executive committee. Former partner A.G. McNeese was the bank's chairman.

The Houston firm with the closest and most lucrative ties to local banking was Vinson & Elkins. In 1924, Judge James A. Elkins, William A. Vinson and other V&E partners started Guaranty Trust Bank, which became First City National Bank in 1956. As evidenced by First City vice president W.A. Kirkland's letters in August of 1934 to the more established oil bankers at National Bank of Tulsa and First National Bank of Dallas,[414] Houston's First City was an early participant in the business of loaning to oil producers.

V&E provided legal services to Guaranty, while the two institutions referred clients to each other. In the 1920s and '30s, Elkins bought shares in several other banks and became one of the state's prominent bankers. V&E attorneys often became board members and, thus, the law firm gained more influence and clients.

Houston's "local independent oilmen had never catered to Baker & Botts; they always thought it was too close to the big oil companies and Eastern finance," *Texas Monthly* reported in 1973. "The Judge, wearing his banker's hat as president of First National, gave them loans; VE in turn did their legal work. The firm prospered by carrying them on the cuff while they drilled dry holes and collecting when they finally hit. This neat little arrangement catapulted VE into the big time."[415]

The firm and bank retained close ties throughout the bank's history, it added. "Vinson Elkins is practically synonymous with First City National Bank, where senior partners John Connally and Marvin Collie serve on a board chaired by Judge Elkins' non-lawyer son."[416]

Many an early independent not only accessed capital locally, but also turned to legal counsel in the developing oil financial centers. As the energy-banking industry grew, so too did law firms, working with

---

[414] Thompson letter to Kirkland (August 25, 1934) and McElvaney letter to Kirkland (August 14, 1934).
[415] Smith, Jr., "Empires of Paper."
[416] Smith, Jr., "Empires of Paper."

the banks and producers to structure and document the agreements that tied producers to their capital providers.

Introduction of the Loan Agreement

Up through the 1950s, some bankers, including McElvaney in Dallas and Thompson in Tulsa, who had been around since the days of Dad Joiner's discovery, kept the loan documents simple: a promissory note setting out the schedule for repayment and a mortgage in the event the borrower failed to meet the scheduled amortization. A separate loan agreement was rarely used, unless the loan required some unusual agreement or restriction that didn't logically fit in the note or mortgage.[417]

Unusual agreements might include restrictions on the borrower's salary and dividends or private agreements related to the financial condition of the borrower rather than conditions related to the mortgaged property that would be filed in public records.[418] For most production loans, agreements were not used. Under complicated transactions that required a large amount of time to complete, there was a definite need for the loan agreement.[419] By the end of the 1950s, bank officers were reporting that the use of loan agreements had become almost universal as a written record of all representations made by the borrower to the lender.[420]

---

[417] "Some lenders follow the standard policy of requiring a loan agreement relating to the loan, but the majority of the lenders with which I have had experience prefer to have the covenants and agreements set forth in the note and mortgage unless unusual agreements not suitable for including in a note or mortgage are deemed to be needed in a particular case." Johnson, "Legal Aspects of Oil and Gas Financing," 150.

[418] Johnson, "Legal Aspects of Oil and Gas Financing," 150. *See also*, Scott, "Some Aspects of Oil and Gas Financing," 329. "These [loan] agreements are used merely to set forth the general understanding between the customer and the lender, prior to the closing of a loan and may contain certain provisions operative after the loan is made, such as accounting procedures, allowance for operating expenses, the release of undeveloped acreage from the mortgage under certain conditions, prepayment privileges, moneys suspended or escrowed pending the meeting of legal requirements, future development on the properties and other matters customarily not included in a mortgage, deed of trust or note."

[419] Scott, "Some Aspects of Oil and Gas Financing," 329.

[420] Thompson, "Legal And Other Aspects of Financing The Oil Industry," 38.

The benefits of using a loan agreement in documenting production loans included the ability to provide for additional commitments by the borrower and additional assurances for oil credits. If a borrower were to default under these extra covenants, the benefit to the lender was that the loan maturity could be accelerated, irrespective of the borrower being current with note payments.

For certain banks, the practice was to include the foregoing covenants and agreements in the borrower's original loan application rather than in a loan agreement. Thompson wrote, "The simplest type of loan agreement is to compose an application for credit, addressed to the lender, and include all the negotiated terms, signed by the borrower. Then the lending institution merely approves same in writing on the original application instrument."[421]

A contemporary discussion of provisions in a circa 1957 loan agreement included a recitation of covenants very similar to today's reserve-based loans. These include a negative pledge on properties or other assets not described in the mortgage; a limitation on additional borrowing; restrictions on dividends and salary increases; payment of taxes and compliance with governmental regulations; a limitation on use of proceeds; and requirements for annual audits or more-frequent, periodic financial statements.[422]

In addition, loan agreements were used to govern what part of the monthly production-sales income received by the lender was to be applied to the debt and what was to be done with the balance. Joint letters from the borrower and the bank, instructing the borrower's purchasers of production to make payments directly to the bank, were typically sent out at closing. If such instruction letters were not delivered at closing, the loan agreements would include provisions that required the borrower to update the bank with names and addresses of the purchasers and the conditions under which the bank was authorized to send out the letters for direct payment to the bank.[423]

---

[421] Thompson, "Legal And Other Aspects of Financing The Oil Industry," 38.
[422] Thompson, "Legal And Other Aspects of Financing The Oil Industry," 37.
[423] Kirgis, "Financing an Oil Venture," 504; Thompson, "Legal And Other Aspects of Financing The Oil Industry," 37.

Financial Covenants

For the most part, production loans did not have the standard corporate-credit financial covenants due to the unique nature of the loan's collateral. Some of the larger facilities included some financial covenants. The typical financial covenants found in late-1950s loan documentations included net worth, debt to equity, working capital, net income after depletion, depreciation, taxes and cash flow to debt service.

Given the unique nature of oil and gas accounting, these measures were viewed with a different perspective than with non-oil-company credit. For example, net worth could be extremely low if dry holes and intangible well costs were expensed rather than capitalized and depreciated. An officer of Republic National Bank of Dallas noted in 1966 that, typically, "the Debt to Equity Ratio may be very high, and the company's loan would still be very safe, this Ratio can be as high as 8-to-10, whereas 4 is usually considered high on a normal corporate credit."[424]

By far, the most important ratio under amortizing term production loans was cash flow to debt service. Usually, a certain amount of depreciation and intangible drilling expenses were budgeted and subtracted from the total cash flow to arrive at available cash flow for debt service. Based on credit-underwriting standards of the time, the cash-flow-to-debt-service margin, if carefully arrived at by engineering projections, was required to be only 10% to 20% above the debt service to favorably qualify the credit.[425] As discussed below, following the energy-credit meltdown in the mid-'80s, regulators insisted that oil loans conform to the more conventional corporate-credit financial covenants.

The Promissory Note

The promissory note in early loan documentation was more detailed than the current form of note, if a note is even used today in some

---

[424] Monteith, "Financial Criteria of Oil and Gas Lending," 293.
[425] Monteith, "Financial Criteria of Oil and Gas Lending," 294.

loans. Many of the operational clauses regarding amortization, interest rates, interest-rate calculations, repayment covenants, usury savings, remedies, venue and applicable law, and, later, jury waiver, were included in the "long-form note," which made specific reference to the mortgage or deed of trust securing the payment of the note and describing, in general terms, the properties serving as collateral.[426]

Where loan agreements were not universally included in the loan documentation, the purpose of including these provisions within the four corners of the note was to enable the holder to bring suit on the note against the borrower. Where the note was negotiable, it could be freely transferred to a holder in due course. Under the Uniform Commercial Code, if the note was negotiable, it was more easily enforced when transferred, even if certain terms were missing from the note.[427]

The long-form note would spell out the required monthly payment equal to the greater of a straight amortization payment or a fixed percentage of proceeds from production.[428] In addition, it would have the amortization schedule on the back similar to the following provision:

> All Advances made by Payee to Maker pursuant to the Loan Agreement and all payments by Maker of the principal hereof shall be recorded by Payee on the schedule attached hereto and incorporated herein.[429]

These original notes were held in the bank's energy department. Clerks would hand-mark the payment grid on the back as run-

---

[426] Scott, "Some Aspects of Oil and Gas Financing," 333.

[427] A negotiable note is enforceable on its own term except against real defenses such as fraud in the factum, incapacity, and forgery. *Federal Deposit Ins. Corp. v. Wood*, 758 F.2d 156, 160 (6th Cir. 1985). John M. Nolan, et al. "Texas Annotated Promissory Note," Advanced Real Estate Law Course 2001, Dallas June 20-22, 2001.

[428] Hubert Dee Johnson (Carrington, Gowan, Johnson, Bromberg & Leeds), "Legal Aspects of Oil and Gas Financing," *Institute on Oil and Gas Law* (1958), 156.

[429] Renewal Promissory Note dated March 10, 1982, from Murchison Brothers to First National Bank in Dallas.

proceeds checks were mailed in by the production's purchaser and each payment was applied.[430]

To readily identify the note as the original, it was stapled with a colored back sheet (blue-backed notes) or printed on special, embossed, green-bordered "note paper." As photocopiers became more common, to protect against a photocopy being confused as the original note, some lenders would require that the note be printed on security paper into which "VOID" is specially dithered diagonally across the page. In regular light it is barely visible; when photocopied, it becomes visibly apparent.[431]

Much of the early efforts at protecting the negotiability and integrity of the "original note" have, through expediency and recognition of current practices, been dropped. Today's original notes are no longer printed on the distinctive green bordered "note paper;" if used at all, the notes are printed and processed along with the rest of the closing documents to be electronically scanned and distributed to the borrower and lender.

Today, most of the provisions in the early, long-form promissory note are embedded into the credit agreement itself. The demise of the promissory note as a material agreement in today's loan documentation was described by energy-finance lawyer Robert Shearer in a 2000 paper: "With complex pricing options and pricing grids based on leverage ratios and LIBOR rates so complicated and intricate they can only be fully defined and described in the loan agreement, the promissory note has become the runt of the loan documentation litter, abbreviated in form, shorn of substance and feebly referring to the loan agreement for all the important stuff."[432]

---

[430] Murray Brasseaux, Executive Vice President, Energy Lending, BBVA Compass Bank, interview by the author, May 11, 2011.

[431] As recently as the summer of 2014, on the day of closing, one 30-year energy finance attorney required a messenger pick up necessary security paper at an office-supply store instead of the note on the closing table that had been printed on the same plain common stock paper that the rest of the loan documents were printed on. It did not arrive in time to meet the wire deadline for funding and postponed the closing by a day—much to the frustration of the borrower and its counsel.

[432] Robert Shearer, "Oil and Gas Lending – the Borrower's Perspective" (paper presented at 26th Annual E.E. Smith Oil, Gas & Mineral Law Institute, March 31, 2000), 14.

The Mortgage

Perhaps the most important document in the early loan package was the mortgage or deed of trust that created the lien and collateral rights of the lender with respect to the property securing payment. The legal concept of a mortgage relates back to English common law. Mortgages are recognized in every jurisdiction in the U.S.

Meanwhile, the deed of trust, which existed for a brief period in England around 1800, has been adopted in a large minority of the states.[433] This derivation from the more-traditional mortgage normally involves a technical conveyance to a third person in trust to hold title as security for the payment of the debt. It differs from a mortgage in that title passes to the trustee, while, under a mortgage, the mortgagor retains title.

Deeds of trust contain a private power of sale—i.e., the out-of-court right to private foreclosure—upon default and conducted by public auction by the trustee on the steps of the county courthouse. Foreclosure under a mortgage, on the other hand, is typically conducted under court supervision, typically following a trial and court order, resulting in a public auction at a sheriff's sale, although some "mortgage states" permit private foreclosures. From the lender's perspective, the deed of trust contrasts favorably to a mortgage, giving the lender the right to private versus judicial foreclosure.[434]

Typically, the lien instrument securing an oil and gas loan was a combination of a real estate mortgage, covering the minerals in the ground, which was treated as real property in most producing states, and a personal-property security instrument, covering the oil and gas produced from the wells. Where loans were secured in more than one

---

[433] John A Gose and Aleana W. Harris, "Deed of Trust, Its Origin, History and Development in the United States and in the State of Washington," *Real Property, Probate and Trust* (Summer 2005), 8. Deeds of trust are the most common instrument used in the financing of real estate in Alaska, Arizona, California, Colorado, Idaho, Maryland, Mississippi, Missouri, Montana, Nebraska, Nevada, North Carolina, Oregon, Tennessee, Texas, Utah, Virginia, Washington and West Virginia, whereas most other states use mortgages.
[434] Grant S. Nelson, Dale A. Whitman, *Real Estate Finance Law* (5th ed.), § 1.6 (Thompson West: 2010).

state, multiple-jurisdiction mortgages/deeds of trust would be prepared with input and advice of local counsel in each state.[435]

The nature and rights of oil and gas leases is dependent upon the laws of the state in which the property is located. Some states, such as Texas, hold that oil and gas in the ground belong to the mineral-estate owner and can be transferred under the oil and gas lease, conveying the ownership and exclusive right to produce in the lessee for so long as oil and gas are produced in paying quantities. Thus, in Texas, the oil and gas lease is classified as a fee-simple determinable.

Other states, such as Kansas, hold that oil and gas in the ground is not capable of "ownership" until it has been captured (produced). The owner of the oil and gas lease in these states holds the right to explore and, if discovered, to produce the oil and gas—a nonpossessory interest usually classified as "profit-à-prendre."

The covenants found in some of the earliest oil and gas mortgages and deeds of trust are similar to the basic covenants required under today's loan documentation: compliance with laws and regulations; lease maintenance; compliance with lease obligations; good and workman-like operations; no other liens; payment of taxes; inspection rights; monthly reports on operations; and descriptions of indebtedness and obligations secured, including renewals and extensions of the original note and future indebtedness.[436]

In addition, early deeds of trust granted the trustee the right to cure any covenant breach, which expense would be added to the mortgagor's indebtedness and accrue interest at the default rate. Following any default and prior to foreclosure, the secured lender was granted the right to take possession of and operate the mortgaged properties, without liability to the mortgagor except for acts of bad faith in connection with such operation.[437]

---

[435] Johnson, "Legal Aspects of Oil and Gas Financing," 151.
[436] Scott, "Some Aspects of Oil and Gas Financing," 331.
[437] *See* Deed of Trust and Chattel Mortgage from Richardson Oils Inc. to Great Southern Life Insurance Co. dated August 22, 1938, recorded in Deed of Trust Records Volume 8, page 24, of Winkler County, Texas.

At closing, multiple counterparts of the lien instruments were prepared for filing and recorded in each jurisdiction in which the pledged properties were located. Deeds of trust and mortgages for filing at the county (or parish) level were typically prepared on longer, "legal size" paper, rather than letter size, as the recording fee was typically charged by the page.[438] In addition to per-page recording fees, eight states also charged a recording tax associated with the value of the indebtedness secured by the mortgage.[439] Failure to properly pay the applicable mortgage tax could result in the county clerk's refusal to record the instrument.

Over time, as the credit agreement has become the controlling loan document, the mortgage has evolved similar to the long-form promissory note. Many of the borrower's early representations and covenants related to operation of the oil and gas properties that had been included in the early term-loan mortgages have migrated over to the loan agreement. To avoid any confusion or contradictory covenants, the mortgage form has been truncated—limited to representations as to the borrower's title and covenants to pledge after acquired assets as well as to provisions necessary for the creation and enforcement of the mortgage. Unlike the fate of the promissory note, the mortgage shall always be a required document as the sole means to perfect a lien on the borrower's oil and gas leases.

Early oil and gas mortgages reflected the necessity of multiple recordings triggered by the term-loan structure. In the 1930s, wildcatter Sid Richardson executed 29 separate notes between January 11, 1936, and July 26, 1938, for each loan draw, sometimes making multiple draws in a month and many in amounts no greater than $20,000 to

---

[438] Mortgages and other publically recorded documents such as oil and gas leases, assignments and conveyances, have drifted away from "legal size" paper length, beginning around 1982 when Supreme Court Justice Warren Berger banished legal-size pleadings in all federal courts and state courts soon followed suit. Steven M. Sellers, "Lawyers go Green," *American Association for Justice*, 2013 Westlaw 49-Jan JTLA TRIAL A 22 (Reuters).

[439] Mortgage taxes are assessed by Alabama ($0.15/$100), Florida ($0.35/100), Kansas ($0.26/100), Minnesota ($0.23/100), New York ($1.00/100), Oklahoma ($0.10/100, but oil and gas real property is exempt), Tennessee ($0.115/100), Virginia ($0.20/100 up to $10 million value; more thereafter) compiled by National Conference of State Legislatures Fiscal Affairs Program, September, 2012.

$30,000 at a time, each with different maturities of 60 days to two years.[440] Richardson was famous for augmenting production income by borrowing on any asset a lender would accept as security. The daughter of one rancher who granted oil leases to Richardson said, "My abstracts [of title] are full of liens against Sid Richardson."[441]

In addition to specifically describing the notes secured under the mortgages, most mortgages also included "drag-net" and "all future indebtedness" clauses to secure other obligations owed by the borrower to the bank, including any future advances made by the bank to the mortgagor.[442] In Texas, a future-advance clause is effective between the parties to the deed of trust and with respect to third parties who have notice of such provision, whether or not the lender is obligated to make the advances.[443]

Drag-net clauses, which purport to cover any and all other obligations owing by the mortgagor to the lender, are also enforceable under Texas law, so long as the intention of the parties was clear that the mortgage was to secure such obligations.[444] One commentator in the 1950s expressed caution in relying upon provisions that the mortgage secures renewals and extensions of the original note as a state's law may require amendments be filed in public records to prevent the lien from becoming barred by limitations as far as bona fide purchasers and subsequent lien-holders were concerned.[445]

---

[440] Release from Bank of Manhattan Co. in favor of Richardson Oils Inc. and S.W. Richardson dated August 26, 1938, recorded in Volume 4, p. 262, Winkler County, Texas.

[441] Olien and Hinton, *Wildcatters*, 75.

[442] Release from Bank of the Manhattan Co. in favor of Richardson Oils Inc. dated January 31, 1949, recorded Volume 6, p. 444, Winkler County, Texas.

[443] Nolan, *Texas Deed of Trust Annotated*, 13, citing *F. Groos & Co. v. Chittim*, 100 S.W. 1006, 1011 (Tex. Civ. App. 1907, no writ). Note that treatment of future advance clauses vary from state to state. A future advance clause is effective in Oklahoma, but will not protect the mortgagee against intervening liens if the future advances are discretionary by the mortgagee. *Garey v. Rufus Lillard Co.*, 1945 OK 305, 165 P.2d 344 (Ok S. Ct, 1945).

[444] *First v. Byrne*, 28 N.W, 2d 509 (Iowa Sup. Ct., 1947); Johnson, "Legal Aspects of Oil and Gas Financing," 154. *See* Nolan, *Texas Deed of Trust Annotated*, 14, citing also *FDIC v. Bodin Concrete Co.*, 869 S.W. 2d 372, 377 (Tex. App. – Dallas 1993, writ denied).

[445] Johnson, "Legal Aspects of Oil and Gas Financing," 154 (referencing VATS Articles 5520 and 5522).

In a development line-of-credit loan—unlike a table-funded term loan—future advances were likely to occur rather frequently. The enforceability of any particular future-advance clause was fact-specific and subject to the laws of the state in which the mortgaged properties were located. However, one law commentator noted in 1957 that, on the basis of early Texas cases, lenders taking liens on Texas properties were able to make very liberal use of and rely on the future-advance clause.[446]

Not all are as liberal as Texas. Some states expressly prohibit future-advance clauses. In Oklahoma, for example, a future-advance clause is enforceable as between the mortgagor and lender. However, there is an exception if the lender's future advances are not obligatory—e.g., if the lender retained the discretion whether to make advances, as is the case in any future increase of the borrowing-base determination or advances following a borrower's default.

In such case, a future advance may not be effective in Oklahoma to protect the mortgagee against intervening liens.[447] Accordingly, in documenting multi-state loans, the practice—then and now—required engaging local lawyers, who were familiar with the particulars of their state's law.[448]

Assignment of Production

The third leg of basic oil-loan documentation, in addition to the note and mortgage, was the assignment of production—also called an assignment of the runs. Oil production is sold in the field direct from the storage tanks on the lease and measured by a "gauger," the oil-purchaser's man. Each time the gauger made a run to pick up the producer's oil, he filled out a paper receipt, showing the opening and closing volumes on the producer's tank gauge where the produced oil

---

[446] Johnson, "Legal Aspects of Oil and Gas Financing," 156, citing *Freiburg v Magale*, 7 S.W. 684 (Tex. Sup. Ct. 1888), *First National Bank of Commerce v. Zarafonetis*, 15 S.W. 2d 155, 156 (Tex. Civ. App. 1929), writ of error refused.

[447] *Garey v. Rufus Lillard Co.*, 1945 OK 305, 165 P.2d 344 (Ok S. Ct, 1945).

[448] Hubert Dee Johnson (Carrington, Gowan, Johnson, Bromberg & Leeds), "Legal Aspects of Oil and Gas Financing," *Institute on Oil and Gas Law* (1958), 156.

was stored onsite. The gauger also measured the oil's API gravity, the tank's temperature and the volume of the tank's non-merchantable base sediment and water (BS&W).

The receipt was called a "run ticket." These were made in triplicate—one copy for the producer, one copy for the gauger and the original for the purchaser, typically a pipeline company or a refiner. The purchaser's obligation to pay for the volume reported on the run ticket was called the "runs"—oil-patch jargon for "accounts receivable."

Early production loans required an assignment of the runs to be paid directly to the bank to be evidenced by instruction letters, known as "letters-in-lieu," which were mailed to the purchaser following closing. Purchasers of production typically pay owners of production from a well pursuant to a contract called a "division order" under which the payees agree as to the division of sale proceeds and direct the purchaser where to send the payments. When an interest-owner sold its interest in the lease, the purchaser of production would require the assignee sign a revised division order, reflecting the change in ownership and new place of payment.

Instead of a bank signing a new division order based on its rights under the mortgage, the bank would send instruction letters "in lieu" of a division order, directing that the borrower's share of proceeds be paid to the bank. As payments for term loans were received, the bank would debit the monthly principal amortization and accrued interest amount, record the principal payment on the back of the note and remit the balance to the producer's operating account.

Control of 100% of the producer's proceeds gave the bank control over the producer's income stream, should the loan go into default. Some lenders argued—perhaps with self-serving rationale—that this arrangement of the banker receiving all of the production proceeds should be preferred by the borrower because, when all proceeds are controlled by the bank, the bank has less incentive to foreclose.[449]

---

[449] Scott, "Some Aspects of Oil and Gas Financing," 332.

Under most mortgages and deeds of trust, the assignment to the bank of the proceeds from the mortgaged wells' production was absolute. Under lien instruments, it was not contingent to become effective upon a future event, such as default; it was unconditional from the outset.

A 1925 U.S. Supreme Court case, *Benedict v. Ratner*, raised the question of whether the assignment of production could be nullified in whole or in part if the lender followed the practice of releasing to the borrower a part of the assigned funds.[450] Ratner, the creditor, under an assignment of the debtor's accounts receivable following its bankruptcy, claimed a security interest in such amounts to be applied to his loan. Benedict, the receiver and trustee, claimed the arrangement had been fraudulent under New York law because Ratner had permitted the debtor to retain the receivables notwithstanding the purported assignment to Ratner. The court ruled that a collateral assignment is voidable as inherently fraudulent when the assignor is permitted to retain possession and control over the interest assigned.

In 1956, in *Dupree v. Quinn*, a Texas court of appeals followed *Benedict* under the facts of a non-oil and gas case that also involved an assignment of accounts receivable.[451] However, the Texas Supreme Court reversed the ruling and commented, "The cases make it clear, however, that this doctrine applies only when the power of dominion over the subject matter of the assignment is reserved to the assignor by the agreement of the parties."[452] Holding that there was no express provision in the assignment granting the debtor control over the receivables, the court upheld the assignment in favor of the bank.

At the end of the 1950s and during the beginning of the 1960s, it was not entirely clear to oil and gas lenders' lawyers whether *Dupree* or *Benedict* was applicable to the assignment of production and proceeds under a deed of trust.[453] To avoid any issue, properly drafted deeds of trust covering Texas oil and gas made the assignment of production

---

[450] *Benedict v. Ratner*, 268 US 353 (1924).
[451] *Dupree v. Quinn*, 290 S.W. 2d 329 (Tex. Civ. App. 1956).
[452] *Quinn v. Dupree*, 303 S.W.2d 769, 773 (Tex. 1957).
[453] Maginnis, "Financing Oil and Gas Development," 697.

proceeds absolute and the borrower did not reserve any power of dominion over the proceeds. The borrower's right to receive from the lender a percentage of the runs was limited and conditional.[454]

Subsequent law experts in the early 1960s advised taking the further step to make the assignment of production separate from the granting clause of the mortgage and place it in a separate section in which it was recited that it was given for additional security. Other commentators went further, suggesting the assignment be made in a separate instrument altogether.[455] Today, the common practice is to include the assignment of production as a separate section included within the mortgage.

The proper jurisdiction to file an assignment of proceeds attributable to the production from the mortgaged property was not clear in the early days of energy lending prior to the adoption of the Uniform Commercial Code in 1965.[456] Until then, the interest could either be characterized by the courts as an "interest in real property," "inventory held for sale" or "assignment of accounts receivable," which gave rise to uncertainty and protective, duplicative filings. Accordingly, the recommendation was to file assignments of production both in the chattel-mortgage records and in the real estate records.[457]

Into the 1980s, credit facilities were less often term loans and more often revolving lines of credit that didn't require monthly, principal-amortization payments. Producers wanted more control over their destinies. Moreover, where the producer was the operator of a well and sold production on behalf of third-party non-operating working-interest owners, a substantial portion of run checks were not the property of the borrower. A bank could get into trouble if it applied a third party's money to the borrower's debt.

---

[454] Johnson, "Legal Aspects of Oil and Gas Financing," 160; *see also* Maginnis, "Financing Oil and Gas Development," 697.

[455] James D. Voorhees (Moran, Reidy & Voorhees), "Financing Oil and Gas Operations on Credit Mortgages and Liens," 5 *Rocky Mt. Min. L. Inst.* (1960): 374.

[456] The Uniform Commercial Code was adopted by most states in 1965.

[457] Voorhees, "Financing Oil and Gas Operations," 378.

Over time, bankers agreed to dispense with the requirement of mailing letters-in-lieu to the purchasers at closing. Payments were, instead, permitted to be made directly by the purchaser to the producer.

Banks continued to take a security interest in the proceeds of production under a separate section in the deed of trust, which contained the same words of absolute assignment for purposes of securing the borrower's obligations. And letters-in-lieu were still prepared for execution at loan closing, but the name of the purchaser was left blank as the letters were held by the banker for safe-keeping to be mailed to the current purchasers only at the time of a default.

Supplementing the mortgage provisions, the credit agreement would also spell out that the borrower had fully and unconditionally assigned its proceeds of production to the bank. But it also provided that the bank would permit the borrower to continue to collect such proceeds, if not in default.[458]

Title Due Diligence

Lending to an oil and gas company requires verification of the borrower's ownership to the collateral pledged as security to repay the loan. In all oil and gas loans, the borrower warrants that it owns its oil and gas property. But prudent underwriting requires that the bank and its counsel independently satisfy itself as to the borrower's ownership.

---

[458] "Notwithstanding that, by the terms of the various Security Documents, Borrower is and will be assigning to Lender all of the 'Production Proceeds' (as defined therein) accruing to the Mortgaged Properties covered thereby, so long as no Default has occurred, Borrower is and may continue to receive from the purchasers of production all such Production Proceeds, subject, however, to the Liens created under the Security Documents, which Liens are hereby affirmed and ratified. Upon the occurrence of a Default, Lender may exercise all rights and remedies granted under the Security Documents, including the right to obtain possession of all Production Proceeds then held by Borrower or to receive directly from the purchasers of production all other Production Proceeds. In no case shall any failure, whether purposed or inadvertent, by Lender to collect directly any such Production Proceeds constitute in any way a waiver, remission or release of any of its rights under the Security Documents, nor shall any release of any Production Proceeds by Lender to Borrower constitute a waiver, remission, or release of any other Production Proceeds or of any rights of Lender to collect other Production Proceeds thereafter." Excerpt from 1997 Banc Paribas Credit Facility.

Chapter 4: Elements of Energy Lending

Unlike home loans or commercial real estate loans where banks look to title insurance companies to insure a borrower's title, title insurance is not available for oil and gas mineral properties. The bank—and its counsel—must independently conduct an evaluation by reviewing of the land files and researching public land records.

Further complicating this aspect of loan documentation for energy lenders, oil and gas loans are also unlike home loans and commercial real estate, where the collateral typically consists of one tract of land owned 100% by the borrower. A producer's assets are typically comprised of many wells on multiple tracts involving oil and gas leases from multiple owners of the minerals.

Further, the bank needs its counsel to confirm that the properties examined and described in the mortgage are the same properties being evaluated by the bank's engineer.[459] Early energy lenders did not have engineering appraisals prepared on a well-by-well basis to cross-check against a borrower's title. A bank's approach to title examination in the East Texas Field was described by McElvaney in 1934:

> [T]here are practically no record titles in the East Texas field. They are all limitation titles [i.e. title acquired by the landowner by adverse possession], and where we find that we are depending almost entirely on the collateral we, of course, insist on proper examination of title either by our own attorneys or other attorneys whom we regard as entirely reputable. In the case of relatively small loans where the interest has not been under attack for say a period of a year and a half or two years we usually waive title examination, relying in these instances upon the examination of the attorneys for the [crude oil] purchasing company, who are ordinarily fairly careful in their examination, with the result that at least most of the outstanding irregularities in the title have been heretofore cured.[460]

---

[459] Maginnis, "Financing Oil and Gas Development," 697.
[460] McElvaney letter to Kirkland (August 14, 1934).

A more homespun analysis of correlating the value of title to the value of the well is attributed to Jim Hogg who, after retiring as Texas' governor, went into the business of prospecting for oil. After the Spindletop discovery, Hogg, like many others, started taking leases around Patillo Higgins' original well. Hogg was larger than life in many ways and commanded attention and respect wherever he went.

A local said of Hogg's stay at Beaumont's most respected hotel, "He used to sit in front of the Crosby House with a little old battered straw hat on top of his head. One time I heard a young man engage him in conversation and I heard him ask, 'Governor, how does a fellow tell oil land?' The governor lapsed into the backwoods vernacular, in which he often spoke, and said, 'Well, son, it's about this way: if it hain't no good for nothing else, it's a good sign; and if the title is bad, it's a cinch.'"[461]

As energy bankers and their analyses became more sophisticated with the use of petroleum engineers evaluating the proposed collateral on a well-by-well basis in the 1950s, it was the lawyer's responsibility to tie the borrower's title in the wells to the values evaluated by the engineer. Even today, this is not always an apples-to-apples exercise. The perennial problem is matching reserve-report well names—typically generated by the borrower's engineering department—to the well descriptions in the borrower's title files—typically generated by the borrower's land department. Bank lawyer Hubert Dee Johnson reported in 1958:

> Property descriptions furnished by the borrower to the lending officer and valuation engineer are usually inadequate as legal descriptions. When accurate legal descriptions of properties are furnished, the lender's attorney and the valuation engineer may have some difficulty in being certain that the legal descriptions cover the same properties as those included in the engineer's valuation. Reconciling legal descriptions with

---

[461] Hinton and Olien, *Oil in Texas*, 33.

rather general descriptions sometimes used in pipe line division orders may present a problem before the loan is closed or later in connection with maintaining accurate records when payments are received under division orders. To avoid these difficulties with respect to property descriptions the lender's attorney must work closely with the lender's engineer and with the lender's representative who handles oil and gas proceeds received in connection with the repayment of the loan.[462]

By the late 1950s, banks required satisfactory title opinions—both as to the borrower's good title to the mortgaged property and that the mortgage created a valid first lien and assignment of production securing the payment of the borrower's debt. This was commonly referred to as a closing-lien title opinion. Importantly, under an ABC production-payment financing, the seller "A" did not warrant title and "C," the purchaser/borrower, did not have any additional assets to back a warranty to the lender; therefore, title opinions assumed a greater importance in financing these transactions.[463]

A review of the literature from this period provides evidence that banks were much stricter regarding credit compliance prior to funding the loan. The practice up through the '70s was not to fund the loan until title was approved and all security instruments had been properly filed. The standard procedure was for the bank to require that the borrower provide current title opinions or abstracts of title, evidencing his title, and that the borrower execute and record the mortgage, granting the bank a first lien on the collateral prior to closing.[464]

---

[462] Johnson, "Legal Aspects of Oil and Gas Financing," 152.

[463] Richard S. Brennan (Partner, Mayer, Brown & Platt, Chicago, Illinois), "Current Trends in Oil and Gas Financing," 25 *Rocky Mt. Min. L. Inst.* (1979): 16-19.

[464] "In many instances it is desired that the mortgage or deed of trust be recorded and included in the abstract, with the final opinion showing a first and prior lien position in the bank before the money is actually advanced." McElvaney, "Some Aspects of Financing Oil and Gas Transactions," 333 (1954); *see also* Maginnis, "Financing Oil and Gas Development," 698 (The mortgage should be filed for record prior to the closing of the loan).

Only after the mortgage had been properly executed, acknowledged and recorded were the proceeds of the loan delivered to the borrower.[465] Some practitioners by the end of the 1950s were advising that lenders take the extra precaution of having a lawyer at the county courthouse verify by telephone that no instruments had been filed of record since the last date the title records had been examined as reflected in the title opinion. The lawyer's call from the public phone booth outside the county clerk's office, confirming that nothing had been filed in the public records, would then trigger the closing, which Denver-based lawyer Frederic Kirgis described in 1959 as "rapid-fire [and would] cause the almost instantaneous transfer of funds."[466]

Under instructions over the telephone, the lawyer stationed at the courthouse would, then, record the lien instruments, which had been previously executed and acknowledged. Where multiple counties or parties were involved, practitioners recommended that the bank's lawyer prepare a closing memorandum to establish priority of closing steps and as a check-list of closing mechanics and responsibilities.[467]

Documentation at Closing

Following closing and funding, division orders or letters-in-lieu, providing instruction to the producer's purchasers, were executed, including a file-stamped copy of the recorded mortgage. These instruction letters enclosed an acknowledgment copy, which the bank requested be returned to it to insure the purchasers would pay the bank in the future for the production purchased.

Practitioners were warned that prompt and satisfactory completion of these post-closing procedures was as important as any other legal aspect of making and closing the loan because, Johnson wrote, "failure to do so or delay in doing so can affect adversely the proper performance of the loan."[468] This was timeless advice for banks' law-

---

[465] Thompson, "Legal And Other Aspects of Financing The Oil Industry," 38.
[466] Kirgis, "Financing an Oil Venture," 505.
[467] Kirgis, "Financing an Oil Venture," 506.
[468] Johnson, "Legal Aspects of Oil and Gas Financing," 162.

yers to pay attention to the details, especially after the bankers and oilmen have moved onto their next deal.

Certain aspects of perfecting liens on the bank's collateral were simplified by the adoption of a uniform set of rules across all states. The Uniform Commercial Code was published by the National Conference of Commissioners on Uniform State Laws in collaboration with the American Law Institute in 1952 after 10 years in draft.[469] The UCC was a model code and had no legal effect unless adopted by the individual states as statutes. By 1965, it had been adopted by 39 states, simplifying certain questions created under each state's unique laws regarding personal and real property.

The UCC was welcomed by finance lawyers, who felt a uniform system of lien registration could provide protection in states in which the law was unclear as to whether the security interest created by the mortgage covered an interest in real or personal property. In some jurisdictions, there was a danger that a production payment under the ABC structure might not be classified as a real-property interest. Whether or not the production payment would be classified as real property in a particular state, the lender was assured a perfected lien on the accounts receivable attributable to the production, if it complied with the applicable UCC requirements.[470]

The eventual adoption of the UCC in whole or in part by each of the 50 states simplified the process of perfecting liens on the portion of oil and gas property that is personal-property collateral—principally oil and gas produced from the wells and the related accounts receivable. Some producing states, such as Mississippi and Louisiana, were noticeably slow adopters of the UCC, with Mississippi adopting in 1972 and Louisiana not until 1990.[471] This resulted in complications in documenting production loans in multi-state transactions during this period.

---

[469] The American Law Institute, Past and Present ALI Projects, (as of October 2015) Ali.org.

[470] Beatty, "Selected Problems in Oil and Gas Financing," 114.

[471] Louisiana R.S. 10:9-101, Sos.la.gov.

CHAPTER 5

Lending Into the 1970s

"To finance the Seventies we will need to use all
money raising devices of the past and then still more."
A.G. Gueymard

With the demise of the ABC loan structure following the 1969 Tax Reform Act, some energy lenders were instantly nostalgic for the good old days. In 1971, Tom Stephens, a senior loan officer in the petroleum and minerals department at First City National Bank in Houston, was ready to pronounce the death of oil and gas development financing.[472]

But, in 1972, A.G. Gueymard, Stephens' boss at the time, concluded that there remained a great need for new sources of oil and gas capital as U.S. production was declining while worldwide demand was growing. "To finance the Seventies we will need to use all money raising devices of the past and then still more," he reported to the Rocky Mountain Mineral Law Foundation Institute.[473]

Gueymard also discussed the myriad alternative financing options available to oil and gas companies, drillers and pipeline operators. He was optimistic about sourcing additional capital, but he was equally concerned with the magnitude of the task ahead for the industry, writ-

---

[472] Stevens, "Current Developments in Petroleum Financing," 203.
[473] Gueymard, "The Seventies-An Era of Transition," 575.

ing, "The enormity of the figure is staggering, even to an American oil banker!"[474]

He noted that forecasts predicted $180 billion of debt capital would be needed in the next decade to meet the capital needs of the industry—in addition to cash from operations and sales of equity. This implied "that by the end of the decade the industry will be borrowing in excess of $20 billion a year. Historically the industry has borrowed only about $5 billion per year."[475] He concluded:

> The capital needs of the 1970's cannot be met by cost reduction. Instead, they must be derived from increased profits coupled with either equity sales or increased debt burdens. *The more desirable solution lies in increasing revenue in the form of world-wide increased prices.* The consumer of petroleum energy is destined throughout the free world to pay far more dearly in the future for this readily usable form of energy which he took for granted in the past. [emphasis added][476]

The latter part of the statement was somewhat prescient. The average price of oil in 1970 was $3.18 a barrel; by the end of the decade, it had multiplied to $17 a barrel.[477] The increased commodity prices wished for at the beginning of the decade by energy lenders—and producers—resulted in a global transfer of energy muscle from Texas independents to the sheiks in the deserts of the Middle East. It also resulted in less-favorable treatment at home, evidenced by Congress' imposition of the Windfall Profit Tax on oil companies.

Bankers got their wish: World oil prices increased. But this would not be without substantial costs and unintended consequences. With the demise of the ABC loan and with rising commodity prices caused

---

[474] Gueymard, "The Seventies-An Era of Transition," 575 (noting that historically most capital needed by oil companies during the 1960s was generated out of cash flow and the industry had borrowed only about $5 billion a year).

[475] Gueymard, "The Seventies-An Era of Transition," 573-4.

[476] Gueymard, "The Seventies-An Era of Transition," 575.

[477] U.S. EIA, Independent Statistics & Analysis. "Petroleum & Other Liquids." Accessed March 6, 2016. Eia.gov.

by global disruptions, there was more demand by producers for capital and more competition by lenders to meet the demand.

Energy loans were still some of the most profitable and, when
properly documented, least risky for oil-patch and money-center
banks. With proration laws, advancements in reserve analysis and the
relative stability of commodity prices, loans secured by oil and gas by
the late '60s were a profitable and relatively safe venture for lenders.
Bankers at First City National Bank in New York reported in 1968:

> The loss ratio on oil and gas loans had been historical-
> ly low at oil banks, and these loans are still attractive
> to lenders. We ran a survey of 40 oil lenders which
> showed that about five percent of all types of loans
> made, based on production, became problem loans.
> About 1.75% of these loans involved losses but the
> actual loss experience was *less* than 0.4% of the origi-
> nal face amounts extended.[478]

Surprisingly, with all the tumult in oil and gas prices in the 1970s
up through this century, loans secured by these have remained, on
balance, a relatively safe place for banks to employ capital. Standard &
Poor's reported that, during 1995-2002, lending to the E&P segment
of the oil and gas industry had been relatively safe, compared with
other industries, because of low default rates and the potential for
good recovery on defaulted debt.[479]

For the period between 1996 and 2005, recovery rates on senior
secured bank debt in the E&P sector were excellent.[480] In 2013, S&P
reported that less than 1% of bank loans to the oil and gas industry

---

[478] Gerald E. Sherrod (Vice President, First National City Bank, New York, N.Y.), "What
Makes Those Bank Engineers So Conservative," 1 *Journal of the Society of Petroleum Evaluation Engineers* (1968-69): 18.

[479] Standard & Poor's Ratings Services, "Utilities & Perspectives, Global Utilities Rating
Service," Vol. 11, No. 43 (October 28, 2002).

[480] S&P tracked more than 15 bankruptcies of U.S. E&P companies for the period between 1996 and 2005 and reported that 77% received full recovery, 15% recovered more
than 85% and 8% recovered less than 85%. Standard & Poor's, "S&P's Default And Recovery Analysis Of U.S. Oil And Gas E&P Sector Provides Implications For The Future," March 26, 2006, 7.

had defaulted and the recovery rate was nearly 100% going back to the mid-1990s.[481] Whether the energy-banking industry can maintain this high level of performance remains to be seen in the post-2014 price-collapse environment.

The New Standard—The Borrowing-Base Revolver

By the end of the 1970s, oil and gas loan documentation evolved into the fundamental structure that is used today. Without the tax advantage of the ABC structure, most banks reverted to the traditional term loan, lending against the producer's current cash flow from producing wells to provide drilling capital for the next set of wells.

The 1970s also brought a rapid increase in oil prices. Between 1973 and 1975 the price doubled and, from 1975 to 1980, it increased from $7.67 to $21.59. A producer who pledged his production to secure a loan in 1975 saw the value of his reserves increase threefold,[482] yet his term loan not only didn't increase, it continued to amortize. The only way to unlock this increase in value was to refinance the loan with a new term loan, again locking in the lower collateral price until coming back to refinance again.

Not surprisingly, bankers and their borrowers were looking in the 1970s for ways to streamline the cumbersome process of annually refinancing and increasing term notes with new loan documentation and mortgages. In 1979, Chicago-based attorney Richard S. Brennan reported:

> Bank lenders have become more and more sophisticated in understanding energy businesses and their financing needs. They are showing themselves to be more flexible in their attitudes toward adapting traditional financing techniques. In many cases, they are demonstrating a willingness to assume more business

---

[481] David A. Kaplan et al., "Despite Risks, We Expect Excellent Recovery on Most Reserve-Based Lending Facilities of E&P Companies," *Standard & Poor's Ratings Services* 2 (January 18, 2013), 3.
[482] U.S. EIA, Independent Statistics & Analysis. "U.S. Crude Oil First Purchase Price." Accessed March 6, 2016. Eia.gov.

and legal risks than they have traditionally done. Because of increased competition among bank lenders, and because of the relative profitability of this kind of financing to banks ... we can expect this trend to continue.[483]

Brennan also wrote of a "new more flexible technique" that had been introduced in recent years. This was the borrowing-base, revolving-loan facility, which is the mainstay of almost all secured oil and gas lending today. The structure was derived in part from secured revolving-credit arrangements for merchandisers.

The concept of adjustable credit under an energy loan tied to the value of the borrower's collateral—the borrowing base—was introduced around 1978 by Continental Illinois—likely by Wallace Wilson and Jerry Pearson, both of whom were well respected in the industry.[484] In *Belly Up: The Collapse of the Penn Square Bank*, author Phillip L. Zweig credits Continental Illinois for inventing the borrowing-base revolver, which he calls an "evergreen revolver."

"The method calls for the bank to establish a 'borrowing base' for a customer that was usually about half of the discounted current value of the customer's reserves," Zweig wrote. "The note requires only the payment of interest, with the idea that by the time it matures the reserves can be 'reengineered' and a new loan extended to pay back the previous one."[485]

---

[483] Brennan, "Current Trends in Oil and Gas Financing," 16-20.

[484] Efforts to identify the exact author of the first reserve borrowing-base revolver have been inconclusive. Tom Whitener, founder of Energy Spectrum and formerly senior energy banker at First City National Bank, Dallas, (interview by the author, July 29, 2014) and John Homier, petroleum engineer for Continental Illinois, 1986-1994, (interview, January 29, 2013) both credit Continental banker Jerry Pearson as the author, whereas Tom Fuller, First City banker in the 1970s, (interview, August 31, 2012) credits Continental banker Wallace Wilson. Other sources, such as Jim Cordell (interview, June 18, 2014), head of Continental's Texas lending office in the late '70s and early '80s, remembered that Continental was making small reserve-based revolving loans to larger independents, such as Anadarko Petroleum Corp. and Phillips Petroleum Co., circa 1974 with six- to 12-month redeterminations, depending upon the field's decline curve.

[485] Zweig, *Belly Up*, 72-73.

Chapter 5: Lending Into the 1970s

Jim Cordell, who opened Continental Illinois' Houston office in 1975, said in 2013 that, in 1965, Continental Illinois' "management had tired of competing for loans to major oil companies at low rates and wanted to get into the smaller, independent-producer loan market. The bank hired engineers to evaluate oil and gas collateral and entered the production term-loan market."[486]

As early as 1975, the bank made smaller reserve-based loans with collateral reviews of six months to a year, depending upon the borrower's properties' production profile. By 1978, Continental Illinois was making larger loans, including a $400-million revolving line of credit loan to Davis Oil Co. that had a six-month collateral review.

Once word of this more-flexible structure became known in the oil patch, it was quickly adopted by most of the other energy banks. Tom Fuller, a former First City banker, said in 2012, "Continental Illinois was stealing all our customers and, to compete, we had to offer the same structure."[487]

First National in Dallas also started copying the borrowing-base revolver, "but it was hard to swallow for a conservative bank," recalled Tom Whitener, an energy lender with the bank in the late '70s. "In response to the increasing oil prices, there was a greater need for capital. It didn't seem a smart thing to do. It was like a drug: The more the producers used it, the more they wanted it."[488]

The borrowing-base-revolver structure solved the complications that arose from the traditional production-term loans employed by energy lenders into the early 1970s. In the traditional term loan, the oil company would return to negotiate a new term loan each year to fund the next year of drilling, necessitating new loan documents and mortgages or, at least, amendments to mortgages and title updates each time.[489] Instead, under a revolving line of credit tied to the value of

---

[486] Jim Cordell, author's interview.
[487] Tom Fuller, author's interview.
[488] Whitener, author's interview.
[489] Brennan, "Current Trends in Oil and Gas Financing," Section 1.A; *see also*, C. Stephen Christian (Security Pacific National Bank, Denver, Colorado), "Introduction to Commercial Bank and Non-Bank Institutional Financing In The Minerals Industry," *Mineral Financing* (1982), Section 2-18.

the collateral pledged to the borrowing base, the producer was able to borrow, repay and re-borrow up to the maximum loan amount, which was determined annually—or, at times, more frequently—until the loan matured.[490]

Early borrowing-base loans were structured as a revolving line of credit for a period and automatically converted to amortizing term loans, unless the bank, in its discretion, elected to extend the revolver period.[491] In some later revolving loans, it was the borrower who could elect to convert to an amortizing term loan or pay the facility off at maturity.[492]

This option is not typically seen in current borrowing-base credit facilities, however, perhaps because the borrower, once on a "revolver line," would never opt to convert to an amortizing term loan. Instead, he would likely continue to renew his loan or find another bank to refinance his existing revolver—at least until the borrower decided it was time to sell his properties and pay off his bank line in full.

The borrowing-base revolver answered the borrower's need for more flexible borrowing power and avoided the legal expense of continually amending and re-filing loan documentation. Richard Brennan wrote in 1979, "The technique can greatly simplify a continuous course of lending between one or more banks and its or their customer, and it is proving to be more and more popular with respect to borrowers having constantly increasing borrowing needs."[493]

---

[490] Michael M. Boone (Haynes and Boone, Dallas, Texas), "Structuring and Documenting the Oil and Gas Loan" (paper presented at the Third Annual Banking Law Institute, March 14, 1980), 2-18; see also Christian, "Introduction to Commercial Bank and Non-Bank Institutional Financing," Section 2-18.

[491] Bridges, author's interview.

[492] Boone, "Structuring and Documenting the Oil and Gas Loan," 16. This "convertible" structure is still used today by some regional banks on smaller single-bank facilities. John Lane, Senior Vice President, Manager Energy Lending, First Tennessee Bank, interview by the author, November 7, 2011.

[493] Brennan, "Current Trends in Oil and Gas Financing," 16-3-4.

A bank unwilling to switch from the standard, term loan to revolving lines of credit would often find its customers leaving in favor of more "progressive" banks.[494]

Borrowing-Base Mechanics

Typically, the borrowing base was calculated on the same underlying parameters used in calculating the maximum loan amount under a term loan—with one structural difference. Under a term loan, the borrower begins amortizing principal soon after the funds are advanced. Under a revolving loan, the borrower has no principal-amortization schedule and, in fact, can borrow up to the full amount of the borrowing base on the last day prior to maturity. The borrowing base serves as a way to convert the loan under a revolver to an amortizing, term loan on each borrowing-base redetermination date.

With periodic redeterminations of the borrowing base—today, typically every six months—the borrowing base amount is reset. As originally designed, the bank would review the borrower's most current reserve report as an estimate of the company's future value and, after deducting its anticipated depletion rate through projected production during the coming six months, calculate the borrowing base. If everything goes as expected, even if the borrower drew down the maximum borrowing base under the revolver on the last day before the next scheduled determination six months later, the bank will be "fully secured."

The original theory for establishing a borrowing base equal to the future expected collateral value at the time of the next redetermination has, over time, lost out to lenders' competition for market share. Where multiple banks compete for a borrower's business, more often than not, the determining factor in the borrower's decision will be which bank can offer the highest initial borrowing base. The more conservative bank will usually lose out to the bank with a more aggressive (higher) borrowing base.

---

[494] Christian, "Introduction to Commercial Bank and Non-Bank Institutional Financing," Section 2-18.

Where possible, banks may give some collateral credit to the initial six months of production that would be "rolled off" in the traditional borrowing-base calculation. If the bank's engineers have confidence that the borrower's reserves will be replaced over time from the company's behind-pipe or probable reserves, then there is more confidence in crediting some or all of the initial six months' production. Conversely, a bank may be reluctant to give credit in the borrowing base to the first six months if the borrower is fully drawn or his track record or properties fail to evidence an ability to easily replace reserves.[495]

One variation of the borrowing-base structure acknowledges that the initial borrowing base gives full credit to the properties' collateral present value at closing, but the bank will amortize it monthly—reducing the amount available each month. In this "stretch" borrowing base with six amortizing monthly payments, the reduced borrowing base at the end of the six-month period is the same as the properties' projected present value of the collateral—that is, the "conforming borrowing-base amount."

If borrowing the full amount available and, at the end of the six months, the present value of the collateral has declined, resulting in a reduced borrowing base, the borrower must pay down what is drawn that is above the new determination. For example, if Producer Oil Co. has $500 million drawn on its original $600-million borrowing base and the borrowing base is subsequently determined to be $400 million, the company is required to repay $100 million.

Most borrowing-base loans give the borrower the option to either pledge additional assets to increase the borrowing base to an amount at least equal to the outstanding borrowings or repay the deficiency in one payment or in five equal monthly installments. In this, prior to the next scheduled redetermination, the borrower's outstanding loans would not exceed the expected collateral value.

---

495 Byron Cooley (Senior Vice President Energy, DNB Bank, ASA), interview by the author, January 29, 2015.

While this structure looks very efficient in theory, things can get messy quickly in practice. Typically, a borrower has pledged everything it owns to the bank when the loan is first made, including everything it owns that is classified as "proved reserves." Borrowers rarely have any "extra collateral" available to pledge to the bank. The alternative for curing a borrowing-base deficiency is, then, typically for the producer to start paying down principal on a monthly basis.

In such an event, cash flow must be diverted from other uses. Typically, the producer's first option will be to defer discretionary capital expenditures—that is, future drilling. But new drilling is needed to replace the production that generates the cash flow. In the short term, this may be an option, but, if capex is deferred too long, the producer gets deeper in a hole from which it cannot escape.

"When this happens, either oil and gas prices have fallen or the borrower has been very unlucky in replacing his reserves," Byron Cooley, a senior energy lender, said in an interview. "In either case, he's in some form of financial stress. The several times I have been faced with this situation has always resulted in the beginning of a strong disagreement period between the borrower and bank, which ultimately has led to a work-out situation or even bankruptcy.

"In essence, while it looks good from a theoretical standpoint on paper, it really doesn't work like it should."[496]

Borrowing-Base Determination

Unlike term loans, determining the borrowing base for a revolving loan was not as simple as looking at the reserve engineer's estimate of the borrower's total proved reserves and multiplying that by the bank's advance rate.[497] As the concept has become more sophisticated over the years, rigorous risk analyses by the bank's engineers include comparisons of proved developed producing (PDP) versus proved undeveloped (PUD) reserves, well-value concentration, decline rates,

---

[496] Cooley, author's interview.
[497] Dartez, author's interview.

lease-operating expenses, plugging and abandonment liability, commodity prices and basis differentials.[498] [499]

Some of the early borrowing-base loans provided for a predetermined method of calculating the borrowing base as a straight percentage of reserve values derived from periodic reserve reports, while other lenders—as is the case today—retained sole and absolute discretion in how it is calculated.[500]

According to long-time energy banker Murray Brasseux, Bank of the Southwest was one of the first banks to develop a proprietary statistical analysis for borrowing-base calculations.[501] The late 1960s was a period where an interest in statistics developed as a way of evaluating capital investments. The petroleum industry, with its high-risk investments, began experimenting with various applications.

Frank Dartez recalled a paper written by David Hertz, "Risk Analysis in Capital Investments," which had a general application to most businesses at a time when business schools began adding statistics to their curricula.[502] The premise of the paper was that companies typically calculated cash flow, for example, by multiplying the average of the estimated volume of a product being manufactured by the average price expected for the product, less the average manufacturing cost and the average operating expenses.

---

[498] Basis differentials represent the value of oil and gas depending on where it is produced. Oil produced far from a market fetches a net less price to the producer than oil produced nearer to refineries due to the cost of transportation.

[499] Dartez, author's interview, explaining how Bank of the Southwest developed its proprietary statistical reserve borrowing-base calculations. "In the late 1960s oil companies started using statistics based on a Harvard Business School paper presented by David Purtz which included variables on average prices, profits, etc. The bank sent its engineers to graduate school classes on credit and financial management. I started using statistical analysis to generate probability distributions for the wells and extrapolate as to value for the company's properties. In the 1980s after the price collapse, we would run a base case and a stretch case on prices. The bank was able to see greater value than our competitors." Dartez, author's interview.

[500] Boone, "Structuring and Documenting the Oil and Gas Loan," 16. This "convertible" structure is still used today by some regional banks on smaller single-bank facilities. John Lane, author's interview.

[501] Brasseaux, author's interview.

[502] David B. Hertz, "Risk Analysis in Capital Investments," *Harvard Business Review*, January/February 1964; *see also* Dartez, author's interview.

Hertz showed that a better approach would be to establish a probability distribution around each of those factors. That distribution is likely to be different for each factor and, from these, a composite distribution of the cash flow is developed that indicates the entire range of possibilities. It is a good way to rank and compare various capital-investment proposals.

In the 1960s, Citibank sent Dartez along with its other engineers to a graduate-school course staffed by top MBA professors. Dartez took interest in a statistics course and learned about a technique called Monte Carlo analysis. The technique is a way to accurately duplicate a probability distribution using random numbers.

A previous management study by a Citibank engineer was of problem oil and gas loans and the factors that contributed to those problems. The one factor that stood out was a concentration of risk in a few properties. Dartez wrote his thesis on the analysis of risk that results from spreading the concentration of risk among multiple properties, using the Monte Carlo method.

Dartez explained, "My definition of a safe reserve-based loan is one that will pay out using an acceptable rate of interest—even if the reserve estimate is at the lowest range of projected estimates. For example, if the historical data on a property indicate that a 10% rate of decline is the expected rate, but, on a worst-case basis, the property could conceivably decline at 30%, the loan value should not exceed the present value of the 30%-decline case.

"If two or more independent properties are involved, statistics must be used to determine the minimum case—when the properties are added together. To accomplish this, probability distributions of the present value were developed for each property and the data entered into a Monte Carlo program. The program generated a composite distribution from which the minimum present worth could be determined. The study included the analysis of a number of cases, where the concentration of value was varied."[503]

_____

[503] Dartez, author's interview. Dartez's paper, "Risk Analysis in Non Recourse Petroleum Lending," was selected by the Graduate School of Credit and Financial Management at

Significant modifications were made to simplify the analysis through the use of statistical formulae that could be verified by the Monte Carlo method. The technique was successfully used for more than 20 years at Bank of the Southwest and its successors.

J. Thomas Mullen et al., attorneys with Mayer Brown & Platt, which was Continental Illinois' lead bank counsel, wrote in 1982 of borrowing-base agreements, "The determination of the Borrowing Base shall be made by the Bank in the exercise of its sole discretion in accordance with the Bank's customary practices and standards for loans, the payment of which is serviced by oil and gas properties."[504]

Some banks were more specific in setting forth how the borrowing base was calculated. But it was more favorable—from the lender's perspective—to define it as broadly as possible to provide flexibility in the future should the bank change its economic parameters used in its calculation. Typically, bankers were—and remain to this day—willing to discuss with the borrower how they have calculated the borrowing base and there can be some give and take on the engineer's interpretation. However, the final determination remains the sole discretion of the lender.

In a recent example of formulaic borrowing-base provisions, an Appalachia-based bank that had more than 100 years of experience in lending to coal producers decided to get into oil and gas lending as production in the Marcellus shale play was taking off. Relying on language from a Pittsburgh law firm, the bank agreed to a formulaic borrowing-base calculation in a loan to a Texas-based producer.

Stanford University in July, 1969, as the most outstanding report and received the American Petroleum Credit Association Award for Meritorious Achievement. He employed this risk analysis when he became manager of engineering at Bank of the Southwest in 1979.

[504] J. Thomas Mullen, et al., Mayer, Brown & Platt, "An Introduction to Legal Documentation Used in Bank Financings for the Oil and Gas Industry," Chapter 3 at 28 (paper presented at the Rocky Mountain Mineral Law Foundation, November 1982). An example from a 1980 First National Bank in Dallas $2-million revolver included the requirement: "Bank shall advise Borrower of the amount which Bank's petroleum engineers, in accordance with the customary procedures and standards used by Bank for its petroleum industry customers, have designated as the amount of the Borrowing Base as of such date based on producing wells then existing on the Mortgaged Property." Note that, as indicated by this excerpt, the original borrowing bases were calculated only on producing properties, not undeveloped properties.

In this, the borrowing base was the sum of the present value discounted at 10% of 65% of the borrower's PDP reserves; 35% of its proved, developed, non-producing reserves (PDNP); and 25% of its PUDs. Upon opening a Houston office and hiring an experienced energy lender in 2014, however, the bank seized the first opportunity it had to delete the formula and began to derive the borrowing base solely at its discretion. Notwithstanding the credit-agreement provisions, the course of conduct and communications between the lender and borrower can lead to misunderstandings and, at times, result in lawsuits over the intent and a lender's calculation of a borrowing-base determination.[505]

As loans evolved from single-lender facilities to syndicated facilities with two or more banks involved, different approaches to calculate the borrowing base were used to gain a consensus, but, still, always within the participating banks' discretion. Some credit agreements included more elaborate mechanisms that would toss out the high and the low numbers proposed by individual, participating banks and use the average of the remainder.

In almost all cases, any increase at redetermination requires a unanimous vote—that is, no one lender could be "dragged up" against its own credit standards. Maintaining or decreasing the base requires a consensus of the majority lenders—typically representing two-thirds of the total commitment.[506]

Today, in a standard multi-bank credit facility, one lender typically originates the loan and serves as the administrative agent. Among the agent's responsibilities is to recommend the new borrowing base each season and this is put to a vote. What the producer is not privy to is the vote-canvassing and horse-trading that occurs when there

---

[505] Plaintiff's Original Petition and Verified Application for Temporary Restraining Order, Temporary Injunction, and Permanent Injunction, *The Pfanenstiel Company, LLC v. Independent Bank*, Cause No. DC-16-00601, District Court, Dallas, Texas, filed January 20, 2016.

[506] In recent facilities syndicated among a larger group of lenders, a few facilities have permitted increases in the borrowing-base amount with less than 100% of lender approval (95% approval) provided any bank that does not vote in favor of the increase is not obligated to fund its pro-rata share of the increase.

isn't immediate, unanimous concurrence. Like white smoke from the Sistine Chapel, the borrower only officially knows the amount of his new borrowing base when the agent announces it.[507]

Unlike U.S. borrowing-base determinations, the determination under European reserve-based loans secured by North Sea and other producing areas outside of North America is more formula-driven based on an agreed model established between the borrower and the banks at the time the facility is negotiated. Typically, a "modeling bank" will work with the borrower to set the algorithm—that is, the "banking case"—and compute the resulting base amount during the life of the facility. In a 2014 *Oil & Gas Financial Journal* article, a Société Générale banker and two energy attorneys wrote:

> While the Banking Case will generally be re-run twice a year, and assumption inputs such as hydrocarbon prices and production profiles, etc. will be reset each time the Banking Case is re-run, the model itself will typically not change unless it needs updating (such as when fields are disposed of or new ones are added). … Because there is an agreed model and the assumptions that go into it are carefully tested by the Technical Bank, individual syndicate banks do not typically have their own separate models but agree [to] one single model and banking case at each review. … There is no further or specific right of approval for

---

[507] The admonition of keeping the bank's determination of a borrowing base inside a black box has not always prevailed. In 2011, a private-equity-sponsored oil and gas company negotiated in its credit agreement that the borrowing base amount would be set by the lender "in good faith" based upon information deemed appropriate, exercising reasonable commercial standards and consistent with normal and customary oil and gas lending criteria as exists at the particular time. Further, the provision required the lender to provide to the borrower its "bank price deck" and, upon request, to meet with the borrower to discuss the lender's evaluation of the borrower's reserves and "respective methodologies for valuing such properties and the other factors considered in calculating the Borrowing Base."

lenders over increases in the Borrowing Base Amount
[under the international borrowing-base structure].[508]

A number of European banks that are active in both the U.S. and
foreign energy-lending markets will maintain one set of criteria for
determination of borrowing bases on U.S. reserves and another set for
reserves elsewhere.

While the international model has been used abroad since the beginning of North Sea oil and gas development in the 1970s,[509] the
American model remains separate. There are structural differences
between U.S. reserves on private leases versus international reserves
on land under which the government owns the mineral rights. A U.S.
adoption of the international model appears unlikely at present.

In late 2014, a European bank with a U.S. presence was trying to
build a syndicate of interest in a large, U.S.-reserve-based loan, utiliz-
ing the "banking case" model. Many other energy bankers, even ones
who work for European banks, were not inclined to sign up for this.
Meanwhile, with the current downturn in commodity prices, beginning in mid-2014, banks have the upper hand in how the base is determined and there is little incentive for U.S. bankers to get innovative
to attract new accounts.

Borrowing-Base Deficiency
As borrowing bases are typically reconsidered twice a year, the expectation was that the borrowing base would increase if the borrower had
experienced a net increase in its reserves as a result of drilling or acquisitions or both. Of course, in the oil patch, there are many variables: wells go offline, equipment fails, prices drop or there is some
other event or multiple calamities. Therefore, the loan agreement in-
corporates a mechanism that requires the borrower to take action to

---

[508] K. Price, Société Générale, D. Gonsoulin and Jason Fox, Bracewell Guiliani, "Reserve
Based Finance: A Tale of Two Markets – Part 2," *Oil & Gas Financial Journal*, February
2014.
[509] Kevin Price, et al., "Reserve Based Lending Markets: From Projects to Borrowing
Bases," *Oil & Gas Financial Journal*, August 1, 2006.

cure a deficiency when the value of its collateral falls below what has been drawn under the revolver.

The existence of a borrowing-base deficiency is not an event of default and does not give the lender the immediate right to terminate the loan and accelerate payment. Instead, the loan usually allows the borrower to pledge more collateral or pay down the deficiency in a lump or monthly payments. Since the introduction of the revolver in the late 1970s, the principal variation has been in how long the borrower can take to cure the deficiency. In an example from the 1980s, the borrower was allowed to make monthly payments equal to 90% of monthly cash flow from the collateral until the deficiency was retired.[510]

The problem with this repayment structure was that the deficiency might never be cured if production or prices fell too far. Because the lender would be redetermining the borrowing base again within six months, the general convention came to be to give the borrower a month to pledge additional collateral, pay the deficiency in full or commence payments in five, equal, monthly installments. In this, the borrower would be in compliance during the six-month determination—if there were no further decrease in the base. This timing is consistent with the methodology of the calculation, which is based on what will be the value of the reserves six months later.

No additional loans were permitted as long as there was a deficiency. If a new deficiency existed at the next determination as a result of a further reduction of the borrowing base, the borrower considered the three options again.

Some banks require repayment of any deficiency prior to the next redetermination date, sometimes as quickly as within 30 days.[511] This

---

[510] In a 1980 revolver by First National Bank in Dallas, the borrowing base was reset annually; if there was a deficiency, the borrower either cured the deficiency with a principal payment or pledge of additional collateral. If the deficiency was not so cured as of the date of redetermination, the loan converted to a five-year term loan with monthly payments equal to 95% of net revenues.

[511] Credit Agreement, Mallon Resources Corp., Mallon Oil Co. and Midland Bank Plc, New York Branch, August 24, 1995, p. 15, filed Mallon Resources Corp. 8-K for June 15, 1995, Ex. 1.

is inconsistent with a semi-annual determination structure. However, there is no standard borrowing-base loan; therefore, differences result due to the lender's preference with regard to each client and what negotiating power the borrower has.

Other facilities have gotten further away from original borrowing-base mechanics by immediately assessing a default rate of interest on the deficiency until the date the deficiency is resolved. Under the original structure, a deficiency is not a "default"—provided that the deficiency is made up within the specified period of time. If a lender charges a default rate during the make-up period, the lender is treating it as if the borrower is in default and, during a grace period to cure the default, charging default interest.

As the borrowing-base concept evolved, bankers and, later, borrowers negotiated the right to trigger a special interim "wild card" redetermination at any time during each six-month period or, at least, annually. This is the result of the borrower's desire to be able to access additional availability in the event that the value of its production significantly increased—typically as a result of an acquisition of producing reserves or extraordinary success in development drilling.

At the same time, bankers wanted the ability to reduce the borrowing base in the event of a significant loss-of-production event, commodity-price decline or sale of the producing reserves. For the lender, if market conditions rapidly deteriorate or the borrower's cash flow is severely diminished for one or more other reasons, its wild card is a ripcord, accelerating discussions on how to resolve what is becoming or may have already become an upside-down loan.

This flexibility in favor of the lender was the basis for Standard & Poor's criticism of the reserve-based loan—sometimes referred to as an RBL—versus more-standard asset-based credit facilities in which the formulae for available credit are more predictable. In 2012, the ratings service reported:

> We believe the volatile nature of oil and natural gas prices combined with RBL lenders' unilateral discretion to change the assumptions that go into a compa-

ny's reserves valuation can limit a borrower's ability to access those funds, especially during a period of stress. As a result, we view RBL facilities as a weaker form of liquidity [for the producer] than traditional asset-based lending facilities. We also believe that companies' overreliance on these facilities creates a vulnerability, particularly for companies whose creditworthiness is already weak.[512]

However, knowing the downward spiral a sudden borrowing-base reduction would create for the producer's operations, banks have rarely triggered this—even when commodity prices dropped precipitously in 1985, 1998, 2008 and 2014.[513] This is rather surprising, given the thousands of oil and gas loans and more than 100 oil and gas company bankruptcies during this timeframe. Of course, banks recognize that precipitating a rapid reduction in the borrowing base, thereby triggering the mandatory amortization of a borrower's loan, may do more to harm the banks' ultimate recovery of a non-performing loan.

While the concerns expressed by S&P's analysis has not been observed in dramatic, mid-term, borrowing-base reductions, the power of the bank to be able to exercise such a right still has an effect upon over-stretched producers. Even as oil prices were nearly halved at the end of 2014 from a June 2014 high, few banks, if any, triggered an interim redetermination.

This did not, however, stop lenders in 2015 and into 2016 from previewing for borrowers what the redetermination season would likely bring, as prices failed to recover. This early warning signal from the banks can give producers time to get their financial house in order—usually, if available, by selling public or private equity or debt securities or reducing the principal with cash on hand.

---

[512] David A. Kaplan, "Unique Feature in Oil and Gas Reserve-Based Lending Facilities Can Increase Companies' Default Risk," *Standard & Poor's Ratings Services,* May 1, 2012, 7.
[513] Rich Gans, Senior Vice President, Wells Fargo Bank, interview by the author, November 1, 2013.

Chapter 5: Lending Into the 1970s

On the other side of the coin, a borrower wants a wild card for the opposite reason. In the event the borrower's production significantly increases as a result of drilling or buying producing reserves, the borrower can expedite an increase in the availability under its borrowing base, usually to fund the acquisition or the capex needed to further drill.

Other modifications that have been added to borrowing-base provisions are automatic triggers for redetermination when a certain threshold of the borrower's collateral is sold—typically the sale of properties exceeding 5% of the reserves calculation—and monetization of forward hedges. Additional modifications include the borrower's ability to elect a lower borrowing base than its collateral's value permits.

Another option allows the borrower to reduce the borrowing base at the time of a redetermination. Under most credit agreements, a borrower pays to maintain a revolving credit facility for the undrawn amount—the "commitment fee." To the extent a borrowing base exceeds the borrower's projected capital needs for the next six months, the borrower might elect a lower borrowing base to spare the expense of the unused fee.

The earliest recommendations by bank counsel in presentations from the 1970s, when borrowing-base revolvers were introduced, were that the lender should retain wide latitude in determining the borrowing base. While most credit agreements during the past 35 years have generally followed this advice, some borrowers have negotiated limitations on the lender's "sole discretion" from time to time.

One seemingly innocuous, but common, modification provides that the lender's determination, albeit in the lender's sole discretion, "shall be based upon the value of the borrower's engineered proved reserves in accordance with the lender's customary internal standards and practices for valuing and redetermining the value of oil and gas properties in connection with reserve-based oil and gas loan transactions."

While it is the practice of most, if not all, energy lenders to be consistent in its determinations, it could prove problematic in the event of a dispute with a disgruntled borrower over its redetermination. A discovery request by the borrower's trial attorney may ask for all of the bank's documents concerning how the number was derived—including internal policies and procedures as applied to all loans and all clients.

A similar embellishment is sometimes added that a determination shall be "consistent with such standards as applied to similarly situated borrowers." Again, anything short of "sole and absolute discretion" is an opportunity for a borrower's counsel to get its nose under the tent and peek into the bank's black box for calculating the base.[514] Of course, bank's counsel would have a substantial argument that, given the many variables included in the calculation of any one borrower's base, such a blanket search of all the bank's loans would be an exercise in futility.

The subjective and unchallengeable "sole discretion" standard, when modified by the objective standard of the lender's "customary standards and practices," can give rise to differences of interpretation by the lender and borrower—or, in litigation, by a jury. This issue is most likely to arise during a precipitous fall in commodity prices when a borrower is faced with a deficiency and its back to the wall. In this case, a borrower may choose to contest the redetermination in court, putting default at bay, especially if it sees no means of remedying the deficit in the time required by the agreement.[515]

---

[514] This demand for production of documents was filed by a borrower contesting the bank's methodology for calculation of its borrowing base. The plaintiff asked for "Documents sufficient to identify your customary practices and standards, as they pertain to Borrowing Base determinations and as in effect at the time of each Borrowing Base Determination you made, for Similar Loans," and the bank was ordered by the court to produce original credit memoranda, as approved by the bank's energy credit committee, for such borrowers. *The Pfanenstiel Company, LLC v. Independent Bank*, Cause No. DC-16-00601, District Court Dallas County, Texas. Order March 10, 2016.

[515] In January, 2016, following the drop in oil prices, a lawsuit was filed against a bank for alleged failure to properly calculate the borrowing base. *The Pfanenstiel Company, LLC v. Independent Bank*, Cause No. DC-16-00601, District Court Dallas County, Texas, filed January 20, 2016.

But where the determination is in "the lender's sole and absolute discretion," without reference to any stated standards, the success of a borrower's attack on the lender's determination may hinge on which state's laws govern the loan. A borrower in Texas will have little basis to seek judicial relief. This can be the case even if the borrower can prove the lender acted outside of its "customary standards and practices."

Moreover, in Texas, at least, the lender's discretion is not constrained by any court-imposed subjective standard that it be in "good faith." There is no implied duty of good faith among parties to a commercial contract absent a "special relationship" between the parties. Credit agreements between sophisticated lenders and oil and gas producers do not create a "special relationship."[516] Under Texas law, a redetermination by a lender having "sole discretion" is unlikely to be found wrongful, so long as the lender complies with the express terms of the credit agreement.

Despite this, many lenders—especially those participating in syndicated oil and gas loans—prefer to select New York law as governing the obligations of the parties. The preference for New York law is for the ease of syndicating large, commercial loans by money-center banks, which tend to be headquartered—and their in-house counsel licensed—in New York. Under New York law, the duty of good faith is much broader than in Texas. In some instances, the duty may even be violated where the lender has complied with the letter of the contract.

This was illustrated by the 2003 holding of a New York court in a commercial dispute where the court stated, "Even where one has an apparently unlimited right under a contract, that right may not be exercised solely for personal gain in such a way as to deprive the other party of the fruits of the contract. This limitation on an apparently unfettered contract right may be grounded … on the purely contractual rule that even an explicitly discretionary contract right may not be

---

[516] *Victoria Bank & Trust Co. v. Brady*, 779 S.W.2d 893, 902 (Tex. App.-Corpus Christi 1989), rev'd on other grounds, 811 S.W. 2d 931.

exercised in bad faith so as to frustrate the other party's right to benefit under the agreement."[517]

In another case, involving a dispute between a Colorado-based producer and a New York bank over an oil and gas, reserve-base loan, the borrower brought a securities claim against the lender based on what the borrower asserted was "the false pretense that the Borrowing Base would be determined in good faith." The loan agreement provided the base would be determined "in the lender's discretion" and further that "it is expressly understood that Lender has no obligation to designate the Borrowing Base at any particular amount."[518]

Notwithstanding the explicit discretion reserved by the bank, the New York court held that, "although the Credit Agreement explicitly permits Midland [Bank] to determine the Borrowing Base upon values assigned to Mallon [Resources]' assets 'in its discretion,' Mallon's allegations that its business was successful and that its reserves had substantially increased … are sufficient allegations, for the purposes of this motion, that Midland may have assigned values to Mallon's assets not in its discretion but in bad faith."[519]

The trial court refused the bank's summary-judgment motion to dismiss the borrower's claim prior to trial on the merits.[520]

---

[517] *Richbell Information Services, Inc. v. Jupiter Partners, L.P.*, 309 A.D.2d 288, 302, 765 N.Y.S.2d 575, 587 (Sup. Ct., App. Div. 2003) (majority shareholder exercised express contractual rights to the detriment of the minority shareholder).

[518] The Credit Agreement provided: "Lender shall determine the amount of the Borrowing Base based upon the loan collateral value which it in its discretion assigns to the various items of Collateral at the time in question and based upon such other credit factors (including without limitation the assets, liabilities, cash flow, business, properties, prospects, management and ownership of each Borrower and its Affiliates) as Lender in its discretion deems significant. It is expressly understood that Lender has no obligation to designate the Borrowing Base at any particular amount, whether in relation to the Maximum Loan Amount or otherwise." Credit Agreement, Mallon Resources Corp., Mallon Oil Co. and Midland Bank Plc, New York Branch, August 24, 1995, p. 15, filed Mallon Resources Corp. 8-K for June 15, 1995, Ex. 1.

[519] *Mallon Resources Corp. v. Midland Bank, PLC, New York Branch*, 1997 WL 403450 (S.D.N.Y. 1997).

[520] Denial of a summary judgment motion to dismiss is not a finding that the borrower's allegations are correct. It only means that the plaintiff has alleged sufficient issues of fact, which the court will consider prior to determining the merits of the plaintiff's claims.

Bank Price Decks

Following effective implementation of proration rules by the latter part of the 1930s, early reserve-based underwriting used the field's posted price the borrower was receiving for his production at the time without provision for a future price increase. "The appraiser, in reducing his estimated barrels of future reserves to dollars must adopt a unit per barrel price, which is usually the current price at the time the appraisal is made," Tulsa-based banker Russell Hunt wrote in 1953.[521]

Given that these loans were made on current production and that, typically, the wells were located in the same field, it was logical to use the posted price against a two- to four-year maturity. But prices were subject to fluctuation and the banker had to consider the possibility of a decline even during a few years. Hunt noted, "A repayment schedule must consider 4 or 5 years during which period prices could be subject to material changes.

"If, for example, the present price of the oil from a certain lease is $2.50 per barrel after excise taxes, and the appraiser's estimate of the further operating costs is an average of 60 cents per barrel, the net figure is $1.90 per barrel, but if the price should decline 50 cents per barrel to $2.00, or a decline of 20 percent, and the operating cost figure of 60 cents be deducted, the net return is reduced to $1.40 per barrel, or a decline of 30 percent … ."[522]

Impact on Other Loan Provisions

The borrowing-base loan served to reduce, somewhat, the due-diligence role of the bank's lawyer. After the demise of the large ABC transactions, in which warranties of title were not given by sellers of properties, attorney Richard Brennan observed that, "under certain circumstances, principally where costs would be prohibitive or time considerations are paramount, bank lenders might be willing to make loans solely or in part in reliance on title warranties, without seeking independent title assurances.

---

[521] Hunt, "A Banker's Viewpoint on …," 20.
[522] Hunt, "A Banker's Viewpoint on …," 21.

"Nonetheless, title opinions are required by lenders in most reserve oriented financing transactions, and in any such transaction involving a group of bankers or sizable loans the advice and guidance of local counsel continues to be crucial."[523]

An explanation for this lower due-diligence threshold may have been the recognition of a changing balance of power between the lender and the borrower. With a table-funded term production loan, the borrower—effectively, if not literally—walked out of the bank with all the money he was ever going to get under the loan. He wasn't going back to the bank for any more money—at least, not until the term loan was about to mature. From the banker's perspective, there is more incentive for the borrower to promptly and fully comply with covenants, such as providing additional collateral or evidence of title, on an ongoing basis, if that borrower needed continued access to the bank's credit under a revolver.

Additionally, as the borrowing-base structure continued to evolve, provisions were added into the loan agreement. These assured that the lender, at any time it determined the borrower did not have "acceptable title" to its oil and gas properties, could reduce the borrowing base by an amount attributable to the title-defective property. This power reduces, but by no means obviates, the necessity for complete title due diligence prior to closing.

The Role of the Internet

Digital access to public information, real-property records and other technological inventions have also drastically changed how energy lending and borrowing are done. Joe Bridges recalled his efforts at introducing technology to his employer, Humble Oil & Refining Co., in the late 1960s: "I managed to get approval of the purchase of the

---

[523] Brennan, "Current Trends in Oil and Gas Financing," 16-19; *see also*, Fuller, author's interview. As an example from a 1980 credit agreement, a condition precedent to funding included "The Title Opinion of Colorado counsel satisfactory to Bank, … including the opinion that the Bank Liens are first and prior liens and that there are no other superior or equal Liens against any of the Mortgaged Property except Permitted Liens."

first Wang, suitcase-sized calculator with four remote terminals to allow calculations using exponentials and logarithms.

"In 1968, I would travel to the Production Research Center across Houston to use their computer at night for reservoir calculations for the Katy Gas Field. In 1971, I purchased First City National Bank's first HP-35 handheld calculator to use for evaluating oil and gas properties that secured the bank's loans. These instances were each like the dawn of a new age."[524]

Petroleum engineer E.W. Schafer, a Bank of New York officer, reported to the Society of Petroleum Evaluation Engineers in 1970 the concept of using digital technology in connection with computing the value of a company's reserves. In his presentation, he encouraged fellow reservoir engineers to finagle time-sharing access to their banks' computer to process data.[525] He said, "Newer terminals are now able to receive data at 30 characters per second, which is three times the speed of the teletype terminals. ... This terminal weighs about 27 pounds and is completely portable; all you need is a telephone and you are in business."[526]

Joe Vilardo, an energy-finance attorney who began his career as a reservoir engineer for American National Pipeline Co. and was, later, a banker with Continental Illinois, recalled calculating reserves on a desk calculator in the late '70s.[527] Tim Murray, an engineer with Atlantic Richfield Co. prior to his career as an energy banker, said, "While a major oil company could afford to invest in expensive mainframe computers, most bank engineers were still using hand-held calculators and Big Chief tablets. It wasn't until 1984-85 that engineers could ac-

---

[524] Bridges, author's interview.
[525] E.W. Schafer (Assistant Vice President and Petroleum Engineer, Bank of New York, New York), "Computer Time-Sharing and the Petroleum Evaluation Engineer," 3 *Journal Of the Society Of Petroleum Evaluation Engineers* (January 1970), 26.
[526] Schafer, "Computer Time-Sharing and the Petroleum Evaluation Engineer," 26.
[527] Joe Vilardo, Partner, Haynes and Boone LLP, and former reservoir engineer, ANR Pipeline Co., 1976-1980, and Continental Illinois Bank, 1980-1989, interview by the author, March 1, 2016.

cess remote computers through GE phone modems and access IBM XT computers with floppy-disk capability."[528]

Also, advances in computing technologies in the 1980s and '90s added a new tool in how geologists explored for oil and gas by being able to process and analyze 3-D seismic images of Earth's subsurface. In the mid-1960s, when 3-D technology was being developed, the ability to process huge amounts of seismic data required investment in room-sized mainframe computer systems at a staggering cost.[529] With continued technological advances, the cost of processing the raw data from the field had decreased by up to tenfold between 1983 and 2007.[530]

Schafer's remarks in 1970 were prescient. He cited attempts by certain computer companies and others to establish nationwide communications systems, including computer instructions being sent via satellite, and proposed the creation of "virtual data rooms." He said, "Why would it not be feasible for a group of companies to go together and prepare data banks of lease production history, well histories including logs, pressure history, etc. This information stored in one location would be instantly available at each remote terminal to be typed out or displayed on a CRT device."[531]

It was not just the processing of engineering data that was slow; the work of the lawyers' word-processing before computers was done by typewriter. Exchanging drafts of and negotiating an oil loan was time-consuming. To prepare just a transmittal letter, it would take even the most efficient lawyer a few hours to handwrite or dictate the letter, get the initial draft typed, review it and, as necessary, further mark it up. A secretary would retype the letter, assemble the enclosures, address the envelopes and have a runner deliver the package across town or, if opposing counsel were out of town, send the documents via air mail through the U.S. Postal Service.

---

[528] Tim Murray, Benefit Street Partners LLC, interview by the author, March 28, 2015.

[529] Olien and Hinton, *Wildcatters*, xx.

[530] Olien and Hinton, *Wildcatters*, xix.

[531] Schafer, "Computer Time-Sharing and the Petroleum Evaluation Engineer," 28.

Chapter 5: Lending Into the 1970s

Even if the drafts were ready to send to opposing counsel early in the day, odds were that it would take at least a day or more to reach their destination. And, if the client needed to review drafts prior to sending them to opposing counsel, the process could take a week or more.

In the 1940s through the 1960s, the protocol for closings was to have original counterparts of all documents for each party and its counsel—plus multiple mortgage counterparts executed for filing in each county—in the bank's offices for banker and borrower to sign in front of their lawyers and a public notary. Although the loan documents back then were shorter in length, each was typed, with up to four carbon sheets, requiring a secretary to, literally, pound away on the manual typewriter so each copy would be legible.[532]

Down in the secretarial pool, alongside the stack of sheets of onion paper, yellow draft paper, carbon paper, bottles of Liquid Paper (invented by a Dallas bank secretary) and ubiquitous, overflowing ashtrays, multiple typists would work on all nature of legal documents.[533] A young law associate responsible for having a loan agreement or mortgage typed went down to the pool, took a number and got in line.

Young lawyers and paralegals were not spared tedium beyond the logistics of working with the typing pool. At larger law firms, in addition to typing pools, were teams of young college-age proofreaders (modern day "spell-check") and first-year law associates with wavy-edged "red-lining" rulers and red ink pens, manually red-lining changes on hard-copy drafts (modern day "track changes").

---

[532] IBM invented the Selectric, an electric typewriter that was further improved upon in the 1970s with magnetic memory cards (mag-cards), each capable of storing up to 5,000 characters per card (about the number of words on one single-spaced, typewritten page) that quickly became standard law-office equipment.

[533] Author's description of Butler, Binion, Rice, Cook and Knapp typing pool on the 10th floor of the Mille Esperson Building circa 1982. The heaven-sent, magical, error-fixer that became branded as Liquid Paper was invented in 1951 by Bettie Nesmith, a secretary at Texas Bank and Trust in Dallas, in her kitchen to correct typing mistakes by painting over them with white tempera paint. The income from her invention allowed her to retire from her secretarial career and allowed her son, Michael, to pursue a musical career, including a role in the 1966-68 television show, "The Monkees."

Before law firms had websites and e-mail, they had cable and tel-ecopier addresses. Telecopiers still in use in the 1960s and '70s were replaced with facsimile machines that were added to the law firm's standard equipment by the mid-'70s. These machines were the size of a small oven and, initially, because of their cost, were limited to one or two per firm, manned by the mailroom clerk. Anyone wanting to send a document by fax transmission was required to fill out a cover sheet, clip it to the top of the document and place it in the queue with all other out-going faxes.

Each fax was hand-loaded one page at a time on the drum; an-other machine printed in-coming faxes from other law firms. While this means of rapid document exchange was a boost in office efficien-cy, care had to be taken with early faxes that were printed on thermal paper. Any coffee spilled on a stack of faxed documents would im-mediately and permanently bind them together, rendering all but the first page inaccessible. And, even if encountering no calamity, once placed in the law firm's files, the sheets quickly faded and became brit-tle after one or two years, disintegrating if touched by hand.

Bankers also had their own horror stories of trying to work re-motely with the exchange of loan documents with their lawyers. Joe Bridges recalled:

> In the mid- to late '80s, I traveled with my own fax machine in an aluminum Halliburton suitcase because hotels did not routinely have fax machines and, in any event, they were not secure enough for sensitive transactions. Before this, in 1985, while on spring break with my family in Maui, five hours removed from New York, I did not yet own my own fax ma-chine. The lawyers, at about 8 p.m. Hawaii time, would fax loan documents and purchase agreements to the Honolulu office of Bowne Printers, which would then put it on the shuttle from Honolulu to Maui, where I would pick the documents up at about 10 p.m. after dinner. I would mark up the documents with my comments and, at about 2 a.m. (7 a.m. in

New York), call in my comments. We repeated this
cycle every day the week of spring break and, on my
return to Houston, we closed the purchase of Sunny
South Oil & Gas, together with the loan that funded
the purchase. The next day, I bought my own fax machine and the Halliburton suitcase.[534, 535]

As for document delivery, the introduction of Federal Express in
the early 1970s and its rapid adoption was a mixed blessing to lawyers
who were trying to close oil and gas loans. The exchange of drafts was
sped up to out-of-town destinations, but, often, they were not ready
by FedEx's late-afternoon deadline as a result of typing, correcting,
retyping and collating copies.

This required eager young associates to know how to get packages to the city's last-deadline FedEx office downtown or, failing this, to
the FedEx terminal at the airport before midnight. The early career of
many finance attorneys at the time was more often an exercise in logistics, document distribution and information management than the
practice of law.

Following public access to the World Wide Web beginning in
1991,[536] much of the old way of loan negotiation and document distribution was radically changed and sped up. Telephonic and electric
communication obviated the need for in-person negotiations.[537] Initially, e-mail was used to exchange drafts among lawyers and, as other

---

[534] Bridges, author's interview.

[535] Oilfield-service pioneer Erle Halliburton commissioned the manufacture of aluminum
cases in 1938 for protecting his garments and documents in the field. The luggage division was purchased by Zero Corp. in 1952. The brand continues to carry the Halliburton
name. Zerohalliburton.com.

[536] Martin Bryant, "20 years ago today, the World Wide Web opened to the public,"
TNW, August 6, 2011. Accessed May 1, 2016, Thenextweb.com.

[537] Setting up a conference call as late as the 1990s required a day's advance notice to
make a reservation with the AT&T conference operator, who would call each participant
at an appointed time the following day to initiate the call. Curiously, no one at the time
seemed concerned that Ma Bell was listening in on client-confidential conference calls.
Simpler times.

industries adopted e-correspondence, drafts were sent simultaneously to bankers' and borrowers' desktop computers as well.[538]

With the easy exchange of electronic copies, the expense of word processing was significantly reduced by the ability to "cut and paste" without need of scissors, tape and a Xerox machine. Photo-copying had greatly facilitated the preparation of mortgage-property descriptions by allowing landmen and lawyers to copy recorded assignments or prior mortgages to attach to execution counterparts for the closing.

But multiple iterations of copied property descriptions became the bane of county recorders in most producing states. Often, they could no longer read the original, typed lease information that had been recorded, copied, cut and pasted and re-recorded with extraneous page numbers and information in the margins. Electronic manipulation of Word files, containing an inventory of the producer's oil and gas properties, that were printed to a hard copy produced a much more legible product for county clerks to index.

Not only was the preparation of lengthy mortgage-property descriptions made easier by e-distribution; more importantly, it greatly accelerated the evolution of loan documents. For lawyers, the facility and immediacy of computer-drafting meant no loan document was too long—thus, no covenant was too unimportant to not include in a credit agreement.

The 25-page loan agreements of the 1970s ballooned into 100-plus-page documents by the early 2000s. And the ability of lawyers to adopt—i.e., crib—language and provisions in similar documents from other law firms' and lenders' documentation in whole cloth from the Internet was a temptation too great to resist. Because many of the larger, credit facilities were syndicated, most syndicated credit agreements had coalesced into a "market form."

Borrowers and their counsel also gained quick insight via copies of other banks' loan agreements—and even their own bank's agree-

---

[538] The day of lawyer-to-lawyer-only professional-communication courtesy is a vestige, slain by the age of mass e-mail communication in which bankers and producers are copied on all correspondence.

ments with other customers. Pre-Internet, this would have taken months or years to extract from public domain; today, it is instantaneous.

This quick access to changes in documentation inured to the borrower's benefit at the bargaining table. Borrowers, no matter how small, wanted the loan provisions they had seen the bank give its larger customers, which had been able to negotiate special exceptions.

Through the 1990s, closings were still held in person, typically at the bank lawyer's office with final loan documents signed and exchanged at the closing table. Over time, this formality has succumbed to the convenience of remote closings whereby signed documents were exchanged via fax and, later, scanned and e-mailed as an attachment, followed by overnight delivery of the originals. More recently, signatures may be attached to PDFs and, possibly, the documents never printed by any party—lender, attorney, opposing attorney or borrower. Recently, a millennial-age law associate expedited a closing by using a photograph of the signature page from the banker's iPhone to serve as evidence of the lender's consent.

The formality of in-person negotiation and closings for the most part has gone the way of the archaic English "livery of seisen" ceremony.[539] Even prior to e-mail, in-person negotiations were seen as an unnecessary expense and delay when drafts could be negotiated via exchange by fax and execution counterparts delivered by FedEx, obviating the need for the borrower's executives to fly to the bank's offices to sign the loan documents. E-mail has just made the process much more convenient and instantaneous and the documents more lasting than those printed on thermal paper.

---

[539] Prior to 1536, under early English common law, a transfer of real property was conducted by a formal ceremony called "livery of seisin" between the grantor and the grantee and witnesses—typically the youngest members of the serfs or tenants who worked the land. The grantor would hand the grantee a twig or clump of soil from the land symbolizing the transfer of property. Whereupon, the youngest witnesses were sharply beaten in order to ensure that they would remember the ceremony. Leslie Kiefer Amann, "A Survey of Transfer and Ownership Law for Trustees," Texas Bankers Association Wealth Management and Trust Division, Graduate Trust School, July 18, 2007, 9, Naepc.org/journal.

With the advent of e-mail, many states adopted and, in 2000, Congress enacted a law that made the use of e-signatures as good as their paper equivalents.[540] This has further reduced the necessity of "in office" closings.

Some banks still require possession of a signed original prior to funding. However, many of the larger, syndicated, energy loans governed by New York law collect separately signed promissory notes only for such banks that request an original, viewing the loan agreement itself as sufficient evidence of the loan. This can greatly facilitate administration of loans in which there may be as many as 30 or more participating banks—and avoids the necessity of drafting a "lost-note affidavit" at loan payoff in the event any of the banks is unable to locate its original promissory note.[541]

---

[540] *Electronic Signatures in Global and National Commerce Act*, Pub.L. 106-299, 114 Stat. 464, 15 U.S.C. ch. 96 (enacted June 30, 2000). Texas adopted a similar statute in 2007. *Uniform Electronic Transactions Act*, Tex.Bus.Comm.Code Title 10, Subtitle B, Chapter 322, Section 322.007.

[541] Upon payment in full of a promissory note, the best practice is to return the original note to the maker with the note marked "Cancelled. Paid in Full." This practice originally arose where promissory notes were "negotiable instruments" that evidenced the maker's absolute obligation to pay to the holder of the note the obligation evidenced by the note. As previously discussed, most notes today would fail to constitute a "negotiable instrument" and, therefore, would not constitute prima facie evidence of the maker's obligation to pay the holder of the note if the original note were to fall into the hands of some third party. Nevertheless, once a borrower has paid his obligations in full, he is entitled to and should expect (and his new lender will typically require) that his original lender return his original note. More often than should be the case, the bank is unable to find the borrower's original note and the bank's counsel will be called upon to prepare an "Affidavit of Lost Note" reciting that, upon due investigation, the bank has been unable to locate the original note and that, if and when the original note is ever located, the bank will mark the original note "Paid in Full" and return the note to the borrower.

CHAPTER 6

1980s: The Decade of Destruction

"I think we'd better get ready for the biggest Texas tornado we've ever seen, because it's going to tear this state apart."
Gene Gray

From 1958 to 1970, prices for oil and natural gas were relatively stable. Oil hovered around $3 a barrel; interstate gas prices were regulated by the Federal Power Commission under the Natural Gas Act of 1938, thus the price showed little change during these years.[542]

In retrospect, the seeds were being sown for an upheaval in world energy markets. The balance of power to set oil prices was changing. The Organization of the Petroleum Exporting Countries was formed in September 1960[543] with five members—Iran, Iraq, Kuwait, Saudi Arabia and Venezuela—and accounted for more than 80% of the world's oil exports. The structure of OPEC was based upon that of the Texas Railroad Commission, which Venezuela's oil minister, Juan Pablo Pérez Alfonzo, studied while in exile in the U.S. in the 1950s.

---

[542] The U.S. natural gas wellhead price in 1958 was 12 cents an Mcf and rose to only 17 cents by 1970. U.S. EIA, Independent Statistics & Analysis. "U.S. Natural Gas Wellhead Price." Accessed March 6, 2016. Eia.gov.
[543] "Brief History," Organization of the Petroleum Exporting Countries, accessed May 1, 2016, Opec.org.

OPEC's formation had been precipitated by Standard Oil of New Jersey's announcement of a 7% reduction in its posted price for Middle Eastern crudes. Alfonzo, who had been lobbying with the major Middle Eastern oil producers to form a cartel, knew this would be the straw to break the camel's back, resulting in the formation of the international kind of Railroad Commission he had been promoting.

Initial reaction by the major oil companies was to pretend OPEC did not exist. "'We attached little importance to it,' said Howard Page of Standard Oil, 'because we believed it would not work,'" Daniel Yergin wrote in *The Prize*.[544]

The inability of exporting countries to control oil prices appeared to be confirmed in the short term when Egypt and Jordan invaded Israel in 1967 in what became known as the Six Day War. Arab states, in support of Egypt and Jordan, called for an oil embargo against countries friendly to Israel, particularly the U.S. and U.K.[545]

The call had little palpable impact, however. In 1967, the U.S. and other producing countries had spare capacity to make up for the loss from the Middle Eastern states. In the U.S., in response to the embargo, the Railroad Commission lifted proration restrictions and, with corresponding action by other producing states, U.S. daily output surged by almost 1 million barrels.[546] In addition, Venezuela and Iran did not cease exports.

The immediate needs of the market were met and the "Arab oil weapon" was discredited.[547] But the anemic response of Texas' more mature wells to produce in excess of their allowables raised doubts about U.S. producers' ability to answer future Middle Eastern crises.

The Rise of OPEC

The tide turned in the 1970s. The sun set on the Texas Railroad Commission's influence on global oil prices as it was exposed in a

---

[544] Yergin, *The Prize*, 494, 502, 504 and 523.
[545] Saudi Arabia, Kuwait, Iraq, Libya and Algeria banned shipments of oil to the U.S., Britain and, to a lesser degree, West Germany. Yergin, *The Prize*, 537.
[546] Yergin, *The Prize*, 539.
[547] Yergin, *The Prize*, 556-67.

1971 test by the commission that was to demonstrate the state's capacity to produce 2 million extra barrels a day. The test failed, revealing that the state's reserve capacity was only 10% of that amount.[548]

The following year, proration was set at 100%; wells could flow unrestricted for the first time since proration.[549] But daily production grew by only a few thousand barrels. An independent producer said, "It was a desolate truth to be proved right on this—in that we had to admit in the United States that we were suddenly beholden to foreign sources for oil that we had resisted so hard, so futilely for so many years."[550]

The power to control oil prices shifted from Texas, Oklahoma and Louisiana to OPEC; there was no more meaningful spare capacity in the U.S.[551] In addition, six other nations had joined OPEC: Qatar, Indonesia, Libya, the United Arab Emirates, Algeria and Nigeria. The next time Syria and Egypt invaded Israel, which was in October of 1973, OPEC again called for cuts in exports and an embargo against nations supporting Israel.

Overall, OPEC daily exports were curtailed by 4.4 million barrels—about 14% of internationally traded oil. The price of Iranian oil increased more than 300% in a two-month period from $5.40 per barrel in October to $17 in December.[552] Through the decade, culminating with the Iranian Revolution and the disruption of its exports, further price increases were sustained by a real or perceived shortage of U.S. supply.

In the midst of a shortage of imported supply and despite higher oil prices, U.S. production declined from a peak of 9.64 million barrels

---

[548] "Back in 1969, the district chief engineer and I, at Humble Oil & Refining's office in Rosenberg, Texas, plotted the production response as producing days for prorated wells were increased from eight days to full production. The production curve flattened out and became virtually horizontal by the time we hit 20 days. So much for full production." Bridges, author's interview.

[549] Prindle, *Petroleum Politics*, 96.

[550] Texas State Library and Archives Commission, "Introduction," modified August 17, 2011, accessed January 20, 2015, Tsl.texas.gov.

[551] Yergin, *The Prize*, 596; James L. Williams, WTRG Economics, "Oil Price History and Analysis," Wtrg.com, accessed March 16, 2016.

[552] Yergin, *The Prize*, 596-97.

a day in 1970 to 8.6 million in 1980.[553] Oil prices began to recede after 1980 from more than $40 a barrel, but this was not conceded to be fact until 1986, when the price reached a low of $10 and remained, on average, between $15 and $25 until the end of 1999.[554]

The 1980s proved to be a tumultuous time for U.S. oil and gas producers—and their lenders.

Changes in U.S. Bank Regulation and Environmental Laws

In addition to global changes in energy supply, energy bankers were watching changes in banking regulation that would alter the landscape of energy loans. It was reported in 1982 that, of the nearly 15,000 commercial banks in the U.S., approximately 300 were making some type of energy loans and nearly 100 had extensive energy departments.[555]

Historically, energy loans to independents were originated by banks located in the oil patch. First City National and Texas Commerce Bank in Houston and First National and Republic National in Dallas were recognized as the leading Texas energy banks.[556]

Major oil companies, publically traded with investment-grade ratings, typically had direct banking relationships with the money-center banks in New York. Since the 1940s, the New York banks had technical staffs to evaluate the majors' oil properties and to finance the ABC acquisition loans. They did not go "down market"—that is, making smaller, direct, secured loans to independents until the 1970s.

---

[553] U.S. EIA, Independent Statistics & Analysis. "U.S. Field production of Crude Oil." Accessed March 6, 2016. Eia.gov.

[554] U.S. EIA, Independent Statistics & Analysis. "Cushing, OK Crude Oil Future Contract 1." Accessed March 6, 2016. Eia.gov.

[555] Christian, "Introduction to Commercial Bank and Non-Bank Institutional Financing," Section 2.2.

[556] Leavenworth, "Big Texas Banks Vie for Energy Loans," published the results of a 1979 informal telephone poll of the top energy-company CFOs, including integrated and independent oil companies, voting for the best Texas energy bank in the following order: First City National (Houston) and Republic National (Dallas) each with 26.5%; First National (Dallas), 16%; Texas Commerce, 10.5%, Bank of the Southwest, 9.5%, First National (Midland) and Fort Worth National (Fort Worth), each 5.5%.

Of course, some of the independent producers were just as happy to stay with their local lenders that bankrolled their first grubstakes. No better example is the relationship between H.L. Hunt and First National Bank in Dallas. In the 1930s, First National's president, Nathan Adams, made Hunt a $50,000 unsecured loan to purchase Dad Joiner's Daisy Bradford discovery well and surrounding leasehold in East Texas.[557] That loan and First National's confidence in Hunt bought the bank a very lucrative and long-lasting relationship that many a New York banker found impregnable.

Frank Dartez started his banking career with Citibank in New York in the 1960s and recalled making numerous calls on representatives of the various Hunt entities, including Placid Oil. "H.L. Hunt had a large, extended family—both legitimate and illegitimate—and most were involved in the energy business in some way," Dartez said. "This resulted in numerous, significant bank accounts, all of which were at First National. By the 1960s, several Hunt entities had been very successful, particularly Placid Oil, Hunt International and Penrod Drilling, one of the largest drilling companies in the country, all jointly owned by three of Hunt's sons—Herbert, Lamar and Nelson Bunker."

This immense wealth attracted the attention of the money-center banks in New York and Chicago. "In the 1960s, branch banking was still not legal in Texas and the Texas banks were dwarfed in size by the money-center banks. Some said the Hunt relationship accounted for about two thirds of First National's portfolio. Still, with its relatively low legal limit, First National was able to control both the credit and deposit relationships with the Hunts, probably with passive participations to other friendly banks who promised not to contact their customer.

"At Citibank, we called on their key lieutenants frequently in hopes of developing a relationship with the Hunt brothers. We would also make a courtesy call on the bank in Dallas; it had a large energy department. When we called on the bank, they knew all about our call

---

[557] Burrough, *The Big Rich*, 75-81.

on the Hunts and suggested that we might want to go through them before making any further calls.

"Finally, in about 1970, the financial needs of the Hunts exceeded what First National could do. After all of our efforts, we were shocked to learn that Penrod Drilling had set up a major credit facility with First National Bank of Chicago after the senior management of FNB Chicago hosted a lavish dinner for the Hunt brothers. One of the cardinal rules of business development was to call on the person who could make a decision and we had not done that—because we could not get access to the brothers. It was a bitter lesson."[558]

By the end of the 1970s, many local banks were in the business of making energy loans to the smaller independent producers. The state's fifth-largest bank, Mercantile National of Dallas, re-entered the field of energy lending in 1976, hiring Jim Hamilton to head the new department. He was quoted in a 1979 *Texas Business* article: "Mercantile was active in oil financing in the 1930's and '40's, but when foreign crude made domestic oil operations marginal years later, the bank made the decision to not be aggressive in oil financing. By the '70's, it was clear that Mercantile had missed an opportunity."[559]

A number of other local banks actively making loans to producers included Bank of the Southwest, Allied Bank of Texas, First National Bank of Midland, Frost Bank and others. During the 1960s and early 1970s, many of the money-center banks relied on oil-patch banks to originate direct relationships with smaller producers and would lend as an "over-line" participant. But, by the mid '70s at least, Continental Illinois was directly marketing in the Texas and Oklahoma energy banks' backyard and, in 1974, opened a loan-production office in Houston.

However, the New York bankers who stayed in their headquarters were able to leverage their "passive participation" role to key lender and sometimes become the primary lender. Byron Cooley said of the beginning of his banking career with Continental Illinois in

---

[558] Dartez, author's interview.
[559] Leavenworth, "Big Texas Banks Vie for Energy Loans."

1976, "From the mid-1970s, the larger New York banks and Continental Illinois were focused on agenting Texas deals and not simply take overlines from Texas banks.

"Yes, they still did take participations from Texas banks (mainly from lesser banks when they saw an opportunity to work into the agent role), but their main objective was to displace Texas banks on large relationships, where they had a lot of success. My recollection was that Texas banks were fine as long as a borrower's need fit into their 'box.' Over the years, the fit became not so good.

"Continental and New York banks were more imaginative. They were willing to design financing packages to better fit borrower's needs—and, as a result, landed many large relationships. Did we go dangerously out on the risk curve? I don't think so. Being innovative and approaching loans from a different perspective than before? Yes. But assuming undue risk? No."[560]

Ben Love, formerly the chairman of Texas Commerce Bank, wrote in 2005 of his bank's loan to Big Three Industries Inc., an oil-field-service company whose chairman was a member of the bank's board. When the company's financing needs exceeded Texas Commerce's loan limit in 1968, Chase Manhattan was brought in as a participant to provide the "over-line credit."

Within months Big Three needed to finance a loan in Europe. Love called Harold Young, his contact at Chase Manhattan, for assistance and was unpleasantly surprised. Love wrote:

> He would *let us* participate? Big Three was *our* loyal customer! Worse yet, Harold called back in a few days and said it would be best if Chase took over as Big Three's primary bank because the company was expanding far beyond our loan limit and overall capabilities. Well, that was like being punched in the nose by an ostensible ally.
>
> However, it clearly exemplified the problem of our lacking the lending capacity and international ex-

---

[560] Cooley, author's interview.

pertise our Texas-based customers needed—plus the inevitable risk of losing those customers to the money center banks. We could do little about it unless Texas banking laws were modified.[561]

Cooley recalled a similar story as a Continental Illinois banker in the late 1970s. "We banked a wide number of Texas energy corporations—and not as a participant but as an agent. We banked those because we were smarter and more innovative than our Texas counterparts, who pretty much 'stuck by the book.'

"When I first joined the Houston office in 1977, I was assigned as back-up on a new loan participation with oil producer and refiner Howell Corp., a long-time Houston relationship agented by First City. Within six months of closing the loan participation, the chief financial officer of Howell personally came to our office and asked if we could take over the agency, as he was tired of dealing with First City.

"So we did. And this happened frequently on a number of occasions."[562]

A new era in banking in Texas and other states began in 1970 when President Nixon signed an amendment to the federal Bank Holding Company Act of 1956, permitting the formation of holding companies. However, Texas continued to harbor the anti-monopoly and "anti-big" sentiment from the earliest days of its history; therefore, efforts by the larger Texas energy lenders to grow under the holding-company structure were challenged in the state legislature.

The Independent Bankers Association and the Texas Bankers Association, both organizations historically dominated by small banks, actively lobbied legislators for protection. In 1974, the Texas legislature convened a constitutional convention to rewrite the state's un-

---

[561] Ben Love, *My Life in Texas Commerce* (Texas A&M University Press: 2005), 151.
[562] Cooley, author's interview. In the late '70s, Continental Illinois banked Coastal States Gas, Quintana, Sanchez-O'Brien, Kendavis Industries, Valero, Tesoro, Texas City Refining and others.

wieldy, 1876 constitution that had been driven by the Grange political organization that promoted agrarian, populist goals.[563]

The state's 1876 constitution prohibited banks from establishing branches and expanding their scope and reach. Texas' "unit banking" regulation had the effect of protecting the smaller, locally owned institutions. Over time, it also had the effect of concentrating loans in oil and gas and commercial real estate at big-city banks, which forfeited the consumer-banking business to the more customer-convenient suburban banks and the home-mortgage business to the S&Ls, which had unlimited branching powers.

Amendments were proposed that were so strict as to require the larger Texas banks to divest existing holdings. The 1974 legislature, like its brethren a century earlier, determined big was bad and that the bank-holding companies would gobble up any and all small-town banks. But the legislators' efforts came to naught as the convention failed to garner sufficient votes to submit a document to the public for a vote.[564]

In the subsequent legislative session, the debate was taken up again. This time, the Texas Bankers Association reversed its "anti-big-bank" position, allowing Texas banks to expand their footprint across the state under the holding-company structure.[565]

To the extent that the amount of the loan made by one of these banks exceeded its legal lending limit, these banks would parcel out to one or a couple of overline banks the excess portion. Typically, these

---

[563] D. Sven Nordin, *Rich Harvest: A History of the Grange, 1867–1900* (University Press of Mississippi: 1974). The Grange was an organization founded in 1867 for farmers and their wives that was strongest in the Northeast and promoted the modernization not only of farming practices but also of family and community life. Membership soared from 1873 (200,000) to 1875 (858,050) as many of the state and local granges adopted non-partisan political resolutions, especially regarding the regulation of railroad-transportation costs.

[564] *Handbook of Texas Online*, Mary Lucia Barras and Houston Daniel, "Constitutional Convention of 1974," accessed February 20, 2016, Tshaonline.org.

[565] Love, *My Life in Texas Commerce*, 179-186. In 1987, Texas' law was brought current with those of other states to permit branch banking, but it was too late to save many of the state's major banks.

were Chase Manhattan, Manufacturers Hanover, Citibank and Morgan Guaranty in New York or Continental Illinois in Chicago.[566]

By the early 1970s, intrastate, multibank, holding-company systems had developed in Texas, particularly in metropolitan areas and encouraged by state prohibition of branch banking. These "group-banking systems" or "bank-holding companies," about a dozen of which were multi-billion-dollar statewide entities, were destined to become the dominant corporate organizational form for banks in Texas. By the summer of 1985, some 130 such systems controlled almost half of the more than 1,800 separately incorporated banks and held nearly three-quarters of bank deposits in the state.[567]

While Texas banks were growing, they still lacked the ability to underwrite the larger producer loans. With the rise in commodity prices, more out-of-state capital was coming to Texas. And where these money-center banks controlled the agent role, they preferred other out-of-state banks as syndicate members because they could take larger portions of the loans.

"As far as Continental was concerned, we preferred to overline deals with other out-of-state banks instead of Texas banks, as the Texas banks would try to steal the relationship," Cooley recalled. "Favorite overline banks for Continental were Bank of Montreal and Barclays. Such banks didn't have a legal limit issue and could, and were willing to, take massive overline amounts."[568]

Beginning in the mid-1970s, competition heated up between major Texas-based banks and out-of-state capital—especially from New

---

[566] Gordon Sorrels, former Head of Oil and Gas Lending at Allied Bank of Texas, interview by the author, April 7, 2016. To the extent a loan to any borrower exceeds the bank's regulatory lending limit (no more than 15% of capital to any one borrower), the bank "would share the loan with another bank. This is known as participation. The originating bank would perform the credit evaluation, collect all necessary documentation, obtain mortgages over the collateral and service the loan by collecting payments and passing them on to the participating bank. The larger bank would provide funding for its share of the loan and pay a commission to the originating bank." Shauna Ferris, "How to Destabilize the Financial System: A Beginner's Guide," *Variance* 4:1, 2010.
[567] *Handbook of Texas Online*, Lawrence L. Crum, "Banks and Banking," accessed March 31, 2016, Tshaonline.org.
[568] Cooley, author's interview.

York and Chicago. But, as the next decade would show, events would overtake the proud tradition of Texas-grown energy banking.

The 1970s may be characterized as the beginning of the modern era of energy lending; the 1980s, however, brought many bank failures due to wild swings in oil prices and interest rates and, later, in collapsing real estate markets. The events left in their wake a trail of capital and job destruction and depressed economies in energy states, principally Texas, Oklahoma and Louisiana.

Texas had entered the decade as the proud and unequalled leader of the U.S. energy industry and the capital of energy-lending. But, by the end of the decade, many of the well-respected Texas energy banks—and other oil-patch banks—failed or were folded into national bank-holding companies at the insistence—and with the assistance—of federal regulators.

As the '80s began, rising oil and gas prices inflated the optimism held by producers and their lenders. In fact, to some, particularly in the Northeast, it looked as if oil companies were making too much money. Just three months into the new decade, the U.S. enacted the Crude Oil Windfall Profit Tax Act as part of a compromise between the Carter Administration and Congress over deregulation of oil prices.[569]

The act was intended to recoup the "windfall" revenue earned by oil producers as a result of the sharp increase in oil prices brought about by the OPEC embargo of 1973, Iranian curtailment in 1979 as a result of the revolution, and its and Iraq's curtailment in 1980 as a result of the Iran-Iraq War.[570]

---

[569] Yergin, *The Prize*, 675.

[570] The term "windfall profit" had its origins in Colonial America. The English prized large timbers for use as masts for its naval fleet and the Colonies had abundant supplies of tall and straight white pines. The Massachusetts Bay Colony charter in 1691 forbade anyone without a license from the Crown to cut down any tree greater than 24 inches in diameter. Similar laws were passed by Parliament in 1711, 1722 and as late as 1772. It had as much popular support as the Tea Tax and led to the Portsmouth, New Hampshire, White Pine Tree Riot of 1772, a precursor to the Boston Tea Party a year later. However, if a tree were blown over by wind, the landowner was free to use it for his own profit.

From 1978 into the beginning of 1981, U.S. oil prices soared. Prices were forecast to potentially exceed $100 a barrel, fueling a drilling frenzy.[571] By 1982, the number of rigs drilling had more than doubled—funded in large part by "rig loans," which would soon become toxic for some energy banks.

At the end of the Arab Oil Embargo in March of 1974, the rig count was less than 1,500. It rose steadily with oil prices to more than 2,000 in 1979. The count exceeded 4,520 at year-end 1981.[572] Not only were commodity prices rising rapidly; by December 19, 1980, the prime lending rate hit an historic high of 20.5%.[573]

Natural gas generally tracked oil's price run-up, but for different reasons. Subsequent to the *Phillips* decision in 1954, the Federal Power Commission had been regulating interstate gas prices. Throughout the 1960s, interstate prices were frozen at 1959 levels, resulting in a decline in drilling.

Zweig quoted Oklahoma producer Robert A. Hefner III in *Belly Up*:

> "There were twenty-five to thirty years of regulation of [natural gas] that kept its price below the marginal cost of finding it," Hefner said. This arrangement disrupted the "whole energy infrastructure of the country." A shortage was created, most notably in the interstate markets because producers couldn't afford to drill for gas at the regulated wellhead price, and, indeed, 1967 was the last year there was a net addition to gas reserves according to the American Gas Association.[574]

---

[571] U.S. EIA, Independent Statistics & Analysis. "U.S. Crude Oil and Natural Gas Rotary Rigs in Operation." Accessed March 6, 2016. Eia.gov.

[572] J. Thomas Mullen, Mayor, Browne & Platt, "The Future of Bank Financing of the Oil and Gas Industry" (paper presented at Eastern Mineral Law Foundation, 9th Institute, May 1988), Section 19.02[3].

[573] "Prime Rate History," FedPrimeRate.com, accessed March 4, 2016.

[574] Zweig, *Belly Up*, 19.

U.S. production would not reverse this long, slow decline until the potential of the U.S. shale-gas revolution became evident some 40 years later.[575] Meanwhile, because intrastate gas prices were relatively free of price controls, the price for this gas grew to exceed interstate prices severalfold. Thus, producers dedicated their gas production to intrastate pipelines and, whenever possible, diverted gas away from interstate markets.

Lack of gas supply in Northeastern markets led to an energy crisis there during the winter of 1970-71. In response, the FPC raised ceiling prices and, in 1974, adopted further regulatory changes intended to increase interstate-gas supply. However, bowing to political pressure, the FPC set rates at about half of then-current intrastate price. Interstate shortages continued.

By 1978, 41% of gas sales were intrastate in Texas, Oklahoma and Louisiana, meaning that the 45 other Lower 48 states were sharing less than 60% of the nation's supply.[576] Congress responded, passing the Natural Gas Policy Act in 1978, which provided for a phased deregulation of prices through 1985, except for gas produced from wells drilled prior to 1977, which remained under price controls. The price for "deep gas" from formations below 15,000 feet was immediately decontrolled.

By 1981, the price of deep gas soared above $10 per Mcf—more than four times the price of regulated, shallow gas.[577] Deep-gas producers, primarily in Oklahoma's Anadarko Basin, responded with the drillbit—financed by their energy bankers.

Flush production from these deep wells and price escalation from deregulated markets—along with regulatory actions that includ-

---

[575] U.S. EIA, Independent Statistics & Analysis. "U.S. Crude Oil and Gas Reserves, 2013." Accessed March 5, 2016. Eia.gov. With the growth from shale-gas development, U.S. gas would begin to see a first dramatic increase in reserve additions in 2008 since 1967 and surpassed each year thereafter through 2014 (the most recent EIA data as of publication).

[576] "In 1965, a third of the nation's proved reserves were earmarked for intrastate consumers; by 1975, almost half of the proved reserves were committed to intrastate consumers." "The History of Regulation," Natural Gas Supply Association, accessed March 1, 2016, Naturalgas.org/regulation/history.

[577] Zweig, Belly Up, 90.

ed President Carter's efforts to address the energy crisis, which he dubbed the "moral equivalent of war"—encouraged conservation and switching to coal power, depressing demand for gas as a power-plant boiler fuel and contributing to huge gas surpluses by the mid-1980s.[578] By this time, gas producers in Oklahoma and other states that had gone into debt on expectations of sustained, high gas prices were hammered by a combination of the overall U.S. economic recession and flush gas supply—as interstate pipelines halved their prices for deep gas and gas prices collapsed with oil prices.

Faced with long-term contracts at the newly above-market price to either take producers' gas or just pay for it, many interstate pipelines invoked "economic force majeure" and "market out" clauses in an effort to avoid payment. Energy bankers had relied upon the guaranteed income stream from the contracts with investment-grade, interstate pipelines when lending to drillers searching for deep gas. Termination or breach of these take-or-pay contracts triggered defaults. Producers were faced with the option to fight it out with the pipelines in lengthy court battles or renegotiate contracts.[579]

In addition to evaluating the enforceability of borrowers' take-or-pay contracts, bankers and their lawyers were also busy during the 1980s with a number of other novel issues, particularly the definition of "prime rate" and the impact of the windfall-profit tax on underwriting and documenting oil and gas loans. In addition, other issues to be addressed included U.S. price controls on "old oil" versus "new oil" and OPEC-pricing policies.[580]

Even the bank's reserve engineer's job was more complicated. Mike Boone, a co-founder of Texas law firm Haynes and Boone LLP, wrote in 1980, "It should be recognized that the estimation of future prices has become a literal nightmare for the engineer due to the gradual deregulation of prices through the various formulas for 'lower

---

[578] Zweig, *Belly Up*, 41-66.
[579] Federal Deposit Insurance Corporation. Division of Research and Statistics (FDIC), *History of the Eighties – Lessons for the Future* (Washington, DC: Federal Deposit Insurance Corporation, 1997), 298-299.
[580] Boone, "Structuring and Documenting the Oil and Gas Loan," 5.

tier' and 'upper tier' oil, the relevance of stripper prices and future changes in OPEC pricing policies."[581]

By 1983, a slumping world economy, conservation, fuel competition from coal and nuclear power, and federal regulations led to falling oil and gas prices. Burrough wrote, "In Texas, drill bits began whirring to a halt. Across the state, wildcatters who had borrowed heavily to drill expensive deep wells saw the value of their collateral fall. Banks began calling in loans; many of the new wildcatters born during the 1970's began to go bankrupt or, like George W. Bush's renamed Bush Exploration Co., limped into shotgun mergers.

"As oilmen failed, Texas banks weakened. In October 1983, just eight months after the OPEC price reduction, the state's largest independent bank, First National of Midland, collapsed. In the next decade nine of the ten largest Texas Banks would follow suit. Texas Oil, the engine of the state's economy, coughed, then sputtered, then began, with a series of violent backfires, to die."[582]

Producers were not the only ones hit by the rough economic times. The early 1980s saw a rash of bankruptcies by oil and gas purchasers.[583] Bankrupt purchasers owed royalty-owners and operators for the oil and gas they had purchased and sold. Many of the producers became unsecured creditors as they discovered too late that they had neglected to obtain or perfect security interests in their accounts receivable owed to them by the purchasers.

As such, bankruptcy laws left these interest-owners' holding virtually worthless, unsecured claims.[584] Judge Marvin Isgur noted in a case 30 years later, "The Texas Legislature responded to the (first) 'oil and gas bust' of the early '80's by enacting the non-standard language we now know as section 9.319 [of the Uniform Commercial Code]. The bankruptcies of several large oil and gas operators and purchasers

---

[581] Boone, "Structuring and Documenting the Oil and Gas Loan," 9.
[582] Burrough, *The Big Rich*, 407.
[583] In 1982, Basin Inc., Brio Petroleum Inc., Compton Petroleum Corp. and Gratex Corp. filed bankruptcy petitions. Cynthia Grinstead, "The Effect of Texas U.C.C. Section 9.319 on Oil and Gas Secured Transactions," 63 *Tx. L. Rev.* 311, 322 (1984).
[584] Grinstead, "The Effect of Texas U.C.C. Section 9.319 ...," 323.

had a considerable impact on Texas royalty and non-operation working interest owners … ."[585]

The legislature passed an amendment in 1983 to Texas' creditor laws to provide "automatic perfection" of a security interest in favor of the producers and royalty owners in the production and sales proceeds held by the first purchaser. The coverage of the statute was expanded in 1987 when the definition of "first purchaser" was amended to expressly include the operator who disburses proceeds of production.[586] This lien was crafted by the legislature to be a "consensual lien" based solely on standard contracts for the purchase and sale of oil and gas documentation used in the oil and gas industry.[587]

Under the "producer's lien," perfection is "automatic" in the sense that it did not require the filing of a standard financing statement.[588] The statute transferred the risk of loss associated with the crude purchaser's bankruptcy away from the producers—and their creditors—and onto the other creditors of the crude purchaser.[589] Other producer states have adopted similar non-standard statutory protections for producers and royalty owners.[590]

The effectiveness of these producer-lien statutes to protect royalty owners and producers were not substantively challenged until 2008, when the creditors of oil-purchaser SemGroup LP challenged them in

---

[585] *In re Tri-Union Development Corp.*, 253 B.R. 808, 811 (Bankr. S.D. Tex 2000) (citing Official Comment 1 by Colin Kaufman (Vernon 1991)).

[586] Terry I. Cross, "Structuring and Documenting Oil and Gas Financing Transactions, Part Two," *Texas Oil and Gas Law Journal*, (Butterworth Legal Publishers, Austin Texas) Volume 6, No. 4, (1992), 63 (hereinafter, "Cross Two").

[587] *Clarks' Security Transactions Monthly* (Matthew Bender & Company, Inc., Vol. 25, June 2009).

[588] *See* Tex. Bus. & Com. Code § 9.319(a)(1991). Terry Cross, "Oil and Gas Product Liens - Statutory Security Interests for Producers and Royalty Owners under the Statutes of Kansas, New Mexico, Oklahoma, Texas and Wyoming," 50 *Consumer. Fin. L.Q. Rep.* 418 (1996).

[589] Cross Two, 62.

[590] Kansas, *see* Kan. Stat. Ann. Section 84-9-339a; New Mexico, *see* N.M.S.A. Section 48-9-2 et seq. (1973) (statutory non-uniform commercial code lien); North Dakota, N.D. Cent. Code Ann Section 35-37-04; and Oklahoma, *see* Okla. Stat. Ann. tit. 52, Section 548 (originally adopted in 1988, the statute was repealed in 2010 and replaced with a statutory lien outside the scope of the state's uniform commercial code).

bankruptcy court in Delaware.[591] Until then, however, most energy bankers welcomed the improved status their producer-borrowers enjoyed and included a collateral assignment of such lien rights as additional collateral under the producer's deed of trust or mortgage.

In addition to adjusting to changes in world energy markets, producers and their lenders wrestled with increasing federal and state environmental regulations. A number of significant statutes were adopted in the 1970s, including the Clean Water Act of 1972, Safe Drinking Water Act of 1974 and the Resource Conservation and Recovery Act of 1976.[592]

But the environmental law with the most direct impact on producers—and, potentially, their lenders—was passed in December of 1980 in response to the Love Canal disaster. Congress adopted the Comprehensive Environmental Response, Compensation, and Liability Act (CERCLA).[593] Known as the "Superfund Act," it created the specter of strict liability for any owner or operator of property contaminated by hazardous substances.[594]

Although petroleum and its constituents were exempt by statute under the "petroleum exclusion," a number of hazardous chemicals and substances used in operations for oil and gas exploration and

---

[591] *In re: SemCrude, L.P., et al.*, Case No. 08-11525 (Bankr.D.Del. 2008). The court held against the producers in favor of the oil purchaser's secured creditors, finding that Delaware creditor laws controlled and not local laws in the states where the producers delivered and sold their oil.

[592] Respectively, 33 U.S.C. §§1251-1387, 42 U.S.C. §§ 300f-300j and 42 U.S.C. §§6901-6992k.

[593] 42. U.S.C. §§ 9601-9675, subsequently amended by the Superfund Amendments and Reauthorization Act (SARA) October 17, 1986.

[594] Love Canal was a waste dumpsite for Hooker Chemical Co.'s nearby chemical facility between WWII and the 1950s. After the site was closed and the canal covered with soil, it was sold to the city of Niagara Falls for $1.00 with disclosures of its prior use and statements that the area should be sealed off to prevent any human or animal contact. But the land was developed for low-income housing and adjacent elementary schools were built. By 1979, the environmental hazards associated with the site were made public. All across America, the public, public officials, businessmen and lenders became acutely aware of the affect and liabilities associated with ownership of contaminated real property. Love Canal was removed from the Superfund List on September 30, 2004, after a 15-year remediation effort. "Superfund," United States Environmental Protection Agency, accessed October 20, 2015, Epa.gov.

production were not.[595] Because the liability for clean-up was strict, joint and several and retroactive, the potential costs to a responsible party could be catastrophic.

Secured lenders were expressly excluded, so long as they did not exercise or participate in management of a contaminated facility. But early judicial decisions following enactment of the act raised questions about what level of a lender's management participation could take it outside of the safe-harbor "secured lender" exclusion and what would be the consequence of the lender's foreclosure and post-foreclosure activity.[596]

The "secured lender" exclusion was cast into doubt in 1986 in a court ruling that recognized secured lenders as "owners" and "operators" under CERCLA in certain circumstances—typically involving the lender's participation in the debtor's business beyond what was merely necessary to protect a security interest in the collateral.[597] These lenders' actions ranged from management of the property for several years after foreclosure to participation in the financial management of the property to such a degree that the lender was able to influence the debtor's treatment of hazardous waste.

In such cases, the lenders began to look more like a conventional owner or operator by "participating in the management." Thus, they were held liable under CERCLA as owners or operators of contaminated sites.[598]

Much time, credit-committee angst, legal analysis and environmental due diligence was expended by energy lenders, their lawyers and environmental consultants over these issues and over what steps could best insulate their collateral and—more importantly, the lender directly—from liability. New, lengthy provisions covering representations and affirmative covenants were added to credit agreements and

---

[595] "Superfund," U.S. EPA, accessed October 20, 2015, Epa.gov.
[596] Butler & Binion, *Environmental Law Simplified: A Practical Guide for Oil and Gas Operations* (Pennwell Corp., February 1993), 77.
[597] *United States v. Maryland Bank & Trust Co.*, 632 F. Supp. 573, 579 (D. Md. 1986).
[598] *United States v. Mirabile*, 15 Envtl. L. Rep. (Envtl. L. Inst.) 20,992 (E.D. Pa. Sept. 4, 1985): 20,994.

deeds of trust to document the borrower's compliance and due-diligence inspection of the oil and gas properties. Indemnities to lenders were also added in the event of any liabilities caused by violations of environmental laws.

The importance of obtaining environmental assessments ("Phase I") covering the collateral was almost as imperative to the bank's due diligence as assuring the company's title. This requirement was strictly enforced by most energy banks soon after the adoption of CERCLA.

However, producers found it difficult to comply, primarily because accepted bank protocols for Phase I assessments were written for commercial real estate loans. In a typical real estate loan, generally, there was no more than one owner of a single tract of land of less than a few acres, typically located in an urban area. The typical collateral for an energy loan includes hundreds of leases in multiple fields in many jurisdictions and each potentially having multiple owners.

It was often unclear to the lending officer and his counsel what level of due diligence satisfied the bank's new environmental policies, much less what would satisfy the CERCLA standard of "all due inquiry" and, thereby, protect the bank from successor liability as an "innocent purchaser" should it become the owner following a foreclosure.

By the end of the 1980s and into the 1990s, the urgency to insure and document compliance with environmental due diligence in documentation of oil and gas reserve-based loans decreased, as producers and environmental regulators became more familiar with the requirements. For energy lenders, many nagging questions under the Superfund Act were answered in 1982 by the U.S. Environmental Protection Agency's lender-liability rule, which provided that a lender can retain its secured-creditor exemption, unless its management control extended to the borrower's environmental compliance or extended to substantially all of the operational aspects of management, whether or not specifically including environmental compliance.

The rule also clarified what actions lenders could take in foreclosure and, subsequent to foreclosure, to preserve its status of remaining within the security-interest exclusion.[599] Legislation in 1996 provided some clarification of what constituted participation in management by distinguishing between pre-foreclosure activities and post-foreclosure activities and provided "safe harbors" for specific lender activity that may be necessary in loan administration.[600] For mortgage lenders that foreclose, the act clarified that Superfund liability does not attach as long as the lender seeks to sell, release (for lease-finance transactions) or otherwise divest itself of the property at the "earliest practicable, commercially reasonable time, on commercially reasonable terms, taking into account market conditions and legal and regulatory requirements."[601]

Before the 1980s concluded, however, an oil-spill disaster created further regulatory oversight of oil and gas operations. In 1989, the *Exxon Valdez* tanker ran aground in Alaska's Prince William Sound and spawned the Oil Pollution Act of 1990.[602] While OPA was aimed at protection against marine spills, its jurisdiction covered all "navigable waters of the United States."[603] Accordingly, compliance with OPA's reach became another item for bankers and their counsel to address in the covenant and representation package of energy loan documents.

On the whole, the energy industry has shown serious and sincere concern for the environment and has had decades to incorporate the environmental protections covered by these statutes into their policies and procedures. As a result, the typical banker's sensitivity to environmental issues has become much less of a focus in loan due diligence and documentation since the 1980s.

---

[599] Butler & Binion, *Environmental Law Simplified: A Practical Guide*, 77.

[600] Nolan, *Texas Deed of Trust Annotated*, discussing the *Asset Conservation Act of 1966* (42 U.S.C.A. Section 9601(20)(E)-(G).

[601] 30 42.U.S.C. § 9601(20)(E)(ii).

[602] *Oil Pollution Act of 1990*, 33 U.S.C. §§2701-2761. This was not the first time an oil spill triggered adoption of new federal environmental laws. The National Environmental Policy Act (NEPA) was adopted after the Unocal oil spill in 1969 from Platform A in the Dos Cuadras Field offshore Santa Barbara, California. Among NEPA's provisions was the requirement of extensive environmental-impact studies prior to drilling on federal lands. Olien and Hinton, *Wildcatters*, 136-137.

[603] *Oil Pollution Act of 1990*, 33 U.S.C. 2701, 2702(a).

Alternate Loan Structures

At the beginning of the '80s, the borrowing-base revolver loan was becoming the favored structure, yet term loans and production loans continued.[604] The advantage of the term loan was that, by its nature, banks could typically lend against a higher percentage of the borrower's proved reserves because production would commence to amortize principal immediately.[605] For this reason, term loans were better suited to fields in which there was little to no additional capital-expenditure requirements for incurring production to sustain cash flow.

If additional development was planned, the revolver loan was used. With this, the borrower could access borrowed funds to supplement cash flow from existing production to fund drilling new wells, which were to result in additional reserves and, thereby, a higher borrowing base upon subsequent determinations.[606]

Other reported forms of oil and gas loans at the time included the "completion line," which was dedicated, short-term credit to finance\ costs incurred in completing identified wells, and the "lease line" to finance the acquisition of undeveloped oil and gas lease inventory.[607]

Under "lease lines," typically not more than 50% of the leasehold cost would be financed by banks and maturities were limited to six months, within which the borrower would covenant to complete the geological and geophysical work to package the leases for resale or to make further investment within three to six months. Lease lines were not favored as collateral and extended only to borrowers having other, reliable sources of repayment and who were experienced in promotion and sales of lease inventory.[608]

---

[604] Boone, "Structuring and Documenting the Oil and Gas Loan," 15; *see also* Christian, "Introduction to Commercial Bank and Non-Bank Institutional Financing," 2-16.
[605] Christian, "Introduction to Commercial Bank ...," Section 2-16.
[606] Christian, "Introduction to Commercial Bank ...," Section 2-16.
[607] Mullen, "The Future of Bank Financing," Section 19.02[3][b].
[608] Christian, "Introduction to Commercial Bank ...," Section 2-22-23.

Zweig wrote, "Traditionally, oil and gas lenders have regarded the lease as being of dubious value in securing a loan. In leasing oil and gas property, the purchaser pays the mineral owner a bonus up front, and agrees to a royalty on any production. ... But if oil and gas are not found, or if the lease expires before drilling begins, the value of the lease evaporates. ... As one veteran lender put it, 'You don't know oil and gas are there until you drill.'"[609]

Another popular financing structure was subscription loans to limited drilling partnerships that solicited investors to secure a portion of their capital commitments with letters of credit issued by each investor's bank. Investors put up 25% in cash and the balance of their capital investment was covered under L/Cs from their banks. The partnership would pledge the limited partners' L/Cs as collateral in, typically, a two-year term loan to acquire leases and prove up acreage through drilling.

In concept, by maturity, the term loan would convert to a production loan when, it was hoped, income from production would pay off the term loan and the L/Cs would not have to be called. This loan structure was introduced by Continental Illinois as a result of 1976 revisions to the Internal Revenue Code for tax-sheltered investments and was popular with high-net-worth investors who could shelter 70% of their investment against drilling costs incurred by the partnership.[610]

As Zweig described this, "someone in the 50% tax bracket making the minimum $150,000 investment would be able to write off $75,000 by putting up only 25% or [$37,500], in cash. People recognized that even if they had to fund on the letters of credit, they would be able to take the deductions immediately and pay later in inflated dollars, allowing them in many cases to finance their tax bills with no cash out of pocket."[611]

---

[609] Zweig, *Belly Up*, 14, *see also*, Mullen, "The Future of Bank Financing," 19.02[3][b].
[610] Zweig, *Belly Up*, 86.
[611] Zweig, *Belly Up*, 82.

The structure was bastardized by bankers at Penn Square Bank for their borrower-drillers whose prospective investors claimed their local banks didn't understand L/Cs. The prospective investors got Penn Square to issue the L/Cs on their account in favor of Penn Square to secure their investments in the Penn Square-banked drilling partnership.

Essentially, if the drilling wasn't successful, which was often the case, Penn Square would be in the position of having to honor the L/Cs on behalf of the limited partnership to pay itself and other banks participating in its agented loans. Seminars on this tax-shelter investment were popular. In Oklahoma City, Lewis Mosberg, a leading local oil and gas attorney, conducted 18 seminars a year; there was demand for him to have done more, but these were all that time permitted.[612]

The investments were packaged as private offerings to wealthy investors in blind pools in which the investor had no idea of where the wells would be drilled. According to Mossberg, 95% of the promoters were real estate developers, who had no prior experience in oil and gas operations.[613]

When Penn Square was taken over by the FDIC in 1982, it refused to honor the letters of credit and banks that had participated in the Penn Square-generated, public limited-partnership loans found their collateral L/Cs worthless.[614] Even where Penn Square was not the issuer, the drilling-partnership lenders had a hard time collecting.

The lending banks relied upon prompt payment by the issuing banks, but they had failed to review the creditworthiness of the issuing banks. Where the issuing banks were insolvent, the lending banks went directly after the investor limited partners. To enjoin payment on their letters of credit, the limited partners alleged that the lending banks were involved in a fraud and conspiracy with the general-

---

[612] Zweig, *Belly Up*, 87.
[613] Zweig, *Belly Up*, 87.
[614] Zweig, *Belly Up*, 81-89 and 426.

partner oil company. The result was expensive litigation chasing limited partners across the U.S.[615]

While banks were agreeable to offering producers a more flexible structure under borrowing-base revolvers to provide easier access to capital, they still insisted on a tight security package. In addition to the standard deed of trust, many lenders were folding security-agreement language into the deed of trust under the new rules permitting perfection of liens under the Uniform Commercial Code on produced oil and gas and proceeds from the sale thereof.

Bank counsel Mike Boone wrote in a 1980 paper, "Structuring and Documenting the Oil and Gas Loan," that, in addition to the filing requirements under Texas' version of Article 9 of the Uniform Commercial Code, there was not universal agreement among bank lawyers regarding the applicability of the Texas Business and Commerce Code section. This section provided for special filing with the Texas Secretary of State's office and notice requirements in connection with perfection against personal property and fixtures owned by a "utility."[616]

Boone wrote, "Although the apparent intent of the statute was directed towards public utilities, the broad definition of 'utility' caused some bank lawyers to question the true meaning of the statute. Compliance with the statute on typical producer secured loans was not consistent among banks or their law firms, and some bank attorneys did not require such compliance when the borrower was clearly not a 'utility' within the common meaning of the term."[617]

Borrowers resisted such filings, considering them unnecessary and problematic. If a borrower filed a security document that characterized itself as a public-utility common carrier, it potentially subjected itself to onerous state-utility reporting requirements and the need to share its gathering system with third-party producers. Amendments in 1987 clarified the definition of a "utility" to provide that a person is

---

[615] Mullen, "The Future of Bank Financing," Section 19.02[3][d].
[616] Texas Business and Commerce Code, Section 35.02.
[617] Boone, "Structuring and Documenting the Oil and Gas Loan," 21.

not a utility, unless and until such person files a security instrument with the Texas Secretary of State that states, conspicuously, on its title page, "This Instrument Grants a Security Interest By A Utility."[618]

The more important feature of the security package was the assignment of production. Banks continued the practice under the original production term-loan structure, which required direct assignment of production proceeds to pay down amortizing loans. Even under revolver loans, without a monthly principal amortization requirement, banks required letters-in-lieu, which required that purchasers' payments for production be directed to specially designated operating accounts controlled by the bank.

The letters would be held by the bank for safe-keeping and the borrower would have direct access to such proceeds, so long as no event of default occurred under its credit agreement. Following an event of default, the letters could be delivered by the bank and the borrower's access to such funds could be restricted. The sale proceeds that were paid directly to the bank could be applied against obligations owed under the loan.

In 1981 and 1984, decisions in commercial real estate cases regarding assignment of rents raised concerns among bank lawyers as to the enforceability of the assignment-of-production clauses.[619] The cases held that an assignment of rents that was only effective following an event of default was an additional remedy in securing repayment of the debt obligation.

However, it was felt that, because minerals were personal property once produced, the rulings regarding rent payments should be inapplicable. Instead, under Section 9.502(a) of the Texas Business and Commerce Code, a lender should be entitled to collect the proceeds

---

[618] Cross Two, 57.
[619] *Taylor v. Brennan*, 621 S.W2d 592 (Tex. 1981) and *Matter of Village Properties, Ltd.*, 723 F.2d 441 (5th Cir.) cert. denied, *Wolters Village Ltd. v. Village Properties, Ltd.*, 104 S. Ct. 2350 (1984).

of production from the purchaser "when so agreed and in any event upon default."[620]

In revolvers, the bank retained the flexibility to determine when to exercise its right to notify the purchaser and, in most cases, would "not exercise this right until such time as it feels insecure."[621] It could be more administratively expedient, when the borrower was also an operator for third-party producers, for the bank to permit the borrower to continue to receive checks where the gross-proceeds receipts belonged not only to the borrower but to the non-operating working-interest- and royalty owners as well.

Bankers were concerned with capturing and retaining funds that did not belong to their borrower. Adhering to the lessons of key court holdings, more conservative lenders, to be able to capture the borrower's share of proceeds upon exercise of remedies, would require that all proceeds be paid into a specified depository account—a "lock box"—over which the bank, at any time, could take control. But, until such control was exercised, the proceeds would flow through the lock-box account into the borrower's operating account, which was also maintained with the bank.[622]

Downfall of the Energy Lenders

By 1982, major commercial banks active in the oil patch devoted between 20% and 30% of their loan portfolios to the energy industry. Some 300 of the nearly 15,000 commercial banks in the U.S. were involved in some type of energy financing and nearly 100 had extensive departments. Foreign banks also jumped into the market.[623] Only four foreign-headquartered banks had an office in Houston in 1973; by 1981, 64 were in the city.[624]

---

[620] Terry I. Cross (Haynes and Boone LLP), "Structuring and Documenting Oil and Gas Financing Transactions: Part One," *Texas Oil and Gas Law Journal*, Volume 6, Number 3 (1992) (hereinafter "Cross Part One"), 50.

[621] Boone, "Structuring and Documenting the Oil and Gas Loan," 21.

[622] Cross Part One, 50.

[623] Christian, "Introduction to Commercial Bank ...," Section 2.2.

[624] Bernstein, "Houston & Oil: The Feast, The Famine, The Future." Foreign-owned bank assets in the U.S. increased from $24 billion in 1972 to $98 billion in 1978.

Chapter 6: 1980s

The public-equity and public-debt markets were open to the majors and the largest independents. But commercial banks continued to represent the primary source of long-term debt capital for small and mid-size producers.[625]

The halcyon days of the early '80s for them—and their lenders—began to grow gloomy by the middle of the decade. From 1982 to 1985, OPEC attempted to set production quotas low enough to stabilize prices. In 1982, it established its first quotas; in 1983, it cut its target price to $29 a barrel. These attempts met with repeated failure as various members did not adhere.

By August of 1985, Saudi Arabia—tired of its role as the swing producer—linked its oil price to the spot market for crude and, by early 1986, increased its output from 2 million barrels a day to 5 million. By the middle of 1986, oil prices plummeted below $10 per barrel. Of course, every dark cloud has its silver lining: On August 23, 1988, amid low oil prices, President Reagan repealed the Windfall Profit Tax.[626]

It was small comfort, however; there were precious few profits and certainly not any windfall among the producers left standing by then. From 1982 to 1992, 51% of oil and gas exploration and production jobs were eliminated. In 1983 alone, 131 producers, drilling contractors and other energy service companies filed for bankruptcy.[627] The U.S. petroleum industry lost more than 400,000 jobs.

A former landman sold subscriptions to his monthly report on Harris County, Texas, foreclosure postings, which included the homes of many out-of-work oilfield workers and professionals. Some 16,600 Houston-area mortgages were foreclosed in 1985—more than the previous two years combined. In 1986, there were nearly 3,000 foreclosures in February alone. Almost 30% of Houston's office space was empty, including a number of recently completed towers dubbed "see-through buildings" for that they lacked interior walls or tenants.

---

[625] Christian, "Introduction to Commercial Bank ...," Section 2-2.
[626] *The Omnibus Trade and Competitiveness Act of 1988*, P.L. 100-418.
[627] Bernstein, "Houston & Oil: The Feast, The Famine, The Future."

Houston restaurateur Steve Zimmerman, owner of the upscale La Colombe d'Or, pegged the price of his four-course lunch to the price of a barrel of West Texas Intermediate and called it the *"C'est la Vie* Oil Barrel Special." The regularly priced $35 meal became a bargain by April 1986. *Newsweek* reported, "Zimmerman isn't making money, but he's having fun. Energy Bankers have forgotten what fun is. They are spending most of their time writing off bad loans and fending off rumors about mergers with big money-center banks."[628]

1986 ushered in the most severe depression ever experienced by the U.S. petroleum industry. Unemployment in oil-patch states soared; the industry lost 35,000 jobs in April of that year alone.[629] Louisiana led the nation with a 13.2% jobless rate. Oklahoma's was 7.8%. Texas, Louisiana and Alaska were each projecting $1-billion budget deficits.

As the entire petroleum industry sustained tremendous damage, independents, particularly those whose operations included contract drilling, were hit especially hard. Independents coped through Chapter 11 and Chapter 7 bankruptcies, layoffs, salary freezes, office closings and asset sales. Drilling rigs sat idle and rusting in equipment yards, while roughnecks and roustabouts applied for unemployment benefits. Houston's Allied Bank rented an old airstrip in West Texas near Big Spring to store repossessed rigs and other equipment.[630]

Penn Square: The Canary in the Coal Mine

Even before the Saudis' punitive action, there were signs that not all was well in the world of oil and gas lending. During the 1982 Fourth of July weekend, Penn Square Bank was shut down by the FDIC, becoming the largest FDIC payoff in history at the time.[631] Within a year of the bank's failure, more than 150 Penn Square borrowers, owing the FDIC $352 million altogether, filed for bankruptcy.[632]

---

[628] "Banking's Dry Hole," *Newsweek*, April 14, 1986.
[629] Olien and Hinton, *Wildcatters*, xiv.
[630] Scott Clark, "Banks Made Oil Bash Possible, Now Share Hangover," *Houston Chronicle*, June 2, 1985.
[631] Mullen, "The Future of Bank Financing," Section 19-3.
[632] Mark Singer, *Funny Money* (Knopf: May 12, 1985), 146.

Chapter 6: 1980s

Penn Square, which became a household name when it collapsed, had very modest beginnings. The bank was located in a suburban shopping mall and was formed in 1960 by Penn Square Mall's developer and prominent Oklahoma City oil families: Robert S. Kerr and Dean McGee.[633] Bill P. "Beep" Jennings, the son of a small-town bank president, moved to Oklahoma City in 1960 as Penn Square's first president, but he left within four years to pursue other banking opportunities. Jennings, with the support of a few investors, returned to acquire the bank in 1975 and he became its chairman.[634] Penn Square became an energy lender in the spring of 1976 when Jennings declared at a loan-committee meeting that he wanted to start an oil and gas department.

One of the bank's loan officers, Bill Lakey, offered to start the department. He reported, after the bank's demise, "Nobody else knew anything about oil and gas lending. I didn't either, but at least I was interested."[635] The bank's capital was $4 million, which limited it by law to a maximum loan to any one borrower of $400,000.

By 1982, Penn Square's energy portfolio had grown to $2 billion and it was reporting assets of almost $500 million.[636] To put this suburban, mall-headquartered bank's energy portfolio in perspective, money-center banks Manufacturers Hanover Trust and Chase Manhattan had, at year-end 1981, energy-deal exposure of approximately $4 billion and $3.5 billion, respectively.[637]

The sad history of incompetence, mismanagement and lack of controls that brought about the downfall of Penn Square is documented by Mark Singer in *Funny Money* and Zweig in *Belly Up*. Although more than 30 years have passed since Penn Square was shut down, there are many lessons that can still be learned by energy bankers and bank lawyers alike. Singer wrote of what one Penn Square

---

[633] Singer, *Funny Money*, 16.
[634] Zweig, *Belly Up*, 27-30.
[635] Singer, *Funny Money*, 17.
[636] Singer, *Funny Money*, 21.
[637] "Penn Square Bank, Maverick Oil Lender," *American Banker*, April 26, 1982.

lending officer had to say about Jennings, perhaps illustrating how the bank epitomized the worst of energy lending:

> "Beep was a can't-say-no-guy. His attitude toward everyone was 'Come in, we'll talk to you.' The way it worked was, he'd give a verbal commitment to someone and if I didn't want to make the loan I'd turn it down. He didn't want to be the one to do that. Beep would call me and say 'We want to lend So-and-So four hundred thousand.' I'd ask him: 'By when?' He'd say 'Today.' He'd say, 'Just lend it and get the information later.' Well hell, I might need to spend a little more time than that. If you work that way and find out six months later you've got a problem, but you're still trying to get the documents and collateral together—if you haven't got everything filed and recorded and secured, but meanwhile the guys you banked already have the money, they aren't necessarily going to be interested in cooperating with you. Beep would take on people that a lot of other bankers wouldn't touch."[638]

Four months prior to Penn Square's implosion, *American Banker* reported, "According to conversations with senior officials of some of Penn Square's competitors and downstream correspondents, the upstart bank appears to have violated some of the taboos of energy lending and correspondent banking. They believe it has based its reserve lending on an overly optimistic view of oil prices and interest rates, that it lends on brand-new properties and to inexperienced oil and gas operators — criticisms dismissed as 'sour grapes' by Penn Square officials.

"Correspondent bankers say that Penn Square's volume of participations exceeds their own 'comfort level' because of what they called the customary 'moral obligation' of a loan originator to buy back loans that go bad, particularly loans sold downstream. They point out that

---

[638] Singer, *Funny Money*, 18.

most of their own downstream participations are not made as over-lines but rather as accommodations to their country banker customers."[639]

Energy lenders who were active in the late 1970s and early 1980s with major Houston and Dallas banks recalled in interviews 30 years later that Penn Square would come by their banks, peddling packages of energy loans. None merited any more than a cursory review to know the loans would not meet the institution's standards for credit underwriting and loan documentation.[640] Byron Cooley recalled that Bill Patterson, a senior Penn Square energy lender, "called me in Houston at one point, asking if we would be willing to take an overline on an Oklahoma-based rig loan related to our Coastal States Gas exposure, which we sharply declined."

Others did participate, however, and surprisingly included Continental Illinois' Midcontinent division out of Chicago. In 1976, Roger Anderson, the newly appointed chairman of Continental, announced his intention to grow it into one of the top national banks within five years. The bank's growth-oriented strategy, coupled with the departure of its seasoned energy lenders in 1980,[641] led to changes in the special-industries department shifting responsibility to less-experienced energy lenders, including John Lytle, who was in charge of the Midcontinent division, handling Oklahoma and surrounding areas.

The bank's energy department had four divisions—Eastern, Midcontinent, Western and Houston. Cooley recalled of working at the time out of the Houston division, "There was a bit of a power struggle going on between the groups and a certain competitive spirit de-

---

[639] "Penn Square Bank, Maverick Oil Lender," *American Banker*, April 26, 1982.

[640] James Kipp, Managing Director, Wells Fargo Bank, and formerly an energy lender for First City Bank from 1979-1992, interview by the author, September 7, 2012; Whitener, author's interview.

[641] "Continental Illinois' Most Embarrassing Year," *BusinessWeek*, October 11, 1982, 82: "An exodus of talent from the Special Industries Dept.—in charge of lending to energy, mining, utilities, and transportation companies—cause a reliance on less-experienced officers and other banks to bring in business. And with no bona fide chief operating officer riding herd on operations, responsibility for problem areas could be passed back and forth."

veloped of who could grow their portfolio the fastest. Lytle headed the Midcontinent group and handled Oklahoma City and the Penn Square relationship. At least one senior Continental energy lender, Dennis Winget, resigned from our bank and had joined Penn Square. So, how to quickly grow the Midcontinent portfolio? Partner with Penn Square and Dennis Winget and take overlines."[642]

By 1982, Continental held more than $1 billion of Penn Square-originated loans of which $842 million were charged off or classified as non-performing by the end of 1983.[643] How could a reputable, conservative, experienced bank like Continental Illinois fall into this? *BusinessWeek* reported in 1982, "Former and current executives pinpoint this as the time Continental began relying heavily on Penn Square to generate energy-loan volume.

"Even when the processing departments detected a multitude of problems with Penn Square's documentation—the legal documents that spell out precisely the asset collateralized, along with the proper signatures, descriptions and limitations—they 'let the exceptions grow to a point where they became unmanageable,' confides one insider. Says this executive: 'That's what allowed the disaster to happen.'"[644]

Jerry Pearson, who was among the seasoned Continental Illinois bankers who had left, was described by Zweig as "a traditionalist who was uneasy with any energy loan that was not based on well-engineered, proved reserves. He was death on rig and lease line loans, recognizing that their collateral value in a downturn could easily be reduced to almost nothing.

"... Continental after Pearson was willing to do lease lines because they were never able to attract the top tier independents that for years had been cozy with Texas banks like the First of Dallas and Texas Commerce. Penn Square and lease line deals were the cornerstone of Continental's strategy for getting in on the basement level with the Oklahoma independents. Said one observer, 'They figured if

---

[642] Cooley, author's interview.
[643] Ferris, "How to Destabilize the Financial System," 81, 94.
[644] "Continental Illinois' Most Embarrassing Year," 82, 86.

they're not financing the guy who's doing leases, they'd miss out on a lot of other stuff after the ball got rolling.'

"But it was lines of credit secured by leases that would eventually kill Continental Illinois. Most traditional energy lenders avoided lease deals because their value can evaporate so quickly under adverse conditions. ... Not only did Penn Square lend for lease acquisitions, it lent 100% of the purchase price, something a prudent bank wouldn't even do on a new car loan to a creditworthy customer."[645]

Cooley takes exception to Zweig's broad paintbrush as including all of the bank's energy lenders with the failures of Lytle's Midcontinent division. "From my recollection, none of the other three divisions were involved in the banking 'atrocities,' such as inadequate or non-existent documentation, lack of proper analysis, no checks and balances, etc.," Cooley said.

"The lease-line loans were strictly a Midcontinent issue. The Houston division under Jim Cordell never compromised on documentation or analysis and Cordell wouldn't think of ever doing a lease line. In Houston, we were able to attract plenty of top independents. The Midcontinent division under Lytle banked lease lines because Penn Square did and they were offered on a participation basis, which increased its portfolio."[646]

Certainly, much more than documentation exceptions in its Penn Square overline participations caused Continental's energy loans to go bad, not the least of which was the downturn in oil prices. But the checks and balances of proper loan documentation and discipline of carefully underwritten credit analysis were missing in Penn Square's procedures and, equally, of those overline banks content to take carte blanche participations in the loans.

This go-go mentality in the Midcontinent division and the lack of experienced, competent oversight were recommended under a 1976 study by McKinsey & Co. that resulted in two profound changes in

---

[645] Zweig, *Belly Up*, 140,156.
[646] Cooley, author's interview.

philosophy: Management zeroed in on high-growth markets and it emphasized an aggressive approach that meant taking greater risks.[647]

Continental gained a reputation of being the most aggressive energy lender and, overall, it was the fastest-growing lender in the country. *BusinessWeek* reported, "In energy, the bank gradually stretched the traditional rule of lending a maximum 50% of a particular project's anticipated cash flow. By the end of the decade, competitors say, Continental was doling out up to 25% more credit against the same balance sheet and reserves in oil and gas production. Says a Texas banker: 'Continental was making a lot of risky loans but got caught when inflation turned down.'"[648]

Yergin noted in *The Prize* that the bank was winning awards for good management; its chairman was named "Banker of the Year." It was the bank to beat.[649] He cited an energy lender, who said Continental was "eating our lunch."[650]

To keep up, other energy lenders were forced to relax their underwriting standards and embrace the new borrowing-base revolver as the standard loan structure, which was reset annually at the time. "But that wasn't fast enough," Tom Whitener, formerly a senior energy lender with First National Bank in Dallas, recalled in an interview in 2014. "So it was redetermined semi-annually and, just before the crash, borrowing bases were being redetermined every 90 days."[651]

Zweig wrote in 1985, "Continental was subversive in its dealings with the other banks in trying to gain control of a credit. [A] Texas banker said, 'Continental fought the efforts of other banks to demand tough covenants and improve the credit. They'd never feel their way along, they were always ready to do whatever the company wanted. ... Continental made life difficult for us,' he said. 'They didn't seem to understand the ups and downs of the industry.'"[652]

---

[647] "Continental Illinois' Most Embarrassing Year," 82, 89.
[648] "Continental Illinois' Most Embarrassing Year," 91.
[649] Yergin, *The Prize*, 714.
[650] Yergin, *The Prize*, 714.
[651] Whitener, author's interview.
[652] Zweig, *Belly Up*, 74.

The bank was willing to cut corners to attain its objectives of rap-id growth and improved profitability. Although this appeared to be a very successful strategy for Continental Illinois in the short term,[653] lending institutions are not in the business for the short term and, somewhere, senior management lost this guiding principle and suf-fered the consequences.

Following the demise of Penn Square and during the continued deterioration in oil prices, Continental was unable to recover from its massive losses in the Midcontinent division. In May of 1984, rumors in the press of Continental's impending failure caused a run on the bank; by July, the FDIC nationalized Continental through an "open bank" transaction, acquiring 80% of the bank's stock.

At the time, Continental was the U.S.' seventh-largest bank by deposits. The FDIC believed it was "too big to fail,"[654] but was unable to find a solvent bank willing to buy it and its toxic loans. Contrary to its treatment of energy banks in the Southwest a few years later, the FDIC did not close Continental. It gave depositors and general credi-tors a full guarantee—above the statutory $100,000 on deposits—and injected billions of dollars, diluting existing shareholders. Ultimately, the FDIC sold its position in 1991, with a cost to its insurance fund of approximately $1 billion—considerably less than the $4.5-billion orig-inal estimate.

Jody Grant, chief executive officer of Texas American Bank in Fort Worth, argued in his memoir, *The Great Texas Banking Crash: An Insider's Account*, that the "open bank" restructure was more efficient and vastly less costly to taxpayers—and the FDIC's insurance funds—than what the FDIC wrought upon the staid Texas and Oklahoma banks that were brought down a few years later by the one-two punch of oil and real estate crashes.[655] The result was that a bank that blindly

---

[653] Ferris, "How to Destabilize the Financial System," 81, 96.

[654] In the congressional hearings two months following the FDIC's takeover of Continental Illinois, U.S. Rep. Stewart B. McKinney declared that the government had created a new class of banks—those "too big to fail." Eric Dash, "If It's Too Big to Fail, Is It Too Big to Exist?" *The New York Times*, June 20, 2009.

[655] Joseph M. Grant, *The Great Texas Banking Crash: An Insider's Account* (University of Texas Press, 1996), 259.

bought, say, $1 billion of Penn Square loans was saved, while more-prudent, experienced and conservative energy banks that refused to participate in Penn Square's poorly documented loans were shut down by the FDIC and sold at fire-sale prices to out-of-state banks and investors.

Penn Square's practice of participating out oil and gas loans was not unique to it. Many small Texas and Oklahoma banks that were, like others, subject to regulation that prohibits them from lending more than 10% of its capital to any one borrower also aggressively participated out their bank-generated loans. Beep Jennings turned banking regulation that was intended to protect the solvency of depositary institutions into a license to steal.

Shauna Ferris, a lecturer in actuarial studies, wrote in 2010, "Penn Square might just keep 1% of a large loan, selling participations for the remaining 99% of the loan. If the commission for the participation was 1%, then Penn Square could make as many loans as it wanted to, without any need to fund the loans from its own deposit base. In fact, it appears that, sometimes, Penn Square passed on *more than* 100% of a loan, a practice known as 'over-participations.'"[656]

Eighty-eight banks participated in Penn Square loans. Seattle-First National Bank (SeaFirst) took its rig loans, predominantly. It saw half of its capital wiped out and reported writing off $378 million of loans purchased from Penn Square.[657]

SeaFirst's losses were, perhaps, more excusable than Continental's, as the bank was a relative newcomer to energy lending. Between 1978 and 1981, SeaFirst grew its energy-loan portfolio from $11 million to more than $300 million with more than $50 million in participations with Penn Square. Like a greenhorn at the big-stakes poker game in the local saloon near closing time, SeaFirst bought another

---

[656] Ferris, "How to Destabilize the Financial System," 94.
[657] The actual amount of SeaFirst's losses is not consistently reported. G.C. Hill, "Losses from Penn Square Bank Failures Total to $1.2 Billion and are Still Growing," *The Wall Street Journal*, April 12, 1984, reported that SeaFirst wrote off $343 million. Zweig, in *Belly Up*, puts the number at $366 million. Zweig, *Belly Up*, 338.

$350 million of loans from Penn Square in the last two months of 1981—six months before the Oklahoma City bank blew up.[658]

By the end of 1982, SeaFirst's energy loans totaled $1.3 billion, more than one-eighth of its entire loan portfolio.[659] After it wrote off more than 90% of Penn Square-originated loans, the FDIC was able to orchestrate its acquisition by Bank of America.[660]

SeaFirst and Continental were not alone when the music stopped. Northern Trust Bank reported holding more than $120 million of Penn Square-originated loans. Michigan National Bank wrote down $100 million out of $200 million. Chase Manhattan held $275 million and wrote off some $100 million. Overall, banks participating in the Penn Square loans suffered $1.5 billion in losses.[661]

Some losses were due to incomplete or absent documentation—an error that was repeated in home-mortgage lending in the 2000s that was brought to the public's attention in the Financial Crisis of 2008. Bank investigators, sifting through mountains of Penn Square records in Oklahoma City, determined that "some 3,000 loans were improperly documented, making the mess tough to untangle."[662]

Employees forged promissory notes from bank customers to provide collateral for loans. They also allowed borrowers to pledge the same collateral for two loans, which were then participated to different banks. And, to keep borrowers from going into default, Penn Square would make interest payments out of its own funds. This was euphemistically called "upstreaming the interest."[663]

"Whenever participating banks expressed concern about the quality of the loans," Ferris wrote, "Penn Square assured them that they could not lose—because PSB promised to take back any loans

[658] Zweig, *Belly Up*, 263.

[659] Martin H. Wolfson, *Financial Crises: Understanding the Postwar U.S. Experience* (M E Sharpe Inc, June 30, 1986), 95.

[660] Zweig, *Belly Up*, 436-438.

[661] Singer, *Funny Money*, 155-57; *see also* Yergin, *The Prize*, 732, and Ferris, "How to Destabilize the Financial System," 94-95.

[662] R. Rowan, "The Swinger Who Broke Penn Square Bank," *Fortune*, August 23, 1982, 122.

[663] Ferris, "How to Destabilize the Financial System," 95

which became too risky. These promises were, of course, unofficial. If the buy-back agreement had been included in the official participating agreements, Penn Square would have been in trouble with the regulator."[664]

In 1980-81, oil loans were being based on projections of prices escalating 10% per year to a maximum of $80 per barrel.[665] Continental's success at gaining market share in the backyards of more conservative energy lenders in Oklahoma and Texas caused a relaxation of underwriting standards by local energy lenders to protect their turf. There was frenetic lending on the part of many banks.

U.S. Banker reported in 1985, "For example, in 1981 officials of Republic [National] Bank of Texas were feeling pressure from members of the board of directors to preserve the bank's market share in energy lending. It was reported that Chairman James D. Berry summoned the bank's top energy lenders to his office and told them he wanted to make more energy loans.

"The lenders, who knew the industry was gripped by a gold-rush psychology, all sat there and blinked at the chairman, like a bunch of owls in a tree. But lenders at other institutions were assuming the price of oil would climb to $60 a barrel or more and had lowered their lending standards to grab new business. Republic's customers were going to those other banks."[666]

The closing of Penn Square started a contagion in the oil patch. At Abilene National in Central Texas, $50 million in deposits were withdrawn in the three days following a negative article in *The Dallas Morning News,* in which sources alleged that many of the bank's loans were bad.[667] The bank failed soon afterward.[668]

[664] Ferris, "How to Destabilize the Financial System," 95.

[665] Brian A. Toal, "Credit Where Credit Is Due," *Oil and Gas Investor* 7 (9), April 1988, 30.

[666] FDIC, *History of the Eighties – Lessons for the Future,* 299 (quoting Robert Dodge, "The Long Road Back in Texas," *United States Banker,* July 1985, available: LEXIS, Library: NEWS, File: USBANK). Republic National wound up merging six years later with its cross-town rival, InterFirst Bank, formerly First National Bank in Dallas, and, within a year, the merged bank known as First Republic Bank was closed by the FDIC—in large part due to oil and gas loans.

[667] Grant, *The Great Texas Banking Crash,* 24-25.

[668] Ferris, "How to Destabilize the Financial System," 108.

Chapter 6: 1980s

First National Bank of Midland failed in October of 1983, with more than $1.4 billion in assets. Federal Judge Lucius Bunton, who oversaw the fall-out litigation in this second-largest bank failure in U.S. history, wrote, "First National Bank was like a monument in the Permian Basin. It was a large, independently-owned bank. Sturdy and strong, the First National Bank was paid perhaps the highest compliment that can be bestowed upon an institution. It was said to be stronger than an acre of garlic."[669]

First National had had a long history of lending to the oil and gas industry under the watchful eye of its president, C.J. Kelly. Jody Grant wrote in 1996, "But Kelly had retired during the 1970s, and his successors had steered the bank away from traditional, conservative energy-production loans, secured by oil and gas reserves, and toward loans to finance oil field equipment, most notably drilling rigs. When the drilling business collapsed in 1982, rigs no longer in use or in demand could not bring $.10 on the dollar at auction."[670]

In the post-Kelly years under Charles Fraser and during the boom in oil prices, loans at First National had grown at a meteoric rate. *Time* reported in 1983, "Euphoric about the energy boom, the bank departed from prudent banking practices in evaluating loans; for example, it allowed customers to determine the value of their own collateral. The bank was known for its 'handshake' loans made on long-shot oil and gas ventures."[671]

Frank Dartez remembered being contacted by First National of Midland to possibly join its staff as a senior petroleum engineer with a promise of substantial salary and benefits. The bank had a large staff of engineers, but it was having trouble with keeping up with loan demand. Dartez recalled, "The bank's officers were brimming with confidence in their ability to evaluate every aspect of the Permian Basin. They felt they could be more aggressive than other banks because

---

[669] *FDIC v. Eagle Properties, Ltd., et al,* 664 F. Supp. 1027 (US D W. Dist, Midland-Odessa Division), 1985.
[670] Grant, *The Great Texas Banking Crash,* 25.
[671] "Burying Mother; Oil Woes Break a Texas Bank," *Time* (October 24, 1983). Available: LEXIS, Library: NEWS, File: TIME.

they were familiar with their customers' leasehold and drilling equipment and could put value on them.

"With this superior knowledge, they could make quick decisions. A customer or prospect could bring in his logs and maps on a newly completed well and often get a decision the same day. I was told by one of the bank's officer that it took a senior vice president's approval to decline a loan! It wasn't hard to see what might happen—even with just a modest downturn in the industry—and there was no way I wanted to be a part of that environment."[672]

When Kelly stepped down and Fraser took over, the bank and Midland were experiencing a boom on top of a boom. Judge Bunton wrote in his 1985 decision, "However, by 1982, the boom had bottomed, and the bank, which had grown so large, experienced unsettling troubles with its liquidity posture. The sources of these troubles included: an inordinate concentration of loans in the energy and associated industries area; less than careful lending practices; and imprudent growth."[673]

First National's problems were becoming well known in Midland and among its overline banks, which were concerned about their rights under their loan participations if First National were to be taken over by the FDIC. Charles Beckham, a bankruptcy attorney involved in a number of West Texas bank failures at the time, recalled that, six months before the bank failed, Texas Commerce and InterFirst Bank demanded that First National convert their participations in First National's $100-million loan to MGF Oil Corp. into direct assignments as syndicated loans.

First National was removed as the lead bank and replaced with Texas Commerce as the agent and InterFirst as collateral agent for the three-member syndicate. The MGF loan was the single-largest credit for First National at the time of its failure and one of a few the participating banks were able to seize leadership on prior to the FDIC taking control.

---

[672] Dartez, author's interview.
[673] FDIC v. Eagle Properties, 664 F. Supp. at 2.

Chapter 6: 1980s

After First Midland was declared insolvent by the U.S. Treasury Department's Comptroller of the Currency, the FDIC began a lengthy process of trying to collect on many defaulted loans. Given all the defaults, agency officials calculated that, if they took immediate action, they would have foreclosed on 365 homes, 12 commercial buildings, 1 million acres of land and 139 drilling rigs, resulting in the shuttering of 451 businesses and putting 6,500 people out of work in Midland and Odessa.[674]

Beckham represented Bank One in the 1980s and recalled its efforts to collect on a $20-million loan to a Midland-based producer. The effort forced the company into bankruptcy, but not before some unusual banking activity. The day before the company filed, its CEO drove up to the bank's drive-thru window and withdrew $100,000 in cash from the company's accounts.

In a deposition a few weeks later, the CEO was asked what he did with the $100,000. He responded that he had put the money in a brown paper bag. When asked what he did with the bag, he responded that he gave the bag to Oliver North. The line of questioning was not pursued further. Whether Oliver North actually received the cash was never discovered, but the producer's Chapter 11 was quickly converted to a Chapter 7 liquidation based on a finding of "poor management decisions."[675]

The FDIC took a more deliberate approach, but many independents were wiped out in the end nevertheless. One particular collection effort further highlighted the problems the bank encountered. In its waning days, Fraser sought to shore up the bank's capital by selling its headquarters for $75 million under a loan to a number of Midland's most prominent citizens.

The buyers discovered that their civic gesture was not enough to save the bank. They also learned, when sued on the note, that the bank's 24-story headquarters, 10-floor parking garage and drive-thru

---

[674] Robert Reinhold, "U.S. Helps Texas Survive Death of Bank," *The New York Times*, October 14, 1984.
[675] Charles Beckham, interview by the author, April 23, 2016.

motor facilities were worth considerably less than $75 million. The buyers asserted numerous defenses, but Judge Bunton was not persuaded. Prior to shooting down each defense, he put the case in perspective. He wrote of the bank and its lead banker:

> The Court, in considering this bankground [sic], is reminded of the circumstances and the fate of the captain of the transatlantic liner *Titanic*. The analogies are poignant. The First National Bank, like the vessel, was a magnificent, extravagant, enviable Camelot. It was regarded as unsinkable, said to be designed and engineered to withstand the formidable forces of natural laws. Each was led by an individual who was said by all as born to command – a captain who had risen through the ranks and left aside other individuals of lesser capabilities and greater disabilities. Each captain was aided by capable, attractive and knowledgeable officers and engineers. Each was asked to take his monument through a routine and pleasant passage. But, as did the captain of the ship, so did the chief of the bank, fail to heed the hints of conditions in the West that suggested the course might be other than propitious. Each, although having received warnings, decided to follow the prevailing practice of relying on a sharp lookout rather than reducing the speed of his Camelot. So each office saw an unyielding force and ordered a turn of direction. But, the sheer size of what each commanded and the momentum that was carried meant a lapse of time before a turn could be manipulated. Each monument encountered damage and began to lose its buoyancy. The advisors for each group were called and said the unsinkable ship was badly damaged but that her other sections would hold her up. Such was not the case. So, each commander's monument sank in the morning hours to the depths of ignominy to the brutal shock of their respective communities.[676]

---

[676] *FDIC v. Eagle Properties*, 664 F. Supp. at 3-4.

At the outset of 1982, Midland had seven banks: four independents and three holding-company subsidiaries. Neighboring Odessa also had seven: three independents and four holding-company banks. At the close of 1987, all four independents in Midland and the three in Odessa had failed. But for the support from their holding companies, the subsidiary banks likely would have succumbed to a similar fate.[677]

The peril of asset-based lending on non-producing oil and gas properties—thus lacking current cash flow for repayment—became painfully obvious. Shut-in wells, coupled with decreased revenue caused by lower prices from producing wells, would not service the repayment of loans.[678] And, unlike commercial loans made against a manufacturer's inventory, if wells were not drilled, the underlying leases could expire due to lack of development; thus, collateral could disappear.

Meanwhile, bankers partial to rig loans financed up to 80% of the rigs' construction; later, decent rigs were being auctioned for as little as four cents on the dollar of their original cost. Rigs were repossessed and stacked.[679] Making matters worse, banks had to pay any past-due state and local property taxes on the repossessed rigs or find the liens primed by state or local property-taxing authorities and potentially other lien claimants.[680]

Joe Bridges recalled rig bone yards popping up like mushrooms wherever there was sufficient acreage to hold the unwanted equipment, including alongside Interstate 10 west of Houston. Years later, Bridges was talking about those days with Howard Parker, who had long since retired from Parker & Parsley Petroleum Co., a Midland Basin producer.

---

[677] Grant, *The Great Texas Banking Crash*, 26.
[678] Mullen, "The Future of Bank Financing," Section 19.02[2].
[679] FDIC, *History of the Eighties – Lessons for the Future*, 312. "[A]t the end of 1981, when the number of drilling rigs operating in [Oklahoma] was at its peak, there were nearly 900 of them, but as of May 1986 there were only 128. Oklahoma's gas industry also suffered from plummeting prices ... and producers began to shut down their wells."
[680] Mullen, "The Future of Bank Financing," 19.02[3].

Parker related the story of a call from a New York investment-banker acquaintance of his. "Howard, we can buy rigs today by the pound for practically nothing. We should buy them up and when the business comes back, we will have the lowest-cost rig company in the business." Parker said he would think about it and called a drilling manager he knew to ask him what he thought.

"Mr. Parker," the drilling manager said, "in 1980, we had to have two armed guards on any rig if we even stopped moving it for night-fall. Today, we can park a rig on any road for as long as we want and no one will bother it. If they aren't worth stealing, they sure aren't worth buying."[681]

Had energy prices remained stable, Penn Square may have been an aberration, a footnote in the history of energy banking. From 1983 through the end of 1985, oil had stayed in a relatively narrow band of between $28 and $30 a barrel and reached $31.75 on November 20, 1985, on Nymex—an historical high, belying the threat of a price collapse.

By the fall of 1985, Saudi Arabia, tired of fellow OPEC members' cheating on agreed-to production quotas, increased its daily production from 2 million barrels to 4 million.[682] As a result, on January 2, 1986, the contract for West Texas Intermediate delivered to Cushing, Oklahoma, closed at $25.56; on March 3, $12.27; on March 31, $10.42.[683] This price had not been seen since April of 1970.[684]

The prognosis for leveraged producers was not good. With the drop in prices, Allied Bank's chief financial officer, Jay Crager, predicted in a *Newsweek* article in April of 1986 that borrowers "who've been in intensive care aren't going to make it out of the ward."[685]

Natural-gas prices fared no better. In a 1997 publication, the FDIC reported, "Subsequently, natural gas prices collapsed along with

[681] Bridges, author's interview.
[682] Yergin, *The Prize*, 730.
[683] U.S. EIA, Independent Statistics & Analysis. "U.S. Crude Oil and Natural Gas Rotary Rigs in Operation." Accessed September 19, 2015. Eia.gov.
[684] U.S. EIA, Independent Statistics & Analysis. "U.S. Crude Oil First Purchase Price." Accessed October 15, 2015. Eia.gov.
[685] "Banking's Dry Hole," *Newsweek*, April 14, 1986.

oil prices. For example, after a 33 percent decline in natural gas prices in 1985, from January through mid-May of 1986 spot market prices for natural gas dropped another 34 percent (from $1.90 to $1.26 mmBTUs)."[686]

The collapse in oil and gas prices caught many bankers by surprise. In early 1986, Fred Moses, president of Liberty National Bank and Trust Co. in Oklahoma City, observed, "This happened so damn quickly—in 90 days. We all expected a dip, but none of us assumed it would be such a precipitous drop."[687]

The times were tellingly reflected in the prevailing bumper stickers. A sticker that stated "$85 in '85" was pasted over by late 1986 with "Chapter 11 in '87."[688] In Houston, it became vogue among the *nouveau* poor to hold bankruptcy parties, acknowledging the times and accepting the new paradigm.

When incoming Texas American Bank chairman Jody Grant polled his senior officers in January of 1986 on their expectations for the coming year, they were uniformly pessimistic. Grant quoted Gene Gray, the bank's senior credit officer, as telling him, "Jody, we've been through hell. I don't know what it was like during the Depression, but it couldn't have been much worse, and it damn sure isn't over yet.

"We survived the crash in oil and agriculture in pretty good shape, but this thing we're in right now—no one knows where it's going. Only thirty days ago, oil was at $30 a barrel, now it's at $20. Hell, it could go to $10 in another thirty days.

"If that happens—and, I think it could very easily—what's that likely to do to the rest of our energy portfolio? And, then, what's going to be the effect on the rest of the economy? Real estate could go much deeper into the tank than it already is. I think we'd better get

---

[686] FDIC, *History of the Eighties – Lessons for the Future*, 299.

[687] FDIC, *History of the Eighties – Lessons for the Future*, 312, sourced from John Morris, "Banks of Mid-America Treads Water, Waits for Cheap Oil to Subside," *American Banker* (April 30, 1986), 8.

[688] "A Dream Dies in Texas, Once a Land of Unlimited Promise, the Lone Star State Has Lost its Shine and Now has a Barrel of Troubles," *People* (November 10, 1986).

ready for the biggest Texas tornado we've ever seen, because it's going to tear this state apart."[689]

Notwithstanding the precipitous drop in collateral values, some energy bankers remained sanguine about the market's ability to bounce back, which only further compounded their problems. "RepublicBank [sic] remains committed to the energy industry; it will make new loans based on expectations that oil prices will soon rebound to about $18 a barrel," Eugene Fiedorek, executive vice president of Republic National, told financial analysts in March of 1986.[690] Bankers at Texas Commerce, InterFirst Corp. of Dallas and Mid-America of Oklahoma expressed similar sentiments.[691]

So, instead of an aberration, Penn Square became the canary in the coal mine. By the mid-1980s, the Texas, Oklahoma and Louisiana banking industry began to experience a traumatic downturn caused by credit overextension and loose lending to real estate, energy and energy-related industries. The initial surge in the number of oil-patch-bank failures was caused, primarily, by problems with energy loans. The second wave into the late 1980s was the result of the crash that followed the oil-boom-driven expansion of real estate lending, especially among Texas banks.

At the beginning of 1987, one in six homes and apartments in Houston stood vacant. Because of the associated plunge in property values, the county's tax rolls had declined by an estimated $8 billion. Property values collapsing more than 50% in some suburbs caused many to walk away from their homes and their mortgage payments. In some communities, foreclosure rates were in excess of 60%.[692]

In 1983, only three Texas banks failed; in 1988, the number was 175 and having assets of $47.3 billion—practically a quarter of the state's 1987 year-end bank assets. The following year, there were 134 more failures, with assets of $23.2 billion. In 1988-89, Texas account-

[689] Grant, *The Great Texas Banking Crash*, 14.
[690] FDIC, *History of the Eighties – Lessons for the Future*, 300.
[691] FDIC, *History of the Eighties – Lessons for the Future*, 300.
[692] FDIC, *History of the Eighties – Lessons for the Future*, 309.

ed for 85% of total, U.S., failed-bank assets. All told, from 1980 through 1989, 367 Texas commercial banks failed.[693]

In Oklahoma City, First National Bank & Trust, the state's third-largest bank, failed on July 14, 1986, and was sold to Los Angeles-based First Interstate Bancorp. A week later, BancOklahoma Corp. was reported to be seeking assistance from the FDIC. A few weeks later, the FDIC announced its second "open bank" assistance transaction: This one was with BancOklahoma's Bank of Oklahoma, injecting $130 million of capital and acquiring substantially all of the stock as well as warrants convertible into 55% of the parent's common stock.[694]

Grant wrote of the times that, "while [these] were the first major Southwest banks to succumb to the aftermath of the 1986 oil price dive, they were only a precursor of many others to follow."[695]

Meanwhile, Louisiana's banks were less exposed to loans to oil producers. The FDIC reported in a 1997 summary of the 1980s, "One reason for this, according to [bank consultant] Michael D. Charbonnet … was that Louisiana banks were not big enough to finance the major oil and gas development projects. Texas and Oklahoma banks mainly kept that business to themselves."[696]

Louisiana banks concentrated on lending to oilfield-service companies, which faced mounting difficulties. Bank failures in the state soon escalated. Between 1980 and 1994, there were 70 bank failures in

---

[693] FDIC, *History of the Eighties – Lessons for the Future*, 292, 321. "The sequence in which the states are listed reflects the severity of each state's banking crisis. From 1980 through 1994, Texas had 599 bank failures and $60.2 billion in failed-bank assets (43.8 percent of the state's total bank assets); Oklahoma: 122 failures, $5.8 billion in failed-bank assets (23.8 percent of total state banking assets); Louisiana: 70 failures, $4.1 billion in assets (17.4 percent of total); New Mexico: 11 failures, $568 million in assets (9.5 percent of total); and Arkansas: 11 failures, $161 million in assets (1.5 percent of total). (Note: The number of bank failures refers to FDIC-insured commercial and savings banks that were closed or received FDIC assistance. Asset data refer to assets of banks existing in each state at year-end 1979 plus assets of newly chartered banks as of the date of failure, merger, or December 31, 1994, whichever is applicable.)."
[694] Grant, *The Great Texas Banking Crash*, 26.
[695] Grant, *The Great Texas Banking Crash*, 26.
[696] FDIC, *History of the Eighties – Lessons for the Future*, 311.

Louisiana, equal to 22.4% of the state's banks; their assets totaled $4.1 billion.[697]

Out of the Frying Pan, Into the Fire

On the ropes from the decline in oil prices, banks in the Southwest were dealt a knock-out blow by excessive losses tied to real estate. As the oil price began to steadily decline in the 1980s, banks in the Southwest redirected their lending efforts to booming real estate markets, particularly commercial real estate.

But real estate markets, especially in the Southwest, were both a trailing indicator of the energy industry and artificially inflated by regulatory changes. By 1986, the inflated real estate crisis became manifest and, to add a *coup de grâce*, Congress changed the tax incentives that had supported much of the bubble in real estate.

In large part, many energy banks were also competing with the recently deregulated savings and loan institutions in real estate lending.[698] The Depository Institutions Deregulation and Monetary Control Act of 1980 (DIDMCA) and the Garn-St Germain Depository Institutions Act of 1982[699] greatly increased the investment and lending powers of S&Ls, which—along with substantial tax breaks included in the Economic Recovery Tax Act of 1982—fueled a boom in Southwest real estate markets outside of the thrifts' traditional business of making home-mortgage loans.[700]

DIDMCA increased the limits of federal deposit insurance from $40,000 to $100,000 and phased out limits on the interest rates S&Ls could pay for deposits. Garn-St Germain allowed S&Ls to stretch into all facets of real estate and outside the S&L's community market.

Following relaxation of regulatory controls on S&Ls, charters for new banks and thrifts were encouraged under the Reagan Administration. Before the 1980s, new charters had been granted on the basis of community need. Federally chartered stock associations were required

---

[697] FDIC, *History of the Eighties – Lessons for the Future*, 312.
[698] FDIC, *History of the Eighties – Lessons for the Future*, 292, 302.
[699] *Garn-St Germain Depository Institutions Act of 1982*, Public Law 97-320.
[700] FDIC, *History of the Eighties – Lessons for the Future*, 312.

to have at least 400 stockholders. No one individual could own more than 10%, no group could control more than 25% and at least 75% of the stockholders had to reside within the S&L's market area.[701]

Net-worth requirements were lowered, so a $2-million initial investment could be leveraged into $1.3 billion in assets by the end of the first year in operation.[702] And the initial capital could be in the form of "non-cash" assets—a boon to real estate developers holding land on their books that they couldn't develop.[703]

Under Reagan, the Federal Home Loan Bank Board and the Office of the Comptroller of the Currency approved any application "as long as the owners hired competent management and provided a sound business plan." To keep market share, state-chartered S&Ls, which typically had more relaxed standards than the federal regulations, competed with yet more-liberal regulations.[704] Between 1980 and 1986, 492 new S&Ls were chartered.[705]

In *Inside Job: The Looting of America's Savings and Loans*, journalists Stephen Pizzo, Mary Fricker and Paul Muolo wrote, "The ink wasn't dry on the Garn-St Germain legislation, deregulating the thrift industry, before high-stakes investors, swindlers, and mobsters lined up to loot S&Ls. They immediately seized the opportunity created by careless deregulation of thrifts and gambled, stole, and embezzled away billions in an orgy of greed and excess."[706]

To grow, the new S&Ls advertised and used in-house "money desks" to solicit deposits, often paying more than 100 basis points above bank certificates of deposit. To grow more quickly, S&Ls worked with money-brokerage firms to acquire large bundles of de-

---

[701] FDIC, *History of the Eighties – Lessons for the Future*, 175.

[702] James R. Barth, *The Great Savings and Loan Debacle* (Aei Pr, 1991), 54.

[703] Stephen Pizzo, et al., *Inside Job: The Looting of America's Savings and Loans* (McGraw-Hill, 1989), 12-13.

[704] FDIC, *History of the Eighties – Lessons for the Future*, 176. Referred to as the "competition in laxity," California, Florida and Texas had some of the most liberal laws for state-chartered thrifts.

[705] FDIC, *History of the Eighties – Lessons for the Future*, 178, Table 4.3.

[706] Pizzo, *Inside Job*, 4. "By 1987, when Texas thrifts finally were failing in large numbers, 50 percent were run by managers who had entered the business after 1979 (over 80 percent were former real estate developers)." Pizzo, *Inside Job*, 20.

posits. The brokered deposits were known as "hot money," as they could be deposited one day and withdrawn the next in search of an even higher interest rate.[707]

Unlike commercial lenders, the S&Ls could take high, front-end fees on loans and up to 50% direct-equity interest in real estate loans as compensation in addition to interest. The act also permitted S&Ls to make loans of up to 100% of appraised value. Banker Jody Grant noted the impact on commercial banks that the S&Ls had with their newfound regulatory freedom:

> As a consequence, by obtaining liberal and fraudulent appraisals, borrowers were able to obtain loans far in excess of the amount actually paid for a real estate property and put the difference in their pockets. Although legal, it was a fraudulent concept. With deregulation, the lure of the S&Ls became irresistible to opportunists who recognized the advantages of the new powers under the Garn-St Germain [Act]. To the real estate entrepreneur, the only thing better than borrowing from an S&L was owning one. To the less than honest, owning an S&L was a license to steal. ... The bacchanalian orgy of the mismanaged S&Ls produced a hangover of unprecedented proportions,

---

[707] FDIC, *History of the Eighties – Lessons for the Future*, 175-182. In its discussion of Penn Square's addiction to 'hot money' and subsequent regulatory corrective, the FDIC reported: "In many institutions during the banking crisis of the 1980s and early 1990s, brokered deposits became a problem. When institutions faced liquidity shortages, they frequently turned to brokers for large sums of cash in a hurry. The FDIC believes deposit brokering became a problem following the enactment of the Depository Institutions Deregulation and Monetary Control Act (DIDMCA) of 1980. ... [D]epository institutions began to compete for large amounts of deposits through the offering of high interest rates, and many depositors found the highest rates through the services of deposit brokers. In 1989, Congress passed the Financial Institutions Reform, Recovery, and Enforcement Act (FIRREA), which limited some use of brokered deposits simply by prohibiting troubled institutions from accepting brokered deposits. In 1991, Congress passed the Federal Deposit Insurance Corporation Improvement Act (FDICIA), which amended the 1989 statute by prohibiting troubled institutions (that is, institutions that did not meet applicable minimum capital requirements) from accepting funds obtained directly or indirectly by or through any deposit broker. Those institutions were similarly prohibited from offering a rate of interest significantly higher than other area banks." FDIC, *History of the Eighties – Lessons for the Future*, Chapter 3.

leaving no participant untouched. The impact on Texas' major banks, all of which were active participants, was particularly severe.[708]

A lack of experience and discipline among thrift executives caused many of the thrifts' losses. But outright fraud was also well documented.[709] Pizzo et al. described how the thrifts were able to create inflated profits by flipping loans:

"I remember one closing we had," said a real estate salesperson, describing how they flipped land to raise its value. "It was in the hall of an office building. The tables were lined all the way down the hall. The investors were lined up in front of the tables. The loan officers would close one sale and pass the papers to the next guy. It looked like kids registering for college. If any investor raised a question, someone would come over and tell them to leave, they were out of the deal." At the end of the day's flipping, huge loans, based on the inflated valued created by the flip sales, would be taken out on the properties.

… To keep those loans from going into default, [Dallas'] Vernon Savings—and their sister thrifts like State/Lubbock and Sunbelt—made the loans large enough to allow for an interest reserve that could cover the payments for a year or so. When that money ran out Vernon renewed the loan. And each time Vernon renewed a loan it was able to book new loan fees.

… By the time Vernon failed on March 20, 1987, an unbelievable *96 percent* of all its outstanding loans were in default. Virtually every loan Vernon had made was a bad loan.[710]

---

[708] Grant, *The Great Texas Banking Crash*, 32-33, 38, 42.
[709] "More than 1,000 bank and S&L executives were convicted of felonies." Financial Crisis Inquiry Commission (FCIC), *The Financial Crisis Inquiry Report, Authorized Edition: Final Report of the National Commission on the Causes of the Financial and Economic Crisis in the United States* (Public Affairs, January 2011), 36.
[710] Pizzo, *Inside Job*, 207, 209, 226.

S&Ls' aggressive practices prompted more-competitive behavior by commercial lenders.[711] They reacted to oil-price weakening by increasing their real estate portfolios, fueling substantial growth in real estate development in the Southwest. By the mid-1980s, markets in Houston and Dallas were overbuilt. Grant wrote, "With inflation of the late 1970s and early 1980s and with the more permissible lending resulting from the enactment of the Garn-St Germain [Act] in 1982, the traditions that had governed real estate lending gave way to a new set of standards. ..."

He added that, "by the early- to mid-1980s, most of the old-timers had retired, and [the new lenders] were young and inexperienced. None of them had seen really seen tough times, and most had gained experience only during the highly inflationary days of the 1970s. In those days, it was hard to make a mistake, or at least mistakes were hard to recognize, as inflation bailed out one ill-advised deal after another."[712]

Then, Congress passed the Tax Reform Act of August 1986. "[It] was the final blow for many of the Texas banks and S&Ls. Already weak and vulnerable from five years of economic battering, they could not endure the ensuing 30 to 40 percent devaluation of real estate values. The carnage was devastating," Grant concluded.[713]

Lawrence Crum, a finance professor at the University of Texas at Austin, wrote in a Texas State Historical Association account, "As commercial real estate returns and values declined, developers were unable to find permanent financing from non-bank investors, leaving the banks holding real estate loans as non-performing assets. The percentage of non-performing assets held by Texas banks increased on average from 1.75% to 6.6% between 1982 and 1987. Texas banks that failed during this period had a non-performing ratio greater than 10.4%."[714]

---

[711] FDIC, *History of the Eighties – Lessons for the Future*, 315.
[712] Grant, *The Great Texas Banking Crash*, 48, 49. *See also* FDIC, *History of the Eighties – Lessons for the Future*, 185.
[713] Grant, *The Great Texas Banking Crash*, 216.
[714] Crum, "Banks and Banking."

The seeds that led to the S&L debacle were planted well before any impact of the oil crisis. Pizzo et al. wrote:

> When thrifts began to collapse in large numbers in the mid-1980s, federal and state officials tried to blame the failures on a depressed oil economy. But in California oil played a very minor role in the state's robust business climate, yet thrifts nevertheless failed. The oil excuse, we suspected, was a slippery way of avoiding the real issue—fraud.[715]
>
> ... Bad as things were, Vernon wasn't an exception in Dallas, it was the rule. FBI officials scoffed at Federal Home Loan Bank Board statements that the losses were attributable to the oil recession. Vernon, for example, was already in trouble in 1983, over two years before oil prices collapsed. Government auditors and Justice Department investigators estimated that there were $15 billion in losses in institutions in the Dallas area that were under criminal investigation. In Houston half the failed institutions there were under investigation as well. Every time investigators looked at a failed thrift, they found fraud.[716]

Regardless of the culpability, by the time energy banks in the Southwest switched their focus from oil and gas to real estate, the S&L debacle—which cost taxpayers an estimated $160 billion[717] with almost 3,000 commercial banks and thrifts closed—and changes in tax laws had dealt a double whammy. Banks that chose to compete were doomed to fail.

Legacy of Loss of Texas Banks

Seven of the 10 largest commercial banks in Texas failed between 1987 and 1990 and control of two others was acquired by out-of-state

---

[715] Pizzo, *Inside Job*, 76.

[716] Pizzo, *Inside Job*, 227.

[717] U.S. General Accounting Office, *Financial Audit: Resolution Trust Corporation's 1995 and 1994 Financial Statements*, Report to the Congress, July 1996, 13.

banks, a sad legacy that has affected Texas energy lenders ever since. Texas Commerce Bancshares was the first major bank to seek acquisition by an out-of-state organization in the 1980s.

Led by chief executive officer Ben Love, Texas Commerce and other major state banks persuaded Governor Mark White to call a special session of the legislature in the summer of 1986. The legislature finally passed a bill to allow interstate banking. In November, voters approved a constitutional amendment to permit limited branch banking. The new law allowed out-of-state banks to purchase Texas banks; however, they were not allowed to establish branches in Texas nor enter the state by chartering and establishing new banks—that is, *de novo* banks.

The interstate-banking law took effect on January 1, 1987.[718] On May 1, 1987, Texas Commerce merged with Chemical New York Corp. Following Texas Commerce's lead and subject to the same economic realities, Allied Bancshares announced its merger with First Interstate Bancorp of Los Angeles on May 21, 1987.[719] Seven other energy banks adjudged insolvent were absorbed by out-of-state interests and recapitalized with assistance from the FDIC.

In the case of the 1987 merger of InterFirst Bank and Republic, forming First Republic Bank Corp., the merger of equals was a merger of the equally weak.[720] In less than a year, it sought FDIC assistance and, with National Bancshares Corp. out of San Antonio, was purchased by North Carolina-based NCNB Corp., forming NCNB Texas National Bank.[721]

MBank, an amalgamation of Mercantile National Bank, which traced its Dallas roots back to 1917, and Houston's Bank of the Southwest, established in 1907, was sold to Banc One of Ohio in Jan-

---

[718] Acts 1986, 69th Leg., 2nd C.S., ch. 14, at 71.

[719] The closing was delayed until January of the next year while the deal was retraded due to continuing deterioration of the Houston and Texas economies.

[720] Grant, "The Great Texas Banking Crash," 74.

[721] FDIC, OCC and FRS Joint News Release, "Regulators Announce Approval of Acquisition of Subsidiary Banks of First Republic Bank Corporation, Dallas, Texas, by NCNB Corporation, Charlotte, North Carolina," PR-148-88 (July 29, 1988), 1.

uary of 1990 after the FDIC declared MBank insolvent and in need of a $2.8-billion bailout.

Fort Worth's Texas American Bancshares vainly pursued an 18-month effort to find an "open bank" solution via a combination with National Bancshares of San Antonio and new capital from Texas investors. Instead, it was taken over by the FDIC in 1989, forming Texas American Bridge Bank, which shortened its name to Team Bank. In 1992, Team Bank was merged into Chicago-based Bank One.

Roughly a third of Houston-based First City Bank's $2.1-billion energy portfolio was extended to oilfield suppliers and rig operators.[722] But First City had not only bulked up on oilfield loans in the go-go days of the early '80s. Between year-end 1976 and year-end 1983, the bank's commercial real estate loans increased from 3.11% to 10.71%.

The FDIC reported, "Although the decline in energy markets led directly to asset quality problems for First City, most of the increase in nonperforming assets was associated with commercial real estate lending. As Texas commercial real estate markets declined after 1983, so too did First City's earnings and assets."[723]

By 1986, it was experiencing financial problems; in April of 1988, it received a $1-billion injection from the FDIC in "note capital" and a more than $500-million equity investment by a group headed by A. Robert Abboud, who had been ousted in 1980 from his role as head of Continental Illinois' cross-town rival, First Chicago Corp. Ironically, First Chicago's board had criticized him for losing ground to Continental, which was larding up on Penn Square loans.

In his quest for redemption, he and co-investors purchased First City with the plan of turning it around into a global powerhouse. Abboud directed the bank's attention away from its Texas base, making loans to the likes of Federated Department Stores Inc., Drexel Burnham Lambert and Circle K Stores Inc., each of which later fell into

---

[722] "Banking's Dry Hole," *Newsweek*, April 14, 1986.
[723] John O'Keefe, "The Texas Banking Crisis Causes and Consequences 1980-1989," FDIC Division of Research and Statistics, July 1990, 47. Fraser.stlouisfed.org.

bankruptcy. By 1991, First City was reporting that more than 4.2% of its assets were nonperforming and reported common equity at an anemic 2.6% of assets.

The downfall of First City could no longer be blamed solely on energy loans. In addition to forays into new areas of commercial lending, it continued to feel the impact of a slow real estate recovery in Texas and generally depressed local economy. Paul M. Horvitz, a professor of banking and finance at the University of Houston, told *The New York Times* in 1991, "First City is, after all, a medium-sized bank, and Abboud wanted to be a major player. The losses for the most part were not from doing their knitting in Texas."[724]

In the years between his jobs at First Chicago and First City, Abboud wrote a book, *Money in the Bank: How Safe Is It?*, that was an apologia about his stormy departure at First Chicago. He often cited his book in interviews upon arriving in Houston. The title of the first chapter is "We're Only Human;" the next, "Learning the Hard Way." Federal and state regulators closed First City and its 20-bank system in 1992.

Grant wrote, "Thus ended the long and painful saga of First City, which began about twelve years earlier with the decline in the oil business and the accompanying recession in Houston. This action also brought to a close the golden era of banking in Texas, when the large Texas banks had been the envy of the country. With the closing and sale of First City, nine of the ten largest Texas banks had ceased to exist as Texas-based-and-managed entities due to merger or sale."[725]

The only Texas-owned bank left standing after the carnage was Frost Bank, the tenth-largest in the state. Frost began in 1868 as a wool warehouse in San Antonio and became a nationally chartered bank in 1899. In 1977, it merged with Houston-based Cullen Bank, which was started in 1969 by the heirs of Hugh Roy Cullen, a success-

---

[724] Thomas C. Hayes, "Abboud Out as Chief at Houston's First City," *The New York Times*, March 27, 1991.
[725] Grant, *The Great Texas Banking Crash*, 248.

ful wildcatter who built his career on the discovery of Pierce Junction Field near Houston.

Cullen/Frost reported $23 million in energy-loan losses in 1983 and entered merger negotiations with First City. As Jody Grant observed, because Cullen/Frost was working on cleaning up its problem loans and dressing up the bank for its merger, it was on the sidelines when other Texas banks shifted focus to real estate loans.

"As it developed, it was an extremely opportune time not to be making real estate loans," Grant wrote. "Subsequently, the merger was called off because of First City's troubles, but the timing of these events probably saved Cullen/Frost."[726]

In a way, Cullen/Frost's survival serves as "Exhibit A" for the proposition that the collapse of Texas banks in the 1980s was not due solely to poor oil and gas loans. The '80s brought together a confluence of events, including the collapse of oil and gas markets, changes in tax and energy regulations, an over-heated real estate bubble, deregulation of S&Ls and high interest rates, to name a few. When combined, these ingredients created a toxic stew that took down the state's strongest banks.

If Texas' largest banks had been able to weather the economic stress of the 1980s, the U.S. banking landscape may have been significantly different today. Texas Commerce's Ben Love wrote in his autobiography:

> The tragedy for the state, though, is that Texas could have been one of three financial centers in the country. … [B]eginning in 1970, with bank holding companies, the rules changed. The five largest Texas banks were consolidating the state's fragmented banking system, providing us with a currency (i.e., stock price and stock liquidity) that would enable us to expand into other states, if only the Texas legislature had allowed it.

---

[726] Grant, *The Great Texas Banking Crash*, 229-30.

... [I]f Texas interstate banking laws had been enacted as, for example they were in North Carolina, [Texas Commerce Bank] would have had the inside track to merge with these select, large, Energy Belt, out-of-state banks quickly, diversify our markets, and increase our size rapidly. Merging with those banks would have catapulted Texas Commerce onto the list of the ten largest banks in the United States. ... Instead, oil prices collapsed and the Texas economy took a very rough bump, forcing Texas banks to merge with or be acquired by large out-of-state banks after failing and having federal bailout money injected. ... Today [in 2005] not one of the nation's top fifty banks is headquartered in Texas. ... The historical tragedy of this era was that every large Texas bank was lost.[727]

There was no shortage of anger and dissatisfaction among the largest Texas banks' directors, officers and shareholders, who felt that the deck was stacked against them by federal regulators. Prior to Texas Commerce's merger with Chemical New York, Love visited with Bill Taylor, the Federal Reserve's chief of staff at the time, in Washington to discuss the bank's options. Love protested that the New York banks—with their loans to South American countries during the Latin American debt crisis—were more exposed than Texas Commerce.

Taylor responded, "Ben, I've told you all I'm going to. Don't worry about those Latin American loans. As an element of government policy, the Federal Reserve will not let [the 10 largest banks in the nation] fail. That's the way it is. But I will tell you one other thing: If we think it is proper, we *will* let any Texas bank fail because not one Texas bank is among the ten largest banks in the nation."[728]

Taylor's advice to Love about merging with Chemical or Chase was "You get out of here and get that done." Love added that Taylor

---

[727] Love, *My Life in Texas Commerce*, 309 and 310.
[728] Love, *My Life in Texas Commerce*, 236.

also told him, "You Texans always think what you have in Texas is worth one hell of a lot more than any of the rest of us do."[729]

Bankers trying to find solutions with the FDIC's staff and chairman, Bill Seidman, felt there was a bias against Texas and Texans. Grant wrote, "The popular television series *Dallas* had done much to stereotype Texans, and we had not helped ourselves with bumper stickers during the energy crisis that said 'FREEZE A YANKEE.' Third, there was probably a tendency to indict the entire state for the sins of the fraudulent S&L operators. Thus, a bailout of Texas financial institutions wouldn't have been politically popular."[730]

Grant's motivation for chronicling his time at the helm of Fort Worth's Texas American Bank, which was formed in 1873 and had weathered its share of banking crises, was to expose the indifference, if not outright bias, among federal regulators against Texas banks. Over a period of 18 months, Texas American and San Antonio's National Bank fought a Kafkaesque duel with Seidman to find a buyer that could salvage the Texas roots of two venerable, but battle-weary, institutions.

Grant's narrative is a tale of broken promises and frustration wrought by national politics and regulatory insouciance to a growing real-estate-banking problem. In the ensuing litigation between Texas American and the FDIC over the FDIC's method of taking over the banks in Texas American's organization, U.S. District Judge Barefoot Sanders held that the FDIC had overstepped its regulatory authority:

> The facts of this case indicate an ... egregious use of the FDIC's extensive powers by manipulating the recovery of affiliated banks on the obligations owed to them in order to make those banks insolvent as well. ... The closure and sale of solvent banks through ar-

---

[729] Grant, *The Great Texas Banking Crash*, 100.
[730] Grant, *The Great Texas Banking Crash*, 102.

bitrary devaluation of their assets in another bank cannot be fair.[731]

Even Bill Taylor, who succeeded Seidman as FDIC chief, admitted as much in a back-handed way in a 1992 interview with *The Dallas Morning News*. "The person who says things got a little aggressive in Texas probably isn't all wrong," he said.[732]

Not long after the effects of Texas' real estate bust manifested itself in the collapse of its homegrown and Texas-proud lending institutions, the FDIC faced similar challenges in the Northeast and Florida. Ultimately, it realized that local leaders' continued ownership of and involvement in U.S. banks was a critical element in minimizing the ultimate cost to the FDIC's insurance fund and, ultimately, U.S. taxpayers.

Looking back a quarter-century, Love asks in his autobiography, "What if I had been able to convince the Texas independent bankers and politicians in the 1970s to support our efforts to equip our state with three or four financial institutions that could and should compete with Citicorp and the other major money center banks that were invading the Texas market? What if timing of the oil bust had been different, or its impact had been less severe?

"What if federal regulators had treated our bank in a more even-handed way? What if several of the major Texas banks could have found their way to a merger that would have created a strong Texas bank?

"Such questions are interesting to think about, but as the person responsible for the fate of Texas Commerce and its shareholders, I had the responsibility to act in the 1980s. ... I had to play the cards dealt me. All these years later, ... I feel, though, a certain sense of frustration and even sadness that I didn't have the chance to finish the

---

[731] *Texas American Bancshares, Inc. et al., v Robert Logan Clarke, Comptroller of the Currency,* 740 F. Supp 1243 (U.S. District Court, N.D. Texas Dallas Div., June 25, 1990). Judge Sanders holding was reversed by the Fifth Circuit, 954 F. 2d 329 (U.S. 5th Cir. 1992).
[732] Grant, *The Great Texas Banking Crash,* 234.

job of building an internationally competitive bank based in Houston."[733]

Even if the 1875 Texas Constitutional Convention members had been able to foresee that their efforts to protect hometown banking would backfire more than 100 years later, it likely would not have changed their agrarian-populist agenda of the time. Texans and Texas energy bankers may wish to blame their failure on a conspiracy between federal regulators and the "Eastern Banking Establishment." But the reality is that a root cause was Texas' own state law.

Newsweek reported in April of 1986, just before the eleventh-hour special legislative session called by Governor White that permitted interstate banking, "Texans have fierce, populist objections to interstate banking. But they may have to swallow those objections—and write it off as another dose of humility brought on by the great oil bust of 1986."[734]

The state had ample opportunities in the 1970s to rectify the regulations that hobbled its banks from becoming national leaders.[735] But relief was too late and the problems too massive for Texas' energy lenders to right their course. The personal sting of losing local control of their banks was not limited to the banks' presidents and their boards. There was a palpable loss to each community and to the state.

Grant observed, "The fact that control of the state's major banking resources has passed into out-of-state hands has been traumatic for Texans. The engine that drove the commercialization and industrialization of the state, and provided the early entrepreneurs with seed money to build some of today's leading businesses, is gone."[736]

He provided a clear example of the importance of local bankers and their board members as leaders in the community. In 1972, Tom Vandergriff, the mayor of Arlington, Texas, was angling to get the professional baseball team, the Washington Senators, to move to the city, which sits between Fort Worth and Dallas.

---

[733] Love, *My Life in Texas Commerce*, 250.
[734] "Banking's Dry Hole," *Newsweek*, April 14, 1986.
[735] Love, *My Life in Texas Commerce*, 227.
[736] Grant, *The Great Texas Banking Crash*, 251.

Grant recalled how the mayor needed $8 million to close the deal and Vandergriff said it was the can-do civic spirit of the local Dallas, Fort Worth and Arlington bankers that gave the confidence for the city to pursue its dream. Vandergriff said the bankers told him, "'You get the franchise – we'll provide the money.' Without the bankers' full-speed-ahead spirit and action, we simply could not have done what we did in those days."[737]

Most of the out-of-state banks that acquired Texas banks kept the local energy-banking teams pretty much intact. But there was a competitive difference between homegrown bankers, who were capable of walking down the hall to discuss a loan with credit-committee members, and those who would have to fly to out-of-state meetings or discuss the importance of lending to a local producer over a long-distance conference call.

More than just in energy lending, there was a loss that could not be replaced when the banks' directors were no longer local business-owners, who were to become the next generation of board members, civic leaders and benefactors of their cities and state. More than the tangible loss, there was a loss of Texas pride.

The state that, for several decades, set the world price for oil and had most of the experienced and capable oil and gas bankers was humbled as its financial institutions were sold to holding companies in Ohio, North Carolina and New York. Producers and their bankers were forced to adjust to the new reality.

Energy Lending Takes a Back Seat

Texas bank assets fell from $209 billion at the end of 1985 to around $170 billion at the end of 1991. The banks tightened their lending policies.[738] Like their counterparts elsewhere in the nation, they began selling existing loans and other assets in secondary markets. In 1985, even before the full brunt of the energy meltdown was known, Zweig

[737] Grant, *The Great Texas Banking Crash*, 251.
[738] Crum, "Banks and Banking."

wrote, "Within the commercial banking industry, the least tangible long-range impact of the debacle may also be the most significant.

"The morning after the [1982] failure [of Penn Square], bankers throughout the country began sifting through their portfolios of loan participations and analyzing their loan review procedures, internal controls, and lending authorities. The result has been, by most accounts, stricter lending standards, a phenomenon that inevitably translates into increased difficulty for marginal borrowers in obtaining funds."[739]

The impact of the oil and real estate crashes was felt for more than a decade. Yergin wrote in 1993, "With the collapse of Continental Illinois, energy lending instantaneously went out of fashion. Any banks still willing or able to lend to energy companies rewrote their guidelines so restrictively that getting an oil and gas loan was not much easier than passing through the proverbial eye of the needle. And without capital, there was no fuel for exploration and development, let alone a boom."[740]

Looking back at the 1980s, Olien and Hinton wrote in 2007 in an introduction of a new release of their 1984 *Wildcatters*, "During 1988 more than half [of] all Texas banks were rated as problem banks, undercapitalized and with a host of non-performing loans. Those banks surviving concentrated on collecting old loans and were understandably reluctant to make energy loans. Thus, when North Carolina National Bank [NCNB] took over Republic Bank of Midland, local oilmen joked that its NCNB stood for 'No Cash for No Body.'"[741]

The disarray caused in established U.S. energy-lending markets created an opportunity for foreign bankers. The Texas Constitution specifically restricts deposit-taking activity by foreign banks, making federal or state charters of foreign branches impossible. But the foreign banks were not looking for local depositors. Instead they were drawn to the international energy business in Houston where they

---

[739] Zweig, "Belly Up," 443.
[740] Yergin, *The Prize*.
[741] Olien and Hinton, *Wildcatters*, xv.

could establish banking relationships for overseas loans as well as participate in domestic loans through their U.S. offices, typically located in New York.

Before 1985, foreign-bank activity was confined to nonbank subsidiaries and representative offices that carried out business in Texas incidental to foreign business or international trade. In 1985, the Texas legislature passed the Foreign Bank Agency Act, which specifically authorizes foreign banks to establish one agency in the state—that is, a place where loans could be booked and related activities performed.

After 1985, a number of foreign banks staked out a significant presence in Texas, particularly in Houston. They made strong inroads in the vacuum of the U.S.-lender meltdown. Building "local teams," the foreign banks hired veteran loan officers from failed Texas banks. The officers, in turn, lured their clients as new borrowers that had become disgruntled by the shift in U.S. bank-lending criteria. In 1996, commercial lending by foreign agencies in Houston represented 43.5% of such lending by Houston-area banks.[742]

A number had been participants and, sometimes, leaders of oil and gas credits in the 1970s. Brad Richards, a Houston-based finance attorney with Haynes and Boone, said, "As I recall, there were five original foreign banks, three of which were Japanese: Fuji Bank, Sanwa Bank and Bank of Tokyo. Baker Botts represented Fuji Bank, Sanwa Bank and Union Bank of Switzerland at that time and I am pretty sure they were three of the original FBAs. I know both Fuji Bank and UBS were because I continued to represent them until they left Houston."[743]

Energy-banker John Lane moved from First City National to open French bank Banque Indosuez's Houston agency in 1986. Lane recalled, "At that time, all the Texas banks were failing, which created a significant opening for foreign banks because many trade and infrastructure customers (such as Brown & Root and Halliburton) had

---

[742] "Foreign Banks Bring Global Links to Houston," Federal Reserve Bank of Dallas, Houston Branch, March 1997, Dallasfed.org.
[743] Brad Richards, Partner, Haynes and Boone LLP, interview by the author, February 1, 2016.

bonding and letter-of-credit needs that the Texas banks could not meet because their credit was not accepted by beneficiaries.

"At Banque Indosuez, we confirmed MBank LC's, allowing them to keep a large portfolio of trade customers in exchange for 25% participations in each of their relationships. When MBank failed, we ended up with the whole portfolio. We had a lot more direct-lending relationships at Indosuez than participations—as we had a local LC group and could issue and negotiate letters of credit locally.

"This, combined with the bank's global presence, gave us a great avenue into trade credits as well as bonding. Over seven years, we built up a very profitable $2-billion energy-focused portfolio with no bad loans."[744]

Other foreign banks included Bank of Montreal which had a well-established energy lending group operating in Houston since 1962. It was joined by other Canadian banks, including Canadian Imperial Bank of Commerce (CIBC) in 1985, Toronto Dominion in 1989 and Scotia Bank. France's Crédit Lyonnais opened shop in Houston in 1977, followed by Société Générale (1979), Banque Paribas (1980) and Banque Indosuez (1986).

Norwegian and Scottish banks gained familiarity with oil and gas banking in the 1970s, while lending to North Sea producers. Bank of Scotland opened in Houston in 1975 and Norwegian banks Den Norske Credit Bank and Christiania Bank joined the Houston energy market in 1979 and 1987, respectively. Christiania Bank closed a year later and Den Norske closed its Houston office and, subsequently, reopened as DnB Nor Bank ASA in 2006.

Creative Financings for Energy Projects

Early post-crash prognosticators predicted—and correctly so—that rig loans and completion- and lease-line facilities would be rare and only to very strong borrowers.[745] But others could have not been

---

[744] Lane, author's interview.
[745] Jane Fleck Romanov and James L. Irish (Thompson & Knight, Dallas, Texas), "An Overview Of Sources Of Capital And Structuring Investments In Oil And Gas," 34 *Rocky Mt. Min. L. Inst.* (1988): Section 13.26.

more wrong in asserting that it would spell the end of the secured, borrowing-base structure. J. Thomas Mullen, an attorney with Continental Illinois' lead bank counsel, predicted in 1988 that the borrowing-base loan would only be available to major companies under a monthly, reducing, borrowing base with required, periodic, amortization installments. "It will be less available to independents and smaller companies," he wrote.[746]

The bank failures of the '80s spawned congressional investigations, reports and academic studies about improvements needed in banking regulations and lending management. Many of these reforms were effective—for a while—but they did not prevent the crisis of 2008. "As time goes by, the lessons of past failures are forgotten—and then we must learn them again," Shauna Ferris reported to an actuarial society in 2010.[747]

In addition, money-center banks, previously content to take passive participations in the originating lender's loans, began to require a direct assignment and their own, separate notes from the borrowers to avoid any "Penn Square problems" should the originating bank become insolvent. After the Penn Square fiasco, the Office of the Comptroller of the Currency ordered national banks to improve their risk-management practice for taking participations. The banks were instructed to perform their own, independent evaluation of credit quality, including financial health and collateral, instead of simply relying on the judgment of the bank that originated the loan.[748]

---

[746] Mullen, "The Future of Bank Financing," Section 19.03[2]. While this prediction proved incorrect, Mullen accurately noted, "Engineers and bankers are now running sophisticated computer programs with various projections to show the cash flow sensitivity per dollar per barrel movement in the price of oil. This compares favorably to the rough estimates made using hand held calculators in the early 1980s."

[747] Ferris, "How to Destabilize the Financial System," 81,110. The 2008 crisis also resulted from inflated asset prices; subprime lenders and lending too much against the value of inflated collateral; the sale of loans to third parties, undermining lending standards and spreading risks throughout the banking system; investors relying upon risk assessments of intermediaries with conflicts of interest; and regulators that were too slow to take effective action.

[748] Ferris, "How to Destabilize the Financial System," 81, 97.

Before Penn Square, there was little definition or characterization of the relationship between the lead bank and the participating banks. The lead bank would originate and close the loan with the borrower as the sole lender and holder of the borrower's note and liens on the collateral. The originating bank was, thus, both the legal and equitable owner of the entire loan.

After the loan was closed, the bank would sell an undivided share of the loan and collateral to participating banks. Often, the borrower was neither involved nor informed of the participation and— importantly under the bankruptcy code—the borrower's other creditors were not notified of the additional claims to the borrower's collateral.

In a bankruptcy, the participating banks' legal rights were in question: either the participants were creditors of the lead bank or the lead bank was holding the debt and collateral for the benefit, and as a fiduciary, of the participants.[749] After Penn Square's failure in 1982, Kevin Fisher and Elizabeth Muratet wrote in a *Tulsa Law Review* article:

> Consequently, the day of the undisclosed participation should be over. Ideally, the participants are best protected when the borrower executes and delivers separate promissory notes to each participant for its pro rata share of the loan. The banks would then execute an intercreditor agreement specifying the details of the administration of the loans. ... To further assure that adequate notice is given, the participant should give direct notice to the borrower of its ownership interest. In the future, bank counsel should ... use an intercreditor participation agreement which not only identifies the relationship between the lead and the participants but also establishes the relationship between the participants themselves.[750]

---

[749] Jeffrey D. Hutchins, "What Exactly is a Loan Participation?" 9 *Rutgers-Camden L.J.* 447 (1978): 463-74.
[750] Kevin Fisher and Elizabeth Muratet, "The Aftermath of Penn Square Bank: Protecting Loan Participants from Setoffs," 18 *Tulsa L.J.* 261 (1982): 271-272.

First National Bank of Midland had sold loan participations to Texas Commerce and InterFirst, among others. After rumors began to circulate about its financial health; the participant banks demanded the borrower issue direct notes to each lender.[751] Fisher and Muratet were correct about the direct assignments. However, instead of a separate intercreditor agreement among the banks, the convention became to use a syndicated loan facility administered by the lead bank as "agent."

The agented form of syndicated credit facility included provisions, which established the agent's role as well as the rights of the lenders vis a vis the borrower and amongst themselves. As energy-lending markets returned, more of the credit facilities would be shared among a small group of energy lenders (club deals) or larger, more widely syndicated facilities (syndicated loan facilities), where all lenders held directly a note from the borrower for their share of the aggregate commitment and a vote in the administration of the credit facility to the oil and gas producer.

By the end of 1980 and into the '90s, as bankers became more comfortable with the concept, most borrowing-base loan agreements were documented as syndicated loans with an administrative agent—even at times when the original loan was a single-bank facility.

Upon the Penn Square failure, energy lawyers in general and energy-banking lawyers in particular were busy with reviewing existing loan facilities or trying to help their clients locate new sources of capital. The Rocky Mountain Mineral Law Foundation held a special institute in 1982 focused solely on "creative financings" of mineral projects.

"The present environment for mineral industry financing can be described simply: harsh," Vance K. Maultsby, Jr., a partner with accounting firm Peat, Marwick, Mitchell & Co. in Dallas, reported. "The current recession has affected the mineral industry drastically. There is less money available from outside the industry, less demand for products, and less internally generated money.

---

[751] Charles Beckham, author's interview.

Chapter 6: 1980s

"Commercial bankers examine loan requests with a jaundiced eye. One can hardly blame them after observing the collapse of the Penn Square Bank in Oklahoma City and the ripple effect therefrom on major money center banks around the country. ... In short, the industry has probably never been faced with a more challenging environment in which to arrange financing. Indeed, creative financing may be the key to near-term survival for many oil and gas companies."[752]

Alternatives to standard bank lending examined at the special institute included non-traditional capital structures. One was described as the "exploration retainer," which was paid by an established oil and gas company to a smaller firm with special expertise. The smaller company developed prospects to sell to third parties at a promoted cost and to its lender-sponsor on a non-promoted, "heads up" basis.

Another was "open roll-ups." With changes to the federal tax code, tax benefits of the drilling partnerships were adversely affected. "Roll-ups" were structured where stock in a new public corporation was offered to holders of the limited-partner interests. Assets were operated by a common operator to simplify operations and accounting.

Also, "equity-kickers" were being included, in addition to interest and principal payments, typically to non-bank lenders, such as insurance companies, merchant bankers and pension funds. "Equity-kickers" can provide additional value to a lender from the borrower. For example, a borrower can issue stock warrants that the lender can choose to exercise to purchase equity in the borrower at some later date. For producer borrowers, equity-kickers can also be created as direct interests in the borrower's properties and wells in the form of overriding royalty interests, net profit interests and similar interests.[753]

Mullen summarized in 1988 that the changes in lending philosophy would result in banks only lending to strong borrowers; portfolios would become more diversified and there would be a greater focus on

---

[752] Vance K. Maultsby, Jr., Partner, Peat, Marwick, Mitchell & Co., Dallas, Texas, "Overview of Mineral Financing, Conference on Mineral Financing," Section 1-1 (paper presented at the Rocky Mountain Mineral Law Foundation, November 1982).
[753] Maultsby, "Overview of Mineral Financing," Section 1-12-14.

the primary source of repayment. "That is - cash from operations, and collateral will be viewed only as a secondary source of repayments," he reported.[754]

Loan-documentation changes included tighter descriptions of collateral, changes in interest-rate pricing definitions and provisions incorporating the availability of oil and gas price hedging. With the advent of digital technology in the oil patch, deeds of trusts were revised to include pledges by the producer of all seismic and geophysical data as well as its rights in all computer software and hardware as collateral.[755]

In the midst of soaring and, then, sinking oil and gas prices, producers and their lenders were also faced with extreme volatility in the cost of borrowed funds. Interest rates climbed steeply in the 1970s with prime at around 15.25% in December of 1979 and 20% four months later. The rate fell to 11% in July of 1980 and the year closed at 21.50%, which has remained the historical high.[756] For the producer, the applicable interest rate was almost more important in his decision to borrow than was the bank's advance rate against reserves.

Meanwhile, in January of 1986, the British Banking Association began to report the interest rates top-tier banks would offer in interbank loans and adopted the London Inter-Bank Offer Rate (Libor) as a much-needed benchmark for short-term interbank loans. The entry of foreign banks and increased competition for business from large, corporate borrowers caused many domestic lenders to utilize Libor indices or the U.S. federal-funds rate.

In turn, the availability of alternate rates often resulted in large corporate borrowers receiving subprime rates.[757] Smaller, "prime rate" borrowers challenged the banks in court for fraud and breach of contract on a variety of theories based on the premise that a lender's *pub-*

---

[754] Mullen, "The Future of Bank Financing," Section 19.03[1].

[755] Mullen, "The Future of Bank Financing," Section 19.04[3].

[756] "Prime Rate History," accessed March 20, 2016, Fedprimerate.com. Prime rates began to decline after 1981, but did not get below 10% until May, 1985.

[757] Edward F. Mannino, *Lender Liability and Banking Litigation* (ALM Properties, Inc., Law Journal Press, 1989), Section 1.04[2], 1-20.

lished prime rate should be its lowest and best rate to its commercial borrowers.[758] In reaction to these lawsuits, lenders and their attorneys adopted several approaches. Some eliminated the use of the term "prime rate" altogether and instead used "base rate" or "published rate."

To provide greater transparency, some smaller banks used the prime rate published daily by *The Wall Street Journal*. Other lenders, in their loan documents, expressly qualified *prime rate* to be "not necessarily the lowest rate charged by the bank as legal notice to the borrower that he may not be receiving the *lowest* commercial rate."[759] These changes in interest rates continue today as energy lenders offer "base rate" and "Libor" pricing.

Paradigm Shift: Nymex Hedges Producers' Price Risk

The 1990s brought the second-most important change in oil and gas lending since the introduction of the borrowing-base revolver. With the advent of oil- and gas-futures contracts, the borrowers' ability to lock in near-term prices for their future production provided banks with greater confidence in how much to lend.

Hedging of oil was not entirely new. Oil exchanges sprang up almost as soon as oil was discovered in commercial quantities, following Colonel Drake's well in Titusville, Pennsylvania, in 1859.[760] By 1870, the industry's big refiners and most shippers and oil-brokers were no longer buying crude at the wellhead. At nearby Oil City, an informal oil exchange formed on unpaved Center Street where producers, buyers and brokers traded certificates representing 1,000-barrel lots.

---

[758] *Michaels Building Co. v. Ameritrust Company, N.A.*, 848 F.2d 674, 676 n.2 (6th Cir. 1988). Associated Press, May 3, 1985 (reporting on a settlement by Manufacturers Hanover Trust Co. to a class action challenging the bank's lending practices of overcharging customers with loans pegged to the company's prime lending rate, potentially affecting tens of thousands of borrowers).

[759] Mannino, *Lender Liability and Banking Litigation*, Section 1.04[2], 1-20.

[760] The description of early oil exchanges is taken from The American Oil & Gas Historical Society. "End of Oil Exchanges," accessed October 14, 2014, Aoghs.org.

The firm of Rockefeller, Andrews & Flagler had just reorganized as Standard Oil Co. and was buying for its refinery in Cleveland. Jacob Vandergrift and George Forman—as Vandegrift, Forman & Co.—bought crude as shippers at first, but they began buying for themselves too for their new Imperial Refinery on the other side of the railroad tracks.

Lockhart & Frew was buying for its Pittsburgh refineries and its new Atlantic Refinery in Philadelphia. The back room of its Oil City office served as a makeshift meeting area for the "street exchange." The Oil City Exchange was organized as a corporation in 1874, three years after the formation of the Titusville Oil Exchange, which was the first U.S. oil exchange.

The exchanges allowed oil to be purchased either on a "spot"—or cash—basis or on a deferred-delivery basis of 10 days. The exchanges also made markets in futures transactions that could be used for speculation and could settle differences in prices.

By 1875, additional exchanges were formed in New York. In 1884, the petroleum exchanges of New York, Pittsburgh and Oil City formed the Conference of Oil Exchanges, adopting uniform rules. The exchanges were affecting the market price for oil. John Rockefeller warned in 1882 that oil prices were "a dangerous speculation," although the main currency of the exchanges were certificates issued by his own Standard Oil against oil stored in its pipelines.

In 1884, trading on the exchanges exceeded physical production with certificates representing more than 40 million barrels traded in New York, 27 million in Oil City and 20 million in Pittsburgh. In the early 1890s, hundreds of thousands of barrels were being traded daily on the exchanges.[761]

On January 23, 1895, Rockefeller declared to producers that Standard would buy oil only at prices "as high as the markets of the world will justify" and not necessarily "the price bid on the oil ex-

---

[761] Jerry W. Markham, *A Financial History of the United States: From Christopher Columbus to the Robber Barons (1492-1900)* (M.E. Sharpe, 2002), 314-315.

change for certificate oil."[762] In other words, Standard Oil would quote its own prices.

Soon after, with Standard Oil buying 90% of total production in the region, transactions on the exchanges stopped. The Titusville exchange was dissolved. "Its members are scattered far and wide, but the glory of the days when fortunes were made and lost in hours and minutes, will ever be a memory with them and thousands of others," *Oil City Derrick* reported in 1896.[763]

Standard Oil was the price-setter for the Appalachia-Ohio region, but its market share eroded to 70% as competitors gained, such as Pure Oil in the East, The Texas Co. and Gulf Oil on the Gulf Coast, Cities Service and Sun in the Midcontinent, and Union Oil in California. In addition, demand for petroleum products was increasing more rapidly than Standard's ability to expand. In 1911, it controlled only 44% of production in the Midcontinent, 29% in California and 10% on the Gulf Coast.[764]

In 1872, just after the Titusville Oil Exchange was formed, the predecessor to the New York Mercantile Exchange (Nymex) was formed, initially trading dairy products.[765] In 1978, it started trading heating-oil futures—not so much out of a grand vision of what it would become, but more out of an act of desperation.

Nymex had been seen as a less sophisticated exchange. It was perceived more often as a place for licensed gamblers and rogue traders, not all of whom were overly concerned about efficient and transparent markets. By the early 1970s, the primary commodity it traded was the Maine potato, accounting for 80% of all trades. Traders had

---

[762] "End of Oil Exchanges," Aoghs.org.
[763] "End of Oil Exchanges," Aoghs.org.
[764] Harold F. Williamson, *The American Petroleum Industry: The age of energy, 1899-1959* (Northwestern University Press, 1963), 4-14.
[765] Yergin, *The Prize*, 706-707. Originally known as the Butter and Cheese Exchange, the name was changed to the New York Mercantile Exchange in 1882. "History of the CFTC: US Futures Trading and Regulation Before the Creation of the CFTC," Cftc.gov.

pegged potato futures to the less-abundant Maine potato to better manipulate the price in the trading pit.[766]

J.R. Simplot, known as the "Potato King of Idaho," was the largest supplier of French fries to McDonald's and wanted Nymex to also trade Idaho potatoes. Traders objected because the supply of Idaho potatoes was more abundant, less susceptible to manipulation and principally controlled by Simplot. Simplot was not one to take "no" for an answer.

May was the biggest month to trade potatoes on the exchange and traders were aware that an anonymous buyer had gone short on some 1,000 contracts—representing 50 million pounds of Maine potatoes—for May 1976 delivery. Traders who suspected Simplot was behind the short positions bet long, expecting to squeeze the short before the contracts expired.[767] On the last day of trading the May contract, Simplot didn't dump his position. He defaulted on his obligation to deliver the potatoes at a personal loss of between $3- and $5 million and was later fined $50,000 by the Commodity Futures Trading Commission (CFTC).[768]

But Nymex was hurt more. It exposed Nymex's inability to honor the contracts. "There had never been a default anywhere in the entire 150 year history of the U.S. commodities market," Michel Marks, who became chairman shortly after the fiasco, told Leah McGrath Goodman in *The Asylum: The Renegades Who Hijacked the World's Oil Market*. "The essence of an exchange is the sanctity of its contract, regardless of how it is managed."[769]

---

[766] Leah McGrath Goodman, *The Asylum: The Renegades Who Hijacked the World's Oil Market* (William Morrow, February 15, 2011), 39.

[767] *Leist v Simplot*, 638 F. 2d. 283 (2nd Cir., 1980); Kara Newman, *The Secret Financial Life of Food: From Commodities Markets to Supermarkets* (Columbia University Press, December 4, 2012), 133-134.

[768] Goodman, *The Asylum*, 50-51.

[769] Goodman, *The Asylum*, 51.

Chapter 6: 1980s

The CFTC banned potato-trading on the exchange—contracts that had accounted for 80% of its business.[770] *The New York Times* reported:

> "The problem we faced," Mr. Marks said, "was that it took two to three years at that time to get a new contract through the Commodity Futures Trading Commission for a good exchange, and this was not a good exchange." The Merc was thus left to look through its many failed contracts. It landed on two possibilities, currencies and heating oil. Since currency futures were already flourishing on the Chicago Mercantile Exchange, "it was oils [sic] or it was nothing," Mr. Marks said. The exchange modified delivery on the heating oil contract to New York harbor from Rotterdam, and reintroduced it as quickly as it could.[771]

In November of 1978, Nymex trading in heating oil began. President Reagan deregulated oil prices in January of 1981 as his first executive order just days after his inauguration. In October of 1981, the exchange began trading leaded gasoline as well.[772]

It expanded its suite of energy contracts further, creating the first "open market" for oil futures since the previous century. Reagan's price decontrols allowed oil prices to fluctuate with market forces, permitting the kind of volatility needed to fuel demand for a futures market. The Iranian revolution threw the supply situation into tur-

---

[770] There is a certain irony that McDonald's "Spud King" singlehandedly took down the former "Butter and Cheese Exchange," which had also been an egg-trading forum, five years after McDonald's introduction of the Egg McMuffin. Down but not out from the destruction and despair caused by the fiasco of the lowly spud, Michel Marks, at age 27, was elected vice chairman of Nymex and, two weeks later, succeeded to the role of chairman, following his predecessor's untimely death by heart attack.

[771] James Sturngold, "Merc Leaves Potatoes Behind," *The New York Times*, February 10, 1986.

[772] Goodman, *The Asylum*, 89. Heating oil began trading on November 14, 1978; unleaded gasoline, in December, 1984. Nymex continued to trade leaded gasoline for two years *after* leaded-gasoline sales were made illegal in the U.S.

267

moil—just the kind of uncertainty that makes commercial oil dealers go to a futures market to lock in future prices and assure supply.[773]

On March 30, 1983, the contract for West Texas Intermediate for delivery to Cushing, Oklahoma, commenced trading.[774] Only 949 contracts—each representing 1,000 barrels of oil as did the certificates of the late 1800s—were traded during the first month; in all of 1983, some 37,000 contracts were traded. By the end of 1984, an average of 7 million barrels—or 7,000 contracts—for oil traded daily and, on a heavy trading day, as many as 20 million barrels, which represented 25% more oil than the production ceiling set by OPEC.[775]

The exchange's timing was fortuitous—for it and for independent oil producers. This transparent pricing was in direct competition with the posted prices dictated by the major oil companies and OPEC.[776] After Saudi Arabia doubled its daily output from 2 million barrels to 4 million in the fall of 1985, prices for U.S. oil collapsed to $10. "Once the oil-trading companies realized they were holding all this overpriced oil, they had to find a place to get rid of it," Marks told Goodman. "What happened to all that extra oil supply was that it was sold on NYMEX, often at bargain-basement prices. The transition was fascinating. We basically became this huge liquidation center."[777]

Nymex upset the control held by OPEC and the oil majors; for them, the party was over: They no longer had a corner on global oil prices. The demise was reported in *The New York Times* in December of 1984:

> OPEC continues to set its basic official prices, of course - but it has had increasing trouble making them stick. ... The Merc's influence on oil prices was dramatically demonstrated last month. On Oct. 31, in an attempt to firm sagging oil prices, members of the

---

[773] Sturngold, "Merc Leaves Potatoes Behind."
[774] Goodman, *The Asylum*, 91.
[775] Stuart Diamond, "Setting Crude Prices in the Pits," *The New York Times*, December 9, 1984.
[776] Goodman, *The Asylum*, 71.
[777] Goodman, *The Asylum*, 92-93.

Organization of [the] Petroleum Exporting Countries set a lower ceiling on the amount of oil each could produce. Merc oil traders did not believe the OPEC quotas would stick, and did not bid up prices on contracts for future delivery of oil.

All during November, despite continual predictions by OPEC officials that prices would rise, the cost of oil futures on the Merc actually fell. The spot market followed. By Dec. 1, spot and futures prices for many oil grades were 5 percent lower - a drop of about $1.40 - than at the time of the OPEC announcement.

"The Merc has become the new benchmark for oil," said Gary M. Becker, director of the Paine Webber Energy Futures Group in Houston. "A visible and centralized pricing mechanism has been put in living rooms and offices around the world."[778]

Recognizing the power of the market established by Nymex, *The Dallas Morning News* quoted the head of First National Bank of Tulsa's energy section in November of 1986: "Banks, as well, might use options to protect themselves against non-performing energy loans. Robert A. Walker said options 'will provide us with more flexibility at a lower cost than hedging with futures contracts itself.'"[779]

Nymex began trading oil options in November of 1987 and natural-gas futures in April of 1990, further allowing borrowers and their lenders to be assured of the future price of borrowers' expected production. While open-market trading has been criticized for unnecessarily amplifying price gyrations at times—and usually in response to economic and political headlines—it "also encouraged a 'wait-and-see, better safe than sorry' mentality among independents who might otherwise have gone ahead with exploration and developments," wrote Olien and Hinton in 2007.[780]

---

[778] Diamond, "Setting Crude Prices in the Pits."
[779] Anne Reifenberg, "Crude Oil Futures to Hold New Options," *Dallas Morning News*, November 9, 1986.
[780] Olien and Hinton, *Wildcatters*, xv. (2007 edition).

Yergin wrote that "the Great Game" had shifted again, this time from the Middle East to traders on the Nymex floor.[781] Goodman added in *The Asylum*, "With the influx of competition, they no longer had a corner on global oil prices. Much worse, a failed potato market run by a kid [Marks, who became chairman at the age of 27] they'd never heard of was blatantly eating their lunch.

"And he wasn't based in any of the major oil towns, like Houston or Vienna or Riyadh, but in a rat-infested trading pit in downtown Manhattan inhabited by misfits and pranksters and gun-toting gangsters who had absolutely no knowledge of the oil business."[782]

Nymex traders were brash and young, but set in their ways. Refusing to modernize and adopt newer electronic methods of trading, Nymex's success was quickly copied in 2000 by Intercontinental Exchange (ICE), whose investors included Goldman Sachs and Deutsche Bank, Duke Energy and Reliant Energy, and Royal Dutch Shell and BP.

Technically, ICE was a foreign exchange, although it operated out of Atlanta. Instead of traders physically bidding in a pit, contracts were exchanged on the Internet, where traders could bet on much larger quantities of commodities than on Nymex—and without having to report to the CFTC. Goodman wrote, "In short order, ICE would become the eBay of the energy market. But the NYMEX traders didn't know it yet."[783]

Nymex's monopoly in open-market energy-futures trading began to erode. By 2006, its board merged it with the Chicago Mercantile Exchange. Today, "Nymex" is little more than a brand used by CME Group.

While gone but in name only, what began as an exchange's effort for survival continues to be a critical element of oil and gas lending today. Underwriting reserve-based loans to oil and gas companies requires assessing three fundamental risks: whether the properties con-

---

[781] Yergin, *The Prize*, 707.
[782] Goodman, *The Asylum*, 93.
[783] Goodman, *The Asylum*, 202.

tain the projected amount of resource (reserve risk), whether the borrower can efficiently produce the reserves within the timeframe and cost estimate (operational risk) and whether the borrower would receive a price for his production sufficient to make a profit and repay the loan (price risk).

The accuracy of reservoir engineering has continually improved during the years—particularly in the 1990s with the advent of 3-D-seismic analysis. Since the days of the first production loan, evaluation of operational risk had been the lender's principal role. As McElvaney wrote in 1954, "It's people who sign the note, it's people who promise to pay, it's people who pay or fail to pay; and the banker's ultimate judgment above the ground in the matter of oil loans is no less important than the engineer."[784]

As for price risk, hedging offered borrowers and bankers an ability to manage, if not control, this. The ability to secure an economic, future price also became material in decisions on buying producing properties and planning the next year's drilling program. Where the lender could reduce price risk, an opportunity was created for it to reduce the interest rate charged or decrease the discount of the collateral's value, thereby increasing the borrowing base.

By the late 1990s, hedging was no longer an exception to reserve-based loans; it became a fundamental component. Hedges and provisions related to what a borrower could and could not do with its hedge contracts became integral to the terms of the loan documentation to the point where bankers began to require a minimum amount of hedging, especially where the bank had the capability—and economic incentive—to be the producer's hedge counterparty.

It started out in the 1990s as a simple covenant of "thou shall not enter into speculative hedges in excess of anticipated production." Today, it has developed into multiple provisions that lenders, borrowers and third-party hedge providers have weighed in on, regulating the permutations of and interaction between the two financial products: loans and commodity hedges.

---

[784] McElvaney, "Some Aspects of Financing Oil and Gas Transactions," 321-24.

When banks first started to include the borrower's hedges in calculating the base, it or an affiliate was providing the hedge in most cases. Early on, the critical issue was to secure the hedge affiliate's exposure under the contracts to the borrower to insure that the borrower's hedge obligations were secured on equal status as the primary loan—that is, *pari passu*.

Not all banks were capable of providing hedging to their borrowers and would share collateral with third-party hedge providers, such as BP, Royal Dutch Shell or Lehman Brothers. Or they would bring in additional lenders with this capability, such as Macquarie Bank or Union Bank of California, that were willing to take a non-leading role in the syndicate in trade for expanding their hedge-market base.

Removing most of the commodity-price risk from the banker's calculus became an integral feature of reserve-based lending by the end of the 1990s. Since the advent of the borrowing-base revolver, no other event so transformed the relationship between banker and producer.[785] Not only did hedges provide a floor to support the banker's risk of commodity-price collapse, hedges exceeding current-market prices became an asset that could be monetized by borrowers in a declining market if looking to raise cash.

Producers were incentivized to hedge with their lenders. Hedging with its lender (above the bank's price deck) allowed the lender to give the borrower a higher borrowing base. Moreover, hedging with a third party could lead to immediate cash calls if the market price for the hedged hydrocarbons exceeded the hedged price. In such case, the producer's hedges would be "out of the market" and it would owe the counterparty for sales as each month's hedge contracts closed and the counterparty would make a margin call to secure the payment obligation.

Unlike a secured-lender hedge counterparty, the third-party hedge counterparty demanded collateral—usually in the form of a cash deposit or a letter of credit—to secure the obligation owed by

---

[785] Arthur "Buzz" Gralla, interview by the author, February 19, 2015.

the producer in the event of out-of-the-money hedges. The lender counterparty secured by the producer's oil and gas properties as collateral did not require additional collateral because the underlying value of the producer's oil and gas properties would increase as its hedges accrued obligations for being out of the money.

Notwithstanding the criticisms that speculators in the futures market exacerbate price fluctuations, producers' and their lenders' ability to fall back on the hedge counterparty's obligation has enabled lenders to be more aggressive in determining how much they are comfortable lending.

CHAPTER 7

1990s: Energy Banking Reinvented

"mezzanine – noun | mez·za·nine | \ 'me-zə-,nēn, ,me-zə-'\ "
Merriam-Webster Dictionary

If it can be said that the 1980s began with irrational optimism, "the decade ended with irrational pessimism," Paul Hilliard, president of Badger Oil Corp., said in a 2004 article. Hilliard was chairman of the Independent Petroleum Association of America from 1989 to 1991. "During my term, it was just about the bottom – in IPAA membership, revenue, even morale. Independents were trying to pay back $30/bbl debt with $12/bbl oil."[786]

Although there was a brief spike in world oil prices following the Iraq invasion of Kuwait in 1990 to more than $40 a barrel, oil began a new, steady decline in price. By the beginning of 1994, the inflation-adjusted price was at its lowest level since 1973.

World oil prices affected the major oil companies as well as the independents; all were facing a new oil-price paradigm. Cost-cutting was the game of the day. As market expectations were revised, the industry down-sized and its lenders adjusted; credit once again became accessible to the industry.

Olien and Hinton wrote, "Gone were the days when a major like ARCO [Atlantic Richfield Co.] would try to be everywhere and do

---

[786] Leslie Haines and William Pike, Editors in Chief, *America's Independents: From Black Gold to Diamond Jubilee, the 75th Anniversary of IPAA* (Hart Energy Publishing, LP, 2004), 73.

everything; cost cutting and efficiency were the new goals, and they often mandated what amounted to disintegration. As major oil companies rationalized their operations and focused on their most profitable sectors, they began to part with a significant proportion of their domestic reserves of both oil and gas."[787]

The "non-core" assets the majors sold in the 1990s were often sold to the engineers and geologists who had been laid off or took early retirement and knew these resources best. A 2004 special report upon the IPAA's 75th anniversary noted, "With this sea change, hundreds of new independents were born, merger and acquisition advisory firms were formed, public-equity markets were tapped and private-equity providers were launched."[788]

Joe Foster, founder of Newfield Exploration Co., said in the report, "During the late 1980s and early 1990s there was a significant drive by the major oil companies to reduce their unit costs. This drive to cut costs led to the disposition of many properties that were burdened with very high DD&A [depreciation, depletion and amortization] expenses.

"This opened a world of opportunity for independents like Newfield. Further, workforce downsizing by the majors made many highly qualified technical people available to work for independents, often on properties where they had ideas that did not get implemented by the previous employers."[789]

Pam Pierce, president of Huber Energy LP and who had been with Arco's Vastar Resources Inc. unit until it was rolled up by BP in 2004, said, "An important event in the 1990s was the number of people in this business who worked for major oil companies and were laid off as properties were sold or as the majors consolidated. Many of these people learned how to be independents.

"There was a flow of assets and of skilled and knowledgeable people from the majors. The majors trained us very well. They gave us

---

[787] Olien and Hinton, *Wildcatters* (2007), xvii-xviii.
[788] Haines and Pike, *America's Independents*, 91.
[789] Haines and Pike, *America's Independents*, 91.

the best tools and the ability to try new ideas, to use technology to learn."[790]

Jim Flores, who, with Billy Rucks, formed Flores & Rucks Inc. in the early '90s, successfully capitalized on the sea change. The independent became Ocean Energy Inc., an international E&P that was sold to Devon Energy Corp. in 2003. Flores said of the role innovation in exploration played in the growth of the new independents, "Coming off the oil crash of the 1980s, the majors were restructuring their business and an abundance of high-quality properties were available.

"Then, new technologies – 3-D seismic and lateral drilling – brought the risk of oil and gas operations down, and we started attracting capital. That equation was a perfect storm for independents to be able to make money. Prior to that, we didn't have technology, we had tons of risk, and we didn't have any good properties. That's why so many independents went broke in the 1980s."[791]

The availability of quality assets, coupled with the growing ranks of willing buyers with access to capital, led to a growing market for acquisitions and divestitures (A&D) of oil and gas properties. Randall & Dewey Inc. was one of the first "A&D advisory" firms to take advantage of this opportunity. Both of its founders—Jack Randall and Ken Dewey—had left Amoco Corp. during one of the major's rounds of down-sizing.

Other new A&D shops were formed, including The Oil & Gas Asset Clearinghouse and Madison Energy Advisors Inc. In business since 1979, Ebco U.S.A. Inc. had appraised and marketed oilfield equipment; it joined in marketing oil and gas properties.

Keith Fite, executive vice president of Taos Resources LLC, worked at Ebco. He said in the 2004 report, "The A&D market was very new in the early 1990s, and there were a lot of properties on the market. The sellers weren't quite as sophisticated in the sales process

---

[790] Haines and Pike, *America's Independents*, 92.
[791] Haines and Pike, *America's Independents*, 94.

as they are today, so there were probably better deals to do then than there are today. The majors didn't always know what they had."[792]

Out of the transformation of the majors, who turned their focus to international opportunities, new life and new blood were injected into the ranks of the U.S. independents, creating the next cycle of E&Ps and a new wave of bank borrowing into 2008.

Bank Credit Markets Recover

Producers in the 1990s saw a lot of new ways to access capital. The formerly Texas-based energy banks consolidated under out-of-state ownership, albeit employing mostly the same energy bankers, but with newly issued lapel pins and business cards. Oil and gas mortgages circa 1990 provide graphic testimony to the tumult of the late '80s as exemplified in this Team Bank example as to the provenance of the mortgagee's lien priority, under the granting clause:

> [T]o Team Bank, a state banking association (successor to Team Bank, N.A., formerly known as Texas American Bridge Bank, N.A., assignee of the Federal Deposit Insurance Corporation as receiver for Texas American Bank/Fort Worth, N.A., a national banking association).

Notwithstanding some predictions to the contrary,[793] reserve-based loans under borrowing-base structures continued to be the principal conforming commercial-bank structure. But traditional bank capital was not as widely available as had been the case in the early 1980s—and rightly so. Less-seasoned energy companies had to look elsewhere to build a mature stable of "bankable properties"—i.e., proved, producing properties with current cash flow.

---

[792] Haines and Pike, *America's Independents*, 97.
[793] Jane Fleck Romanov and James L. Irish (Thompson & Knight, Dallas, Texas), "An Overview Of Sources Of Capital And Structuring Investments In Oil And Gas," *34 Rocky Mt. Min. L. Inst.* (1988): Section 13.26.
[793] Mullen, "The Future of Bank Financing," Section 19.03[2].

Lenders and bank examiners were more focused on sustainable operating cash flow as a source of repayment and collateral was viewed more as a secondary source of repayment. Also, bank engineers were able to run their calculations on computer programs to project cash-flow sensitivity per dollar change in the price of oil and gas.[794]

Joe Vilardo, the energy-finance attorney who was a Continental Illinois banker, recalled in an interview that, after so many oil and gas loans soured in the 1980s, financial covenants were developed in response to requirements imposed by bank regulators. "When the regulators took a hard look at the industry, they were shocked to find out that there were no financial covenants in most of the RBL deals. Their approach was that all industries must be required to meet some financial hurdles in their senior secured loan agreements to instill discipline on management and protect the banks."

The thinking was that the unique aspects of the oil and gas industry should be taken into account when crafting an appropriate set of financial covenants. "Since a debt/cap covenant didn't work for the industry—and that's due to the difference between FMV and GAAP book value of oil and gas reserves—the banks came up with the debt/Ebitda covenant," Vilardo said. "I believe they also wanted to see a better indicator of liquidity than the typical current-ratio test, so minimum-interest or fixed-charge coverage covenants [Ebitda /Interest Expense or Fixed Charges] started to appear in a lot of RBL deals as well coming out of the '80s."[795]

Many non-Texas and non-Oklahoma national banks that acquired traditional oil and gas lending institutions continued an energy-finance practice. However, the activity was muted in the latter half of the 1980s and in the early 1990s, consisting primarily of traditional senior oil and gas reserve-based loans. The void created opportunities for new providers of capital from numerous sources and sources far different than the traditional reserve-based loans.

---

[794] Mullen, "The Future of Bank Financing," Section 19.03[2][b].
[795] Vilardo, author's interview.

Chapter 7: 1990s

An in-house attorney at Enron Corp. reported in 1995, "The changing landscape of the energy industry has prompted an evolution of creative financing devices. ... Financing providers have funded capital to the producer market by providing an array of financial products ranging on the continuum from purchasing reserves, i.e., purchasing of Production Payments or NPIs [net profit interests], taking a secured position in producing reserves and financing development drilling activity to investing in partnership arrangements or making other equity investments."[796]

In addition to straight debt, new capital providers were offering structured-finance loans in the form of volumetric production payments (VPPs), NPI conveyances, prepaid gas contracts and other structures.[797] Several mezzanine-capital providers raised money from institutions that had not recently participated in energy financing and, in the process, provided these new investors with significant returns.

Former Texas energy bankers, investment bankers and oil and gas executives developed these funds. Industry players—notably pipelines operators, such as Enron—also entered the business, initially as a means of securing physical gas supply to support its gas-trading operation. Subsequently, Enron and others became energy lenders, earning a fixed rate of return, and later became "financial players" as well, taking an equity interest in bankrolling management teams to gain exposure to greater participation in the upside.

Much of the capital for the growth and consolidation of the industry in the early '90s came from these new sources. Many of these funds were investing in oil and gas reserve acquisitions through debt securities with equity returns. Private placements of subordinated debt were used in conjunction with senior bank financing to make acquisi-

---

[796] J. Heintz, Enron Capital & Trade Resources Corp., "Production Payments and Other Energy Financing Alternatives" (paper presented at the Rocky Mountain Mineral Law Foundation Institute "Oil and Gas Acquisition," November 1995), 10B at 13.
[797] Heintz, "Production Payments ...," 10B-1. *See also* Nick Snow, "The VPP Option - It's Back," *Here's the Money: Capital Formation 2004, Oil and Gas Investor,* May 2004, 23, "VPPs were born in the 1980's when commercial banks were having problems with their real estate and oil and gas loans. Producers found it hard to access funds."

tions to bolster balance sheets in order to prepare producers to take their companies public.

Rise of the Mezzanine Lenders

In addition to the existing structures under production payments financed by insurance companies and pension funds, exploration and development financing was provided by merchant bankers and mezzanine lenders. Mezzanine capital is junior to the traditional senior secured loan under borrowing-base revolvers, but ahead of equity investors in terms of repayment—thus, an intervening level designated "mezzanine" because it occupies the middle portion of the capital spectrum for oil and gas producers.

Into the 1980s, pension funds seeking passive income were increasingly drawn to oil and gas. They would typically buy a note from an oil company, secure it with production and get a royalty interest on the back end—once the principal and interest were paid—as a loan-enhancer known as an equity-kicker. This mezzanine structure is still used today. Indeed, many of the current private-equity providers, such as EnCap Investments LP, started out as providing mezzanine capital and—over time, to increase the return on its investors' dollars—migrated to providing straight equity.

Early entrants to mezzanine-lending to oil and gas producers were Trust Company of the West (TCW) in 1982 and Resource Investors Management Co. (Rimco) in 1986. The period from 1989 to around 1993 produced more growth in mezzanine finance to independents. Bill Weidner, a private broker of capital to oil and gas producers, wrote in 2002 of that period, "Oil was still in the mid-teens, the gas bubble hadn't popped, commercial banks were tight, and private-equity funds were a novel concept. Thus began an outstanding five-year mezzanine investment period, which eventually ended in 1993 with new technologies and a flood of capital."[798]

---

[798] William Weidner, Cosco Capital Management LLC, "Mezzanine Capital Flows Appear to be Changing," *Oil and Gas Investor*, June 4, 2002.

Chapter 7: 1990s

As the 1990s progressed, these mezzanine pioneers were joined by a number of other capital providers. Primarily, these included traditional banks through their unregulated subsidiaries, pipeline operators seeking to secure supply from portfolio producers, physical commodity traders and other capital providers that were not constrained by the regulatory restriction that prohibited commercial banks from taking equity-kickers on loans.[799]

These new capital providers were willing to lend on riskier ventures or take junior secured liens behind their more-conservative senior-bank brethren because they could take direct interests in their borrower's equity or prospects, increasing the return on their investments. Equity-kickers were taken in various forms, including warrants, overriding royalty interests, net-profits interests and volumetric production payments.

A financier was cited by *Oil and Gas Investor*: "Many generalist equity firms started looking at oil and gas. At the time, I think TCW and First Reserve Corp. offered debt with equity-kickers. In fact many of the deals back then were mezzanine in nature. The banks were just gone.

"Everybody's thinking was colored by inflation. Mezzanine became very attractive to institutions. Alas, as the bust lengthened through the 1980s, capital dried up. Natural gas was priced too low to be economic to drill. Clever new ideas began to emerge—they had to. This turmoil spawned new opportunities, as turmoil always does."[800]

This was the era when private equity came to the fore in a new way. First Reserve was formed in 1983 by Bill Macaulay and John Hill, initially investing mostly in the oilfield-service sector and, later, moving into oil and gas production. In 1988, Ken Hersh, Gamble Baldwin, David Albin and Richard Rainwater started Natural Gas Partners LLC. Also in 1988, four former Republic National energy bankers

---

[799] B.F. Clark, Jr., "Convergence of Capital," *Oil & Gas Financial Journal*, March 2006. Wells Fargo Bank formed mezzanine lender, Wells Fargo Energy Capital (1998); Enron (1992), Tenneco (1992) and Williams (1996), pipeline companies, formed lending subsidiaries.
[800] *Oil and Gas Investor*, June 2002.

formed EnCap: Bob Zorich, Gary Petersen, David Miller and Marty Phillips.

These groups were creating a new business model: aggregate capital from large institutional investors, manage direct-equity investments in oil and gas for them and grow new E&P companies. Through the 1990s, the recession and the real estate bust led to other changes. Insurance companies had to keep more capital in reserve, which tied up capital they might have invested in oil and gas. Meanwhile, the banking industry, especially for energy, was only beginning to recover.

Firms that made a business of advising institutions flourished, such as RPI Institutional Services and Rimco. Producers' choices now included asset-based lending, preferred and common stock and direct joint-venture (JV) participation in exploration and development drilling. Funders moved down the balance sheet from notes to preferred equity to common stock. Large pension funds, such as those of AT&T Inc. and General Electric Co., started taking net-profits interests in structured financings as a way to invest in oil and gas, while retaining tax-exempt status.

Meanwhile, the mezzanine firms that traditionally supplied debt with equity-kickers were being joined by big industrials, utilities and major gas producers and traders that saw opportunity as well. Royal Dutch Shell formed Shell Capital Inc., Enron formed Enron Capital & Trade Inc. and Duke Energy began a producer-finance unit, Duke Energy Capital Partners.

Mezzanine debt was either in a straight-term structure fully funded at closing or, more often, drilling-development lines of credit, which were drawn down over time, subject to lender-approved capital expenditures. Once advanced, moneys repaid from the proceeds of production could not be reborrowed, as would typically be permitted under revolver loans.

If the borrower had the collateral or balance sheet to justify a conventional borrowing-base loan, but needed access to additional capital for an identifiable development program, a mezzanine lender would make a loan secured by a second lien on the borrower's collateral that was junior in payment to the conforming borrowing-base facility.

Alternatively, the mezzanine facility might be the borrower's only debt facility, if it lacked bankable, producing collateral. In this case, the borrower and lender would expect the mezzanine debt to be taken out in a short period—12 to 24 months—after the proceeds were used to drill prospects that became bankable, cash-flowing reserves.

Of course, the greater the risk taken by the mezzanine lender, the more expensive was the capital. Typically these mezzanine loans were structured with an interest rate that was a couple percentage points higher than the first-lien debt, a portion of which could be paid in kind (PIK) by rolling accrued interest into the outstanding principal amount.

For riskier loans, additional consideration was charged that would typically kick in upon retirement of the loan. These equity-kickers were warrants to acquire equity in the borrower or direct interests in the borrower's oil and gas properties in the form of overriding royalties, net-profit interests and production payments.[801]

Documentation of the straight-mezzanine single facility or second-lien facility was similar to the standard revolver in many ways, except they were single-draw or non-revolving lines of credit and the use of proceeds was more closely controlled by the capital provider. The second-lien mezzanine facilities basically copied the bank's senior-facility documentation as far as representations, covenants and events of default.

However, the typical mezzanine facility would have a maturity date of at least six months after the senior facility's maturity. Financial covenants would conform to the senior facility, but financial ratios would be relaxed by at least 15% from the senior's principal financial

---

[801] Cross, Part One at 69; Amiel David and James Kipp, First City Bank Texas, "Risk Factors in Oil and Gas Lending—New Alternatives," *Journal of Petroleum Technology* 1490 (December 1991): 1491.

covenants and include an additional financial covenant, testing the borrower's ratio of asset value to total funded debt.

Asset value was typically a function of the company's PV10 reserves, based on the average three-year swap price quoted on Nymex, with parameters set on percentage caps for the value of proved non-producing reserves (PDNP) that could be included in the total asset value. An asset-value coverage ratio of less than 1.5 times total secured debt was typically used by the second-lien lender to control the amount of secured debt ahead of the second lien.

Where the mezzanine capital was layered behind senior facilities as second-lien paper, additional documentation in the form of an agreement between the senior lender and the junior, mezzanine lender was required to establish the lenders' competing rights to the borrower's collateral that secured the facilities. The customary inter-creditor agreement between the first- and second-lien lenders had four primary elements: prohibition on the right to take action to enforce the second liens for some period of time, i.e. a "stand-still" or "blockage" period; restriction to not challenge enforcement or foreclosure actions by the first-lien-holder; restriction to not challenge the enforceability or priority of the first lien; and waivers or limitations on the second-lien-holder's rights to exercise or take actions in a bankruptcy against the borrower and its property.

In second-lien facilities, if documented simultaneously with the senior loan, counsel for the second-lien lender would typically follow the lead of the senior bank's counsel on due diligence and document preparation to reduce the overall transactional cost of the two facilities. However, it was—and remains—incumbent upon the second-lien lender's counsel to be vigilant on both title due diligence and mortgage-lien coverage to a greater degree than the first-lien lender's counsel.

The typical underwriting requirements for the senior-lien facility were "satisfactory title to at least 80% of the borrower's oil and gas properties by value" and "mortgages covering at least 80% of borrower's proved reserves, by value." The senior lender's underwriting had a substantial, built-in equity cushion with senior-loan borrowing bases being capped at between 55% and 65% of the present value of the borrower's oil and gas assets. This meant that the senior-lender counsel's due diligence did not have to chase down title to every last one of the borrower's properties but could focus, instead, on the high-value properties.

Additionally, in senior credit facilities, a borrower is typically required to evidence satisfactory title to at least 80% of its proven oil and gas reserves by value and, similarly, is required to pledge at least the same amount under the mortgage to secure repayment of the borrowed money. Under the production loans and ABC loans, 100% of the borrower's properties served as the collateral and title requirements and mortgages covered all of such property.

Under a borrowing-base structure, the loan was made to the producer who had multiple properties in varying stages of development. Some properties were little more than goat pasture—no established reserves and, therefore, very little economic value to the producer and even less collateral value to the lender. The cost to verify a producer's ownership of these undeveloped properties could exceed the collateral value the banker placed on the properties. Even the time and effort to properly describe all of the borrower's low-value assets sufficient for legally effective mortgage-property descriptions might not be cost effective.

Recognizing this contingency, early reserve-based credit agreements would require the borrower to mortgage substantially all of its properties but, in no event, not less than 80% and provide evidence of title to at least 80% by value of its oil and gas properties. Over time, borrowers and their counsel pushed the mortgage threshold down from "substantially all" to just the 80% level as the maximum. As a rule of thumb, first-lien bankers and their counsel have been willing to accept this amount as the minimum threshold.

The empirical basis of this rule of thumb can be traced back to an Italian economist, Vilfredo Pareto, who observed in 1906 that 80% of the land in Italy was owned by 20% of the population. He later observed that 20% of the peapods in his garden yielded 80% of the peas at harvest.

His observation, now known as the Pareto Principle or the "80/20 rule," has been applied to many business strategies and been exhibited by many social phenomena. For example, a 1992 United Nations report showed that the richest 20% of the world's population controlled 82.75% of the world's income. More recently, *The Wall Street Journal*, in a story on communicable diseases, reported that scientists observed that "super-spreaders," who make up roughly 20% of the population, accounted for the transmission of about 80% of certain infectious diseases.[802]

Closer to the energy industry and following major oil companies' consolidations at the end of the 1990s, James Mercurio, who was the head of Banc of America Securities' natural-resources group, commented on his expectation for an increase in independents' borrowing demand as the majors applied the 80/20 rule to their asset portfolios: "... [T]hose that no longer meet their return-on-investment hurdles—there should be more opportunities for efficient independents to make acquisitions."[803]

The 80/20 rule in title due diligence in oil and gas lending is applied by the senior lender to achieve cost-effective acquisition of satisfactory title and lien coverage. Typically, for any oil and gas company, not all wells are of equal value. Applying the Pareto Principle, the top 20% in number of the most valuable wells will, on average, account for roughly 80% of the aggregate collateral value of all of the company's producing properties—also known as the "vital few and the trivial many." Credit agreements require that the borrower:

> Deliver satisfactory title information in form and substance acceptable to the Administrative Agent covering the Oil and Gas Properties evaluated by such Re-

---

[802] Sumathi Reddy, "The 20% Who Spread the Most Disease," *The Wall Street Journal*, December 15, 2014.
[803] Brian A. Toal, "Capital Malls," *Oil and Gas Investor*, April 29, 2000; Jon Hughes, "Mile High Capital," *Oil and Gas Investor*, July 1, 2008.

serve Report, on at least 80% of the total net present value (determined by a discount factor of 10%) of the proved Oil and Gas Properties evaluated by such Reserve Report.

The senior lender further haircuts the collateral value in arriving at its borrowing base to somewhere between 55% and 65% of the proved reserves' total value. In a perfect world, the second-lien lender, by definition, is lending against the remaining 45% to 35% value of the borrower's proved reserves and any probable and possible reserves, which do not factor into the senior lender's borrowing-base calculation. The junior lender can only expect to be paid out of that portion of the borrower's collateral after the senior facility has been paid in full.

If payment of the senior loan requires more than 65% of proceeds from the forced sale of the borrower's collateral assets by value, the junior lender has to wait until all senior debt is paid. Accordingly, the junior lender has much less "equity cushion," if any, to rely on for repayment. Moreover, the second-lien lender's cushion is easily deflated following a default.

In the event of a foreclosure, properties typically don't fetch "top dollar" in a fire sale nor even in an "orderly liquidation." Further, if the second-lien lender did not take the effort to place liens on the remaining 20% of the borrower's properties not mortgaged under the senior facility, it could find itself unprotected and unsecured, fighting over these lower-valued, but nevertheless valuable, assets in a bankruptcy scenario along with the hoi polloi of the borrower's unsecured creditors.

Knowing this, mezzanine lenders' advance rates were more heavily weighted towards proved undeveloped acreage or enhanced-recovery projects, tapping into future value that senior lenders did not typically lend against. Accordingly, second-lien lenders and their counsel tend to be more comprehensive in their review of the borrower's title to this property and more careful to mortgage substantially all of the borrower's properties.

Senior lenders welcome and can take comfort in some level of additional debt burden added by the mezzanine debt where the mezzanine lender's liens are subordinate to the senior facility, creating a further "cushion" for repayment. Plus, as an added benefit—because the senior-loan covenants do not permit the borrower to grant liens to the mezzanine lender without first granting senior lien on the same collateral as security for the senior facility—the senior lender benefits from the additional effort of the mezzanine lender's counsel on both title due diligence and collateral coverage.

Too much junior debt, however, can cause the producer to default under the weight of the interest payments. This especially can be manifest in markets where net income tied to oil and gas prices falls precipitously. Accordingly, because the senior lenders are looking to cash flow to keep their loans current on interest payments, the senior facility's borrowing base is typically haircut by an amount equal to between 20% and 25% of the second-lien debt to account for the burden of current interest payments on this debt.

The VPP: Entry of Utilities as Capital Providers

Demand for new financing structures was also driven by regulatory changes in the natural-gas market in the late 1980s. Following adoption of the Natural Gas Policy Act of 1978, the Federal Energy Regulatory Commission (FERC) promulgated a series of orders to break the monopoly of interstate pipelines over the resale of gas. The result forced them into the role of "transporter" instead of merchants.

Local distribution companies (LDCs) could no longer count on pipelines for long-term gas-supply contracts and became responsible for lining up their own supplies at reasonable prices directly from producers. FERC Order 636 made it easier for large gas consumers to enter these contracts directly with producers.[804]

Some utilities jumped directly into the business of owning, exploring for and developing gas reserves. But, as reported by the mid-

---

[804] Paul E. Strohl, "Gas Into Gold: The New Alchemy of Financing Oil and Gas Acquisitions in the 1990s," 39 *Rocky Mt. Min. L. Inst.* 16-1 (1993): 16.5-6.

1990s, there were certain drawbacks to direct acquisitions of reserves by large gas consumers. Very few utilities had appreciable experience in oil and gas operations and many of them were daunted by the considerable price, reserve and operating risks associated with working-interest ownership.

Some LDCs and, in the Midwest, some industrial end-users had moderate success in the E&P business. But most of the large gas consumers were not inclined to diversify out of core businesses into a business that, even in the best of times, was extraordinarily fickle.[805] Instead, many of these made loans to producers in the form of volumetric production payments (VPPs), locking in long-term sources of gas to meet expected demand over many years.

Although the ABC production-payment structure was not as popular after tax-code revisions in 1969, a number of capital providers continued to use the production-payment structure in oil and gas transactions as an alternative to bank debt. The granting of the production payment had beneficial tax treatment to the producer.[806] The producer's sale of the specified volume of future production was not treated as a taxable sale under the tax code; rather, under the property laws of most producing states, and if properly documented,[807] VPPs were treated as a sale of real property.

In addition, the producer could deduct as an expense that portion of the production proceeds that correlated to interest. And the producer remained the owner of the working interests—thus, entitled

---

[805] Strohl, "Gas Into Gold: The New Alchemy," 16.12.

[806] Cross Two at 66 and Strohl at 16.16-17. "A production payment is a non-operating interest entitling its owner to a share of oil, gas, or like hydrocarbons (or proceeds from the sale of such hydrocarbons) produced from a described tract of land, free of the costs of production at the surface, and terminating when a specified volume of hydrocarbons has been produced (or a specified amount of proceeds from the sale of such hydrocarbons has been realized). The owner of a production payment has a direct ownership interest in the underlying oil and gas reserves, at least in jurisdictions that have embraced the ownership-in-place theory." Strohl at 16.16-17.

[807] The tax benefits could be jeopardized if the production payment did not meet the Internal Revenue Code and regulatory requirements, including that there be sufficient reserves at the time of grant for a reasonable expectation of repayment and the repayment could not come from any other source than the burdened reserves (i.e., no guarantees from the grantor nor liens on associated equipment). Cross Two at 67.

to deduct the intangible drilling cost (IDC) and depletion from its taxes.

Additional tax credits were available for producers who qualified, serving as a basis for specialized structured finance. For example, Section 29 of the Tax Code gave the producer a federal tax credit for production from qualified tight-sands gas, coal-seam gas, Devonian-shale gas and tar-sands oil through 2002 from wells spud before year-end 1992.

These tax-advantaged VPP financings were structured by the producer—who, because of net-operating-loss carry-forwards or alternative minimum tax, was not able to use the tax credits, which would expire if not used in the year generated—to monetize the credit. This had the effect of reducing the cost of funds to the producer by compensating the cash investor for the use of its money in part with otherwise-unusable Section 29 credits.[808]

Importantly to the VPP purchaser and if properly documented,[809] the prevailing assumption among lending lawyers was that the production payment should be outside the debtor's estate, if the owner of the working interests went into bankruptcy under section 541(d) of the Bankruptcy Code.[810] This is because the production payment is a direct ownership interest in the burdened oil and gas leases—thus, a real property interest. In 1994, Congress amended the bankruptcy code to exclude production payments from the property of a debtor's

---

[808] Cross Part One at 67-68, see also, F.B. Cochran, "Financing with Oil and Gas Derivatives," *41 Rocky Mtn, Min. L. Inst.* (July 21, 1995): 16-47-8.

[809] In the ATP Oil & Gas Corp. bankruptcy case involving federal Gulf of Mexico leases out of which ATP had sold highly structured VPP interests, the bankruptcy court refused the VPP-holders' summary judgment motion regarding the real property nature of their volumetric overriding royalty, holding that issues of material fact existed regarding whether the instrument creating the VPP could be properly characterized as a disguised financing rather than a real property interest. *NGP Capital Resources Co. v. ATP Oil & Gas Corp. (In re ATP Oil & Gas Corp.)*, No. 12-3443, 2014 Bankr. LEXIS 33 (Bankr. S.D. Tex. January 6, 2014). At the time of publication, this issue had not been resolved by any final order from the bankruptcy court.

[810] Cross Part One, at 67, citing *Standard Oil Co. of Texas v. Marshall*, 265 F. 2d 46 (5th Cir. 1959); *States v. Quintana Petroleum Co.*, 133 S.W.2d 112 (Tex. 1939); *Tennant v. Dunn*, 110 S.W.2d 53 (Texas 1937).

estate, thereby giving these lenders even greater comfort with the pro-ducer's credit risk.[811]

Commercial banks that wanted to remain active in financing in-dependent producers were developing competitive capital structures of their own. In addition to their traditional revolving senior debt, banks were providing bridge loans or "stretch loans"—i.e., a second tranche of senior, but non-conforming, borrowing-base availability with a higher-interest coupon.

Basically, these loans went beyond the bank's credit parameters for traditional—i.e. conforming—borrowing-base limits and stretched to loan additional funds. And some banks, through their unregulated subsidiaries, began providing mezzanine capital and equity funding, primarily to finance acquisitions of large blocks of developed oil and gas properties.

According to Loan Pricing Corp., bank syndications for oil and gas companies totaled $22 billion in 1995, $36 billion in 1996 and more than $55 billion in 1997. In December of 1996, under Chairman Alan Greenspan, the Federal Reserve Board permitted bank-holding companies to own investment-bank affiliates with *up to 25%* of their business in securities underwriting—up from 10%—expanding the loophole created by the Fed's 1987 reinterpretation of Section 20 of Glass-Steagall and effectively rendering Glass-Steagall obsolete.

In August 1997, the Fed eliminated many restrictions imposed on national bank's "Section 20 subsidiaries" and stated that the risks of underwriting had proven to be "manageable" and that banks would have the right to acquire securities firms outright. As a result, banks also began to underwrite high-yield debt securities, which provided much of the capital for acquisition activity as oil and gas producers bulked up to launch their IPOs.

More-established producers were able to access public markets either under traditional common-stock offerings and debentures or newer structures of publicly traded master limited partnerships (MLPs), which replaced the royalty-trust structure that was more

---

[811] Bankruptcy Code §541

prevalent in the early 1980s.[812] The capital investments in the 1990s were more driven by cash flow and the prospect of success than as a vehicle to take advantage of specific tax benefits. Investors and lenders—both singed by the conflagration of the '80s—were more cautious with less of an appetite for long-term maturities or exit plans and more apt to concentrate on shorter-term, lower-risk investments.

Interaction Between Borrowing Base and Hedging

Following the introduction of oil futures on Nymex, mezzanine lenders and other financial investors used sophisticated structures to manage the commodity-price risk of the VPP through a hedging strategy.[813] The ability to hedge was, perhaps, the most important new element introduced in the 1990s in underwriting oil and gas reserve-based loans. Commodity-price volatility after the 1970s had become accepted by industry and capital providers as commonplace.

Discussing how banks looked at a borrower's ability to repay, long-time energy financier Arthur "Buzz" Gralla said in a 2004 article, "In the 1970s, we calculated loan values but we did not do the type of detailed financial analysis that we do today. In the early 1980s, we really didn't examine the what-ifs on price as we do today. Into the 1990s, there became a much heavier emphasis on hedging as a risk mitigant for companies that have any significant degree of leverage."[814]

The advent of Nymex and its public, transparent trading of oil contracts for delivery in future periods of time provided price clarity to bankers by giving them a benchmark for what production might be sold for in the future.[815] Actual prices in the future might prove Nymex wrong, but it, at least, established a common yardstick by which all reserves could be measured.

---

[812] *See* Romanov and Irish, "An Overview of Sources of Capital and Structuring Investments in Oil and Gas," 34 *Rocky Mt. Min. L. Inst.* 13-18 (1988).

[813] F.B. Cochran, "Financing with Oil and Gas Derivatives", 41 *Rocky Mtn, Min. L. Inst.* Chapter 16, (July 21, 1995): 16-42.

[814] Haines and Pike, *America's Independents*, 100-101.

[815] The futures contracts traded on Nymex were regulated by the Commodity Futures Trading Commission on a cleared exchange that guaranteed both sides of every trade, providing transparency on pricing and certainty of execution.

Jack Randall, co-founder of asset-marketing firm Randall & Dewey, remarked in 2011 that the market changed after Nymex. Previously, the majors each had their own, internal forecasts and bank loans were based on the posted price of oil or gas. Following Nymex and the ability to hedge future production, "all of that changed.

"It's kind of academic now. You want to know what oil and gas cost five years out? Here's the futures market. And, you go and lock in the price in the derivatives market. It's not what a group of employees at a conference table some place with a crystal ball think."[816]

This new certainty created demand for bankers' capital, as hedging facilitated buying oil and gas properties. Joe Foster was one of the early beneficiaries of this, as he and other ex-Tenneco Oil Co. executives founded Newfield Exploration in 1989. In the same 2011 article, he said, "Nymex was one of the greatest things that happened. It simplified the valuation. When you're looking at buying a property, you have to look at what prices are going to be over a period of time. That was difficult to do.

"Nymex sort of takes that out of it. It gives you a strip. The strip may be right or the strip may be wrong, but it gives you a basis upon which to make an intelligent bid, based on a price that you think will be pretty similar to what your competitor will use. It really takes the oil and gas price out of the game and makes the emphasis more on the reserves and what you perceive the upside to be."[817]

Yergin wrote that, when oil trading on Nymex was introduced in 1983, it was initially dismissed by established oil companies as "a way for dentists to lose money."

> But the practice – of futures trading, not dentistry – moved quickly in terms of acceptability and respectability. Within a few years, most of the major oil companies and some of the exporting countries, as well as many other players, including large financial houses, were participating in crude futures on the NYMEX.

---

[816] Nissa Darbonne, "Game-Changers, 1981-2011," *Oil and Gas Investor*, August 2011, 81.
[817] Darbonne, "Game-Changers, 1981-2011," 83.

… Once [price setting] had been [by] the Texas Railroad Commission system in the United States and the
majors in the rest of the world. Then it was OPEC.
Now price was being established, every day, instantaneously, on the open market, in the interaction of the
floor traders on the NYMEX.[818]

In the first year of trading, average daily volume represented 1.7
million barrels of oil; by 1990, the barrels represented by Nymex contracts exceeded that year's global oil production; and, by 1994, the
daily volume had risen to 106.8 million barrels when world production
was 70 million.[819]

Bankers were more comfortable in lending when price-risk was
reduced. However, not all producers were comfortable with mitigating
this risk: It was perceived by many as capping their upside—if oil
prices would rise. Early on, the use of price-risk-management tools
was not even supported by Wall Street.

"There was a lot of criticism of companies that would hedge and
guess wrong," Scott Schroeder, chief financial officer of Cabot Oil &
Gas Corp., said in a 2004 article. "You had Wall Street saying that
hedging was always a lose-lose bet. If you guessed right and commodity prices fell, the whole sector was down anyway, so your stock wasn't
being rewarded. If you guessed wrong, you got whacked because you
hedged away the upside."[820]

However, commercial banks increasingly began to insist on it
and, by the end of the 1990s, it was an integral part of banks' credit
documentation as well as being another product offered in their fi-
nancial-service suites. Larry Holden, a Citibank lender, said in a 2007
article, "Since 1999, the use of hedging has really increased. Our current total portfolio is hedged 60%-70%. In the 1990s, we saw very
little hedging being done."[821]

---

[818] Yergin, *The Prize*, 725.
[819] Jeff Fleming and Barbara Ostdick, *The Impact of Energy Derivatives on the Cured Oil Market*
(The James A Baker III Institute for Public Policy of Rice University, April 7, 1998).
[820] Haines and Pike, *America's Independents*, 100.
[821] Jeannie Stell, "Banking Up," *Oil and Gas Investor*, September 6, 2007.

The shift was evident in the Office of the Comptroller of the Currency's standards for underwriting. In the 1980s, the OCC opined on the permissibility of national banks' engagement in interest-rate, currency and commodity-price-index swaps and caps.[822] In the 1990s, it recognized that national banks may advise, structure, arrange and execute transactions as agent or principal in connection with interest-rate, basis-rate and cash-settled commodity swaps, caps, collars, floors, swaptions, captions and other option-like products.[823]

Traditionally, energy banks used a conservative estimate of future cash flow based on the borrower's producing reserves and a "price deck" of estimated future prices, discounted on a PV basis. To manage price risk in underwriting loans with maturities of up to three to five years, the price deck was conservatively below market, which reduced the available borrowing base. But, if a borrower could lock in a future price higher than the bank's deck by means of hedges, it would be able to get the bank to increase the base.

As the value of hedges was calculated into the estimate, bank lawyers were directed to make adjustments to the standard reserve-based loan papers. Language was added to credit agreements to include covenants that the borrower would not engage in speculative hedging, i.e. hedging volumes in excess of anticipated physical deliverability; would hedge only with "approved hedge providers," e.g. the lenders, their affiliates or other credit-worthy counterparties; would not grant liens or credit support to any hedge providers other than the lenders and lender affiliates; and would maintain a certain level of

---

[822] OCC No-Objection Letter No. 87-5 (July 20, 1987), *reprinted in* [1988 - 1989 Transfer Binder] Fed. Banking L. Rep. (CCH) ¶ 84,034; OCC Interpretive Letter No. 462 (December 19, 1988), *reprinted in* Fed. Banking Law Rep. (CCH) ¶ 85,686; OCC Letter from J. Michael Shepherd, Senior Deputy Comptroller, Corporate and Economic Programs (July 7, 1988) (unpublished).

[823] OCC Interpretive Letter No. 725 (May 10, 1996), *reprinted in* 1995-1996 Transfer Binder Fed. Banking L. Rep. (CCH) ¶ 81,040; *see also* OCC Letter from Jimmy F. Barton, Deputy Comptroller Multinational Banking, to Carl Howard, Associate General Counsel, Citibank, N.A. (May 13, 1992) (unpublished); OCC Letter from Horace G. Sneed, Senior Attorney, Legal Advisory Services Division (March 2, 1992) (unpublished); OCC No-Objection Letter No. 90-1 (February 16, 1990), *reprinted in* [1989-1990 Transfer Binder] Fed. Banking L. Rep. (CCH) ¶ 83,095.

production hedged for a certain period, e.g. between 60% and 75% of expected volumes for the next 12 to 36 months.

As borrowers became more accustomed to coordinating their hedging strategies with their capital requirements, loan agreements were further expanded to include covenants that borrowers not terminate or modify hedges the lenders had used in calculating the borrowing base. In addition, borrowers were required to deliver periodic reports of their hedge positions and expressly granted lenders a security interest in the contracts under agreements that were revised to include, as collateral, liens on the contracts.

The preferred structure, at least from the perspective of the banks, was that the producer hedge directly with the bank, which allowed the bank to balance collateral-value swings. As the reserves decreased in value as a result of price decreases, the hedges would *increase* in value. In contrast, if prices increased, the rise in reserve values would more than offset hedge liabilities. Simply stated, when it came to dealing with the banker's commodity-price risk for underwriting production loans, the hedges provided the lenders "right way risk."

Non-lender, third-party hedge providers could be accommodated. But this required a separate agreement between the bank and the provider, regarding administration of the collateral under an intercreditor agreement. In the event of a default under the credit agreement or the hedges, this could hamper the bank's ability to work out a restructuring of the borrower's obligations—both under the loan and under the hedge.

In larger, syndicated facilities, only a couple of the larger banks would usually have hedging capability. This created an opportunity for the members of the bank group to have different types of exposure to the borrower. However, under standard syndicated-loan documentation, a syndicate bank's hedge exposure was paid back *pari passu* with the principal loan exposure and the bank providing the hedges was not given any greater weight in voting on administration of the facility.

Further, in the event the lender exited the facility, it would no longer share in collateral for any new hedges it entered into with the producer. But it would remain secured for hedges that had been entered into while the bank was a member of the syndicate. In a 2007 article, long-time energy lender Tim Murray wrote, "Capital availability has always lagged the cycles in the E&P sector. What has changed during the past 10 years has been the maturation of the commodity hedging market.

"Price volatility now can almost completely be factored out of the risk equation. Prior to this, lenders suffered large losses through commodity cycles, which discouraged new entrants and moderated the aggressive stance of existing lenders. With hedging protection afforded all lenders, perhaps this boom-bust cycle won't repeat."[824]

Loan Syndications

Following the bank mergers of the 1980s, a revolver with Chase Bank would have represented a blue-chip syndicate among Chase, Manufacturers Hanover, Chemical, Texas Commerce and First City National of Houston. Similarly, a Bank of America-led facility would have included a syndicate of Republic National, InterFirst, Nations Bank, Security Pacific and SeaFirst.

But the appetite for lending to any one borrower did not equal the predecessor banks' aggregate legal lending limits. In the case of Chase, pre-consolidation, each might have taken $25 million of a producer's loan facility, aggregating to $125 million. One banking lawyer reported in 2000 that, if Chase was considering a loan to a medium-size independent with a low investment-grade rating, it would still only want to hold to its pre-merger limit of $25 million, if that much.[825]

Historically, in the days of single-bank loans, each bank had its own form of loan agreement. Overline banks took loan participations subject to the idiosyncrasies of the correspondent bank's form of documentation. But, as the size of the loans grew beyond any one bank's comfort hold level, the banks and their counsel gravitated to a

---

[824] Tim Murray, "The Ins and Outs of Mezzanine," *Here's the Money: Capital Formation 2007, Special Supplement to Oil and Gas Investor*, May 2007, 31.
[825] Shearer, "Oil and Gas Lending – the Borrower's Perspective."

market form of agented, reserve-based loan agreement more universally accepted and, therefore, easier to syndicate.

The transition to a "market" conforming loan document was an evolutionary process. Two models that became the standard were the "Bank of America form" and the "Chase form." Even in smaller, single-bank loans, most of the first-tier lenders would typically use the syndicated bank form of credit agreement as its initial draft, with the expectation that the loan would eventually grow in size and additional banks would be added.

It is much easier from a loan-documentation standpoint—for the agent, borrower and the new participants—to bring a bank into a facility that is already structured for syndication than to rewrite the agreement, which requires renegotiation with the borrower and its counsel.

Broader adoption of "market terms" was greatly facilitated by the exchange of drafts in electronic form—in WordPerfect and, then, in Word—to the other lenders' counsel and to the borrower's counsel via "floppy disks" and, later, via the Internet. Once the loan was closed, the electronic drafts became a part of bank counsel's database as a template to cut and paste revisions on the next credit agreement.

In addition, with the advent of Internet access, copies of publicly held borrowers' loan agreements are posted at the SEC's website.[826] With e-communication, borrowers became savvier about trends and changes in market terms, enabling them to shop and compare what

---

[826] SEC filings were submitted on paper and were available only by paper copy. In the 1970s, the SEC contracted with a third party to create and distribute microfiche copies to designated SEC public reference rooms. Obtaining copies of these documents was cumbersome and expensive. An individual had to either make hard copies one page at a time in the reference rooms or order copies from service bureaus, which, in turn, had to make and sell hard copies as requested. In short, immediate access was virtually impossible except at an extremely high cost. In 1984, the SEC allocated $30 million to start the EDGAR (Electronic Data Gathering Analysis and Retrieval) pilot program. Its purpose was to create an electronically accessible database, providing a more efficient and less-costly method, whereby the investing public could get the information it needed. A gradual phase-in schedule was established, mandating public corporations to file SEC documents electronically. As of Fall 1995, more than 92% of all public companies were filing with EDGAR. Help.edgar-online.com.

they considered to be their peers' loan terms against what they were being offered.

Meanwhile, prior to the 1980s, loans were not contemplated to be sold like stocks or bonds in a secondary market—other than the overline facilities maintained by correspondent money-center banks. The Loan Syndications & Trading Association Inc. (LSTA) was formed in 1995 by a number of financial institutions to standardize certain provisions of syndicated agreements to promote best practices in both the primary market—where agent banks originate syndicated loans—and in the secondary, loan-trading market. Standard documentation further facilitated the ability of financial investors to more efficiently trade in such credits.

Since its formation in 1995, LSTA has published "standard" forms for commitment letters and certain "model" credit-agreement provisions, covering issues such as lender's increased costs and taxes, rights for the borrower to replace lenders, rights of set-off, sharing of payments by lenders, Libor defaults, agent responsibilities and loan-agreement-syndication assignments.[827] As a result, as these provisions have become more accepted as the standard, it became more difficult to negotiate material changes to them.[828]

As LSTA is not focused on any specific industry, it is not likely that the market in the near future will arrive at a "standardized" reserve-based syndicated facility. Nevertheless, with the consolidation of energy lenders into the major money-center banks and ready e-access to comparable market terms, much of the syndicated facilities generated by lenders and their counsel have many common provisions and structures.

Bank Deregulation

Following the stock-market crash of 1929, one in every five American banks failed. Many of these failures and the market crash itself were

---

[827] "LSTA," accessed May 11, 2016, Lsta.org.
[828] James W. McKellar, "Oil and Gas Financing, 'How It Works'" (paper presented at the 32nd Annual E.E. Smith Oil, Gas & Mineral Law Institute, March 31, 2006).

blamed on the conflict of interest brought about by commercial banks' promotion of securities offerings, while lending to the very companies they were underwriting in public offerings.

In 1933, U.S. Sen. Carter Glass and U.S. Rep. Henry Steagall introduced legislation that limited such conflicts of interests and banned commercial banks from underwriting securities. The Glass-Steagall Act forced banks to choose to be a lender or a securities underwriter. A generation later, memory of the reasons for these protections began to fade.

In the 1960s, bankers lobbied Congress to allow them to enter the municipal-bond market. By the 1970s, investment banks, led by Merrill Lynch, began to encroach on traditional banking territory by offering "cash management accounts," which were interest-bearing, money-market accounts against which their customers could write checks.

Lines were further blurred in the 1980s when the Federal Reserve Board of Governors reinterpreted Section 20 of the Glass-Steagall Act to permit banks to have up to 5% of gross revenues derived from investment banking. The new rules permitted banks' non-bank subsidiaries to hold certain securities that were not permissible for national banks to invest in or underwrite.[829]

The 3-2 vote overruled Chairman Paul Volcker. In late 1987, President Reagan replaced Volcker with Alan Greenspan, a former J.P. Morgan director and a staunch proponent of deregulation.

In 1989, the Federal Reserve increased the percentage of permitted investment-banking revenues to 10% and approved applications by J.P. Morgan, Chase, Bankers Trust and Citicorp to expand the Glass-Steagall loophole to deal in debt and equity securities in addition to municipal securities and commercial paper. In 1996, permissible investment-banking income was increased to 25%, effectively giving commercial banks free rein to actively participate in investment-banking activities.

---

[829] FDIC, *The Financial Crisis Inquiry Report*, 35.

In August of 1997, the Fed eliminated many of the firewall restrictions imposed on "Section 20 subsidiaries," finding that the risks of underwriting had become "manageable." Bankers Trust promptly acquired investment bank Alex. Brown & Co., becoming the first bank to acquire a securities firm.

The death knell to the Depression-era protections of Glass-Steagall was sounded when Sandy Weill of Travelers Insurance Co., which owned investment bank Salomon Smith Barney, announced a $70-billion merger with Citicorp, parent of Citibank, to create Citigroup Inc., the world's largest financial-services company. For the merged entities to stay intact, a repeal of Glass-Steagall was necessary.

Lobbying efforts pitted the competing interests of the insurance, banking, real estate and investment-banking industries against each other in the midst of 1998 elections. Investment-banking interests were successful in repealing Glass-Steagall in 1999 with the Gramm-Leach-Bliley Act. Following the 2001 failure of Enron Corp., Mark Jickling, a specialist with the Congressional Research Service, reported to Congress:

> One part of the fallout from Enron's demise involves its relations with banks. Prominent banking companies, notably Citigroup and J.P. Morgan Chase, were involved in both the investment banking (securities) and commercial banking (lending and deposit) businesses with Enron, and have suffered from Enron's collapse. The two activities had been separated by the 1933 Glass-Steagall Act, until P.L. 106-102 (the Gramm-Leach-Bliley Act) allowed their recombination. Observers have begun to question whether that 1999 repeal of Glass-Steagall encouraged conflicts of interest and unsafe bank lending in support of the investment banking business with Enron.[830]

---

[830] Mark Jickling, Coordinator Specialist in Public Finance, Government and Finance Division, "The Enron Collapse: An Overview of Financial Issues," *Congressional Research Service, The Library of Congress* (March 28, 2002): CRS-5.

The wall that separated commercial lending and investment banking had crumbled.[831] Energy lenders in Houston and Dallas reinvented themselves as "investment bankers" and cast aside their "vice president" titles and iconic lapel pins for "director" titles and suspenders.

When an oil and gas producer went shopping for credit, his banker could offer a lot more "capital products"—from investment banking to M&A to private placements to underwriting public equity and debt. "If all an oil and gas company wants is my money—and no other services—that's not a deal for me," a banker said bluntly in a 2002 article.[832] Large money-center banks also added acquisition and divestiture advisory shops, regional investment banks, commodity-hedge desks and mezzanine to their suites of products.

The larger money-center banks saw reserve-based lending as a springboard for more-lucrative fee-generating transactions by the holding company. This development was not all bad for borrowers. More and more, bankers were able to help steer independent producers through the entire capital food chain. A producer and his "banker" could start with a mezzanine facility or, perhaps even, a direct equity investment in the borrower by the non-regulated side of the bank to establish sufficient collateral to finance development drilling or an opportune acquisition.

In time and with drilling success, the company's collateral could support a conforming borrowing-base senior-lien facility. And, where the banker had the backroom support to administer a syndicate of lenders, the same bank could further increase the size of the facility from a few million dollars into tens and hundreds of millions as the company's reserves and production increased.

To protect the borrower from the downside of commodity-price cycles and lock in a higher borrowing base, the larger banks were capable of providing hedges secured by the same collateral that was securing the bank facility. As the company matured further, its lender

---

[831] FDIC, *The Financial Crisis Inquiry Report*, 56.
[832] Toal, "Capital Malls."

could lead it in accessing the public debt and -equity markets, providing even more capital to help it grow.

All the while, the commercial bank's revenue potential grew to well above what it would have made on just interest payments. A Wells Fargo banker at the time, Tim Murray said in an article, "The best success story I can tell is one where we take an operator from an initial $1 million loan to a $100 million credit facility—and in the process introduce that client to acquisition opportunities, advisory services and investors that can help grow that company."[833]

An example of the long and close relationship between producer and bank is illustrated by a loan in which Wells Fargo financed the management team of a small private producer in 1997. The following year, Wells Fargo introduced the team to EnCap Investments, in which the bank was a fund investor, to provide additional capital in the form of preferred and common stock to finance the company's further growth.

As the company grew, the bank also provided oil and gas hedges and advised the producer in an equity investment by a Canadian royalty trust and, with the bank's investment-banking team, in its IPO as a master limited partnership. Later, the bank advised the producer in a $3-billion merger with another MLP.

The producer's borrowing base had grown from the initial $37 million in 1997 to $2.5 billion by 2014, all the while with Wells Fargo as its lead bank. In the borrower's merger, Wells Fargo served as the borrower's investment advisor, underwriter, administrative agent and arranger and was also the administrative agent for the acquired company. Following the steep oil-price decline in early 2015, the borrower accessed an additional $1 billion in second-lien debt and preferred-equity investments—again with the assistance of Wells Fargo's bankers.[834]

---

[833] Toal, "Capital Malls."
[834] Over the years, the Wells Fargo energy investment-banking group came to be led by James Kipp upon Wells' acquisition of Wachovia Bank after the 2008 financial crisis. Kipp began his career as a commercial energy banker in Houston First City National Bank's energy department.

As the century came to a close, the availability of credit and enthusiasm to put capital to work was affected by the "Asian contagion." Similar to the Texas real estate boom in the early '80s, the Asian real estate market "was overleveraged in the overheated and overbuilt condo and office building sectors" in the 1990s, particularly in Bangkok, which triggered a collapse in July of 1997 of Asian currencies and stock markets.[835]

"By the end of 1997, a vast panic was raging over large parts of Asia, and the contagion spread beyond Asia," Yergin wrote in *The Quest: Energy, Security, and the Remaking of the Modern World.* "In August 1998, the Russian government defaulted on its sovereign debt ... and Wall Street teetered on the edge when the highly leveraged hedge fund Long Term Capital Management collapsed ... [and Brazil's precarious financial position threatened] what U.S. Treasury Secretary Robert Rubin called an 'engulfing world crisis.'"[836]

Central Bank intervention by developed countries by the spring of 1999 was able to turn the panic and contagion around.[837] But U.S. producers felt the disruption in the world's financial markets. The Nymex price for West Texas Intermediate was more than $26 a barrel at the beginning of 1997; it fell to less than $11 by the end of 1998. Meanwhile, the Nymex price for natural gas fell below $2.

"Bloodbath" was an understatement, Yergin wrote, citing a Wall Street analyst. "Companies slashed budgets and laid off employees. One of the major companies shrank its annual Christmas party to some snacks in the cafeteria."[838]

More than the price decline, the sheer volatility of the markets made it difficult for producers to plan and nearly impossible for bankers to safely underwrite loans without significantly discounting current price decks in calculating prudent borrowing bases. Gene Ames, a wildcatter, reflected in 2004, "In the '90s, the volatility of oil and gas

---

835 Yergin, *The Quest* (Penguin Books: September 20, 2011), 86.
836 Yergin, *The Quest*, 86-87.
837 Yergin, *The Quest*, 86-87.
838 Yergin, *The Quest*, 88.

markets and prices increased the difficulty of access to capital for independents.

"Conventional capital sources dried up during the decade and became increasingly more risk averse by the end of the decade as capital sources were diverted from energy to the high tech, dot.com industries in the high tech boom of '97-'99. The subsequent bust of the high tech market left the capital providers in such disarray that they remained closed to energy until late 2003, and 2004."[839]

The Wall Street Journal reported on September 11, 1998, "Continued low oil prices are straining the finances of energy producers, possibly leading to loan defaults and more oil-patch mergers, some bankers and analysts say. With oil prices down about 40% from a year ago and no rebound in sight, revenue is sliding at many energy companies, which are beginning to feel a cash-flow squeeze. Particularly hard hit are small and mid-size producers that are more dependent on oil than natural gas."

By March of 1999, *The Economist*'s cover story was headlined "Drowning In Oil," with a photograph of three oil-soaked roustabouts wrestling a wellhead spewing oil full-bore. With some exaggeration, the report captured what had become the widespread conviction that prices were going to stay low for the foreseeable future.[840]

Analysts surveyed for the article predicted tighter credit, potential defaults by small oil producers, greater merger activity and vulture-fund buy-outs or short-term loans on more onerous terms. On balance, however, commercial lenders felt they were in a better position to weather this downturn than they were in the previous bust.

The *Journal* reported, "When prices fell in the mid-1980's to near $10 a barrel, oil companies went out of business, taking more than a few banks with them. In those days banks lent money based on companies' reserves, even if they weren't producing oil and gas from them. Now, most loans are based on actual production."[841]

---

[839] Haines and Pike, *America's Independents*, 101.
[840] Yergin, *The Quest*, 88.
[841] Christopher Cooper, "Oil Patch Braces for Losses Amid Price Slump, Mergers," *The Wall Street Journal*, September 11, 1998.

The global financial-market situation and precipitous drop in the price of oil and gas clearly affected U.S. producers—large and small. BP started a merger mania on August 11, 1998, announcing it would merge with Amoco Corp., which was formerly Standard Oil of Indiana. Later, in April of 1999, it announced it would merge with Arco and, in May of 2000, it announced it would roll up the remaining shares of Vastar Resources that it did not already own by virtue of its Arco acquisition.

Exxon Corp., formerly Standard Oil of New Jersey, announced on December 1, 1998, that it would merge with Mobil Corp. In October of 2000, Chevron Corp., formerly Standard of California, announced it would merge with Texaco, which was not a former Standard Oil company but, nevertheless, a long-standing member of "the Seven Sisters."[842]

Conoco Inc. and Phillips Petroleum Co. merged in 2002. Foreign majors merged as well, with Total SA combining with Petrofina SA in 1999 and with Elf Aquitaine SA in 2000.[843]

The consolidations benefited the independents—again, just as during the 1980s—as the majors shed U.S. onshore assets for prizes abroad and in the deepwater Gulf of Mexico. Similarly, this opened new investment and talent-access opportunities for independents in the early years of the new millennium.

The pipeline for public offerings, which had been a source of capital for energy companies earlier in the 1990s and was full to capacity in the first half of 1997, dried up overnight as oil prices began to decline. By the first quarter of 1998, companies that had waited to issue debt found themselves too late to get on the public-markets gravy train and never left the station.

---

[842] "Seven Sisters" was a term coined in the 1950s by the head of the Italian state oil company Eni SpA to describe the seven oil companies that formed the "Consortium for Iran" cartel from the mid-1940s into the 1970s and comprised of Standard Oil of New Jersey (Exxon), Standard Oil of New York (Mobil), Gulf Oil (acquired by SoCal in 1985), Standard Oil of California (following its merger with Gulf, SoCal became Chevron), Texaco, Royal Dutch Shell and Anglo-Persian Oil (BP). Yergin, *The Prize*, 765.
[843] Yergin, *The Quest*, 88-107.

Commercial bankers, who had been agonizing in early 1997 over their inability to compete with the public market's lower cost of funds, were quick to seize on the lack of competition and increased the pricing on their commitments to lend by between 100 and 200 basis points for the same type of credits.[844] More ominous for over-extended producers, banks were also reevaluating borrowing bases and finding the value of their collateral coming up short. A wave of restructurings and insolvencies washed over the industry in 1999 and 2000.[845]

Yet, notwithstanding the bloodletting, of the 19 pure-play E&P bankruptcies between 1995 and 2012, reserve-based lenders recovered their entire principal.[846] In addition to greater underwriting discipline following the lessons of the 1980s and the adoption of the flexible borrowing-base structure, the use of commodity derivatives as a hedge against price fluctuations was credited for the lower loan-loss ratios than experienced by lenders to other industries in that timeframe.[847]

---

[844] Interest rates are typically denominated in basis points equal to 1/100th of one percent.

[845] Some of the E&P companies filing for bankruptcy during this period included National Energy Group Inc. (February 1999), Forcenergy Inc. (March 1999), Alma Energy Corp. (May), Coho Energy Inc. (August), Forman Petroleum Corp. (August), Costilla Energy Inc. (September), Southern Mineral Corp. (October), Abraxas (non-bankruptcy distressed exchange, November), Michael Petroleum Corp. (December) and KCS Energy Inc. (January 2000).

[846] Standard & Poor's Ratings Services, "Despite Risks, We Expect Excellent Recovery on Most Reserve-Based Lending Facilities of E&P Companies," January 18, 2013. S&P noted that its study generally includes only companies that have defaulted with outstanding debt in excess of $50 million and where there is sufficient publicly available information (usually in the bankruptcy filings) relating to recovery. "We believe small companies are often more susceptible to default, due in part to higher cost structure, limited diversification, and less experienced management. It's unclear to us whether the recovery prospects on RBLs of smaller companies differ from those of larger companies within the LossStats sample." Standard & Poor's Ratings Services, "Despite Risks …," 10. Moreover, following the development of the public debt markets for oil and gas companies, Moody's Investors Service noted a day earlier that, while, "senior secured bank debt has superior recovery rates, this comes at the expense of unsecured and subordinated debt holders. Non-senior secured debt holders averaged a recovery of 46% on a weighted average recovery basis on pure E&P company debt." Moody's Investors Service Inc., "Recoveries More Certain for Senior Debt Holders in Oil and Gas," Moodys.com, January 17, 2013.

[847] Charles Kingswell-Smith, Managing Director, Merrill Lynch Capital (presentation to IPAA Private Capital Conference, January 16, 2008), 8.

"We're From the Government and We're Here to Help"

Even the federal government stepped in to offer financial assistance to the beleaguered industry. On August 17, 1999, President Clinton signed into law the Emergency Steel Loan Guarantee and Oil and Gas Guaranteed Loan Program Act to provide federal guarantees of loans to qualified steel companies and qualified oil and gas companies. Originally, the idea was to provide assistance just to the steel industry, but U.S. Sen. Pete Domenici from New Mexico saw an opportunity to extend a helping hand to oil and gas producers as well.[848]

Under the program, the government guaranteed up to 85% of a producer's loan up to $10 million, provided that it met certain conditions. An august board was set up to oversee the program, comprised of Greenspan, Secretary of Commerce Bill Daley and SEC Chairman Arthur Levitt. The board retained an experienced Houston-based energy banker, Charles Hall, to administer the program.

But the program offered little practical assistance. The devil was in the details and very few oil and gas producers and energy lenders were willing to wade through the bureaucratic morass to seek the added credit enhancement of the government's guaranty.

Although Congress had authorized the program to guarantee up to $500 million in oil and gas secured loans, only 15 producers completed the initial applications; six were approved and only three were closed and, eventually, funded. Less than 1% of the federal authorization was ultimately used.[849]

The few guarantees issued was not for lack of trying to generate interest, as Hall made presentations about the program to energy bankers, IPAA members and members of other producer organizations. Because the government did not guarantee 100% of the producer's loan, energy lenders were unwilling to stretch beyond their standard underwriting criteria in connection with partially guaranteed

---

[848] Emergency Oil and Gas Guaranteed Loan Board, 13 CFR Chapter V. CFR Vol. 64, No. 207, October 27, 1999.
[849] Federal Reserve Governor Edward Gramlich, "Loan Guarantee Programs" (speech before the National Economists Club, Washington, D.C., April 24, 2003), The Federal Reserve Board, Federalreserve.gov.

government loans. They would always be on the hook, dollar-for-dollar on 15% of the credit exposure.

And producers who could avoid it had better sense than to be weighed down by the federal bureaucracy.[850] In addition to the cumbersome application process—on top of the standard, bank-application papers—producers faced periodic reporting obligations and still had to show the Oil and Gas Guaranteed Loan Board that there was a reasonable expectation of repayment.

Contrary to what some applicants originally thought, this was not a give-away program. The board saw the program for what it was: a favor to Domenici, a Republican, to gain his support of the true plan, which was to help steel mills and steel-union workers in Appalachia in what had become known as the "Rust Belt." Greenspan administered the plan, as required by Congress, but neither he nor Levitt were interested in squandering taxpayer money.[851]

Many of the producer applicants were not bankable under conventional and conforming lending standards. By and large, they sought governmental assistance because they had been turned down by experienced energy lenders. The reasons were that they were too small for the lender's desired loan portfolio; were seeking dollars for exploration with no current production, thus no current cash flow to cover debt service; or were near insolvent and had no prospects of regaining solvency.

Only the desperate showed up in Hall's office. For those few loans that passed the minimum underwriting criteria, the lenders applying for the guaranty failed to meet commercial energy-lending standards. Many of the applicant bankers had never made a secured oil and gas loan and their clients were no more sophisticated in the process of energy-loan documentation.

Fortunately, for U.S. taxpayers, the board engaged its own counsel to review and approve the applicant bank's documentation that

---

[850] "Laggard Loans," *Oil & Gas Journal*, March 31, 2000.
[851] Charles Hall, interview by the author, November 26, 2013.

was to be guaranteed.[852] The quality and completeness of the documentation submitted for review was lacking. The board's counsel's role was expanded beyond mere loan review and approval to actual drafting of the applicant bank's documentation—coordinating with the borrower on collateral examination and filing of liens to ensure that the loans were properly documented.

The end result was a program that was—perhaps, at best—well intentioned, but so complicated in application and its administration that only the most desperate borrowers and clueless bankers were willing to spend the time and effort to go through the process. Federal Reserve Governor Edward Gramlich reported, "Then oil prices spiked in 2000, the year when applications were submitted, improving conditions in the industry and making credit more easily available.

"When this happened, many lenders, and their borrowers, withdrew their applications. It made little sense for oil and gas lenders and borrowers to go through the federal procedures, not particularly onerous but not trivial either, to get an unnecessary guarantee."[853]

According to Hall, who returned to the ranks of Houston's energy lenders, no U.S. taxpayer lost money on any of the guarantees.[854]

---

[852] Haynes and Boone worked with the board's in-house counsel, Marguerite Owens, to review and work with applicants and their bankers.
[853] Federal Reserve Governor Edward Gramlich, April 24, 2003.
[854] Hall, author's interview.

CHAPTER 8

The New Millennium

"It must be seen in its role in the perennial gale of creative destruction ... ."
Joseph Schumpeter

The arrival of the new millennium brought a collective sigh of relief for borrowers and lenders alike, as computer clocks rolled over from '99 to '00 and a feared, computer-code-based collapse of digital systems failed to materialize. After all of the hoopla, the New Year arrived with a yawn.

The affirmative covenants that crept into loan agreements near the end of the 1990s, requiring that "the Borrower shall take all steps necessary to protect against Y2K" were quickly removed.[855] More importantly, the industry was ready to put the bad memories of the prior couple of years behind them and start the year and century anew.

In the early part of the decade, new loan-agreement clauses were needed and additional forms required after the tragic events of Sep-

---

[855] Typical language for the borrower's representation included "Year 2000 Matters." "In order to avoid a material adverse effect on the Borrower and its Subsidiaries taken as a whole, any reprogramming required to permit the proper functioning in all material respects (but only to the extent that such proper functioning would otherwise be impaired by the occurrence of the year 2000) in and following the year 2000, of computer systems and other equipment containing embedded microchips, in either case owned or operated by Borrower or any Subsidiaries or used or relied upon in the conduct of their business (including, to the Borrower's knowledge, any such systems and other equipment supplied by others or with which the computer systems of Borrower or any of its Subsidiaries interface), and the testing of all such systems and other equipment as so reprogrammed, will be completed by December 31, 1999."

tember 11, 2001. Congress responded to the attacks by enacting certain anti-terrorism laws, including the Uniting and Strengthening America by Providing Appropriate Tools Required to Intercept and Obstruct Terrorism Act of 2001, known in short as the USA Patriot Act.[856] Among many other things, the added language to credit agreements required greater disclosures by borrowers and Know Your Customer (KYC) forms, aimed at deterring money laundering and terrorist financing. [857]

Rising oil and gas prices were welcomed relief from the punishing prices of the end of the 1990s that had crippled many producers or caused them to merge with larger companies. Natural gas rose from less than $2 in the summer of 1998 to between $2.60 and $3.80 during the first six months of 2000 and stretched to $6.80 in January of 2001.[858]

The rig count for drilling gas wells increased from fewer than 400 to almost 900 by the beginning of 2001.[859] But the increase in activity was not producing twice as much gas. In fact, total U.S. gas production was roughly unchanged.[860]

Conventional wisdom was that, with the application of 3-D seismic technology, most of the easy gas had been found and developed. As a result, it became necessary to tap smaller and deeper targets onshore and in the Gulf for which decline rates were high, especially as extraction techniques were improving concurrently.

---

[856] Pub. L. No. 107-56, 115 Stat. 272.

[857] *Bank Secrecy Act and Anti-Money Laundering*, 31 U.S.C. 5318(i) effective July 23, 2002.

[858] U.S. EIA, Independent Statistics & Analysis. "U.S. Natural Gas Wellhead Price." Accessed March 01, 2016. Eia.gov.

[859] There were 371 rotary rigs drilling for natural gas in April, 1999, and 871 in January, 2001. U.S. EIA, Independent Statistics & Analysis. "U.S. Natural Gas Rotary Rigs in Operation." Accessed March 6, 2016. Eia.gov.

[860] U.S. gas production was 18.8 Tcf in 1999; in 2001, 19.6 Tcf. U.S. EIA, Independent Statistics & Analysis. "U.S. Dry Natural Gas Production." Accessed March 6, 2016. Eia.gov.

Chapter 8: The New Millennium

At the same time, U.S. power producers were bringing more gas-fired power plants online, increasing demand.[861] The result was a treadmill in which, despite dramatic increases in drilling, the industry was unable to significantly increase supply. The risk was that rising prices would drive the most price-sensitive users out of the market, thus resulting in demand destruction.

Meanwhile, WTI, which hit a nadir of less than $11 in December of 1998, began what would become a long 10-year path to just shy of $150 in July of 2008. Also, independents and their bankers were encouraged that Texas-oil-patch-grown George W. Bush was elected the U.S.' 43rd president and took office in January of 2001. The son of President George H.W. Bush, "43" grew up in Midland and Houston and had been a wildcatter with Arbusto Energy Co., Spectrum 7 Co. and Harken Energy Corp. in the 1970s and into the early 1990s.

Moreover, Vice President Dick Cheney had most recently served as chairman and CEO of oilfield-services giant Halliburton Co. With the dot-com bust and rising oil and gas prices, capital began flowing to energy companies and they and their investors took heart that new, higher price floors were sustainable.

Despite the good news on the price front, traditional reserve-based lending markets failed to see any significant increase in loan volume.[862] Producers had not forgotten that, in the first quarter of 1999, following banks' reset of their price decks, many of them had greater amounts drawn on their revolvers than their revised borrowing bases. The sting of this borrowing-base deficit was still fresh in the minds of many producers as they entered the new millennium.

U.S. capital markets were still recovering from the Asian contagion and the dot-com hangover; however, producers were wary of spending beyond their means. Increasing oil and gas prices were a double-edged sword for those looking to grow through acquisitions.

---

[861] U.S. natural gas demand for power generation increased from 4.6 Tcf in 1998 to 5.7 Tcf in 2002. U.S. EIA, Independent Statistics & Analysis. "U.S. Natural Gas Deliveries to Electric Power Consumers." Accessed March 6, 2016. Eia.gov.
[862] Brian A. Toal, "Big Deals," *Here's the Money: Capital Formation 2004, Special Supplement to Oil and Gas Investor*, May 2004, 5.

They had stronger cash flows and more asset value to borrow against. But they had to convince their brethren, who were also enjoying improved cash flows, to sell at current prices rather than hold out for, perhaps, higher prices in the near future.

On the banking side, some of the major energy lenders were consolidating. With the money-center mega-mergers, only half as many energy lenders were around in 2002 as five years prior. NationsBank merged with Bank of America in 1998, Deutsche Bank and Bankers Trust in 1999, Chase Manhattan with JPMorgan in December 2000 and First Union with Wachovia Bank in 2001, to name a few.

The mergers left many medium and small independents either squeezed out of their bank or shuffled up to New York offices when they would have preferred local account management. "What's more, the remaining giants of credit burned by Enron-like exposures have become cautious, lowering the percentage of any energy loan they will hold," *Oil and Gas Investor* reported in November of 2002.[863]

These larger banks sought safety and higher fees, thus chasing larger, publicly held oil and gas clients, leaving an opportunity for growth in local bank portfolios. Smaller independents that didn't fit the surviving, national bank's portfolio design had been encouraged to take their business to local or regional banks.

Most of the capital formation in 2000-2001 was in the mezzanine and merchant-banking markets. Mezzanine markets doubled between 1999 and 2001[864] as many of the merchant banks that sprang up in the late 1990s, trying to copy Enron's success, vied for market share in mezzanine and structured-financed transactions.

Many of the utility and pipeline companies that followed Enron's lead used producer financing to enhance earnings as well as comple-

---

[863] Brian A. Toal, "Regional Bankers Court Borrowers," *Oil and Gas Investor*, November 4, 2002. "'During the past 18 months, many money-center banks have up-tiered their energy client focus, neglecting the small-cap independent,' says Arthur R. (Buzz) Gralla Jr., senior vice president and director of all U.S. oil and gas banking for Guaranty Bank." Toal, "Regional Bankers Court Borrowers."

[864] Tim Murray, Wells Fargo Energy Capital, "IPAA Oil and Gas Investment Symposium Private Capital Conference" (presented at 2005 OGIS Private Capital Conference), April 18, 2005.

ment their other business lines, including hedging and trading, commodity sales to power plants and through-put on their pipelines. "In the late 1990s through 2001, the merchant players saturated the market with capital. All of them followed in Enron's footsteps," Kurt Talbot, a veteran mezzanine lender, observed in 2004.

"The quest was for earnings, not necessarily cash returns. In the early to mid-1990's, Enron turned the market on its head with its commodity-risk management and volumetric production payments. These were well structured, low risk and price-competitive. This was a model that was, and should have been, imitated. ... Each of the merchant players was attempting to place $300[-] to $500 million of capital a year in the market.

"There was no deal that could not get done. ... What started as senior debt morphed into subordinated debt, project equity and even venture capital. Ultimately, that's why many of these portfolios blew up."[865]

Spectacularly, Enron blew up. In December of 2001, it filed for bankruptcy, ending months of analysts' queries about opaque financial statements, accounting disclosures and SEC investigations. The company began in 1985 with the merger of two staid pipeline utilities, following FERC's deregulation of interstate pipelines. Houston Natural Gas Pipeline merged with Omaha-based InterNorth Pipeline. In time, Enron became the most innovative and aggressive trading house in the country.

To survive in a deregulated world, Enron reinvented itself in the 1990s with the assistance of a young consultant from McKinsey & Co., Jeff Skilling. Enron began entering long-term, fixed-priced energy contracts and trading natural gas through the use of forward contracts and other instruments. Over time, Enron concentrated on financial instruments and trading markets, straying from its foundation that had been built on hard assets, particularly pipelines and natural resources.

Between 1990 and 2001, Enron Energy Capital Resources Group had invested nearly $5 billion in E&P companies through project fi-

---

[865] Kurt Talbot, Goldman Sachs E&P Capital, quoted by Snow, "Minding the Gap."

nance, equity, mezzanine debt, senior debt, convertible debt, volumetric production payments and other instruments.[866] Its downfall was unrelated to its capital lending and investments in oil and gas assets. Meanwhile, the innovation it brought to financing U.S. independents is largely unknown by the general public or by new, capital-hungry producers that now access capital under debt structures invented and made commercial by Enron.

In 2002, other major power companies and pipeline operators that were trading commodities in competition with Enron also saw these business units fail. Many of them had also launched energy-finance units, including Duke Energy's Duke Capital Partners and Southern Co.'s Mirant Americas. Late-comers, their units were only dabbling in energy finance, relative to Enron's portfolio; their parents, focusing on their own balance sheets, found better uses for their capital and decided to abandon this "non-core" business.[867] In 2006, energy attorney James McKellar reported:

> Their lower debt and equity costs, without the regulatory constraints of banks, allowed them to create large profit margins on their producer financing and their hedging and trading businesses. Securitization of the producer finance portfolios allowed Enron and others [utilities and pipelines] to accelerate profits, which further increased the appetite and lowered the cost for producer loans. The model fell apart with the Enron failure. The rating agencies, who had failed to properly account for the risks that the trading, hedging and financing businesses put on balance sheets, moved quickly to downgrade the ratings of these companies. Production financing and hedging operations were sold, spun off or terminated as these companies went

---

[866] Nissa Darbonne, "A Major E&P Capital Provider, Enron is Busy With Its Own Finances," *Oil and Gas Investor*, January 30, 2002.
[867] Producers, such as Royal Dutch Shell and Range Resources Corp., that had producer-finance units struggled with the capital-allocation decision as well and, ultimately, decided to exit the field. Murray, "The Ins and Outs of Mezzanine," 31.

into bankruptcy or shed assets to improve capital, save credit ratings and avoid bankruptcy.[868]

The mezzanine market had expanded from $200 million in 1991 to $1.3 billion in 2001. During 2002 and 2003, it declined to between $300- and $500 million.[869] The few still standing included three of the original shops: TCW, General Electric Energy Capital and Wells Fargo Energy Capital.

The loss of sources of mezzanine capital meant less competition and higher pricing. Energy-capital broker Cameron Smith said in a 2002 article, "In the classic theory of supply and demand, yes. I'm more concerned, however, that for a while at least, mezzanine capital will simply be much more difficult to find."[870]

Predictions were that, with the loss of Enron, Shell and others, equity-kickers in the form of overrides would cost more.[871] Another energy financier, Scott Johnson, observed in 2002, "The core market of mezzanine investors has been decimated since the beginning of the year. Of five key mezzanine investors last year, only two are left. The mezzanine financing business has certainly been hurt. The remaining investors will be much more selective than ever before, so companies will need to present strong projects and they will need to present them well."[872]

Smith wrote later in 2002, "With the implosion of Enron, Aquila and Mirant, and the withdrawal of Shell, a crucial question may yet be: what assets and team, well-suited to the private-capital psyche, are in, or are about to come into, the market, perhaps as distressed prices,

---

[868] McKellar, "'Oil and Gas Financing, 'How It Works,'" III.B.1.

[869] Wells Fargo Energy Capital Presentation on Mezzanine Debt Markets, IPAA Capital Markets Conference 2004.

[870] Nissa Darbonne, "Where Art Thou Mezzanine Financier?," *Oil and Gas Investor*, June 4, 2002.

[871] Darbonne, "Where Art Thou Mezzanine Financier?"

[872] Darbonne, "Where Art Thou Mezzanine Financier?"

perhaps with books of business yet available for instant gratification?"[873]

The market response to the dire forecast of the dearth of mezzanine providers was quickly answered—perhaps sped on—by the increase in margins that the surviving mezzanine lenders experienced. Within fewer than 24 months, the void was filled by new players: Macquarie Energy Capital, led by former Cambrian Capital bankers; Royal Bank of Scotland, led by ex-Enron lenders; BlackRock Energy Capital, consisting of the producer-finance unit formerly within an E&P company and now known as BlueRock; Petrobridge Investments, led by ex-Mirant and -Shell Capital lenders; Goldman E&P Capital, led by additional ex-Enron lenders; and NGP Capital Resources, formed by private-equity provider Natural Gas Partners.[874]

The Oil and Gas Price Rush of the 2000s

9/11 not only gave rise to new banking regulations; crude oil prices slid on an already-weakened world economy and increases in OPEC production. WTI had exceeded $35 in November of 2000; a year later, it was less than $20 and wouldn't find $35 again until 2003.

Natural gas followed the opposite course, however. The Nymex price had spiked above $10 during in the winter of 2000-2001; after the attack, it fell below $2. But it quickly resumed its steady climb as the winter of 2001-2002 drew down reserves. The price was more than $5 in January of 2003; beginning in December of 2003 and except for a few days, the prompt-month contract did not trade below $5 again until 2009.[875]

---

[873] Cameron Smith, Cosco Capital Management, LLC, "Plenty of Private Capital Available- to the Right Type Companies," *Oil and Gas Investor*, September 4, 2002.

[874] Natural Gas Partners formed NGP Capital Resources in November, 2004, to capitalize on opportunities created by an estimated $2 billion of primarily mezzanine capital that had exited the energy space during the prior three years. Brian A. Toal "Focused On Yield," *Oil and Gas Investor*, April 29, 2005; Amiel David, PeTech Enterprises, IAEE/IELE Conference, Houston Texas December 11, 2003.

[875] U.S. EIA, Independent Statistics & Analysis. "Henry Hub Natural Gas Spot Price." Accessed March 6, 2016. Eia.gov.

Chapter 8: The New Millennium

As for oil and also beginning in 2003, its price consistently grew as well—based in part on commentary that the world had found peak oil-production capacity; thus, no future net supply growth was possible.[876] The inability of the U.S. to replace its oil reserves, much less reduce its dependence on imports, was the topic *du jour*. Not since the Arab-embargo-derived oil crisis of the 1970s had the theory of declining reserves espoused by King Hubbert in 1956 gained so much traction and general acceptance.[877]

In 2005, energy analyst and investment banker Matt Simmons' *Twilight in the Desert: The Coming Saudi Oil Shock and the World Economy* was published, asserting that the limitless Saudi fields were, in fact, limited and that their ability to make up the rest of the world's declining reserves would become a crisis sooner rather than later. Simmons' analysis found support by historically low spare OPEC capacity during 2004-2005.

Bill Weidner wrote in 2008, "The numbers are compelling. In 1986, when OPEC had approximately 17 million barrels of excess daily capacity, the world had consumed 566 billion barrels of crude oil since Colonel Drake drilled his first well in Pennsylvania in 1859. In the … years since 1986, however, the world has consumed almost another 566 billion barrels—and OPEC's excess productive capacity has dwindled to a number almost too small to measure." [878]

The U.S.' perceived dependence upon foreign oil was not just an economic issue; it was a national security issue. In January of 2007, at a hearing before the U.S. Senate Committee on Energy and Natural

---

[876] The root of the advancement was in Hubbert's Peak projection in the late 1960s. It was further propelled by the U.S. invasion of Iraq and post-9/11 economic rebound, rising Asian demand and Gulf of Mexico production disruptions that had been caused by hurricanes Ivan, Katrina and Rita.

[877] King Hubbert predicted in 1956 that U.S. oil production was likely to hit its peak somewhere between 1965 and 1970, a theory, "Hubbert's Peak," that would forever be linked to his name. Yergin, *The Quest*, 237.

[878] William Weidner, "Private Capital Flow," *Oil and Gas Investor*, March 14, 2008, accessed March 1, 2016, Oilandgasinvestor.com. During much of 2004 and 2005, one analyst calculated OPEC's spare capacity to produce oil was less than 1 million barrels per day. James L. Williams, WTRG Economics, "Oil Price History and Analysis," Wtrg.com, accessed March 16, 2016.

Resources, the director of geopolitics and energy at New America Foundation testified, "Simply put, there is no economically plausible scenario for a strategically meaningful reduction in the dependence of the United States and its allies on imported hydrocarbons during the next quarter century."[879]

American production was perceived as being on a terminal decline and dependence upon foreign oil would only increase. Accordingly, the price of oil, which had grown into the $50s and $60s by January of 2007, began to take off on a steep and continuous rise, finding $80 that September and topping out at nearly $150 in July of 2008.

As prices continued their seemingly inexorable rise, oil and gas loans—once perceived as a risky and even "alternative" investment by some bankers—were now highly valued as safe, quality loans. David Reid with Capital One Southcoast Inc. said in a May 2008 article, "The E&P sector has become one of the lowest-risks businesses for banks. For the past decade the loss to the banking industry on proven-reserve-based loans has been virtually zero."[880]

Natural gas was in the money too. Power-generation demand was growing in the 1990s and 2000s as a result of increased use of natural gas, rather than coal; a growing U.S. economy; and increased electricity use via the preponderance of digital services and devices. Hot summers and cold winters piled on, along with a drought in the U.S. Northwest that reduced hydro-generated power supply there.[881]

Further jumps in price during the 2000s were caused by massive losses of production as a result of hurricanes Ivan in 2004 and Katrina and Rita, both in 2005. In December of 2005, the price of natural gas

[879] Dr. Flynt Leverett, Director of Geopolitics and Energy at the New America Foundation, Testimony before United States Senate Committee on Energy and Natural Resources, January 10, 2007.

[880] Gary Clouser, "Regional Credit No Problem," *Here's the Money: Capital Formation 2008, Special Supplement to Oil and Gas Investor*, May 2008, 20.

[881] Mary Ann Capehart, "Drought Diminishes Hydropower Capacity in Western U.S.," *Water Resources Research Center*, accessed on February 15, 2016, Wrrc.arizona.edu.

on Nymex exceeded $15 as a result of reduced supply and the fear of another exceptionally cold winter.[882]

George Mitchell and the Shale Revolution

In the midst of the run-up in natural-gas prices, the marketplace wasn't giving much consideration to newly proven production that was possible from shale. The other Hubbert's Peak—the one Hubbert forecasted in the 1970s for natural gas—was a problem gas producers had persistently faced since the early 1980s. One producer in particular set out to coax gas out of a shale formation, the Barnett, in North Texas.

George Mitchell, a self-made billionaire and social visionary, was born in Galveston, Texas, as the son of a Greek immigrant.[883] After receiving his engineering degree with an emphasis in geology from Texas A&M University and serving in World War II, Mitchell went to work as a wildcatter based in Houston. The company, Christie, Mitchell and Mitchell, eventually became Mitchell Energy & Development Corp.

In a 1998 biography of him and the company, Mitchell said of Harold J. Vance, his petroleum-engineering professor at A&M, "He had a real homespun philosophy. He said, 'If you want to go to work for Exxon (or Humble at that time), fine, then you can drive around in a pretty good Chevrolet, but if you really want to drive around in a Cadillac you'd better go out on your own someday.'"[884]

---

[882] Price figures from U.S. EIA, Independent Statistics & Analysis. "Henry Hub Natural Gas Spot Price." Accessed March 6, 2016. Eia.gov. Storage figures from U.S. EIA, Independent Statistics & Analysis. "Lower 48 States Natural Gas Working Underground Storage." Accessed March 6, 2016. Eia.gov.
[883] Story told by Mitchell to Budd Clark. Mitchell's father took on the name of his railgang paymaster, Mike Mitchell, as he was told that "his name, Savvas Paraskevopoulos, was too damn hard to pronounce."
[884] Kutchin, *How Mitchell Energy & Development Corp. Got its Start*, 187. Ironically, while Mitchell owned a few Cadillacs in his day, he never put on airs or acted like his assets were worth hundreds of millions of dollars. For example, anyone could find him eating breakfast most Saturday mornings in his hometown of Galveston at his favorite breakfast spot with childhood friends and the rest of the local breakfast crowd. And, after pitching to the Galveston City Council a public effort he would underwrite to rebuild the city after

Vance was influential in the careers of many oilmen and oil bankers. As a professor, for example, he taught oil and gas property valuation to Tom Stevens, who in the 1970s became the head of First City's energy group. Later in his career, Vance himself joined the ranks of energy bankers as the head of Bank of the Southwest's oil and gas department. Full circle, Bank of the Southwest was one of the lenders Mitchell relied upon as he was building his company. Vance became a director of the bank.[885]

Mitchell financed his early production from a core of investors who stayed with him for decades. Joseph Kutchin, the biographer, wrote, "Mitchell began his career partnering with his older brother Johnny and wildcatter, Merlyn Christie to form an independent oil company Christie, Mitchell and Mitchell, just like the generation of wildcatters before him. Without any production to speak of they were unable to get bank financing. Instead, he would work up a prospect from geological information and tips, acquire some leasehold on the cheap and try to sell portions of the prospect to local investors."

Mitchell told Kutchin, "I would do the geology and engineering, get the deal together, and then we'd have some land man help us get the leases together and Johnny and Merlyn would go down to the Esperson Drugstore [in downtown Houston] and sell the deals. That's how we started. They'd sell an eighth here and an eighth there, they'd sell over coffee, and the first thing you know, we had a deal that cost $30,000. We'd get maybe at first a 32nd carried interest, and then a 16th carried interest.

"Anyway, first thing you know, we started building, and then we got our quarter net profits, and soon we started taking more of the deals ourselves. So Johnny and I and Merlyn kept building the company gradually. If we'd drill a well, make a well, we'd run to the bank to get some money. If you drill a dry hole, you get nothing."[886]

Hurricane Ike, he and his team rode back in a cab; he jumped in the middle of the back seat.[884]

[885] Tom Stephens, interview by the author, October 12, 2012.

[886] Kutchin, *How Mitchell Energy & Development Corp. Got its Start*, 226-227 (quoting George Mitchell).

Chapter 8: The New Millennium

An early success for the company was the development of Boonsville Field, a gas field north of Fort Worth. The field showed little promise to a number of major oil companies, which had drilled 11 dry holes into the formation and determined the rock too tight to produce; besides, they were looking for oil, not gas.

Based on a tip from a Chicago bookie, Mitchell acquired acreage in the field and began drilling it in 1952. He looked at the geology and knew that a new technology was the answer that prior energy companies exploring in the area failed to employ. He told Kutchin, "Hydraulic fracturing had just come in about two or three years before. Without hydraulic fracturing you couldn't make decent wells. So this is where we combined the engineering with the geology to make it feasible."[887]

After his initial well, Mitchell could see the formation was a large stratigraphic trap. Within 90 days, with help from his go-to investors, Mitchell leased 300,000 acres at $3 an acre.

He needed more money. And just as H.L. Hunt's original loan from First National was based on the bank's president confidence in the East Texas Field, Mitchell found a receptive audience in Vance. B.F. "Budd" Clark had joined the company in 1956 as its chief financial officer and retired in 2002 as its vice chairman. Kutchin quoted Clark, "Fortunately, there was an energy banker [Vance] at Bank of the Southwest who had been George's professor at Texas A&M. He did something that was done very rarely, if at all, in that he lent George money on the basis of the logs showing what reserves were behind each well, even though the well wasn't producing. He saw the logs and the fact that the wells were good, so he had his department lend against them which was highly unusual."[888]

The story of how Clark was hired by Mitchell in 1956 is another testament to the close relationship of oil and gas men and their bankers. At the time, the company was still Christie, Mitchell & Mitchell. Christie wanted to hire a "Harvard man" to help with the company's

---

[887] Kutchin, *How Mitchell Energy & Development Corp. Got its Start*, 5, 193, 228-9.
[888] Kutchin, *How Mitchell Energy & Development Corp. Got its Start*, 66.

business affairs. Clark had received his MBA from Harvard Business School as a Baker Scholar after WWII on the G.I. Bill and had posted his resume with the Harvard Business School alumni group in Houston. Grover Ellis, an energy banker with First City in Houston, passed the resume on to Christie.[889]

The Boonsville Field that Bank of the Southwest agreed to loan against became the foundation upon which Mitchell Energy was built. But, by 1981, after more than 30 years of development and natural declines in the wells' production, the company needed to find more supply to continue to fulfill a contract with Natural Gas Pipeline Company of America that dated back to 1953.

It had been long-known that the source-rock for the gas Mitchell had been producing from the field was the Barnett shale, which had too low a permeability to economically tap with ordinary measures. Beginning with a well drilled in it in 1981, the company failed to produce economic Barnett wells until 1996, when it significantly altered its fracture-stimulation recipe.[890]

As with many discoveries from Columbus on, there were both elements of stubborn perseverance and serendipity in Mitchell's breakthrough. Mitchell had spent millions of dollars and years drilling wells into the Barnett, experimenting with ways to produce the gas he knew was there. His engineers had been using a gel mixture to fracture the shale formation based on the commonly held theory that a water-based fluid would cause the clay in the shale to swell and seal the fractures that were created by the hydraulic pressure.

---

[889] In the summer of 1956, the last person Clark met during a day of interviews with the company was Christie who, deciding it was sufficiently late in the day to start drinking, offered Clark a glass of bourbon. Christie noticed Clark look down anxiously at his Timex wristwatch; he was thinking of how he would make his flight back to New Orleans to his pregnant wife and four young daughters. In his plain-spoken manner, Christie, still holding out the glass of bourbon, said, "Well, do you want the damn job or don't you?" My father accepted both the drink and the offer. For most of his career as the company's executive vice president and chief financial officer, one of my father's primary roles was to keep the channels of capital open to finance the growth of Mitchell's energy operations and, later, to also finance the development of The Woodlands, a planned community north of Houston, maintaining close relationships with many of Houston's and New York's energy lenders over the years.
[890] Darbonne, *The American Shales*, 13.

Chapter 8: The New Millennium

To save on costs, Mitchell's senior completion engineer, Nick Steinsberger, began experimenting with using a lower concentration of chemicals, but still keeping the fluid a gel that would carry the sand (proppant) mixture downhole to prop open the fractures caused by the pressurized solution. But as the engineers reduced the concentration of polymer chemicals, it became more difficult to maintain the gel consistency of the fluid.

In the summer of 1996, on-site for a frac job, Steinsberger noticed that the gel frac mixed by BJ Services Inc.'s crew wasn't cross-linking. "Instead of Jello, it looked more like a slickwater solution."[891]

Recognizing that the fluid wasn't gelling properly, the crew went ahead with the completion anyway. Contrary to the conventional theory, the well's results were surprisingly good *in spite* of the "faulty," watery fracturing fluid.[892] Steinsberger compared notes with other producers, including Union Pacific Resources Group Inc., which was experimenting with its fracs in tight rock in East Texas.

On the S.H. Griffin No. 4 vertical well, Steinsberger and the group finally came up with a mixture of polymers, sand and water that proved a success.[893] The initial rate of production was strong—1.5 million cubic feet a day—and, unlike prior fracs in the Barnett, stayed strong.[894]

As did Columbus, Mitchell had to go hat in hand to his lenders more than once to continue to fund his exploration. And, like Columbus, through determination, perseverance and stubborn luck, he and his engineers turned a mistake into a discovery that changed the world. Along with the Drake well, Spindletop, the Santa Rita No. 1

---

[891] Nick Steinsberger, Vice President-Engineering, Republic Energy, Inc., interview by the author, October 2, 2014.

[892] Gregory Zuckerman, *The Frackers: The Outrageous Inside Story of the New Billionaires* (Portfolio, November 5, 2013), 77.

[893] Steinsberger, author's interview.

[894] In 2012, the S.H. Griffin Well No. 4, which was still producing, had made more than 2.3 Bcf of gas or $11 million worth. It was estimated it could produce another 0.5 Bcf. Russell Gold, *The Boom: How Fracking Ignited the American Energy Revolution and Changed the World* (Simon & Schuster, April 8, 2014), 130.

and the Daisy Bradford No. 3, the S.H. Griffin No. 4 should be added to the pantheon of wells that changed history.

As the breakthrough was under way, a lawsuit against Mitchell Energy and unrelated to the Barnett-shale project was filed in Wise County in the spring of 1996, claiming well-water contamination dating back to, at least, 1978. Plaintiffs won a $200-million judgment and their neighbors filed suits as well.[895]

Mitchell went to his bankers for a $250-million letter of credit to secure the company's appeal bond. Manufacturers Hanover was administrative agent of the credit facility at the time and polled the syndicate for support of the special loan.[896] It was more a "life line" than a line of credit; the company had to fight the court decision lest it and copy-cat suits destroyed the company.

One syndicate member was Bank One. It had inherited the Mitchell account when it bought out Bank of the Southwest in 1990, where Vance had led the energy department. Long-time Bank of the Southwest loan officers Buzz Gralla and Dick Sylvan, working as Bank One officers, supported Mitchell's request, but needed the approval of Bank One's credit officer, "who was not an [oil and gas] guy and he didn't want to do it," Sylvan said in an interview in 2014.

Gralla, Sylvan and bank president Charlie O'Connell favored the deal. As the discussion became heated, Sylvan told the credit officer, "Damn it! George is a director of the bank and he's in trouble. The lawsuit is bullshit. It's time to stick by our customer."

After the meeting, O'Connell admonished Sylvan for being "a little aggressive" with the senior credit officer, but, ultimately, the bank approved the loan.[897] The letter-of-credit facility secured Mitchell En-

---

[895] Kutchin, *How Mitchell Energy & Development Corp. Got its Start*, 68.

[896] Mitchell Energy's principal corporate credit facility, as did many other credit facilities at the time, permitted the company to incur liens to secure appeal bonds. A number of Mitchell's senior lenders did not want to support a separate line-of-credit facility, but they were helpless to prevent it under the terms of the loan agreement.

[897] Dick Sylvan, Credit Officer, BBVA Compass Bank, formerly Credit Officer, Bank of the Southwest, interview by the author, March 28, 2014. Buzz Gralla, Amegy Bank, formerly Energy Lender at Bank of Southwest from 1977-1999, interview by the author, February 19, 2015.

ergy's appeal bond and right to appeal the jury verdict. The appellate court overruled the trial court. A similar lawsuit was ruled in favor of Mitchell in trial. The other lawsuits were dropped by attorneys who couldn't see a means of getting paid by a victory.[898]

Mitchell Energy "had been victorious, but at a high price,"[899] Kutchin wrote. The stock had been under a dark cloud of litigation for more than a year and gas prices fell in mid-1998 to less than $2.[900] Mitchell had exhausted the patience and credit of his lenders. In annual bank meetings during the early 1990s, he and his officers told the lenders of the Barnett's gas potential, but the low production rates were barely breaking even.

Sylvan said, "One year, at the Mitchell bank meeting, Homer Hershey, Mitchell's vice president in charge of North Texas operations, told the bankers, 'Next year, we're going to be drilling a new formation. We have had mixed success so far; to date, returns are flat right now. But we see a lot of potential. The wells are expensive and all need to be frac'd because it is a tight formation.'"

The following year, Hershey reported again. "Homer said, 'We can report good news in the Barnett—our costs to frac are down by a half, plus we are getting two times the returns on production. We are getting a 4-to-1 return. So we are going to drill a lot more wells.' Only later we found out that the 4-to-1 returns were not the average, but

---

[898]*Mitchell Energy Corporation v. Bartlett*, 958 S.W.2d 430 (Tex.Civ.Ap—Ft.Worth November 13, 1997); *see also*, Dan Steward, *The Barnett Shale Play: Phoenix of the Fort Worth Basin: A History* (The Fort Worth Geological Society, 2007).

[899] Kutchin, *How Mitchell Energy & Development Corp. Got its Start*, 69.

[900] U.S. EIA, Independent Statistics & Analysis. "Henry Hub Natural Gas Spot Price." Accessed March 6, 2016. Eia.gov. While the *Bartlett* verdict was under appeal and as gas prices fell from $3.40 in a few months to $1.80, the company was under a dark cloud. Its long-term gas-sales contract, at an above-market, fixed price, with Natural Gas Pipeline had ended. The company also owned The Woodlands, a planned community north of Houston. Stock analysts struggled with valuing the company's shares because it was neither an energy pure-play nor a real estate pure-play. The board told George Mitchell, who owned more than half of the company's stock, that he had to choose between his oil company and his visionary planned community. Although he was the first to admit his heart was in The Woodlands, the gas business was not saleable pending appeal of the $200-million *Bartlett* verdict. Mitchell Energy sold The Woodlands for $543 million. Shortly thereafter, the company made its Barnett-shale breakthrough.

the exception. There were more unsuccessful wells that didn't yield 4-to-1 returns."[901]

Another of Mitchell's lenders recalled, "He was just trading dollars, not really getting back any more from the wells than the cost he spent to drill. (By the end of the '90s), the company had piled on so much debt to afford all its spending that lenders wouldn't offer more."[902]

Mitchell's board concluded it was time to rein in spending, including the company's efforts in the Barnett. By January 1999, Mitchell announced a 20% reduction of its staff.[903] That spring, however, the outlook began to improve with the changed-up recipe in how the Barnett wells were being fracture-stimulated.[904] Upon continued success, Mitchell sold the company to Devon Energy Corp. in early 2002.[905]

Devon took Mitchell's technology and multiplied the results, using horizontal-well technology. "Mitchell's application of water fracs in my opinion proved the Barnett was a viable play. Devon's application of horizontals moved the play into a boom," Dan Steward, a Mitchell geologist, reflected in a 2013 article.[906]

---

[901] Sylvan, author's interview.

[902] Russell Clingman, Wells Fargo Bank, interview by the author, March 26, 2014.

[903] Mitchell Energy & Development Corp., "Mitchell Completes Work Force Reduction, Sets Capital Budget," *PR Newswire*, Feb. 22, 1999, Prnewswire.com.

[904] Dan Steward, "The Shale Gas Miracle: A Tribute to George P. Mitchell" (presented at the Academy of Medicine, Engineering and Science of Texas, January 12, 2012 Annual Conference "Energy for Life," Houston, Texas).

[905] Steward, "The Shale Gas Miracle." By 2000, 186 Barnett wells had been drilled and the play was starting to heat up. Gas prices reached over $9 and landmen checking mineral-ownership records to get oil and gas leases were tripping over each other at county court-houses. Drilling rigs were brought in by the dozen. In 2001, 520 wells were drilled. Mitchell had up to 18 rigs running in its 120,000 acres in the core area of the field. Devon Energy Corp. closed its $3.5-billion acquisition of Mitchell Energy in early 2002. George Mitchell became Devon's largest shareholder. Devon and other operators began experimenting with horizontals in the play. During 2003, 780 wells were drilled; roughly 130 were horizontal and drilled by 27 different operators.

[906] Jim Pierobon, "George P. Mitchell: Founder of Shale Gas — Here's How He and His Team Did It," *The Energy Fix*, August 5, 2013, Theenergyfix.com.

Chapter 8: The New Millennium

As word leaked, other operators began experimenting with horizontal wells and Mitchell's completion recipe.[907] Producers and investors caught shale fever and began searching from basin to basin for the next bonanza—very much like their brethren of a century earlier as wildcatters moved from boomtown to boomtown, buying up leases and chasing one gusher to the next.

However, instead of seeking leases of a couple of acres—or even less, as in the East Texas Field—these new wildcatters were chasing whole basins, encompassing tens to hundreds of thousands of acres and resulting in thousands of wells. The effort required—and continues to require—massive capital.

Signing bonuses for leases in the area of the Haynesville play, for example, had been going for between $200 and $400 an acre before the play was discovered; this grew to nearly $30,000 an acre in the most competitive area.[908] In the Eagle Ford, one South Texas rancher was handed a $1-billion check to drill his 106,000 acres.[909]

To hold leased acreage, an explorer has to make a producing well prior to an agreed deadline or lose the lease. And these shale wells could cost more than $10 million each. Producers quickly stretched all existing capital sources and needed more.

Banks and other sources responded aggressively to the improving commodity-price environment and demand for capital. In 2005, oil and gas loan volume increased 40% from the prior year; in 2006, it grew another 36%. Loan volume in 2006 was $164 billion, compared with $67 billion in 1997. As banks competed to lend more money to

---

[907] Natalie Givens and Han Zhao, "The Barnett Shale: Not so Simple After All," Republic Energy Inc. website, accessed October 2, 2014, Republicenergy.com.

[908] Chris R. Gideon, CPL, interview by the author, March 17, 2016.

[909] DrillingInfo reported that Shell Oil Co. leased Dan Harrison III's 106,000-acre Piloncillo Ranch, spread out over Dimmit and Webb counties, Texas, for a rumored $1 billion in 2010 ($10,000/acre) for Eagle Ford-play development. Just shy of three years later, Shell announced it was selling the lease and taking a $2.1-billion impairment related to its North America shale properties. Proving the old saw that "oil money begets oil money," the Harrison family was one of Texas' original wildcatter families and acquired its original wealth in 1934 when it teamed with J.S. Abercrombie to discover the Old Ocean Field in Brazoria County, Texas.

oil and gas producers, they reduced the cost to record lows, maturities were pushed out and covenants were made looser.[910]

In addition, new mezzanine and private-equity providers were looking for ways to get a piece of the hot energy market. As a result, there was a much deeper and broader pool of capital available to small- and mid-cap E&P companies than historically had been the case. From commercial debt and public-market capital to private-equity funds, the array of capital choices and dollars grew to an all-time high heading into 2008. The number of mezzanine providers increased from a handful after the Enron meltdown in 2001 to some 20 by 2007.[911] Around 2004, in addition to the traditional two-tiered senior-bank-debt/mezzanine-debt structures, traditional energy banks began to compete indirectly with mezzanine by offering a new structure between their conforming senior-lien loan (Tranche A) and the mezzanine (junior-lien) loan.

As commodity prices for oil and gas continued year-on-year increases above historical norms, banks were slow to keep pace in the increases to their price decks used to determine the conforming borrowing base.[912] This meant a considerable gap between bank decks and the 12-month strip—therefore, considerable value above what a borrower could expect from the senior lender's conforming borrowing-base value of its oil and gas assets versus the amount its current cash flow could justify. Thus, an opportunity was created and the lending community responded to fill the void, providing more debt load for the producers to carry.

The structures went by different names, including the "Term B" or "Tranche B" loan, the "Senior Stretch Tranche" and the "Senior Second Out." But these, basically, priced in between senior debt and mezzanine debt—that is, between 100 and 300 basis points over the

---

[910] Brian A. Toal, "Rising Credit Tide," *Here's the Money: Capital Formation 2007, Special Supplement to Oil and Gas Investor*, May 2007, 4. The average spreads for syndicated loans in 2006 were Libor plus 210 basis points versus plus 220 in 2005 and plus 245 in 2004.

[911] Murray, "The Ins and Outs of Mezzanine," 26.

[912] Clouser, "Regional Credit No Problem," 24.

price of the senior bank debt that enjoyed lien and payment priority over mezzanine facilities.

This intermediate capital was typically employed as a stretch piece to help companies in connection with an acquisition of producing and non-producing properties. By making a stretch loan against the borrower's "lesser collateral"—i.e., more heavily weighted to proved undeveloped (PUD) reserves—lenders were able to compete with the alternative, mezzanine sources. These "stretch" loans were usually intended to be short-term debt with around a one-year maturity and with little to no prepayment penalties. But if rising oil and gas prices stopped propping up the producer's loan, just like musical chairs, bankers and producers could find themselves without a seat when the music stopped.

If made by the producer's existing senior bank group, they could be documented under the same credit agreement and secured by the same collateral as the Tranche A "conforming" loan. These loans were an attractive alternative to a company that had a low-value conforming borrowing-base asset mix and didn't want to incur the expense of negotiating a separate mezzanine facility or the cost of issuing public debt or diluting equity.

The Tranche B was typically a term facility—i.e., non-revolver—fully funded at closing with a fixed amortization and maturity earlier than the Tranche A facility. The expectation was that the borrower would refinance the Term B loans within the stated maturity through an increase in the Tranche A borrowing base due to increased production as a result of drilling and development with the dollars provided under the Term B loan and/or through sales of non-core assets.

As the decade progressed, Term B loans were making a strong showing in a number of high-profile transactions from 2004 through 2007. Credit Suisse reported having made three such loans in 2004, five in 2005 and 14 in 2006.[913]

---

[913] Ellen Chang, "Term B Loans," *Here's the Money: Capital Formation 2007, Special Supplement to Oil and Gas Investor*, May 2007, 42. Among the financings were ATP Oil & Gas Corp.'s offshore-drilling program and Venoco Inc.'s acquisition of TexCal Energy (LP) LLC.

Because of the ever-increasing demand among shale pioneers for debt capital, the popularity of the Term B loans did not squeeze out the alternative lenders, who issued billions of dollars of second-lien loans to the industry. This was remarkable growth for a type of financing rarely employed prior to 2000.[914]

But the success and high rate of repayment of second-lien paper encouraged further growth of mezzanine lending during the middle of the decade. These proliferated as institutional money was drawn to the private-equity-type returns on capital that was secured with collateral and governed by debt covenants. As mezzanine loans to E&Ps grew to more than $100 million per borrower, the ability of the alternative lenders to syndicate their second-lien facilities increased liquidity in this market, making it even more attractive to institutional investors.

Syndicated second-lien term loans looked very much like the senior syndicated loan with administrative agents. In addition to a higher cost and looser financial covenants, which were usually limited to just an asset-coverage test, another difference in the market was the composition of the syndicate members. Unlike the senior-loan market, the second-lien market's participating lenders typically were not commercial banks but were insurance and private-funds investors.

An example was the senior and second-lien loans to Ram Energy Inc. agented by Guggenheim Partners LLC, a private investor. To enter the energy-capital market in 2005, Guggenheim hired Tim Murray, who had been the head of Wells Fargo's energy-lending group, to start its Houston office. In connection with Ram's acquisition of Ascent Energy Inc. in 2007, Guggenheim arranged a $175-million senior secured revolving credit facility and added a $200-million senior secured Term B facility from a syndicate of lenders led by Guggenheim. The loan syndicate consisted of more than 15 institutions, including banks, insurance companies, institutional funds and private equity.[915]

As syndicated second-lien facilities became more liquid in the secondary markets, more capital became available to E&P companies.

914 Murray, "The Ins and Outs of Mezzanine," 26.
915 Ellen Chang, "Mezzanine Capital," *Oil and Gas Investor*, March 14, 2008.

Chapter 8: The New Millennium

With the relaxation of Glass-Steagall regulations, the lines between investment banks and commercial banks blurred. Commercial bankers were becoming investment bankers and investment banks were arranging and syndicating senior and second-lien secured energy loans.

Not all investment bankers shared commercial bankers' business model of building lasting relationships, providing daily cash-management services and working through the ups and downs of commodity-price cycles that inevitably come with the oil patch. The investment banks generally did not have the ability to make revolving loans or process the borrower's deposits and distribution checks, much less issue letters of credit needed by producers to support regulatory bonding requirements.

Typically, the investment bank or private-equity shop held little of the actual commitments; instead, they syndicated the facility to a larger group that included not only commercial banks but other non-bank investors.[916] As the origination of loans and holding risks were separated, these facilities lightened up their covenants and closed the price gap between senior-lien and second-lien facilities.

Bill Moyer, IPAA's vice president of capital markets in 2007, said in an article, "The competition resulting from the abundance of capital sources led some providers to be more creative and aggressive – perhaps taking on more risks, sometimes, without the corresponding increase in the rate of return or addition of warrants and overrides."[917]

The harvest of the shale revolution was coming on strong, evidenced by the price-ratio divergence of gas to oil. During 2002 through 2006, the ratio was roughly the traditional 6:1—that is, six million Btu of natural gas are roughly equal to the value of one barrel of oil. In 2007, the 12-month strips were 10:1. In 2008, the ratio widened to 12:1 and, in 2009, would surpass 30:1.[918]

---

[916] Kurt A. Talbot, "IPAA Private Capital Conference" (presented at Private Capital Conference), 10.

[917] Gary Clouser, "More than Plenty," *Here's the Money: Capital Formation 2007, Special Supplement to Oil and Gas Investor*, May 2007, 19.

[918] The crude oil/natural gas price ratio is derived by dividing the spot price of a barrel by the spot price of an MMBtu. U.S. EIA, Independent Statistics & Analysis. "U.S. oil rig count overtakes natural gas rig count." Accessed May 9, 2011. Eia.gov; *see also*, Stell,

The downside of the abundant availability of capital in the earlier part of the decade became evident when global credit markets and both oil and gas prices turned in mid-2008 and into 2009. The producers who needed to work through waivers or amendments found that their second-lien debt had become widely traded and ended up in the hands of opportunistic investors with whom they had no strong relationship, compounded by these investors' minimal experience in E&P. Like public debt notes held by multiple investors, it became impossible to identify and negotiate with the debt-holders to amend the documents—even in the case of a healthy deal.

Much to the dismay of a number of energy companies sitting on a great asset base while facing constrained cash flows to meet debt service during this credit crunch, conference calls to discuss covenant-waiver terms would end up with lenders positioning and arguing amongst themselves, while the borrower died on the vine.[919] One facility, in particular, epitomized the dysfunction of these "loan to own" lender groups when the lead lender's lawyer fired his private-equity-lender client to represent the balance of the lender group with the hope of salvaging a deal to restructure the debt.[920]

Commodity prices kept rising through the first half of 2008 to heights that, to many, seemed unsustainable—and they were. By July, the impact of the global recession and the continued growth in natural-gas supply reversed the price trends for both oil and gas. For those that bet oil prices would fall sooner than they did, the crest came too late. SemGroup LP suffered a $2.4-billion loss on short positions. What had been brewing for months resulted in its Chapter 11 bankruptcy filing in July.[921]

"Banking Up." 2009 data from Oil & Gas 360, "Natural Gas – Where We've Been and Where We're Going." January 17, 2014, Oilandgas360.com. Accessed October 25, 2015.

[919] Kurt A. Talbot, "IPAA Private Capital Conference" (presented at Private Capital Conference), 11.

[920] The loan was ultimately refinanced, the recalcitrant lenders, including the lead lender, were paid off and the oil company was still exploring and producing five years later, albeit after converting some of the original debt into equity as part of the work-out terms.

[921] Christopher Helman, "Inside The Semgroup Bust," *Forbes*, July 28, 2008, Forbes.com.

Chapter 8: The New Millennium

Because SemGroup was a major purchaser of oil, the impact of its bankruptcy was felt by many producers in Oklahoma, Texas, Kansas, New Mexico and elsewhere. Producers' claims, filed in bankruptcy court in Delaware, highlighted the questionable efficacy of a law that had been on the books in Texas and a handful of other producing states since the 1980s regarding the priority and perfection of security interests in oil and gas production and related proceeds.

Prior to the SemGroup bankruptcy, royalty owners, producers and their lenders in these states operated under the assumption that they had a self-perfected priority lien over the production purchaser's creditors.[922] The Delaware court, however, held that Texas' nonstandard provision for automatic perfection in favor of producers would be junior to purchase-money security interests in SemGroup's accounts receivable. Moreover, because SemGroup was a Delaware entity, the law of Delaware governed perfection of liens over the accounts.

When oil prices collapsed in the 1980s, Delaware's legislature did not see fit to follow other states in enacting self-perfecting lien protection for producers and royalty owners. Producers and mineral owners, if any in Delaware, did not comprise as significant a voting block as in Texas.

The only way for them to have a secured lien on SemGroup's estate would have been if they had complied with Delaware's lien laws, which required filing a financing statement with the Delaware secretary of state's office in compliance with Delaware's Uniform Commercial Code—something few, if any, producers had done. Accordingly, many producers—and their lenders—were left with unsecured claims and received 40 cents on the dollar.[923]

As of today, it remains to be seen whether the SemGroup decision affects the credit underwriting and documentation of secured production loans to independent producers. The issue is of greater

---

[922] *In re Semcrude, L.P.* 399 B.R. 388, (Bankr. D. Del., 2009), aff'd 428 B.R. 590 (D.Del.2010).
[923] Chris Moon, "Kansas Oil Producers to Recoup Millions with SemGroup Plan," *Wichita Business Journal*, September 27, 2009.

importance when considering where the producer's assets are geographically concentrated and whether sales of production are to just one purchaser. Likely, given the severe downturn in prices beginning in the second half of 2014, there will be ample data points to see if producers and their lenders learned the lessons of the SemGroup decision.

If a producer's purchaser did become bankrupt, the producer and his creditor should be exposed, at most, for a month or two of production proceeds, if the producer is selling its production under month-to-month contracts. The producer should be able to quickly switch to a solvent purchaser. But even a couple months' production can add up. For example, one producer, Enterra Energy Trust, had a $10-million claim, primarily consisting of sales to SemGroup during June and July of 2008.[924]

Typically, as seen in more-comprehensive mezzanine facilities, there is a requirement that the lender has the right to approve who purchases the borrower's production. Accordingly, under such a covenant, an alert lender might be able to protect its collateral—and its borrower's receivables—if it were aware of that one of the purchasers had less-than-stellar financial credentials. At this point, however, most mezzanine lenders fail to exercise such level of oversight; there is even less monitoring of to whom borrowers sell production under conforming reserve-based facilities.

The collapse of the U.S. housing market in 2007 that marked the beginning of the recession only indirectly affected the energy industry.[925] Many of the companies affected by the credit crisis included some of the energy industry's largest commercial-bank lenders which led to bank consolidation. The toxic nature of poorly underwritten

---

[924] Leslie Haines, "Counterparty and Hedging Risks Grow," *Oil and Gas Investor*, July 29, 2008, Oilandgasinvestor.com.

[925] Housing prices rose from 1997 (110 on the index scale), peaked in April of 2006 (206) and, after a 12-month plateau, precipitously dropped by more than 30% between April of 2007 (202) through May, 2009 (140). S&P Case-Shiller 20-City Home Price Index (SPCS20RSA) reported on Federal Reserve Bank of St. Louis, Economic Research, Research.stlouisfed.org.

home-mortgage loans infected the U.S. and international financial markets.[926]

The effects were multiplied by the use of credit-default swaps and collateralized debt obligations held by hedge funds, money-market funds, investment banks and private-equity funds.[927] Subsequent inquiries by governmental commissions seeking to identify the cause and propose future protections concluded the following in part:

> [T]he banking supervisors failed to adequately and proactively identify and police the weaknesses of the banks and thrifts or their poor corporate governance and risk management, often maintaining satisfactory ratings on institutions until just before their collapse. This failure was caused by many factors, including beliefs that regulation was unduly burdensome, that financial institutions were capable of self-regulation, and that regulators should not interfere with activities reported as profitable.[928]

It was a rebuke that bank regulators would take to heart with respect to oil and gas loans as commodity markets turned south again in late 2014.

BNP Paribas was one of the first commercial-lending institutions to feel the effect of the meltdown; in August 2007, it blocked cash withdrawals from three hedge funds in its U.K. branch, citing "a

---

[926] Subprime home-mortgage originations tripled from an average of between 6% and 8% between 1997 and 2003 to 20% between 2004 and 2006 when it fell to historic norms below 10% in 2007. U.S. Census Bureau. "The total value of mortgaged backed securities issued between 2001 and 2006 reached $13.4 trillion. There was a mountain of problematic securities, debt, and derivatives resting on real estate assets that were far less secure than they were thought to have been." FDIC, *The Financial Crisis Inquiry Report*, 22.

[927] Fratianni and Marchionne explain in their paper, "Large default rates on subprime mortgages cannot explain the depth of this crisis. Subprime mortgages were the accelerant to the fire after the real estate bust short-circuited in the financial house. The fire spread quickly and globally because this house was built with combustible material, such as structured finance and inadequate supervision; a sudden rush for liquidity and fast deleveraging exacerbated by the practice of fair value accounting kept the fire running." Michele Fratianni and Francesco Marchionne, "The Role of Banks in the Subprime Financial Crises" (April 10, 2009), 8. Papers.ssrn.com.

[928] FDIC, *The Financial Crisis Inquiry Report*, 308.

complete evaporation of liquidity."[929] U.S. banks were estimated to have lost more than $1 trillion on toxic assets made up of collateralized subprime debt obligations and other debt derivatives from January 2007 through September 2009.[930]

In 2009, 140 U.S. banks failed.[931] The FDIC estimated that, by the end of the third quarter of 2009, there were 552 "problem institutions" at risk of failure. For seasoned bankers, this was all eerily reminiscent of the mid-1980s, when more than 1,500 U.S. banks failed; this time, however, oil and gas and Texas real estate were not the culprits.

The financial storm that had been brewing hit the financial markets the weekend of September 13, 2008, just as Hurricane Ike made landfall south of Houston. Ike left a trail of destruction over the resort island of Galveston, into Houston and The Woodlands, and north, heading to Dallas, essentially along the Interstate 45 corridor and the energy industry's world capital. Power failures and streets blocked by downed lines and trees prevented many oil and gas executives and their bankers from getting to their offices. Often, Internet access was impossible as well.[932]

As Texas residents were beginning to take stock of the hurricane's destruction in the daylight hours of that Saturday morning, Federal Reserve and Treasury officials were in tense talks in New York with the chairmen of the worlds' biggest investment banks. The goal was to secure a savior for Lehman Brothers, the U.S.' fourth-largest investment bank.

But, when Treasury Secretary Henry Paulson refused to sweeten a Barclays or Bank of America takeover of Lehman with public money, Lehman's fate was sealed.[933] It announced just after midnight the Monday morning of September 15 that it had filed for Chapter 11

---

[929] FDIC, *The Financial Crisis Inquiry Report*, 250-251.
[930] Bloomberg, "US European Bank Write-downs and Losses," November 5, 2009.
[931] "Bank Failures in Brief," FDIC, Fdic.gov.
[932] Clifford Krauss and James C. McKinley, Jr., "Hurricane Damage Extensive in Texas," *The New York Times*, September 13, 2008.
[933] FDIC, *The Financial Crisis Inquiry Report*, 325-339.

bankruptcy protection. On the same day, Merrill Lynch, seeing Paulson's writing on the wall, announced it would be acquired by Bank of America.

The following day, the Federal Reserve organized an $85-billion bailout of AIG for an 80% equity stake that was extended further in October by $37 billion and by another $40 billion in November. On Thursday, the Treasury Department issued a guarantee that $1 in a money-market fund was worth $1.[934]

That same day, Paulson and Fed Chairman Ben Bernanke met in the conference room of the House speaker, Nancy Pelosi, to propose a $700-billion emergency fund, telling her and other leaders of Congress, "If we don't do this, we may not have an economy on Monday."[935] The Emergency Economic Stabilization Act, which authorized the Troubled Asset Relief Program (TARP), was signed into law on October 3, 2008.[936]

Meanwhile, Houston's energy executives and bankers and their employees were also keenly interested in when power would be restored to their homes and offices. It was restored up to weeks later in some of the city's most heavily forested neighborhoods. However, recovery of the nation's credit markets would require more time and much more capital before normalcy would return. The congressional commission studying the collapse reported in 2011, "Before it was over, taxpayers had committed trillions of dollars through more than two dozen extraordinary programs to stabilize the financial system and to prop up the nation's largest financial institutions."[937]

Oil and gas borrowers looking for capital were affected along with every other business; the world's capital markets essentially froze. Bernanke reported in 2011 to a congressional inquiry commission, "I

---

[934] "Treasury Announces Guaranty Program for Money Market Funds," Press Center, U.S. Department of the Treasury, accessed May 3, 2016, Treasury.gov.

[935] Andrew Ross Sorkin, "As Credit Crisis Spiraled, Alarm Led to Action," *The New York Times*, October 1, 2008.

[936] Emergency Economic Stabilization Act of 2008 (Pub. Law No.:110-343).

[937] FDIC, *The Financial Crisis Inquiry Report*, 23.

honestly believe that September and October 2008 was the worst financial crisis in global history, including the Great Depression."[938]

Following a 10-day, $16.7-billion run on Washington Mutual Bank, which had an energy-lending group, the bank succumbed on September 25 when the FDIC placed it into receivership. With more than $300 billion of assets, WaMu was the nation's largest S&L and was roughly tied with Continental Illinois, pre-failure, in terms of relative size to the financial system.[939] It was immediately acquired by JPMorgan Chase.[940]

The same day, Wachovia Bank lost $5 billion in deposits, immediately triggering the FDIC to look for a suitor for it. After a bidding war between Wells Fargo and Citigroup and with further regulatory intervention, Wells Fargo announced on October 3 that it would acquire Wachovia's assets, including the bank's energy-lending team, which was repurposed as an energy investment-banking team. The team, led by James Kipp, had been together since the downfall of First City in 1993.[941]

Credit immediately became less fluid. Banks husbanded their reserves, while unsure of their own exposure to investments in collateralized-debt obligations and other asset-backed securities—and even less sure of fellow banks' investments. Libor more than doubled from 3.11% to 6.44% the day after the Lehman failure. Banks were so wary of lending to each other that, at the end of September, they required an unprecedented premium of 400% above the Federal Reserve Bank's target rate.[942]

Faced with the resulting freeze in interbank lending, the U.S. Treasury was forced to announce on October 14 that, instead of buy-

---

[938] FDIC, *The Financial Crisis Inquiry Report*, 353-356.

[939] William M. Isaac, *Senseless Panic, How Washington Failed America* (Wiley, 2010), 145.

[940] "JPMorgan Chase Acquires Banking Operations of Washington Mutual," FDIC Press Release, September 25, 2008, Fdic.gov.

[941] In another failure, Guaranty Bank was taken over by the FDIC in August of 2009; all of its assets were acquired by BBVA Compass, including the energy portfolio.

[942] The one-month Libor spread over overnight index swap rates showed the strains in interbank lending markets with rates bumping up to 1% in 2007 and early 2008, shot up to more than 3% by fall of 2008, returning to normal rates closer to 0% following the TARP infusion. FDIC, *The Financial Crisis Inquiry Report*, 355.

ing distressed assets, it would recapitalize the U.S. banking system by purchasing up to $250 billion of senior preferred shares in nine large U.S. banks.[943] Soon after this announcement, both the prime and Libor rates came down considerably.

For many foreign banks—principally European banks participating in U.S. reserve-based loan facilities—their cost of funds stayed higher than that of U.S. borrowers, effectively putting them out of competition in energy lending—at least for a while. Even among U.S. banks, any borrower in 2009 that was looking to refinance or ask for any type of amendment to its facility could expect an increase in the price. In many facilities, they also saw a floor on the Libor and prime rates.[944]

Many borrowers were faced for the first time with the concept of "defaulting lenders." Rodney Waller, senior vice president of Range Resources Corp., which had announced a year earlier its horizontal Marcellus-shale discovery well, said in a November 2008 article, "I am concerned that I might have a bank that is going to go away and can't fund its commitment under these conditions from the crunch. JPMorgan, today, on our rollover revolver draws, will no longer give me funds from a bank unless that bank has actually sent that money to them."[945]

Bankers were experiencing this for the first time as well, questioning what right, if any, a participating syndicate lender could continue to enjoy under the loan documents if it was unable to fund its share of borrowing requests when requested. Lehman Brothers itself had only recently begun taking minor commitments in senior reserve-

---

[943] Nabil Khodadad, Dewey & LeBoeuf, "Trends in Financing Mining and Oil and Gas Projects," International Mining and Oil and Gas Law, Development and Investment, April 2009, Conwaygreene.com.

[944] As Libor spiked in October of 2008, there was speculation that even the reported Libor did not reflect banks' true cost of borrowed funds and that reporting banks were under-reporting this, so as to appear to be a better credit risk. This suspicion was proven correct as a few European banks later paid fines in the billions of dollars in the Libor-rate affair.

[945] "New E&P Money-Mall Hours," *Oil and Gas Investor*, November 1, 2008.

based loans.[946] Administering revolving borrowing-base loans in which Lehman, through subsidiary Lehman Commercial Paper Inc., was a lender became very complicated when Lehman filed for bankruptcy. Senior-bank agents became more selective in whom they were willing to invite into a borrower's syndicate.[947]

Prior to Lehman, the language of the standard form of agented reserve-based loan agreement did not contemplate that a *lender* would ever be in breach of its obligations. The credit agreements dealt only with contingencies for if the *borrower* became in default. In syndicated-loan agreements, certain decisions regarding the loan, such as whether to increase the borrowing base, require a unanimous vote of all "lenders." Getting Lehman's bankruptcy trustee or its counsel to focus on a request for a borrowing-base increase in any reserve-based oil and gas loan in which Lehman had less than a $10-million exposure was perceived as impossible in the midst of more than $1 trillion of claims against the estate.

The preferred action was to buy out Lehman's position at par. But, where Lehman also had hedges with a borrower, the process required analysis, review and bankruptcy-court approval. It would take months for the court to permit action that would take Lehman out as a lender.

Following issues with Lehman and questions as to other banks' ability to fund their pro-rata share of borrowings, agent banks and their counsel began adding provisions for addressing "defaulting lenders" in the administration of reserve-based loans. Ultimately, in 2011, the Loan Syndications & Trading Association promulgated "standard language" addressing defaulting lenders that has become a part of the syndicated-loan documentation.[948]

---

[946] This was to share in the first-lien collateral as security *pari passu* for its hedging exposure to its E&P borrowers.

[947] Lehman Commercial Paper Inc. had approximately $11.4 billion of unfunded loan commitments at the end of 2008. Richard M. Gray, Milbank, Tweed, Hadley & McCloy LLP, "Debt Buybacks, Defaulting Lenders and Libor Market Disruption," *LSTA Loan Market Chronicle*, 2009, Milbank.com.

[948] Loan Syndications & Trading Association, Primary Market Committee Model Credit Agreement Provisions 2011, August 2011.

Falling Oil and Gas Prices: The 2008-2009 Edition

Regional energy banks that were not hit as hard by the collapsed home-mortgage market were able to increase their exposure to energy producers by purchasing, at a discount, secured syndicated energy loans from the money-center and foreign banks.[949] These and other healthy banks were able to pick up the slack.

The pullback had begun in August of 2007. *Oil and Gas Investor* reported in January of 2008, "A lot of those banks, [Mark Fuqua, head of Comerica Bank's energy group,] says, recently had problems on some of their underwritings as the credit crunch advanced and the institutional hedge-fund, mutual-fund and insurance-company Term B loan market dried up. 'So now these banks seem more willing to bring other banks like Comerica into deals to spread their underwriting risk.'"[950]

In 2007, the structure and terms of first-lien debt to oil and gas producers were not affected by the liquidity problems suffered by some of the largest energy banks. However, by 2008, borrowers were seeing increases in pricing in response to the generally rising cost of long-term debt capital, especially in the second-lien market. Dorothy Marchand, another long-time energy banker, said in the article, "It appears that the trend we saw in early 2007, in terms of lightening up on covenants, is moderating. Also, because many institutions have pulled back, we see pricing margins or spreads increasing."[951]

Just months before Lehman's failure, Mark Thompson, head of energy lending for U.S. Bank, was cited:

> "I would say that credit structures are getting strong-er," says Thompson. "Even stretch loans are becoming less aggressive and there is pressure in the credit markets to raise loan-pricing grids. Although the Federal Reserve has been lowering short-term rates, long-term rates really haven't followed. So, the liquidity

---

[949] Clouser, "Regional Credit No Problem," 16.
[950] Brian A. Toal, "Lending Trends," *Oil and Gas Investor*, January 1, 2008.
[951] Toal, "Lending Trends."

premium has been expanding and has been since June 2007. ... Now, everyone's cost of funds for long-term money has gone up, including banks' costs of funds, and this will likely lead to an increase in loan pricing for producers."[952]

As oil fell from a July 3, 2008, peak of nearly $150 and gas from more than $13, price decks that had been slow to rise were now also slow to drop and the gap between the 12-month strip and the price deck that had provided a slice of the debt structure for "stretch" Tranche B loans evaporated. While the window for commercial banks to offer Term B loans was closing, non-traditional, mezzanine providers that still had dry powder to lend were happy to keep their windows open.

But the subprime-mortgage crisis wasn't limited to money-center banks; in fact, greater impact was felt by some of the private-equity investors and hedge funds. The institutional players that had begun to invest in the energy-capitalization business in the early 2000s in the midst of rising commodity prices began to drop out due to liquidity issues. Tim Murray said in a March 2008 article, "Debt pricing has increased and some institutional players have dropped out.

"The institutional players I'm referring to are generally funds that have some liquidity issues due to the credit crisis, or have capital that is subject to mark-to-market (derivatives) influences. There are very few institutions pulling back from energy due to poor (energy) investments or lack of confidence in the industry."[953]

In general, mezzanine and other second-lien paper were harder to sell. Lenders had to raise pricing with rates increasing from between 3% and 4% in 2007 to between 6% and 8% in 2008.

B.J. Brandenberger with Energy Spectrum Advisors Inc. wrote in March of 2009, "Anecdotal evidence suggests that each tranche of capital, including senior debt, mezzanine debt and equity, is beginning to require returns comparable to their more risky junior counterparts,

[952] Hughes, "Mile High Capital."
[953] Chang, "Mezzanine Capital."

thus translating into a notable increase in today's aggregate cost of capital for borrowers."[954]

Oil prices had begun falling after June of 2008, further constraining producers' access to capital and willingness to hedge more future production. Just after the mid-September financial-market collapse, Greg Pipkin, a managing director at Lehman prior to its bankruptcy and who immediately moved his group to Barclays Capital, advised, "Start-ups should look for capital from people with whom they have a strong relationship. In a market like we are in today, capital is scarce. Relationships with strong institutions are needed to see an E&P through its business plan, whether three years or 10 years."[955]

With oil prices tanking and general public-equity-market investors' fear of how much the stock market would eventually decline, accessing public markets for capital was too expensive for E&P companies. Capex budgets and acquisitions were cut back. The era of easy credit for the oil patch had ended just as it did for would-be home-buyers.

Range Resources' Waller said, "The E&P side of the energy business had been drilling in excess of cash flow for the last two and a half years. We are going to have to cut back. You can't perpetuate this drilling activity with the credit markets and the fragility of the debt markets. Therefore, that 'wall of gas' (from the shale plays) that everybody wants to talk about, can't get here if nobody wants to drill."[956]

Some acquisitions were restructured and others were cancelled outright. Antero Resources Corp. had announced a $552-million acquisition of Marcellus acreage from Dominion Resources Inc., but had to scale it back due to its difficulty in obtaining follow-on financing "in the current market turmoil."[957]

---

[954] B.J. Brandenberger, "Transaction Activity vs. Nymex," *Oil and Gas Investor*, March 1, 2009.

[955] "New E&P Money-Mall Hours," *Oil and Gas Investor*, November 1, 2008.

[956] "New E&P Money-Mall Hours," *Oil and Gas Investor*, November 1, 2008.

[957] Dominion agreed to "downsize the transaction and increase the amount [paid] per acre." "Financial Turmoil Cuts into Antero's Marcellus Shale Plans," *Daily GPI, Natural Gas Intelligence*, September 25, 2008. "Dominion Ups Marcellus Shale Acreage Price with Antero Resources," Rigzone.com, September 24, 2008.

At the end of September, Forest Oil Corp. completed an acquisition of acreage from Cordillera Energy Partners, but only after amending the deal to reduce the cash portion by $180 million and increasing the stock component of the purchase price. Forest had been trying to sell some properties at the time. Its chief financial officer, David Keyte, said, "The disruption in the credit markets is adversely affecting the timing of our divestiture program as counterparties are challenged to receive adequate financing."[958]

Denbury Resources Inc. announced on October 8 that it would walk away from a $600-million acquisition of Wapiti Energy LLC's Conroe Field, forfeiting a $30-million earnest-money deposit, citing a need to take "significant steps to preserve capital liquidity." It reported:

> In light of the current state of U.S. capital markets, we have taken several measures to assure ourselves that our balance sheet will remain strong during these uncertain economic times. We believe that all of these steps are prudent in light of the current economic environment.[959]

But the "wall of gas" coming online as a result of full-throttle Barnett and Fayetteville production—along with expectations from the recently announced Marcellus, Haynesville and Eagle Ford discoveries—was not to be stopped by anything as *small* as total global recession and a freezing of capital markets. Although the number of active rigs drilling for natural gas dropped in half from October 2008 to October 2009,[960] the shale revolution kept producing results. Annual U.S.

---

[958] "Solich Takes More Stock, Less Cash, To Close Forest Deal," *Oil and Gas Investor*, October 1, 2008.

[959] "New E&P Money-Mall Hours," *Oil and Gas Investor*, November 1, 2008; Denbury Resources Press Release, October 8, 2008.

[960] In September, 2008, the U.S. natural gas rig count peaked at 1,606. Baker Hughes Drilling Rig Report, US NG Rig Count.

natural-gas production continued to grow and was still growing as of the end of 2015.[961]

This was while prices tumbled from more than $10 in the summer of 2008 to less than $2 in the spring of 2012. Wellhead gas prices remained low, but drilling continued as capital continued to flow to gas explorers and producers. Even in the low price environment, wells were being brought online at tremendously economic rates and demand for the gas was growing among power-generation operators and industrials.[962]

In late 2008, Tristone Capital Inc. reported on its survey of approximately 40 energy lenders. "Since starting the survey in second-quarter 2005," it wrote, "the participating banks' oil and gas price decks have continually increased in the extended years from the previous-quarter results. With fourth-quarter 2008 being the first exception to this trend, first-quarter 2009 decks continue to decrease from the last quarter's results."[963] Front-year bank pricing fell 34% for oil and 21% for gas.

All the while, banks became more vigilant in assessing their producer borrowers' ability to repay. Typically, banks set their price decks quarterly, but, as prices changed so precipitously, a number were looking at new decks on a monthly or more-frequent basis. Lenders and borrowers alike were dreading the Spring 2009 borrowing-base-redetermination season.

In addition, the banks themselves had their hands full as borrowing-base season would be soon followed by the national-bank-examination season. *Oil and Gas Investor* reported in March of 2009, "The timing of low oil and gas prices, borrowing-base redeterminations, tight capital markets and the release of E&P audited financial

---

[961] Marketed U.S. gas production increased 18% from 2008 to 2013. EIA.gov, accessed January 12, 2016.

[962] In December of 2015, in what is a usually a high-priced winter-demand environment, the prompt-month Nymex gas contract closed at less than $1.70 an MMBtu as a result of persistent supply and a mild winter. U.S. EIA, Independent Statistics & Analysis. "Henry Hub Natural Gas Spot Price." Accessed March 6, 2016. Eia.gov.

[963] "Energy Lenders' Price Decks," *Oil and Gas Investor*, December 1, 2008, Oilandgasinvestor.com.

results nearly coincides with an important time for commercial banks—their own national bank examination process ... . This confluence of events is unfortunate for distressed companies.

"A bank with E&P clients with borrowing-base deficiencies will soon see those loans downgraded to the high-risk category by examiners, says Tim Murray, Houston-based managing director of private energy capital provider Guggenheim Partners LLC ... . The more high-risk loans a bank holds, the more capital it is required to reserve as bank examiners determine necessary capital ratios to protect depositors from bank failure. ... If a bank can't get additional capital, it has to sell assets, like loans, to shrink its balance sheet to meet mandated capital ratios."[964]

Expectations among both producers and lenders were that borrowing bases would be between 15% and 30% lower—across the board. A number of producers had already cut back on drilling. Thus, their reserve replacements were short of previous projections—another reason to dread the results of the banks' evaluation. But as the results came in, relatively few were dealt a blow.

"Many feared credit limits would be reset below a company's current borrowings and with no cash to make up the difference," *Oil and Gas Investor* reported in May. "The rolling event was supposed to throw a flurry of assets into the marketplace. ... The Redetermination Pandemic resulted in few fatalities in spite of the hysteria.

"Why is this? The simple answer is that banks, also under assault in the current economic battle, have no place and no desire to warehouse all of those E&P assets. Like with the single-family housing foreclosure crisis, banks don't want all these assets coming back on the books and tying up their lending ratios. Better to work it out with an otherwise healthy E&P currently making payments than to repo their assets."[965]

---

[964] Jeannie Stell, "Distressed Finance," *Oil and Gas Investor*, March 1, 2009.
[965] Steve Toon, "Who Put Out The Fire? Banks Soften On Killer Borrowing-Base Redeterminations For E&Ps," May 4, 2009, Oilandgasinvestor.com.

While bankers were wary of bringing more problems to their own credit ratings, 2009 was much different from prior commodity-price collapses. This time, many producers, at the direction of their lenders, had a majority of their production hedged out into 2010 or later and at pre-crisis oil and gas futures prices.[966] Banks were able to factor into their redeterminations the producer's hedged volumes, which were at prices above the banks' lowered price decks. Hedges not only provided borrowing-base support; some producers were able to cash in some of their hedges to provide additional cash.[967]

Although wholesale borrowing-base reductions did not occur, for producers whose borrowing bases were merely "reaffirmed"—that is, kept at the same level as in the fall of 2008—it was merely a stay of execution because, without access to additional capital, drilling would be curtailed. No new drilling meant undeveloped reserves would not be converted into production, thus further reducing the cash flow available for keeping up with interest payments.

Bob Wagner, a former First City and Bankers Trust energy lender, co-wrote in a May 2009 article, "Unfortunately, this is the beginning of a death spiral. With no capacity to develop additional cash flow by developing properties further, they will be like their 1990's brethren, producing depleting assets just to pay interest.

"Their assets will deplete but their debt will not, a problem that will only get worse. The business model they pursued, developing properties toward an asset or company sale, is equally dead, with no buyers in sight at prices that will cover the debt."[968]

Having survived the spring, attention turned to what the fall season might produce. In June, Jeff Forbis, a senior energy lender at Sterling Bank at the time, predicted, "If commodity prices remain at their current low levels, the autumn re-set season may be the most chal-

---

[966] In 2000, only 17% of independent producers used commodity-price swaps to manage financial risk, according to an IPAA survey; in 2010, that number was almost tripled.
[967] Stone Energy Corp., BreitBurn Energy Partners LP and Energy XXI Ltd. unwound top-of-the market hedges to make headway in preparing for a continued capital drought. Nissa Darbonne, "Capital Asset Envy," *Oil and Gas Investor*, April 1, 2009.
[968] Bob Wagner and David Johnson, "Debt Wars," *Oil and Gas Investor*, May 1, 2009.

lenging. Lower capex budgets mean less drilling and reserve additions, and hedges will have rolled off - as such, borrowing bases may be even lower."[969]

More than 25 oil and gas producers had filed for protection under Chapter 11 by that time—more than twice that of the late 1990s.[970] Tekoil & Gas Corp. filed in June 2008, when oil was in the $100s and before its Galveston Bay assets were hit by Hurricane Ike.[971] Lothian Oil Inc., with West Texas assets, filed the following month.[972]

Coalbed-methane producer CDX Gas LLC defaulted under its first-lien agreement agented by Bank of Montreal, accelerating its $105-million senior obligations on September 30, 2008, and triggering default under its $400-million second-lien term-loan agreement agented by Credit Suisse. It filed for bankruptcy on December 15, citing numerous challenges, including commodity prices, depressed credit markets and general economic turmoil.[973]

Also in December, Ausam Energy Corp. and subsidiary Noram Resources Inc., whose assets were primarily on the Gulf Coast, filed for Chapter 11 protection.[974] The Meridian Resource Corp. announced that month that it wasn't in compliance with certain financial covenants and was in default. In April of 2009, its lenders, led by Fortis Capital, further reduced the borrowing base to $60 million. Its outstanding borrowing was $95 million. Unable to cure the deficiency, it incurred an additional event of default under the facility.[975]

---

[969] Gary Clouser, "Banker's Roundtable," *Here's the Money: Capital Formation 2009, Special Supplement to Oil and Gas Investor,* June 2009, 14.

[970] Examples include, Edge Petroleum, Delta Petroleum, Crusader Energy, and Energy Partners Ltd. Wagner and Johnson, "Debt Wars."

[971] Claudia Perez Rivas, "Tekoil Files For Bankruptcy," *Upstream,* June 11, 2008, Upstreamonline.com.

[972] *In re Lothian Oil, Inc.,* No. 07–7012, Doc # 1832 at 2 (Bankr.W.D.Tex. Dec. 17, 2008).

[973] "CDX Gas Defaults on Credit Agreement, Files for Bankruptcy," Bloomberg, December 13, 2008.

[974] "Ausam, Noram File for Chapter 11 Bankruptcy Protection," Rigzone, December 30, 2008, Rigzone.com.

[975] The Meridian Resource Corp., Form 8-K, April 13, 2009.

Chapter 8: The New Millennium

During the year, Meridian entered into a series of agreements whereby the lenders agreed to forbear from exercising the remedies available to them under the loan documents as a result of the events of default. After an exhaustive marketing effort, Meridian was taken private in an acquisition by Alta Mesa Holdings LP.[976]

Edge Petroleum Corp. and Chaparral Energy Inc. canceled their merger plan in December of 2008. In January of 2009, Edge was hit with a $114-million borrowing-base deficit. It initially exercised its option to cure this in six monthly installments of $19 million each. But, without sufficient liquidity, it filed for Chapter 11 protection in October of 2009.[977]

Saratoga Resources Inc., whose Texas Gulf Coast assets were struck by Ike and its Louisiana properties by Hurricane Gustav a couple of weeks earlier, filed on March 31, 2009.[978] Hallwood Group Inc. had had a good run in the Barnett shale, selling its de-risked leasehold positions to Chesapeake Energy Corp. in 2004 and 2005.[979] Its Hallwood Energy LP unit moved onto the Fayetteville play and to West Texas and filed for bankruptcy protection in March of 2009. It reported, "The U.S. and global capital markets are effectively frozen."[980]

Meanwhile, with a $5-million borrowing-base deficit, Crusader Energy Group Inc. also filed in March of 2009, just nine months after its IPO.[981] Another casualty of the Gulf Coast hurricane season, En-

---

[976] "Alta Mesa Holdings Completes Acquisition of Meridian," *Oil & Gas Financial Journal*, May 14, 2010.

[977] Stephen Payne, "Edge Hires Parkman Whaling To Assist In Paying Credit Facility Deficit," *Oil and Gas Investor*, January 16, 2009; "Edge Petroleum to Sell Most Assets, Files for Chapter 11," *Oil & Gas Financial Journal*, October 5, 2009.

[978] "Saratoga Files For Chapter 11 Protection, Cites Hurricane Damage And Lowered Energy Prices As Causes Source," *Oil and Gas Investor*, April 1, 2009.

[979] Darbonne, *The American Shales*, 109-110.

[980] The City Wire staff, "The ups and downs of Arkansas' natural gas production," *Talk Business & Politics*, Mar 6th, 2009.

[981] Crusader's limit had been lowered to $25 million from $70 million. When it missed the first scheduled payment on the $5-million deficiency, it was in default on its senior and second lien loans. Don Mecoy, "Crusader Energy Group Inc. defaults on loan, files for bankruptcy," NewsOK.com, March 31, 2009.

ergy Partners Ltd.'s borrowing base was reduced from $150 million to $45 million and $93 million was drawn; it filed in May of 2009.[982]

By March of 2010, some 60 E&P companies had filed under Chapter 11 or Chapter 7.[983] Delta Petroleum Corp. had a $140-million deficit under its fully drawn, $295-million facility. It held on for a while, but filed by the end of 2011.

In 2008, hedging was more widespread than during the downturn of the late 1990s.[984] So why were there *more* bankruptcies than during the previous cycle? Most bankruptcies occur based on a confluence of events that are set in motion months and years before the filing. Other than a depressed commodity market, this cycle was affected by capital markets that were severely restricted and, for a couple of companies, weather-related interruptions along the Gulf Coast.

Delta, principally a gas producer in Colorado's Piceance Basin, had quadrupled its acreage in 2008 and increased its proved reserves more than 295%. In 2009, it drilled a string of 18 dry holes. Not replacing reserves—combined with what it had that could not be deemed proved under newly lower gas prices—resulted in this collateral declining almost 90%.

Delta's borrowing base under a credit facility agented by JPMorgan Bank in November of 2008 was $590 million. Over time, it was reduced and Delta sold assets to shore up its balance sheet. Notwithstanding, it defaulted on covenants, triggering a workout as its original lenders became fatigued with the company.

It was refinanced by Macquarie Bank Ltd. as an $18-million revolver and $15-million term loan at much higher interest rates. Unable

---

[982] "… Energy Partners incurred debt in 2007 before oil prices began their downward spiral. At the same time, the company was dogged by extended production outages in the wake of Hurricanes Gustav and Ike, which severely damaged some of the third-party operated pipelines Energy Partners relies on." Kimberly Quillen, "Energy Partners files Chapter 11 bankruptcy," *The Times-Picayune*, May 1, 2009, Nola.com.

[983] Nissa Darbonne, "Lessons Learned Offered From the 'Zone of Insolvency,'" *Oil and Gas Investor*, March 1, 2010.

[984] Bertie Taylor, "Mitigating Risk," *Oil and Gas Investor*, April 1, 2010.

to raise additional capital, find a joint-venture partner or a purchaser, it filed for bankruptcy in December of 2011.[985]

TXCO Resources Inc. was an example of a potential shale player that never got out of the gate in an example of "right place, wrong time." The Eagle Ford play had been discovered in South Texas by Petrohawk Energy Corp. in the second half of 2008.[986] But TXCO, which held acreage suddenly prospective for Eagle Ford pay as well, was already under water.

During the second quarter of 2008, when oil was more than $100 and gas was more than $9, TXCO reported net income of $8.7 million, which was improved from a $1.3-million loss in the year-before quarter. Its operating income was $17.3 million.[987] Meanwhile, a 2008-model Eagle Ford well cost more than $6 million—drilled and completed.[988]

TXCO reported in May of 2009 that it was having "substantial difficulties in meeting short-term cash needs," such as to pay vendors; meanwhile, energy prices and "a deteriorating global economy" were preventing it from accessing debt and equity markets.[989]

James Sigmon, chairman and CEO, said in a news article a few days earlier, "There are companies that are ready to talk to us about buying portions of our acreage block or even the whole company. But

---

[985] Declaration of John T. Young, Jr., Chief Restructuring Officer of Delta Petroleum Corporation, In Support of First Day Relief, *In re Delta Petroleum Corporation, et al.* (U.S. Del. Bankruptcy Court, Case No. 11-14006 (KJC) filed December 11, 2011, at 6. "In 2008, Delta acquired an additional 17,300 net acres in the Vega Area, which increased its position to approximately 22,375 net acres, which has over 1,900 net drilling locations based on 10-acre spacing. During fiscal year 2008, Delta increased proved reserves in the Vega Area over 295% to 719.9 Bcfe … and increased production from approximately 25.0 Mmcf/d … at the beginning of the year to approximately 48.0 Mmcf/d at the end of 2008. However, during 2009, as a result of the combined effect of lower natural gas prices through the year and the new SEC reserve pricing rules and Delta's limited capital development plan, proved reserves decreased to 84.7 Bcfe. As of December 31, 2010, proved reserves in the Vega Area totaled 112.6 Bcfe. Net production in the Vega Area currently exceeds 30.0 Mmcfe/d."
[986] Darbonne, *The American Shales*, 227.
[987] "TXCO Resources Reports Record Results and Earnings," TXCO Resources Inc., Form 8-K, filed August 8, 2008.
[988] Darbonne, *The American Shales*, 222.
[989] "TXCO Resources Files Voluntary Bankruptcy Petition Under Chapter 11," TXCO Resources Inc., Form 8-K, May 18, 2009.

that takes time, and in the meantime, our financial situation is deteriorating. We may not have enough time to stay outside of bankruptcy."[990]

The bankruptcy was a lesson for the senior secured lenders. Initial mortgages had been filed against the company's early leasehold position when the loan was closed. Unfortunately, by the time the company filed bankruptcy, a significant number of its vendors were not yet paid. Under Texas law, these "mechanics and materialman" were entitled to liens against the wells they worked on or provided materials to.

Typically, secured banks will be ahead of the "trade" lien-holders by filing their mortgage against the producer's properties before any drilling begins, which is where TXCO's lenders thought they were. As the bankruptcy claims and liens were analyzed, it became apparent that the lenders' mortgages did not keep up with the company's property acquisitions.

Lawyers representing the trade claimed that many of the company's leases and valuable wells were not covered by the original mortgages and the bank group was "unsecured" on such collateral. The banks' lawyers placed mistaken reliance on the mortgage's typical "after acquired property" clause, assuming it would cover new leases after the original-mortgage closing.

After-acquired-property clauses are usually effective to create liens on additional interests acquired by the borrower in the same property already described and covered by the mortgage—for example, where a producer's interest in a mortgaged well is increased after initial drilling and completion costs are recouped. But "after acquired property" granting language is only effective to put third parties on constructive notice to the extent the grant is in the chain of title of the property in question. It doesn't cover unrelated leases acquired by the mortgagor after the original mortgage has been filed.

---

[990] TXCO Resources Inc., Form 8-K, May 13, 2009, referencing the news article, "TXCO nearing bankruptcy," Vicki Vaughan, *Express-News* (San Antonio), May 13, 2009.

The lenders learned this lesson without catastrophic cost, however—because of the value of the *acreage* rather than of TXCO's *wells* after Petrohawk Energy Corp. had made the Eagle Ford discovery well. In a case where the raw land repaid the loan, the underlying value of TXCO's undeveloped leasehold exceeded the amount of its secured debt and creditors were all paid off 100 cents on the dollar.[991]

The lenders, agented by Union Bank, in the Cornerstone E&P Co. LP bankruptcy were not as lucky.[992] In *Cornerstone*, the court held that liens filed by third parties on properties acquired by the debtor subsequent to the original mortgage were subject to the bank's lien only to the extent that the mortgage was in the chain of title prior to the filing of the third party's lien.[993]

Kicking the Barrel Down the Road

By September of 2009, oil had improved to $70, which was roughly the price two years earlier and highly economic for most producers. Gas prices, however, did not improve until after third-quarter 2009; price decks had already been reset by lenders. From its quarterly survey, Tristone Capital reported a first increase in bank pricing for crude oil in September, but gas lost another 7%, providing no help for gas-weighted borrowers.[994]

However, most banks accommodated their borrowers that had good fundamentals and just needed more time to get past the fall in prices via an amendment, waiver or extension of maturity. It presented the opportunity for bankers and bank counsel to temporarily loos-

---

[991] "The secured and unsecured creditors and certain preferred shareholders received a full recovery, including interest on their claims, and the common equity holders received a $10 million recovery." "TXCO Resources, Inc. Recovery for all Secured and Unsecured Lenders," *FTI Consulting*, Fticonsulting.com.

[992] *In Re Cornerstone E & P Company, L.P.*, 436 B.R. 830 (Bankr.N.D.Tex. 2010).

[993] Terry Cross, McClure & Cross, "Statutory Contractor Liens Against Mineral Property," Dallas Bar Association – Energy Law Section, Review of Oil and Gas Law XXX, Dallas, Texas, August 27-28, 2015, citing *In Re Cornerstone E & P Company, L.P.*, 436 B.R. 830, 864 (Bankr.N.D.Tex. 2010).

[994] Front-year pricing for oil rose 11%, but decreased 7% for natural gas. Tristone Capital Inc. Quarterly Lender Price Survey, September 2009.

en covenants—without increasing commitments—in exchange for an increase in pricing, including floors on minimum interest rates.

Meanwhile, with commodity prices at or near the banks' price decks, new hedges could not provide any boost to the borrowing base—as producers who were unhedged were unwilling to do so at sub-$50 oil the previous spring or at sub-$5 gas that spring and into the fall.

For gas-heavy companies, if lower prices held, the future was not going to be pretty. Rolling out the maturity was a way to kick the barrel—or, in this case, the Mcf—down the road in hopes of a price rebound and for the bank to avoid locking in a loss. Meanwhile, oil continued to recover, turning doubtful loans into performers. Under the rubric that "a rolling loan gathers no loss," these amendments were affectionately known by the banking community as "extend and pretend."

Global Recession and the Shale Plays

For many independents, such as TXCO, that were looking to hop onto the unconventional-resource-play train, the market collapse happened at the worst of times. Because producible shale resources can underlie entire counties rather than a few acres and because they are most economical when tapped with horizontal wellbores a mile or more in length, much more acreage is desired and needed. Meanwhile, the cost of drilling and completing a well can be more than $10 million.[995] The most aggressive independents in the shales were carrying massive debt loads in 2008.[996]

A competition between Petrohawk and Chesapeake in leasing the Haynesville shale in the first half of 2008 led to lease-bonus prices of more than $25,000 an acre. Steve Herod, who headed business development for Petrohawk, said in *The American Shales*, that Petrohawk,

---

[995] With the exception of deep-Utica shale-gas tests in Appalachia in 2015, most shale-well costs across all plays declined in 2015 to significantly less than $10 million each as oilfield-service prices declined.

[996] Leveraged producers were carrying a debt load of property value to debt of 0.9x. Wagner and Johnson, "Debt Wars", *Oil and Gas Investor*, May 1, 2009.

alone, paid $2 billion for acreage. "Several billion dollars of lease-bonus money went into North Louisiana in five months. ... It was pretty amazing."[997]

Dick Stoneburner, Petrohawk's chief operating officer at the time, said, "We went toe to toe with Chesapeake from March to August, just a six-month period. But it was an incredible period to be involved in a play like that with Floyd [Wilson, Petrohawk CEO] and Aubrey [McClendon, Chesapeake CEO] going *mano y mano* to see who could end up with the best position. ...

"It was crazy but it worked. I mean, it worked for us. I think it worked for them. It's hard to say. In the long run, it will."[998]

Chesapeake's strategy was copied and envied. To finance its leasing and its drilling to hold the acreage by production before expiration deadlines, it outspent cash flow in all but three out of 34 quarters between 2004 and year-end 2012.[999] During this eight-year period, its spending in excess of cash flow totaled more than $30 billion.[1000]

Meanwhile, the "wall of gas" that was expected to come online as a result of full-throttle shale production was eventually factored into gas futures. Oil futures had rebounded by the end of 2009 to $80.[1001] Gas, however, fell into the $3s by the spring of 2009 and, except for some winter-demand spikes, rarely had a glimpse of more than $5 thereafter.

But most of the shale-gas discoverers and producers knew going in that they would have to drive down their costs via efficiencies of scale in such massive plays. Southwestern Energy Co. amassed 455,000 net acres in Arkansas for an average of about $40 an acre before announcing the Fayetteville play.[1002]

Richard Lane, a Southwestern executive during the discovery, said in *The American Shales*, "Think about doing anything 10,000 times.

[997] Darbonne, *The American Shales*, 200.
[998] Darbonne, *The American Shales*, 200.
[999] Gold, *The Boom*, 194.
[1000] Gold, *The Boom*, 194.
[1001] U.S. EIA, Independent Statistics & Analysis. "Cushing, OK Crude Oil Future Contract 1." Accessed May 9, 2011. Eia.gov.
[1002] Darbonne, *The American Shales*, 139.

If you save a buck here and a buck there 10,000 times, it adds up quickly. That's where the 'manufacturing' think comes in. You control your destiny by driving down cost."[1003]

With banks and oil and gas producers feeling optimistic, the dark days of 2008-2009 were soon forgotten. *Oil and Gas Investor* reported in 2010, "Throughout 2009, banks instituted interest-rate floors; shortened maturities; and tightened financial covenants. The major change for 2010 seems to be some leniency on debt maturities, i.e., four years as opposed to 2009's standard three year maturity."[1004]

Having felt the sting of borrowing-base reductions, producers that had the ability to access public debt and equity markets, when these reopened in 2009, raised money and paid down their bank debt. Between the base-redetermination seasons of the spring of 2009 and the spring of 2010, what was drawn under the senior revolvers had fallen from 64% to 44%. As borrowing decreased, bankers competed harder for new customers; loan syndications were oversubscribed, even for drilling deals. Bank pricing remained relatively firm.

Wells Fargo's Marc Cuenod observed, "Now the market's hunger for new loans has resulted in oversubscriptions on many [syndicated] deals. Deal pricing has remained relatively firm and we're seeing good opportunities for drilling deals, especially in the shales."[1005]

The U.S. was becoming more than satiated with new shale-gas supply. However, there was ample room in the market for new U.S. oil supply. New completion techniques in the Bakken tight-oil play in North Dakota and development of other tight oil after 2008 began contributing significant additional volumes of U.S. oil. Lenders were eager to finance shale-oil development. *Oil and Gas Investor* reported in February of 2013:

[1003] Darbonne, *The American Shales*, 254.
[1004] Gary Clouser, "Banker's Roundtable," *Here's the Money: Capital Formation 2010, Special Supplement to Oil and Gas Investor*, June 2010, 10.
[1005] Bertie Taylor, "Capital Markets Outlook: The Road Ahead," *Oil and Gas Investor*, August 1, 2010.

"The advent of the shale plays has been kind of a game-changer for the mezzanine business," says Mark Green, president of Wells Fargo Energy Capital, in Houston. "… The shales have made mezzanine even more attractive because they have significantly reduced the reservoir risk, and it's become more an issue of execution risk," Green says.

"We've seen hardly any dry holes in the mature plays such as the Barnett and the Bakken. However, it takes a lot more dollars than it used to because of the high well and facilities costs, and our challenge is making sure that the drilling is economic in the current price environment."[1006]

Dodd-Frank and Banking Regulations

In response to the 2008 credit-market crisis, Congress passed the Dodd-Frank Wall Street Reform and Consumer Protection Act in July of 2010. As bank failures had been big; the law is similarly big. *The Economist* wrote, "The law that set up America's banking system in 1864 ran to 29 pages; the Federal Reserve Act of 1913 went to 32 pages; the Banking Act that transformed American finance after the Wall Street Crash, commonly known as the Glass-Steagall act, spread out to 37 pages. Dodd-Frank is 848 pages long."[1007]

The act was more like a set of guidelines than a law[1008] and the task of implementing the law was left to federal regulatory agencies with a one-year deadline. This was delayed and delayed. In 2013, according to one law firm's estimate, 13,789 pages of rules containing 15 million words had completed only 39% of the process.[1009] At year-end

---

[1006] Chris Sheehan, "Mezzanine Moves," *Oil and Gas Investor*, February 1, 2013.
[1007] "The Dodd-Frank act: Too big not to fail," *The Economist*, February 18, 2012, Economist.com.
[1008] Jeff Nichols and Kim Mai, "The Regulation of Swaps and Derivatives and its Impact on Business after Dodd-Frank" (paper presented at State Bar of Texas 11th Annual Advanced Business Law Course, November 7-8, 2013).
[1009] According to Davis Polk & Wardwell, "Over the course of the three years since passage of the Dodd-Frank Act, its initial 848 pages of statutory text has ballooned to 13,789 pages (which amount to more than 10 times the length of Tolstoy's *War and Peace*). That page count, high as it is, represents only 39 percent of the required rulemaking contained

2015, only 68% of the total rule-making requirements had been finalized,[1010] the firm reported in an update. Energy banks responded to the prospective regulation—and repeated investigations and fines by regulators—by getting out of the physical commodities markets.[1011]

The act also prohibited national banks from owning or investing in private-equity funds.[1012] In connection with the relaxation of the Glass-Steagall restrictions on investment banking, beginning in the 1990s, a number of commercial energy banks invested in energy private-equity funds, such as EnCap and Natural Gas Partners, as a means of establishing relationships with these private bankers and, more importantly, with their portfolio companies.

Private-equity sponsors would give their portfolio-management teams the equity capital to make an acquisition or acquire prospective acreage with the intention of quickly turning the investment into proven, producing reserves and a "commercially bankable" company. By investing in equity funds that sponsored start-up E&Ps vetted and underwritten by these experienced investors, the commercial bankers were the first in line when the portfolio companies had sufficient collateral to merit a secured credit facility.

The symbiotic relationship was seen by the commercial bankers as an "energy-loan incubator." For example, Amegy Bank was actively investing in 14 private-equity funds in 2008. Steve Kennedy, senior vice president, said in an article at the time, "This has proven to be a

---

within the legislation." Joe Mont, "Three Years In, Dodd-Frank Deadlines Missed As Page Count Rises," *Compliance Week*, July 22, 2013, Complianceweek.com.

[1010] DavisPolk, "Dodd-Frank Progress Report, Fourth Quarter 2015," Davispolk.com.

[1011] *The Wall Street Journal* reported that the Federal Reserve was considering whether new rules are needed to limit banks' exposure to commodities trading. The article noted that such pressures had triggered a series of high-profile exits from the industry, including J.P. Morgan Chase & Co. Sarah Kent and Daniel Fitzpatrick, "J.P. Morgan to sell Commodities Business for $3.5 Billion," *The Wall Street Journal*, March 19, 2014. Morgan Stanley sold its oil-storage and trading business and Deutsche Bank, Goldman Sachs, Royal Bank of Scotland and UBS had exited or planned to as well.

[1012] A portion of the Volker Rule, Section 619 of the Dodd-Frank Act amends the Bank Holding Company Act of 1956 to add a new section 13(a) that provides in relevant part that: "[u]nless otherwise provided in this section, a banking entity shall not ... acquire or retain any equity, partnership, or other ownership interest in or sponsor a hedge fund or a private equity fund."

very good place to become involved early on with the new, developing companies.

"And, because of our familiarity with these private equity groups, we have been in a position to help several companies find a good equity sponsor. We have made excellent rates of return on these energy private-equity funds to date, so we anticipate continuing this activity for the foreseeable future."[1013]

While commercial banks have ceased making further investments in private-equity funds as a result of Dodd-Frank, the funds and their portfolio clients have not suffered for lack of other investor appetite, filling the void. During each year following 2009, they committed record amounts of capital to invest in the upstream and midstream energy markets.

The banks complied with the restriction on future investments in the funds, but some banks with unregulated subsidiaries have turned to making investments alongside the private-equity sponsors directly in the new companies. At least when banks invested in private energy funds, it was into a diversified portfolio of holdings, thereby spreading risk, much like a private individual lacking the resources to check out every public company will spread risk by investing in a mutual fund. With the prohibitions under Dodd-Frank, which intended to reduce risk to a bank's capital by prohibiting investing in private-equity funds, it can be argued that the level of risk has been increased.

Following on the theme of unintended federal regulatory consequences, banks have also complied with the letter of law under the federal flood-insurance act.[1014] The act requires that any real estate with buildings taken as collateral for a loan must obtain either a certificate that the collateral is not located within a flood zone or obtain flood insurance. The law was intended to fund the federal pool for insuring homes in flood-prone areas.

[1013] Clouser, "Regional Credit No Problem," 24.
[1014] National Flood Insurance Act of 1968 and the Flood Disaster Protection Act of 1973, as amended (42 U.S.C. 4001--4129).

Enforcement of the law took on a sense of urgency after New Orleans and other areas along the Gulf Coast were flooded by Hurricane Katrina. Regulators—hence, banks—became insistent upon literal compliance with the regulation—no matter the kind of real estate involved and even if the real estate consisted of hundreds of oil and gas leases where the value lay thousands of feet underground. Some energy lenders refused to advance funds at closing without the necessary flood survey or flood insurance.[1015]

A work-around for reserve-based loans avoided the act altogether by not taking liens on "buildings" on the collateral. Rather than inspect each oil and gas lease to make sure there were no buildings, the banks modified their lien documents to expressly exclude from the mortgaged properties "all buildings as defined under the Flood Act."

While this has satisfied compliance with federal regulations, it has meant that banks are foregoing liens on any buildings associated with the oil and gas properties. The question that has yet to be addressed is how the collateral's value is affected if buildings on the property are critical to continued operations of the oil and gas production. Have banks solved for the immediate documentary headache only to find that—down the road, following a foreclosure or bankruptcy fight—there is a hole in their collateral?

2013: Buyer's Market at the Capital Bazaar

2013 saw continued competitive pressure on a growing pool of energy-capital providers in search of bankable projects. Public-debt markets chasing yield were open. Even sub-investment-grade E&Ps with B- or CCC ratings were able to access the high-yield bond markets at attractive rates. Accessibility of public debt, combined with a decrease in M&A activity, resulted in lower demand for borrowings from commercial banks.

[1015] In 2012, a New York bank's counsel inquired as to whether a Haynes and Boone LLP producer client had flood insurance. As the producer operated in the Gulf of Mexico, every one of its properties was under thousands of feet of water. The firm advised bank counsel that such insurance was not available to the client.

Chapter 8: The New Millennium

Nevertheless, capital options for the larger independents were as accessible and varied as goods at a Turkish bazaar. Producers were ready to deal as capital providers hawked their products with everyone using $100 barrel oil as the common currency. No one gave much thought to how difficult it would be to untangle the producers' complicated capital structures if oil prices were to fall before all the debt was repaid.

M&A transactions in 2013 were off two-thirds from the prior year: $123 billion in 2012 versus $38 billion in 2013. Not surprisingly, to keep dry powder and moderate floating-interest-rate exposure under credit facilities with fixed-interest-rate bond debt, many borrowers who could do so accessed the public-debt market to pay down their bank revolvers. Commercial energy lenders saw their borrowers' average loan utilization—the ratio of borrowed funds to the availability under the borrowing base—falling as the year progressed. Commercial banks—especially regional and smaller banks lacking capital-markets capabilities to earn fees on the bond issuances—felt the pinch.

Because of the continuing slow recovery in the general U.S. economy and the relative attractiveness of investments in the energy-loan market, a number of new banks entered the reserve-base-lending space, adding further price pressure on loan terms—much to the benefit of producer borrowers. Entrants in 2013 included Pittsburgh-based PNC Bank, which had a long history of lending to the coal industry and, with recent exposure to the local Marcellus-shale play, beefed up its oil and gas lending in Pennsylvania and opened a beachhead in Houston.

Fifth Third Bank out of Ohio, seeing the growth of the Utica-shale play in its backyard, picked up Royal Bank of Scotland's entire Houston team and opened shop in the city. Amegy's Kennedy said in an August 2013 article, "As the capital costs of having an effective presence in a shale/resource play increase, we are seeing more companies narrow their focus into one or two main geologic areas. We are also seeing an increase in private equity investments, as E&P companies realize that the large equity commitments that such firms offer provide a strategic advantage in the new capital intense, acreage intense, shale resource plays.

"For years, companies had to chase conventional reservoir traps, which varied in size, but tended to cover hundreds of acres. Since shale covers thousands, tens or hundreds of thousands of acres, the potentially productive areas are much larger than in the past. Now, one could literally spend a career developing and operating in one continuous geologic play, which was fairly rare in the past."[1016]

BB&T, a large North Carolina bank, was another newcomer to the reserve-based-lending market. Sterling Bank's energy group, led by Jeff Forbis, opened a Houston office for it in 2011.

The structure for reserve-based loans, however, had not changed much during the preceding 40 years—just the pricing and tenor. Forbis said in same the article, "The standard borrowing base revolving credit remains the cornerstone of the energy banking industry. For the most part, new deals are secure, have a five-year term semi-annual borrowing base redeterminations and are priced in the range of LIBOR plus 200 to 275. Covenants are generally: debt/EBITDA -4X, Interest coverage- 2.5X and Current ratio – 1X."[1017]

Another phenomenon affecting not just bank pricing and overall competition for business was the aggressive demands of the larger private-equity funds sponsoring E&P management teams—with some teams having few or no proved reserves. Without the PE muscle behind them, each team would not have commanded much attention of established energy lenders—especially the bulge-bracket banks, such as JPMorgan, Citibank, Bank of America and Wells Fargo.

But, when the profitability of the portfolio company's new loan application was tied to the coattails of a private-equity sponsor's overall commercial- and investment-banking business with these large institutions, equity firms were able to exact pricing and covenant concessions for their portfolio constituents that, a few years prior, would

---

[1016] Gary Clouser, "Bankers' Buzz - Plenty of bank capital available for growth-hungry E&Ps," *Oil and Gas Investor*, August 2013.
[1017] Clouser, "Bankers' Buzz."

have been extended only to the largest independents, such as Devon and Anadarko Petroleum Corp.

Some banks were even willing to document "zero dollar borrowing base" loans. In this, no money would be funded upfront; the expectation was that, once the private-equity-backed borrower found an attractive acquisition, the loan documentation would already be in place, providing ready capital on short notice.

Steve Trauber, head of Citigroup's global energy investment banking, observed in an early 2014 *Oil and Gas Investor* article, "The reality is that, because of the amount of capital out there, the bank market is fairly aggressive. They're giving loans and credit facilities out to companies at rates that don't earn an adequate rate of return on a standalone basis. Instead, they rely upon the other businesses in order to get the rates of return they need on their capital."[1018]

Among smaller banks, their return on committed capital was not augmented by the ability to offer other capital products—lacking investment-banking or hedging capability and having a business model of participating in large facilities agented by the bulge-bracket lenders. Regional and local banks complained of losing clients to more aggressive lenders.

Loans became very cheap for producers, according to David Zalman, chairman of Houston-based Prosperity Bankshares. He told FuelFix.com at the time, "Some banks are offering 10-year payout terms for loans that would normally get five-year terms stretching pricing and payout periods, and we've lost business because of it. What we have seen is some of the banks are even lending money on nonproducing property. That's where it's becoming a bigger issue."[1019]

Phil Ballard, one of Trauber's fellow Citi bankers, said in the *Oil and Gas Investor* article, "It's a very competitive market. Some recent deals have probably been a little more aggressive than they historically have been in terms of covenants and borrowing-base amounts. And

---

[1018] Chris Sheehan, "Margins Pressure Energy Uplift," *Oil and Gas Investor*, February 2014.
[1019] Collin Eaton, "Bank loan standards bending for oil companies amid shale rush," FuelFix, May 22, 2014.

because there are so many new banks coming in, if someone doesn't like it, someone else will step right in to take its place."[1020]

Not only were banks increasing the percentage of borrowing-base value derived from proved undeveloped (PUD) reserves—akin to the raw-land deals banked by the S&Ls in the go-go days of the 1980s—they were also including value to "probable" and "possible" reserves in acreage in the fairways of the more prolific shale plays, such as the Eagle Ford and Marcellus.[1021] Although attributing collateral value to non-proven acreage was similar to the "lease line of credit" from earlier days, proved reserves still made up the bulk of the collateral in these producer loans.

Additionally provisions were added in some facilities to allow the borrower's private-equity sponsors the ability to prop up the client's financial underperformance with equity infusions and thereby cure, albeit temporarily, financial-covenant defaults. These were the very same covenants that were built into credit agreements after the bust of the 1980s to alert bankers to the borrower's ability to remain cash-flow positive, thus able to meet debt service on a current basis.

Serving as advance-warning signals, these periodic financial tests provide banks with the ability to take action early in a deteriorating market to address problems before the collateral dissipates to less than what is needed for repayment. With "equity cure rights" these signals can be overridden and delay the lender's ability to take action.

Seasoned bankers, nevertheless, were not ready to pull back on the throttle. Perhaps this time it really would be different. Just like every other time it was going to be different?

Mark Fuqua at Comerica Bank told *Oil and Gas Investor*, "We have this incredible confluence of tremendous resource base in the U.S. – where we are arguably the largest oil and gas producer in the world and still growing – coupled with this abundance of cheap capital. I've been through a lot of booms and busts, and I don't know exactly

---

[1020] Sheehan, "Margins Pressure Energy Uplift."
[1021] Clouser, "Bankers' Buzz."

where this one is going, but the fundamentals of it still feel pretty good to me right now."[1022]

Some experienced bankers by the beginning of 2014, were sounding words of caution, reporting that the commercial-banking sector was moving into a period of "unparalleled excess liquidity," along with a lack of demand for their capital. Scotiabank managing director Mark Ammerman said, "It sounds funny to say, but you really don't make much money lending money any more, certainly not in as challenging a market as we have with today's liquidity and increasing regulatory capital. You really make your money selling other products and services."[1023]

Regulators began to take notice of the loosening lending standards. In April of 2014, the Office of the Comptroller of the Currency dusted off its 25-year-old loan-examiner's manual, rewriting its handbook on oil and gas production loans and describing supervisory expectations for prudent policies and procedures for lending to the E&P industry.[1024]

More conservative bankers and regulators, however, were out of sync with borrowers' expectations. Producers' management teams began 2014 with much optimism. A February 2014 survey by *Forbes* and CIT of 141 senior U.S.-based energy executives found their short- and long-term outlooks for both oil and gas pricing and profitability to be unabashedly upbeat. More than 80% of the participants described 2013 as profitable and they were predicting an equally profitable 2014. In addition, 91% anticipated they would be profitable during the next three to five years, 66% expected oil prices to rise and 68% expected natural-gas prices to rise.[1025]

Based on ongoing, rosy forecasts and high capital needs, many small and mid-size producers accessed junk-bond markets when they

---

[1022] Sheehan, "Margins Pressure Energy Uplift."
[1023] Sheehan, "Margins Pressure Energy Uplift."
[1024] Office of the Comptroller of the Currency, "Oil and Gas Production Lending," Comptroller's Handbook (April 2014), accessed April 9, 2016, Occ.treas.gov.
[1025] Mike Lorusso, "Lending in a Boom Market," *Oil & Gas Financial Journal*, August 11, 2014.

could to finance drilling. These offerings in the energy space reached $210 billion—roughly 16% of the junk-bond market—a dramatic rise from just 4% of the market 10 years earlier.

The low-interest-rate environment since the financial crash of 2008 and the Fed's $3.5 trillion[1026] of bond purchases, beginning in 2009 and into October of 2014 via its "quantitative easing" program, flooded the markets with debt capital. But unlike equity, debt has to be paid back. And with the availability of different and diverse capital sources, producers ended up with capital structures as complex to navigate as the labyrinth of Istanbul's Grand Bazaar: senior secured first liens under revolver-based credit facilities, second-lien loans from mezzanine providers and various tranches of publicly issued notes held by institutional investors.

The phenomenon that spawned the renaissance of the U.S.' independent producers—the unconventional-resource plays made viable by horizontal, fracture-stimulated wells—continued to feed small and mid-size producers' demand for "easy money." As is the nature of the junk-bond market, lots of money flowed to less-capitalized companies with much-riskier drilling prospects than the larger independents, such as EOG Resources Inc., Pioneer Natural Resources Co., Anadarko, Devon and Apache Corp.

Some of the small to mid-size independents were venturing into untested formations and the marginal edges of unconventional plays, while not having a lot of cash on hand—the same reason they couldn't offer investment-grade bonds. The junk market was over-heated even before the price of oil began to decline after June of 2014. *Forbes* estimated that $500 billion in debt had been advanced to producers, consisting of $300 billion in leveraged loans and $200 billion in high-yield public notes. By 2014, energy claimed 16% of the high-yield market, a fourfold increase from the prior decade.[1027]

[1026] Jeff Kearns, "The Fed Eases Off," Bloomberg QuickTake, September 16, 2015, Bloombergview.com.
[1027] Christopher Helman, "Who Will Get Caught When the Oil Debt Bubble Pops?" *Forbes*, December 19, 2014.

Chapter 8: The New Millennium

A New York-based money manager said in a December 2014 Bloomberg article, "There was too much money going into this space that would have resulted in problems long-term – now that timeline has been accelerated."[1028]

[1028] Nabila Ahmed and Sridhar Natarajan, "Junk Bonds Backing Shale Boom Facing $11.6 Billion Loss," Bloomberg, December 1, 2014, Bloomberg.com.

CHAPTER 9

OPEC Delivers A
Thanksgiving Turkey

"The four most dangerous words in investing are 'This time it's different.'"
John Templeton

As the oil and gas industry proved a century earlier, nothing breeds failure like success. The flush production brought about by each new field discovery since Spindletop has caused local—and sometimes national—prices to collapse.

The current generation of producers and bankers had grown up in an environment where American oil production had been in decline since the mid-1980s. By 2008, production had fallen 40% from a May 1985 high of 9.1 million barrels a day to 5.4 million.[1029]

The force of the shale revolution during the aughts turned the tide in the 2010s. By April of 2015, as the Bakken play expanded and the Eagle Ford, Niobrara, Oklahoma Woodford and Permian Basin unconventional-resource plays developed, U.S. production had reached 9.7 million barrels a day—catching up to a peak not seen since April of 1971, 44 years earlier.[1030]

This growth in U.S. unconventional oil production was un-checked by any state regulatory controls, just like the days before suc-

---

[1029] U.S. EIA, Independent Statistics & Analysis. "U.S. Field Production of Crude Oil." Accessed May 3, 2016. Eia.gov.
[1030] U.S. EIA, Independent Statistics & Analysis. "U.S. Field Production of Crude Oil." Accessed May 3, 2016. Eia.gov. In April, 1971, daily production reached 9.769 million barrels; in April, 2015, 9.694 million.

cessful proration laws kept excess production in line with market demand. Reminiscent of the boom following the East Texas Field discovery, crude-oil storage rose to levels that had not been seen since
the early 1930s.[1031]

Such a prodigious increase in production did not escape the attention of Saudi Arabia and its fellow OPEC members. The U.S. was
turning oil tankers away.[1032] Saudi Arabia's sales to the U.S. had been
reduced to, roughly, the equivalent of as much oil as its own, co-
owned refinery on the Texas coast processed daily.[1033]

As a result of the shale revolution, it was not only OPEC losing
U.S. oil-market share to American independents. Growing U.S. natural-gas production from shale plays had pushed LNG tankers and Canadian supply away as well. Compared with 44 years earlier, domestic
gas production was substantially higher by 2015.[1034]

The Saudis had been hinting during the fall of 2014 that they
were no longer going to be the swing producer that balanced world oil
supply with demand, propped up prices and indirectly subsidized Iran,
Russia and others. The Saudis had played this trump card in 1985
when it increased its exports from 2 million barrels a day to its full
quota of 4 million. The result of the Saudis' actions depressed oil prices well into the 1990s.

While American producers sat down for Thanksgiving dinner in
November of 2014, OPEC members announced that they would not
decrease their output that would have stemmed declining world oil

---

[1031] Brian Scheid, et al., "US crude production to rise to 9.3 million b/d in 2015: EIA,"
Platts, March 10, 2015, accessed May 3, 2016, Platts.com.
[1032] Scheid, "US crude production to rise to 9.3 million." The report added, "The growth
of US production is expected to continue to eat into net imports of crude oil and other
liquids, which fell from 60% of the total share of US liquid fuels consumption in 2005 to
an estimated 26% in 2014. That share is expected to fall to 20% in 2016, which would be
the lowest level since 1968, EIA said."
[1033] John Kemp, "How Saudi Arabia successfully defended its U.S. oil market share:
Kemp," Reuters, February 1, 2016, Reuters.com.
[1034] Natural gas production in 2015 totaled 28.8 Tcf compared with 22.5 Tcf in 1971. U.S.
EIA, Independent Statistics & Analysis. "U.S. Natural Gas Marketed Production." Accessed March 26, 2016. Eia.gov.

prices.[1035] Sometime between the stuffed turkey and the pumpkin pie, the price of oil dropped more than 10%.[1036] And, as world markets digested the news, WTI fell from more than $73 per barrel prior to Thanksgiving to $53 as the New Year began.[1037]

December is normally quiet in the energy-lending business, but, in 2014, bankers' and producers' holiday plans were interrupted by OPEC's declaration and the market's response. Bankers spent the following weeks re-setting price decks and stress-testing their borrowers' loans against the new value of oil reserves by which their loans were secured. Borrowers in turn were busy revising their forecasted 2015 development-capital spending plans and reviewing their long-term drilling contracts.

Responding to lower prices, producers started the year by slashing their capital-investment budgets. Before the New Year, public companies announced, on average, that they were reducing their capex by a third.[1038] The U.S. rig count that had been averaging close to 2,000 dropped steeply. By March, the number of rigs at work had been cut nearly in half.[1039]

Yet, even with deep cuts in drilling budgets, producers continued to outspend cash flow in the first quarter of the year. If not for the value from above-market oil hedges, producers would have had to cut capital expenditures 70% to balance their books.[1040] Capital investments in the field can take between three and 12 months to turn into

---

[1035] "OPEC 166th Meeting concludes," Organization of the Petroleum Exporting Countries, accessed on March 27, 2016, Opec.org.

[1036] U.S. EIA, Independent Statistics & Analysis. "Cushing, OK WTI Spot Price FOB." Accessed March 26, 2016. Eia.gov. WTI closed on November 26, 2014, at $73.70; the following Friday, November 28, at $65.94.

[1037] "Simmons Morning Energy Note," Simmons & Co. International Inc., November 26, 2014, and January 5, 2015.

[1038] Carolyn Davis, "Domino Effect of Lower Oil/Gas E&P Capex Now Hitting Offshore, Midstream," NGO Shale Daily, January 9, 2015, Naturalgasintel.com.

[1039] Between 2011 and 2014, the U.S. oil and gas rotary rig count had been between 1,800 and 2,000. In March, 2015, the number was 1,109. U.S. EIA, Independent Statistics & Analysis. "U.S. Crude Oil and Natural Gas Rotary Rigs in Operation." Accessed March 26, 2016. Eia.gov.

[1040] "Fractured finances, America's shale-energy industry has a future. Many shale firms do not," The Economist, July 4, 2015.

production. Thus, it was no surprise that U.S. production remained resilient during the first part of the year—and even continued to grow.[1041]

Part of the reduction in capital costs came at the expense of the rig contractors, who saw long-term rig leases cancelled or the price renegotiated. Additional pain was spread to every additional member of the oilfield-service industry to bring down producers' operating costs.[1042] Even a Houston law firm that specialized in lease acquisitions and title opinions and had caught a 10-year ride on the shale wave shuttered its doors by the end of 2015 as leasing activity came to a halt.[1043] More than 40 oilfield-service companies went out of business or filed bankruptcy during the year.[1044]

Producers who could reduced staff and focused on preserving cash flow—i.e., doing more with less. Productivity gains were made through greater efficiency with multiple well-pad drilling and completions, faster drilling times and higher production rates through better completions and longer horizontals. Some of the gains were made possible, ironically, by newly lower oilfield-service costs and that, as rig and completion crews were being laid off, service providers retained their best employees to work on what remained.

Importantly, producers in all basins high-graded their drilling inventory, putting aside testing outside of the core of their plays and cherry-picking only the best locations to better insure a return on investors' dollars, profit to pay interest on outstanding debt and proved reserves to support their bank loans.[1045] In early 2015, following their December top-down loan-portfolio review, bankers by and large were

---

[1041] *The Economist*, "Fractured finances;" *also* U.S. EIA, Independent Statistics & Analysis. "U.S. Field Production of Crude Oil." Accessed March 26, 2016. Eia.gov.
[1042] Pamela King, "Workforce: Not all oil industry segments suffer equally as prices slide," *Energywire*, January 26, 2015, Eenews.net.
[1043] Sara Randazzo, "Oil Downturn Sends Texas Law Firm Packing," *The Wall Street Journal*, November 27, 2015. Burleson LLP, formed as an oil and gas title boutique at the beginning of the shale revolution, closed after 10 years at the end of 2015.
[1044] "Haynes and Boone Oil Field Bankruptcy Tracker," Haynes and Boone, LLP, March 1, 2016, Haynesboone.com.
[1045] *The Economist*, "Fractured finances."

still positive that their borrowers could survive oil in the $50s—if it didn't last too long.[1046]

While there was limited concern within the banks, energy-loan-weighted, regional lenders watched as their stock prices lost 20% since oil had peaked at $108 in June of 2014.[1047] Notwithstanding the market sentiment, banks did not take precipitous action to declare "wild card" borrowing-base redeterminations. In general, the consensus was that OPEC would relent and the markets would quickly rebound.[1048]

In fact, even by the scheduled Spring 2015 borrowing base season, the predictions of substantial borrowing base reductions failed to materialize. A survey of producers and energy lenders early in the year predicted borrowing-base reductions would average 25%.[1049] The borrowers' angst was unmerited: Reductions averaged between 10% and 15%, helped in great part by oil hedges that had many borrowers' production still getting more than $90 barrel.

Banks did drop their price decks as the spring-season redetermination approached, but not as aggressively as spot prices would suggest. Typically, banks set their price decks for determining the borrowing base at a discount of around 80% of the current front-year WTI Nymex price and up to 90% of the five-year forward curve, but, because of the precipitous drop in prices, the quarterly price decks set by the banks were *above* the front-year and five-year curves.[1050]

"Industry executives have let out a palpable exhale as we exit the spring borrowing base redetermination season," *Oil & Gas Financial Journal* reported in June of 2015. " ... Ultimately banks settled on modest to no reductions in borrowing bases, [which were accompa-

---

[1046] Julie Steinberg, "Falling Oil Prices Worry Regional-Bank Investors," *The Wall Street Journal*, January 21, 2016.

[1047] Steinberg, "Falling Oil Prices Worry Regional-Bank Investors." For 13 banks with energy loans that comprise more than 5% of their portfolios, shares were down more than 20% on average since June 20, 2014.

[1048] Nicole Freidman, "What Went Wrong in Oil-Price Forecasts?" *The Wall Street Journal*, December 10, 2015.

[1049] "Haynes and Boone, Borrowing Base Redeterminations," Haynes and Boone, LLP, September 18, 2015, Haynesboone.com.

[1050] Macquarie Tristone's Quarterly Energy Lender Price Survey, "Energy Lender Price Survey Q1 2015," Static.macquarie.com.

nied with] numerous amendments that included covenant holidays around [audit opinion] going concerns [exceptions], leverage tests, and asset coverage tests."[1051]

Banks' price decks reflected market sentiment early in the year, which was that prices, while low, would recover. The question being asked on the streets of downtown Houston during the first quarter of 2015 was how quickly prices would recover. Would the recovery be "V" shaped or "U" shaped?

A bump from $43 in March to $60 by May gave markets and producers a false sense that OPEC's turkey didn't have legs. To generate cash on their books, producers with the strongest assets and management went to the public market, selling equity and/or public debt securities. The biggest wave was during the first week of March with 55 energy offerings that raised $50 billion. In all, by the middle of July, 179 equity and debt offerings had raised more than $127 billion for Texas and Oklahoma businesses of which 90% were energy companies.

But as quickly as the opportunity appeared, it was gone. Nymex traders went on Fourth of July holiday with the prompt-month contract for WTI trading at about $57. When they returned to their desks at 5 p.m. Central time Sunday, WTI declined 8%.[1052]

And the price kept declining. "It was like someone turned all the spigots off," William Snyder, head of Deloitte's Texas restructuring practice told *The Dallas Morning News*. "The money just dried up."[1053]

Investors found out the March bump was more of a dead-turkey bounce than a true bottom. In fact, oil prices dipped even lower—into the $30s. Seeking reassurances that the price drop was not permanent, discussions in boardrooms and bank lobbies began to lean toward whether recovery would be "W" shaped rather than the "V"

[1051] Josh Sherman and Sean Clements, Opportune LLP, "Capital Availability for E&Ps," *Oil & Gas Financial Journal*, June 9, 2015.

[1052] U.S. EIA, Independent Statistics & Analysis. "Cushing, OK Crude Oil Future Contract 1." Accessed March 6, 2016. Eia.gov.

[1053] Mark Currriden and Natalie Posgate, "Capital Drying Up for Oil, Gas," *Dallas Morning News*, November 30, 2015.

shape of 2009-10. As prices continued to languish, the feared "U" shape was becoming plausible; the shibboleth "lower for longer" began to creep into discussions.

Producers adjusted again, further cancelling drilling and postponing completion of wells that had been drilled. OPEC's Thanksgiving turkey had created a new specie of oil well—the "DUC" or "drilled but uncompleted."[1054] Because of the relatively higher cost of completing a well with hydraulic fracture-stimulation than drilling it, producers elected to drill but not complete wells until a rebound in prices justified the costs.[1055] Several began to refer to their DUCs as "oil in the bank." When prices improved, they would complete them, bringing on the production when the market price was economic.

Notwithstanding their efforts at cost cutting, many producers' spend continued to exceed cash flow. Facing potential reductions during the fall borrowing-base-redetermination season, many looked to sell non-core assets and to access more expensive capital. Most asset-owners were not willing to accept offers based on the current, depressed market price, so the delta between buyer and seller on the bid and ask meant few sales were consummated.[1056] In some cases, a price was agreed upon, but the buyer walked away after the Fourth of July, even while having to forfeit the earnest-money deposit.

In addition to asset sales, producers looked to capital markets for a lifeline to tide them over until prices rebounded. Public equity and debt markets had closed by July, but, albeit at a higher cost, private equity and debt were still options that some producers were able to secure.

[1054] Industry had called these WOC or "waiting on completion." Securities analysts in 2015 began to call them DUCs and industry adopted the new term.

[1055] Lynn Doan and Dan Murtaugh, "U.S. Shale Fracklog Triples as Drillers Keep Oil From Market," *Bloomberg Business*, April 23, 2015.

[1056] Scott Richardson, RBC Capital Markets, "Volatility Presents Opportunity" (presented to Houston Energy Finance Group, February 17, 2016). In 2014, there were more than 122 property sales of $20 million or more totaling $62 billion; in 2015, the number was 57, totaling less than $24 billion. More than $20 billion of properties put up for sale did not close in 2015.

Chapter 9: OPEC Delivers a Thanksgiving Turkey

"[D]ebt investors are thinking about the best ways to play the next energy-industry distress cycle—but they are doing so with the utmost care," *The Deal* reported. "Why the caution? Mostly because the secondary bond market opportunities aren't what they used to be, so investors are betting on new secured debt, bankrupt companies' bonds, and upside/downside strategies that hold promise in either a best- or worst-case scenario. Other financing structures, such as product[ion] payments, may require further clarity, and opportunities to replace bank lenders haven't started materializing yet."[1057]

Given the precarious leverage of some of the more aggressive shale players, capital providers looked for assurances that their investments would be protected in the event the producer went bankrupt. Off-balance-sheet transactions popular in the late '90s were dusted off. Non-banks purchased volumetric production payments or made loans with equity kickers in the form of convertible overriding royalty payments that, upon repayment of the principal, would automatically convert to net profit interests in the financed properties.

A new twist on the type of drilling dollars majors had contributed to independents back in the 1930s to prove up acreage was the financial-partner "DrillCo" agreement, primarily beginning in mid-2015. Instead of dollars from major oil companies, private-capital providers joined producers in drilling wells in this joint-venture structure in which the producer contributes raw acreage and the financial partner contributes drilling dollars in exchange for a working interest in the wells.

In July, GSO Capital Partners LP closed one of the first such arrangements with Linn Energy LLC in which GSO agreed to finance 100% of the wells, receiving 85% of the net proceeds until achieving a 15% internal rate of return on the wells. After reaching the hurdle, Linn would own 95% working interest and GSO's interest would be reduced to 5%.[1058] Other shale players followed suit.[1059] The DrillCo

---

[1057] Lisa Allen, "Danger Lurks for Debt Investors in the Oil and Gas Fields," *The Deal*, March 27, 2015, Pipeline.thedeal.com.
[1058] "LINN Energy Finalizes Strategic Alliance with GSO Partners," LINN Energy Press Release, July 6, 2015, Ir.linnenergy.com.

structure was favored by investors as a "bankruptcy remote" entity that would be separate from the producer's assets in the event of bankruptcy.

The different layers of debt that producers had been able to access in the heady days of $100 oil added complexity as well as cost to the borrower-producer's capital structure. Energy XXI, a Gulf of Mexico producer, already had a fairly complicated balance sheet. At the top of the market, it acquired EPL Oil & Gas Inc. by merger in June of 2014 with an acquisition price of $2.3 billion just before the price of oil began to fall. At the time, Energy XXI already had six tranches of debt, including its bank revolver and various unsecured public notes issued since 2010 totaling $3.4 billion.

In connection with the merger with EPL, Energy XXI issued another half-billion in public debt. It issued another $1.5 billion of second-lien debt in March of 2015, sandwiched between the senior bank revolver and its public notes.[1060] The March issuance was prompted by an anticipated major cut to its borrowing base and gave these second-lien note purchasers a jump ahead of the existing unsecured debtholders.[1061]

These financings gave some producers a lifeline, while waiting for the hoped-for rise in commodity prices. For those already smothering under the weight of too much debt, the new money was more of a continuation of life support. For those unable to attract more capital,

---

[1059] PR Newswire, "Lonestar Announces Joint Development Agreement With IOG Capital," July 28, 2015, Prnewswire.com; Globe Newswire, "Legacy Reserves LP and Funds Managed by TPG Special Situations Partners Sign Definitive Agreements to Jointly Develop Legacy's Permian Basin Acreage," July 6, 2015, Globenewswire.com.

[1060] Energy XXI Ltd, Form 10-Q Quarterly Report, filed February 2, 2016, for the period ending December 31, 2015, 46. Energy XXI's debt included: (i) a reserve based loan with a borrowing base of $1.5 billion, (ii) $750 million 9.25% senior notes issued December 17, 2010, due December 15, 2017, (iii) $250 million unsecured senior notes issued February 25, 2011, due June 15, 2019, (iv) $5.5 million 4.14% note issued September 2012 due October 2017, (v) $500 million 7.5% unsecured senior notes issued September 26, 2013, due December 15, 2021, and (vi) $400 million in 3.0% Senior Convertible Notes issued November 18, 2013 due 2018, (vii) $510 million in 8.25% Senior Notes due February 15, 2018, (viii) $650 million 6.875% Senior Notes issued May 27, 2014, due march 15, 2024, and (ix) $1.45 billion 11.0% senior secured second lien notes issued March 12, 2015, due March 15, 2020.

[1061] "Distressed O&G Investing," *The Deal*, March 30, 2015, Pipeline.thedeal.com.

the only answer was to seek the protection of bankruptcy courts in the hope of restructuring their balance sheets. By May of 2015, 10 producers had filed for protection; this would triple by August and the year ended with 48 North American producers filing bankruptcy with combined aggregate debt in excess of $17 billion.[1062] By April 14, 2016, Energy XXI, with almost $3 billion in secured and unsecured debt, would become the 63rd North American producer to file for bankruptcy.[1063]

Equity stakeholders and creditors owning first-lien, mezzanine and public bonds issued by these producers were confronted with a rude awakening. Producers had built extraordinarily complex capital structures since 2009 on the back of their properties' worth at $100 oil and now were trying to pay it back with $30 oil. This made the orderly resolution of claims much more complicated by the time their collateral had lost up to two thirds in value.

In the downturn during the '80s, oil and gas bankruptcies were resolved between a small, manageable group of stakeholders: the producer, his banker and his trade creditors. In 2015, like a dysfunctional extended family gathering at Thanksgiving dinner, the party had grown larger and more complex, rife with competing agendas between and among the stakeholders picking over the same carcass. Now, stakeholders at the table had grown to also include any one or all of these: junior secured creditors, including mezzanine lenders and private equity note-holders; holders of secured preferred shares; holders of unsecured preferred shares; and holders of convertible bonds. Especially at the bondholder level, latecomers to the party included distressed-debt buyers that had purchased the notes in the secondary market at a discount with no prior relationship with the borrower.

Further complicating restructuring a producer's debt was the phenomenon where some creditors held more than one class of debt. For example, when an involuntary bankruptcy was filed against Ener-

---

[1062] "Haynes and Boone, LLP Oil Patch Bankruptcy Monitor," Haynes and Boone, LLP, April 4, 2016, Haynesboone.com.
[1063] "Haynes and Boone, LLP Oil Patch Bankruptcy Monitor," Haynes and Boone, LLP, April 4, 2016, Haynesboone.com.

gy & Exploration Partners LLC, it had more than $27 million in trade debt, $375 million in unsecured convertible notes and $765 million of first-lien reserve-based debt. By the time ENXP converted its case to a Chapter 11, a group of the unsecured note-holders had bought into the senior secured debt. As is typical, the senior secured lenders proposed terms under which they would agree to extend credit to ENXP during the pendency of its bankruptcy.

Holding both secured debt and bonds, the "cross-over" creditors had a much different view of the best way to restructure the company than that held by the senior banks, which still held original first-lien debt. Upsetting standard protocol, the "cross-over" creditors proffered their own terms for a competing debtor-in-possession loan that were more beneficial to their unsecured debt-holdings.[1064] Given the precipitous drop in collateral value, the only hope for the out-of-the-money creditors was that the borrower could convert its debt into equity in the restructured company as it exited bankruptcy.

In many bankruptcies, bondholders were wiped out. Junior lenders were unsure of recovery. And even senior lenders were looking at possible impairment of their claims.

New Gulf Resources LLC is an example of a private-equity-sponsored independent that leveraged borrowed capital to jump into the business just before oil prices crested. In May of 2014, it raised more than $500 million to acquire a large position in East Texas. The capitalization consisted of a first-lien RBL from MidFirst Bank with a borrowing base of $50 million, $365 million in 11.75% second-lien notes due in May of 2019 and $135 million in 10%/12% senior subordinated PIK toggle notes due in November of 2019.

Prior to filing bankruptcy, New Gulf explored exchanging the junior debt under the second-lien notes and subordinated PIK notes for notes with higher-ranking seniority in the capital structure (an "up-tier" transaction) in exchange for a reduction in the face value of the junior debt. The company reported, "The debt exchange pricing and the ratios of participating noteholders necessary to provide an ade-

---

[1064] "E&P Top 10 Cases," Haynes and Boone, LLP, April 2016, Haynesboone.com.

quate recapitalization were not economically viable given the then-current price of oil and gas."[1065]

By the spring of 2016, a few producers had already exited bank-ruptcy—reorganized, shorn of most debt and with new owners hoping for brighter horizons. Whether reduction of its debt burden would be enough to permit it to survive to the other side of the lower-for-longer environment remains to be seen.

Producers that were dragged down by more complicated debt structures will be unable to reach escape velocity and will remain in a terminal orbit of intercreditor bankruptcy disputes until their assets are liquidated. No doubt, there were many more companies with billions of dollars of debt yet to file for the protection of the bankruptcy courts before the updraft of the next recovery cycle begins.

Bank Examiners

Since 2014, bank regulators had been more closely scrutinizing underwriting practices for oil- and gas-leveraged loans, publishing a new handbook on this for examiners for the first time in 25 years. The last time guidelines for evaluating oil and gas loans were revised was following the mid-'80s oil-price downturn and subsequent bank failures.

Since the housing-market fiasco and imposition of Dodd-Frank banking regulations, the last thing regulators wanted was to be called before Congress to explain how they missed the next crisis in banking. Given the increasing complexity of independents' capital structures and cognizant of the issues that arose from the shadow banking industry due to collateralized debt obligations carved out of home-mortgage loans that precipitated the 2008 financial crisis, bank regulators focused in on the rising debt obligations of oil and gas producers created by both the banks they regulated and the unregulated private- and public-debt markets.

[1065] Affidavit of Danni S. Morris, Chief Financial Officer, NGR, Declaration in Support of the Debtor's First Day Motion, "In re: New Gulf Resources, LLC, et al., Debtors," USDC Del. Case No. 15-12566 (BLS), 18.

The Federal Reserve reported in November of 2015, "Aggressive acquisition and exploration strategies from 2010 through 2014 led to increases in leverage, making many borrowers more susceptible to a protracted decline in commodity prices. ... Classified commitments—a credit rated as substandard, doubtful, or loss—among oil and gas borrowers totaled $34.2 billion, or 15 percent, of total classified commitments, compared with $6.9 billion, or 3.6 percent, in 2014."

The Fed further warned, "Because of the growing volume of special mention and classified commitments, as well as the significant growth in the leveraged lending portfolio, the agencies will continue to monitor, in particular, the associated underwriting and risk-management processes in the leveraged lending and oil and gas sectors."[1066] In particular, federal bank examiners began to focus on the total debt of the borrower and not just on the senior banks' ability to protect its depositors' money by recovering its first-lien loan. They criticized energy banks on a number of producer loans. Commercial banks appealed some of the criticized loans, but to no avail for the most part.

There was a disconnect between the new regulatory approach and the historical view taken by energy lenders. In addition to looking at a borrower's total debt—both secured and unsecured—regulators were insisting on tighter financial covenants to monitor a borrower's ability to repay. In particular, in discussions between the banks and regulators, including an in-person meeting at Wells Fargo's offices in Houston in September of 2105, regulators insisted that borrowers with a ratio of total debt to Ebitda in excess of 3.5:1 would not be given a passing rating, thus requiring greater bank reserves to be set aside.[1067]

Subsequent to this meeting, bankers and regulators continued to discuss the proper metrics for evaluating energy loans. In preparation for the annual examination in early 2016, energy banks assessed their

---

[1066] "Shared National Credits Review Notes High Credit Risk and Weaknesses Related to Leveraged Lending and Oil and Gas," Board of Governors of the Federal Reserve System, November 5, 2015, Federalreserve.gov.
[1067] OCC Bulletin 2016-9, Occ.gov.

borrowers' loans using a "total funded debt repayment test." Loans to some of the borrowers with significant unsecured public debt were downgraded accordingly.

However, following these loan downgrades, bank regulators came out with *another* set of revised guidelines for examination of oil and gas loans. In this, it appeared that the regulators stepped back from the "total funded debt repayment test." Instead the guidelines indicated that examiners and the regulated banks should evaluate a producer-borrower's ability to repay its total secured debt—not its total secured and unsecured debt.

Bankers were pleased the guidelines for repayment focused on only producer's secured debt, but questions remained. In addition to a "repayment test," the guidelines set out certain financial-ratio tests in evaluating oil and gas loans. Financial-ratio tests measured against the borrower's total debt and not just its secured debt. Whether this was intended to take back with the left hand what the regulators had given bankers with the right hand was not immediately clear.

What is clear is that, as a result of the 2016 guidelines, it will be more difficult for oil and gas producers to obtain bank financing. The impact is already being felt by producers this spring as banks apply the new guidelines in their loan policies and procedures during their spring-season borrowing-base redeterminations.

The guidelines were issued at a time when producers were in the greatest need of flexibility from their lenders on their debt obligations and in need of new bank capital due to the lower commodity-price environment. For some producers on the margins, it may mean the difference between survival and bankruptcy. Although the intent of the regulations is to protect against imprudent lending standards, the end result of the new guidelines for banks may be to cause recognition of greater production-based loan losses than has historically been the case.

High recovery rates in prior downturns were due in large part to the cyclicality of commodity prices. Loans that default at the bottom of the cycle have had a high recovery rate for first-lien lenders that exercise patience and wait for the cycle to recover rather than aggressively exercising remedies when prices are at their lowest. A bank's ability to be patient depends, in part, on what it costs it to hold onto the loan. The worse a loan is classified, the more reserves the bank must hold and, therefore, patience comes at a higher cost.

If bank regulators' new guidelines make it harder for producers to get new financing from commercial banks, this could hinder healthy producers in financing property acquisitions. Without able buyers, distressed-property sales could cause market prices for oil and gas properties to fall lower, resulting in lower loan-recovery rates for distressed producers and their lenders.

Texas endured a very slow economic recovery after the oil-price collapse of the mid-1980s. The S&L-triggered real estate bust put billions of dollars of improved and unimproved commercial properties on the market at a time when financial institutions were least able to help finance a recovery.

A longer-term effect of the guidelines may alter the relationship that has existed between independents and bankers. The new guidelines place banks at a disadvantage when competing against providers of unregulated debt. The ultimate impact is hard to predict. One possible outcome is that banks may choose to no longer compete to be first-lien lenders to producers who also owe—or plan to issue—second-lien and unsecured notes.

Certainly, producers with higher debt leverage will find it harder to get financing from regulated commercial bankers. This does not necessarily mean that oil and gas companies will be without access to borrowed capital. Restrictions imposed by the guidelines on commercial banks will create opportunities for alternative capital sources, including mezzanine lenders and private-equity sources. As a result, producers can expect to pay more for leverage going forward.

CHAPTER 10

In Conclusion

"The Stone Age came to an end, not because we had a lack of stones."
Sheikh Yamani

Sheikh Yamani, Saudi Arabia's oil minister from 1962 to 1986 during the formation and rise of OPEC, predicted the end of the oil age in an interview with *The Telegraph* in 2000. "Thirty years from now there will be a huge amount of oil - and no buyers. Oil will be left in the ground. The Stone Age came to an end, not because we had a lack of stones, and the oil age will come to an end not because we have a lack of oil."[1068]

The same observation can be made that the U.S. didn't stop using the horse and buggy because it ran out of horses. It was gasoline and the internal-combustion engine that drove demand for oil, prompting wildcatters to search for the modern *El Dorado* across the U.S. and the world.

There will come a time when a new disruptive technology will overtake oil as the primary transportation fuel, altering the Hydrocarbon Age paradigm. It is human nature, after all, to innovate, driving perpetuation of our specie. Just as in the early 2000s, as the theory of "Peak Oil" was gaining acceptance within the industry and among policymakers, U.S. producers invented the "Shale Gale," bringing a renaissance to independents and American energy independence.

[1068] Mary Fagan, "Sheikh Yamani predicts price crash as age of oil ends," *The Telegraph*, June 25, 2000.

In contrast, economist Joseph Schumpeter identified another "gale" in the 1940s. The "perennial gale of creative destruction" is the basic architecture of capitalism, he wrote. It "incessantly revolutionizes the economic structure from within, incessantly destroying the old one, incessantly creating the new one. This process of Creative Destruction is the essential fact about capitalism."[1069]

Schumpeter predicted that the same processes that enabled capitalism to succeed the pre-capitalistic framework would also eventually bring its downfall. Innovators would not only push aside "institutional deadwood," but, in the end, destroy the partners and structures upon which the foundations of capitalism were built.[1070]

The many cycles of boom and bust within the oil and gas industry seemingly validate the predicate of Schumpeter's theory. With every new discovery in the industry's early history, producers, investors and even cities went broke. Even today, the innovation that made the Shale Gale possible, resulting in a prodigious increase in U.S. oil production and setting records not seen for 40 years, has caused the bankruptcies of scores of producers and wrought the destruction of billions of dollars of invested capital.

It can be argued that Schumpeter's theory is supported by the effect of capitalistic competition for unconventional-resource acreage at unsustainable costs and the desire to spend beyond cash flow to continually increase reserves and boost stock prices. This drive for profit and market share created the tsunami of U.S. natural-gas production growth that has depressed domestic prices for the foreseeable future. This drive has also resulted in a tsunami of U.S. oil production, putting the global market off its supply/demand kilter.

But like prior cycles, contrary to Schumpeter, this is not the final chapter. Contrary to theories about the demise of the U.S. oil and gas industry, the Shale Gale is emblematic of its reinvention, resurgence and resilience. No matter what happens at the surface, the rocks stay the same. The hydrocarbons that were formed millions of years ago

---

[1069] Joseph Schumpeter, *Capitalism, Socialism, and Democracy* (1942), 83.
[1070] Schumpeter, *Capitalism, Socialism, and Democracy.*

remain, waiting to be produced by new producers with new technology that will make it possible to surface oil and gas cheaper and faster. It is only until some disruptive technology, supported by capitalistic profit motive—not central planning—creates the replacement to fuel today's horse and buggy that hydrocarbons will become the institutional deadwood of a new economy.

Innovation and ingenuity financed by private capital have been the hallmark of U.S. independent producers. From the first rudimentary bit, pounding rock to reach a shallow oil deposit near Titusville, Pennsylvania, more than 150 years ago, the industry has evolved into drilling with precision extremely complex wells down thousands of feet below the surface, turning 90 degrees and steering the bit another mile or farther through hard and dense, hydrocarbon-soaked rock.

Just two decades ago, this rock had been considered too tight to ever produce economic amounts of natural gas. That was disproven in the late 1990s by Mitchell Energy in the Barnett shale. Being a larger molecule, it was believed that it was impossible to extract economic amounts of oil out of tight rock. Lyco Energy Corp. disproved this in 2000 in the Bakken formation in Montana.[1071]

Through such innovation, the technology has changed, but the spirit and drive remains constant. It is the same spirit that drove the early wildcatter to spend his—and his banker's—last dime in search of riches just waiting to be discovered.

With each cycle, capital has been as critical as the producer's determination and his drilling rig. But this capital would never have been as readily accessible if not for the investment opportunities created and nurtured by a stable U.S. legal and regulatory environment—combined with the private ownership of minerals, which has enabled producers to negotiate directly with landowners for the permission and encouragement to drill, develop and produce oil and gas for the past 150 years.

Many countries, including many lesser developed, have equal or greater mineral wealth, but lack the economic, legal or political envi-

---

[1071] Darbonne, *The American Shales*, 48, 63.

ronment that is attractive to private investment. Many countries have stable economic and legal systems, but lack private mineral ownership that facilitates necessary local support for private development.[1072]

Only in the U.S. has there been the combination of an attractive economic environment, private mineral ownership and ready access to capital—the oxygen continuously inhaled by oil and gas producers. The independents' insatiable demand for capital has been answered time and again—by early oil capitalists, passive investors ranging from former governors to Catholic women's associations, public shareholders, local bankers, mezzanine financiers and private equity, all willing to take a calculated risk on an oil and gas wildcatter's ability to produce a valuable prize hidden underground for millennia.

The cycle repeats with each new wave of producers, bankers and other sources of capital. But the producers' and lenders' hard-learned lessons seemingly must be relearned each time. Perhaps that is the answer: It is not until the lessons from the prior circle are forgotten or discounted ("This time it's different") that the same mistakes can be repeated, beginning the cycle anew.

[1072] Bret Stephens, "The Marvel of American Resilience," *The Wall Street Journal*, December 22, 2012, in a Christmas opinion piece reflected on what a future history teacher might identify as important innovations of the early 21st century: "Why, she might ask her students, did the U.S. dominate its peers when it came to all the really big innovations? Fracking would make a good case study. The revolution happened in the U.S. not because of any great advantage in geology—China, Argentina and Algeria each has larger recoverable shale gas reserves. It didn't happen because America's big energy companies are uniquely skilled or smart or deep-pocketed: Take a look at ExxonMobil's 2004 Annual Report and you'll barely find a mention of 'fracturing' or 'horizontal' drilling. Nor, finally, did it happen because enlightened mandarins in the federal bureaucracy and national labs were peering around the corners of the future. For the most part, they were obsessing about the possibilities of cellulosic ethanol and other technological nonstarters. Instead, fracking happened in the U.S. because Americans, almost uniquely in the world, have property rights to the minerals under their yards. And because the federal government wasn't really paying attention. And because federalism allows states to do their own thing. And because against-the-grain entrepreneurs like George Mitchell and Harold Hamm couldn't be made to bow to the consensus of experts. And because our deep capital markets were willing to bet against those experts."

ACKNOWLEDGEMENTS

My wife and family have been extraordinarily patient as time took me away from them while working on this project. For their support and understanding, I am eternally grateful.

In early 2011, one of my law partners, Don Jackson, asked if I would give a presentation on energy finance later that year to the Houston Bar Association's Oil, Gas & Mineral Law Section. The date was far enough into the future that the immediacy of my acceptance seemed a minor commitment of time. Little did I know that agreeing to that presentation would turn into a five-year project, researching the history of an incredibly interesting industry, rich in stories of intrepid wildcatters and iconic energy bankers that directly fueled world events—all of which ultimately centered around an area of law in which I have been fortunate to concentrate my practice for my entire career.

This has been a project that would not have been possible, nor as rewarding, without the help of many colleagues and leaders in the oil and gas and finance industry. It has been my privilege to interview more than 40 bankers, lawyers and producers whose careers span the past 50 years and have made possible the level of energy independence and quality of life that America is able to enjoy to this day. My regret is that I was unable for this book to interview my father, who stood on the front lines of the producers' demand for capital. He passed away in 2005. I know that his experiences would have contributed a great deal more color to this history of oil capital.

I want to expressly thank for their support, encouragement and enthusiasm so many friends, law partners and clients in the industry that gave generously of their time, contacts and recollections. In particular, energy bankers Joe Bridges, Mickey Coates, Byron Cooley,

Frank Dartez, Richard Gould, John Lane, Jim McBride, Tim Murray, Tom Stephens and Dick Sylvan; law partners Terry Conner, Terry Cross, Jeff Nichols, Brad Richards, Joe Vilardo and Charles Beckham; and law professors Chris Kulander and Owen Anderson.

Opinions expressed in this book and any mistakes of facts are solely my own responsibility and nothing in this book reflects the opinion, statement or position of my firm or any of its clients.

I cannot express enough gratitude for the editorial support, advice and assistance provided by Nissa Darbonne, who scrutinized, emended and improved each of my drafts, and for my associate, Kim Mai, who kept me in line with citations of authority, beginning with my initial presentation to the Houston Bar Association when she was a summer associate up through today as a senior associate in Haynes and Boone LLP's Oil and Gas Section.

SOURCES

Interviews

—Barber, Larry, Vinson & Elkins LLP (retired), April 26, 2011.

—Beckham, Charles, Haynes and Boone LLP, April 23, 2016.

—Brasseux, Murray, BBVA Compass Bancshares Inc., May 11, 2011.

—Bridges, Joe, Bridges Family Petroleum LLC, October 2, 2012.

—Browne, Randy, Haynes and Boone LLP, May 5, 2014.

—Clarkson, Jon, First National Bank in Dallas (retired), September 17, 2014.

—Clingman, Russell, Wells Fargo Bank N.A.., March 26, 2014.

—Coates, Mickey, BOK Financial Corp., June 20, 2013.

—Cooley, Byron, Fifth Third Bancorp, March 11, 2013.

—Conner, Terry, Haynes and Boone LLP, January 30, 2016.

—Cordell, Jim, Continental Illinois National Bank & Trust Co. (retired), June 18, 2013.

—Cross, Terry, McClure & Cross LLP, January 4, 2016.

—Dartez, Frank, Bank of the Southwest (retired), March 23, 2015.

—English, John, Baker & Hostetler LLP, July 19, 2013.

—Fuller, Tom, First City Bank Houston (retired), August 31, 2012.

—Gans, Rich, Wells Fargo Bank N.A., November 1, 2013.

—Gideon, Chris, T.S. Dudley Land Co. Inc. May 6, 2014.

—Gould, Richard, Wells Fargo Bank N.A., July 29, 2013.

—Gralla, Arthur "Buzz," Amegy Bank, February 19, 2015.

—Hall, Charles, ING Group, November 17, 2013.

—Harrell, Ron, Ryder Scott Co. LP, retired, September 5, 2014.

—Hilliard, Mike, Winstead PC, April 10, 2016.

—Homier, John, Natural Gas Partners LLC, January 29, 2013.

—Hunter, Elizabeth, Société Générale SA, October 25, 2013.

—Kipp, James, Wells Fargo Bank NA.., September 7, 2012.

—Lane, John, First Tennessee Bank N.A., November 7, 2011.

—Lawrence, Frederick, IPAA, August 27, 2015.

—Marchand, Dorothy, BBVA Compass Bancshares Inc., March 22, 2016.

—McBride, James, Opportune LLP, December 23, 2015.

—McCarter, Terry, Amegy Bank, July 11, 2014 and April 5, 2016.

—Murray, Craig, Enterprise Products Partners LP, April 26, 2011.

—Murray, John, Amegy Bank, July 11, 2014, and April 5, 2016.

—Murray, Tim, Benefit Street Partners LLC, April 21, 2011.

—Nichols, Jeff, Haynes and Boone LLP, October 1, 2015.

—Richards, Brad, Haynes and Boone LLP, February 2, 2016.
—Sears, Larry, Amegy Bank, July 11, 2014 and April 5, 2016.
—Snyder, Martin, Toronto-Dominion Bank, January 8, 2014.
—Sorrells, Gordon, GS Energy Advisors, April 7, 2016.
—Steinsberger, Nick, Republic Energy Inc., October 2, 2104.
—Stevens, Tom, First City Bancorp of Texas Inc. (retired), October 12, 2012.
—Sylvan, Dick, BBVA Compass Bancshares Inc., March 6, 2013, March 28, 2014, and March 22, 2016.
—Trimble, Jim, Tanda Resources LLC, March 2, 2016.
—Vilardo, Joe, Haynes and Boone LLP, March 1, 2016.
—Wagner, Robert, First City Bancorp of Texas Inc. (retired), March 15, 2012.
—Whitener, Tom, Jr., Energy Spectrum Capital, July 29, 2014.
—Wiener, Will, Wells Fargo Bank N.A., May 12, 2011.

Cases

—*Amazon Petroleum Corporation v. Railroad Commission of Texas et al.* 5 F. Supp. 633. 634-637 (E.D. Tex. 1934)
—*Barnard v. Monongahela Natural Gas Company*, 216 Pa. 362, 365, 63 A. 801, 802 (1907)
—*Benedict v. Ratner*, 268 US 353 (1924)
—*Brown v. Humble Oil & Refining Company*, 126 Tex. 296, 83 S.W.2d 935, on rehearing 87 S.W. 2d 1069 (Tex. 1935)
—*Bury v. Pope*, 1 Cro. Eliz., 78 Eng. Rep. (Ex. 1586)
—*Champlin Refining Company v. Corporation Commission of Oklahoma*, 286 U.S. 210 (1932)
—*Comm'r v. Fleming*, 82 F.2d 324 (5th Cir. 1936)
—*Constantin et al. v. Lon Smith et al.*, 57 F.2d 227 (E.D.Tex. 1932)
—*Cowan v Hardeman*, 26 Tex. 217, 222 (Tex. 1862)
—*Cox v. Robison*, 105 Tex. 426 (Tex. 1912)
—*Danciger Oil & Refining Co. of Texas et al. v. Smith et al.*, 4 F. Supp. 236 (N.D. Tex. 1933)
—*Dupree v. Quinn*, 290 S.W. 2d 329 (Tex. Civ. App. 1956)
—*F. Groos & Co. v. Chittim*, 100 S.W. 1006, 1011 (Tex. Civ. App. 1907, no writ)
—*FDIC v. Bodin Concrete Co.*, 869 S.W. 2d 372, 377 (Tex. App. – Dallas 1993, writ denied)
—*FDIC v. Eagle Properties, Ltd., et al*, 664 F. Supp. 1027 (US D W. Dist, Midland-Odessa Division 1985)
—*FDIC v. Wood*, 758 F.2d 156, 160 (6th Cir. 1985)
—*First National Bank of Commerce v. Zarafonetis*, 15 S.W. 2d 155, 156 (Tex. Civ. App. 1929), writ of error refused
—*First v. Byrne*, 28 N.W, 2d 509 (Iowa Sup. Ct., 1947)
—*Frank v. United States*, 220 F. 2d 559, 562 (10th Cir. 1955)

Sources

—*Freiburg v Magale*, 7 S.W. 684 (Tex. Sup. Ct. 1888)

—*Frost-Johnson Lumber Co. v. Salling's Heirs*, 150 La. 756, 836, 91, So. 207, 235 (1920)

—*Garey v. Rufus Lillard Co.*, 1945 OK 305, 165 P.2d 344 (Ok S. Ct, 1945)

—*Griswold v. The President of the United States*, 82 F. 2d 922 (5th Cir. 1936)

—*In re Cornerstone E & P Company, L.P.*, 436 B.R. 830 (Bankr.N.D.Tex. 2010)

—*In re Delta Petroleum Corporation, et al.* (U.S. Del. Bankruptcy Court, Case No. 11-14006)

—*In re Lothian Oil, Inc.* (Bankr.W.D.Tex. Dec. 17, 2008)

—*In re Semcrude, L.P.* 399 B.R. 388, (Bankr. D. Del., 2009), aff'd 428 B.R. 590 (D.Del.2010)

—*In re Tri-Union Development Corp.*, 253 B.R. 808, 811 (Bankr. S.D. Tex 2000)

—*In re: New Gulf Resources, LLC, et al., Debtors*, USDC Del. Case No. 15-12566 (BLS)

—*In re: SemCrude, L.P., et al.*, Case No. 08-11525 (Bankr.D.Del. 2008)

—*Kelly v. Ohio Oil Co.*, 57 Ohio St. 317, 49 N.E. 399 (1897)

—*Kier v. Peterson*, 41 Pa. 357 (1862)

—*Leist v Simplot*, 638 F. 2d. 283 (2nd Cir., 1980)

—*Leonard v. Prater*, 18 SW2d 681 (Tex.Civ.App. 1929)

—*Lilly v. Conservation Commissioner of Louisiana*, 29 F. Supp. 892 (E.D. La. 1939)

—*MacMillan et al. v. Railroad Commission of Texas et al.*, 51 F.2d 400, 404-405 (W.D. Tex. 1931)

—*Mallon Resources Corp. v. Midland Bank, PLC, New York Branch*, 1997 WL 403450 (S.D.N.Y. 1997)

—*Matter of Village Properties, Ltd*, 723 F.2d 441 (5th Cir.) cert. denied, *Wolters Village Ltd. v. Village Properties, Ltd.*, 104 S. Ct. 2350 (1984)

—*Medina Oil Development Co. v. Murphy*, 233 S.W. 333, 335 (Tex. Civ. App. 1921)

—*Michaels Building Co. v. Ameritrust Company, N.A.*, 848 F.2d 674, 676 n.2 (6th Cir. 1988).

—*Michalson v Nutting*, 275 Mass. 232, 175 N.E. 490, 77 A.L.R. 1109 (1931)

—*Mitchell Energy Corporation v. Bartlett*, 958 S.W.2d 430 (Tex.Civ.Ap—Ft.Worth 1997)

—*Moore v. Smaw and Fremont v. Flower*, 17 Cal. 199 (Cal. 1861)

—*NGP Capital Resources Co. v. ATP Oil & Gas Corp. (In re ATP Oil & Gas Corp.)*, No. 12-3443, 2014 (Bankr. S.D. Tex. January 6, 2014)

—*People's Gas Co. v. Tyner*, 131 Ind. 277, 31 N.E. 59 (1892)

—*Phillips Petroleum Co. v. Wisconsin*, 347 U.S. 672 (1954)

—*Pierson v. Post*, 3 Cai. R. 175, 2 Am. Dec. 264 (N.Y. 1805)

—*Queen v. The Earl of Northumberland*, 1 Plowden, 75 Eng. Rep. (1567)

—*Quinn v. Dupree*, 303 S.W.2d 769, 773 (Tex. 1957)

—*Railroad Commission v. Flour Bluff Oil Co.*, 219 S.W. 2d 506 (Tex. Civ. App. 1949) error ref'd.

—*Railroad Commission v. Rowan Oil Co.*, 259 S.W. 2d 173 (1953)

—*Railroad Commission v. Shell Oil Co.*, 206 S.W. 2d 235 (1947)

—*Reagan v. Murphy*, 235 La. 529, 105 So.2d 210, 217 (La. 1958)

—Richbell Information Services, Inc. v. Jupiter Partners, L.P., 309 A.D.2d 288, 302, 765 N.Y.S.2d 575, 587 (Sup. Ct., App. Div. 2003)

—Standard Oil Co. of Texas v. Marshall, 265 F. 2d 46 (5ᵗʰ Cir. 1959)

—State v. Parker, 61 Tex. 265 (Tex. Civ. App. 1884)

—State v. Thrift Oil & Gas Co., 162 La. 165, 110 So. 188 (La. 1926)

—States v. Quintana Petroleum Co., 133 S.W.2d 112 (Tex. 1939)

—Stephens Co. v Mid-Kansas Oil & Gas Co., 113 Tex. 160, 254 S.W. 290 (1923)

—Taylor v. Brennan, 621 S.W2d 592 (Tex. 1981)

—Tennant v. Dunn, 110 S.W.2d 53 (Texas 1937)

—Texas American Bancshares, Inc. et al., v Robert Logan Clarke, Comptroller of the Currency, 740 F. Supp 1243 (U.S. District Court, N.D. Texas Dallas Div., 1990), 954 F. 2d 329 (U.S. 5ᵗʰ Cir. 1992)

—Texas Pacific Coal and Oil Co. v. Comanche Duke Oil Co., 274 S.W. 193, 194 (Tex. Civ. App. 1925) (rev'd).

—The Pfanenstiel Company, LLC v. Independent Bank, Cause No. DC-16-00601, District Court, Dallas, Texas, filed January 20, 2016

—Thompson v. Consolidated Gas Utilities Corp., 300 U.S. 55 (1937)

—Trustees for Alaska v. Alaska, 736 P.2d 324, 335-6 (Alaska 1987)

—U.S. v. Midwest Oil Co., 236 U.S. 459 (1915)

—United States v. Maryland Bank & Trust Co., 632 F. Supp. 573, 579 (D. Md. 1986)

—United States v. Mirabile, 15 *Envtl. L. Rep.* (Envtl. L. Inst.) 20,992 (E.D. Pa. Sept. 4, 1985)

—Victoria Bank & Trust Co. v. Brady, 779 S.W.2d 893, 902 (Tex. App.-Corpus Christi 1989), rev'd on other grounds, 811 S.W. 2d 931

—Westmoreland & Cambria Natural Gas Co. v. De Witt, 130 Pa. 235, 18 A. 724, 725 (Pa 1889)

—Wood County Petroleum Co. v. West Virginia Transportation Co., 28 W. Va. 210 (1886)

Laws, Records & Interpretations

Federal

—Act of March 3, 1807 (Authorizing the Sale of the Northwest Territory), Ch. 46, Sections 2-4, 2 Stat. 445 (1807).

—Asset Conservation Act of 1966 (42 U.S.C.A. Section 9601(20)(E)-(G).

—Bank Secrecy Act and Anti-Money Laundering, 31 U.S.C. 5318(i) effective July 23, 2002.

—Bankruptcy Code §541.

—Clean Water Act of 1972, 33 U.S.C. §§1251-1387.

—Comprehensive Environmental Response, Compensation, and Liability Act, 42. U.S.C. §§ 9601-9675.

—Connally Hot Oil Act 15 U.S.C. § 715 (2000).

—Electronic Signatures in Global and National Commerce Act, Pub.L. 106-299, 114 Stat. 464, 15 U.S.C. ch. 96 (enacted June 30, 2000).

Sources

—*Emergency Economic Stabilization Act of 2008* (Pub. Law No.:110-343).

—*Flood Disaster Protection Act of 1973*, as amended (42 U.S.C. 4001--4129).

—*Garn-St Germain Depository Institutions Act of 1982*, Public Law 97-320.

—*Homestead Act of 1862*, 43 U.S.C. Sections 161 et seq. (repealed 1976).

—Internal Revenue Code § 337.

—*Mineral Leasing Act*, Ch. 85, 41 Stat. 437 (1920) (codified and amended in 30 U.S.C. Sections 181-287 (1982)).

—*Natural Gas Act of 1938*, 15 U.S.C.§§717.

—*National Flood Insurance Act of 1968.* 42 USC § 4129 (2011).

—OCC Interpretive Letter No. 462 (December 19, 1988), *reprinted in* Fed. Banking Law Rep. (CCH) ¶ 85,686.

—OCC Interpretive Letter No. 725 (May 10, 1996), *reprinted in* 1995-1996 Transfer Binder Fed. Banking L. Rep. (CCH) ¶ 81,040.

—OCC Letter from Horace G. Sneed, Senior Attorney, Legal Advisory Services Division (March 2, 1992) (unpublished).

—OCC Letter from J. Michael Shepherd, Senior Deputy Comptroller, Corporate and Economic Programs (July 7, 1988) (unpublished).

—OCC Letter from Jimmy F. Barton, Deputy Comptroller Multinational Banking, to Carl Howard, Associate General Counsel, Citibank, N.A. (May 13, 1992) (unpublished).

—OCC No-Objection Letter No. 87-5 (July 20, 1987), *reprinted in* [1988 - 1989 Transfer Binder] Fed. Banking L. Rep. (CCH) ¶ 84,034.

—OCC No-Objection Letter No. 90-1 (February 16, 1990), *reprinted in* [1989-1990 Transfer Binder] Fed. Banking L. Rep. (CCH) ¶ 83,095.

—*Oil Pollution Act of 1990*, 33 U.S.C. §§2701-2761.

—*Omnibus Trade and Competitiveness Act of 1988*, P.L. 100-418.

—*Safe Drinking Water Act of 1974*, 42 U.S.C. §§ 300f-300j.

—*Stock Raising Homestead Act*, 43 U.S.C. Sections 291-301 (repealed 1976).

—Uniting and Strengthening America by Providing Appropriate Tools Required to Intercept and Obstruct Terrorism Act of 2001 ("PATRIOT ACT"), Pub. L. No. 107-56, 115 Stat. 272.

Spain

—*Reales Ordenanzas para la Direccion, Regimen i Gobierno del Importante Cuerpo de la Mineria de Nueva-Espana, i de su Real Tribunal General*, De Orden De Su Magestad (1783), tit. 5 art. 2.

—Royal Ordinances, May 22, 1783, for the Direction, Regulation, and Government of the Important Body of Mining of New Spain, promulgated by Carlos III, King of Spain.

Texas

—*Act of 1840 January 20, 1840*, (Adoption of Common Law) Republic of Texas.

—Acts 1986, 69th Leg., 2nd C.S., ch. 14, at 71(Texas Interstate Banking Law).

—Acts 26th Tex. Lg. Reg. Session, 1899, Ch. 49, p.8 (Conservation of Natural Gas).

—Texas Constitution of 1876, Article XIV, Section 7 (Release of Minerals to Surface Owner).

—*General Preemption Act of 1841*, Ch. 16, Section 1, 5 Stat. 453 (1841).

—*Relinquishment Act*, (Act of July 31, 1919, Laws 36th Leg., 2nd Called Session, ch. 81, p. 249) Rev. Stats., arts. 5367-5382.

—*Sales and Leasing Act of 1931*, House Bill 358. Acts 42nd Leg., Reg.Ses., Ch. 271.

—Tex. Bus. & Com. Code § 9.319(a)(1991).

—Tex. Nat. Res. Code Ann. Section 111.013 (Control of Pipelines)(Vernon 1978) (original version at 1917 Tex. Gen. Laws, ch. 30, Tex. Rev. Civ. Stat. art. 6019 (Vernon 1962)). February 20, 1917.

—Tex. Nat. Res. Code Ann. Section 81.051 (Vernon 1978) (Commission Jurisdiction)(original version at 1919 Tex. Gen. Laws, ch. 155, Tex. Gen. Civ. Stat. art. 6023 (Vernon 1962)).

—Tex. Bus. & Com. Code, Section 35.02 (Filing of Utility Security Instruments with Secretary of State).

—*Uniform Electronic Transactions Act*, Tex.Bus.Comm.Code Title 10, Subtitle B, Chapter 322, Section 322.007.

Other States

—*Act of 1915*, Okla. Laws 1915, c. 197; Okla. Stat. tit. 52, c.3.

—Article 519 of the Civil Code (Wildlife in enclosures), see La. Civ. Code Ann. art. 3415 (West 2011).

—Article 753 of the Louisiana Civil Code of 1870 (Trapping, Hunting, or Fishing on Preserve).

—Commercial Laws, Secured Transactions, Louisiana R.S. 10:9-101.

—*Digest of the Civil Law Now in Force in the Territory of Orleans*. Article 9, Chapter I, Title II.

—Louisiana Mineral Code,1974 La. Acts No. 50; La.R.S. 31:1 et seq.

—*Town Lot Drilling Act*, Cal. Stat. 1931, c.586.

Public Property Records

—Deed of Trust and Chattel Mortgage from Richardson Oils Inc. to Great Southern Life Insurance Co., August 22, 1938, recorded in Deed of Trust Records Vol. 8, p. 24, Winkler County, Texas.

—Release from Bank of Manhattan Co. in favor of Richardson Oils Inc. and S.W. Richardson, August 26, 1938, recorded in Vol. 4, p. 262, Winkler County, Texas.

—Release from Bank of the Manhattan Co. in favor of Richardson Oils Inc., January 31, 1949, recorded Vol. 6, p. 444, Winkler County, Texas.

Books, Papers, Presentations, SEC Filings, Press Releases & Articles

Sources

—"A Dream Dies in Texas, Once a Land of Unlimited Promise, the Lone Star State Has Lost its Shine and Now has a Barrel of Troubles," *People* (November 10, 1986).

—"Alta Mesa Holdings Completes Acquisition of Meridian," *Oil & Gas Financial Journal*, May 14, 2010.

—"Ausam, Noram File for Chapter 11 Bankruptcy Protection," Rigzone.com, December 30, 2008.

—"Bank Failures in Brief," FDIC, Fdic.gov.

—"Banking's Dry Hole," *Newsweek*, April 14, 1986.

—"Brief History," Organization of the Petroleum Exporting Countries, Opec.org.

—"Burying Mother; Oil Woes Break a Texas Bank," *Time* (October 24, 1983).

—"CDX Gas Defaults on Credit Agreement, Files for Bankruptcy," Bloomberg, December 13, 2008.

—"Continental Illinois' Most Embarrassing Year," *BusinessWeek*, October 11, 1982.

—"Distressed O&G Investing," *The Deal*, March 30, 2015.

—"Dominion Ups Marcellus Shale Acreage Price with Antero Resources," Rigzone.com, September 24, 2008.

—"Drilling Location and Oil Wells Across Texas," Texas-drilling.com.

—"E&P Top 10 Cases," Haynes and Boone, LLP, April 2016.

—"Edge Petroleum to Sell Most Assets, Files for Chapter 11," *Oil & Gas Financial Journal*, October 5, 2009.

—"Energy Lender Price Survey Q1 2015," Macquarie Tristone.

—"Energy Lenders' Price Decks," *Oil and Gas Investor*, December 1, 2008.

—"Financial Turmoil Cuts into Antero's Marcellus Shale Plans," *Daily GPI, Natural Gas Intelligence*, September 25, 2008, Naturalgasintel.com.

—"Foreign Banks Bring Global Links to Houston," Federal Reserve Bank of Dallas, Houston Branch, March 1997.

—"Fractured finances, America's shale-energy industry has a future. Many shale firms do not," *The Economist*, July 4, 2015.

—"Haynes and Boone Oil Field Bankruptcy Tracker," Haynes and Boone, LLP, March 1, 2016.

—"Haynes and Boone, Borrowing Base Redeterminations," Haynes and Boone, LLP, September 18, 2015.

—"Haynes and Boone, LLP Oil Patch Bankruptcy Monitor," Haynes and Boone, LLP.

—"History of 'Big Inch' and 'Little Big Inch' Pipelines Now on Display," Dukeenergy.com.

—"History of IPAA," IPAA, Ipaa.org.

—"History of the CFTC: US Futures Trading and Regulation Before the Creation of the CFTC," Cftc.gov.

—"History: 175 Years," Baker Botts, Bakerbotts.com.

—"JPMorgan Chase Acquires Banking Operations of Washington Mutual," FDIC Press Release, September 25, 2008.

—"Laggard Loans," *Oil & Gas Journal*, March 31, 2000.

—"Legacy Reserves LP and Funds Managed by TPG Special Situations Partners Sign Definitive Agreements to Jointly Develop Legacy's Permian Basin Acreage," Globe Newswire, July 6, 2015.

—"LINN Energy Finalizes Strategic Alliance with GSO Partners," LINN Energy Press Release, July 6, 2015.

—"Lonestar Announces Joint Development Agreement With IOG Capital," PR Newswire, July 28, 2015;

—"LSTA," Lsta.org.

—"New E&P Money-Mall Hours," *Oil and Gas Investor*, November 1, 2008.

—"OPEC 166th Meeting concludes," Organization of the Petroleum Exporting Countries, Opec.org.

—"Penn Square Bank, Maverick Oil Lender," *American Banker*, April 26, 1982.

—"Prime Rate History," FedPrimeRate.com.

—"Reversing the Trend," *The Wall Street Journal*, May 19, 2014.

—"Santa Rita No. 1," Board for Lease of University Lands, University of Texas System.

—"Saratoga Files For Chapter 11 Protection, Cites Hurricane Damage And Lowered Energy Prices As Causes Source," *Oil and Gas Investor*, April 1, 2009.

—"Shared National Credits Review Notes High Credit Risk and Weaknesses Related to Leveraged Lending and Oil and Gas," Board of Governors of the Federal Reserve System, November 5, 2015.

—"Simmons Morning Energy Note," Simmons & Co. International Inc., November 26, 2014.

—"Simmons Morning Energy Note," Simmons & Co. International Inc., January 5, 2015.

—"Solich Takes More Stock, Less Cash, To Close Forest Deal," *Oil and Gas Investor*, October 1, 2008.

—"Superfund," United States Environmental Protection Agency, Epa.gov.

—"The Dodd-Frank act: Too big not to fail," *The Economist*, February 18, 2012.

—"The History of Regulation," Natural Gas Supply Association, Naturalgas.org.

—"The Oil Wars," Texas State Library Archives, Tsl.state.tx.us.

—"The ups and downs of Arkansas' natural gas production," *Talk Business & Politics*, March 6, 2009.

—"Treasury Announces Guaranty Program for Money Market Funds," U.S. Department of the Treasury, September 19, 20018.

—"TXCO Resources Files Voluntary Bankruptcy Petition Under Chapter 11," TXCO Resources Inc., Form 8-K, May 18, 2009.

—"TXCO Resources Reports Record Results and Earnings," TXCO Resources Inc., Form 8-K, August 8, 2008.

—"TXCO Resources, Inc. Recovery for all Secured and Unsecured Lenders," *FTI Consulting*, Fticonsulting.com.

—"Wells Fargo Energy Capital Presentation on Mezzanine Debt Markets," IPAA Capital Markets Conference 2004.

Sources

—Ahmed, Nabila and Sridhar Natarajan, "Junk Bonds Backing Shale Boom Facing $11.6 Billion Loss," Bloomberg, December 1, 2014.

—Alaska Oil and Gas Association, "Member Companies." Aoga.org.

—Allen, Lisa, "Danger Lurks for Debt Investors in the Oil and Gas Fields," *The Deal*, March 27, 2015.

—Amann, Leslie Kiefer, "A Survey of Transfer and Ownership Law for Trustees," Texas Bankers Association Wealth Management and Trust Division, Graduate Trust School, July 18, 2007.

—Baker Hughes Drilling Rig Report, US NG Rig Count.

—Banc Paribas Credit Facility, 1997.

—Bank of Oklahoma, internal bank-communication materials, provided by Mickey Coates.

—Baptiste, Lou-Ann and Gerald Lewis, *Mineral Rights in Trinidad and Tobago: Issues, Challenges and Recommendations*, Land Conference 2011 Conference Theme, The University of The West Indies at St. Augustine, Trinidad and Tobago (2011).

—Barras, Mary Lucia and Houston Daniel, "Constitutional Convention of 1974," *Handbook of Texas Online*, Texas State Historical Association.

—Barth, James R., *The Great Savings and Loan Debacle* (Aei Pr, 1991).

—Beard, Lucile Silvey, "The History of the East Texas Oil Field" (Hardin-Simmons University, June 1938).

—Beatty, John R.A., "Selected Problems in Oil and Gas Financing," 11 *Rocky Mt. Min. L. Inst.* (1966).

—Bernstein, Alan et al., "Houston & Oil: The Feast, The Famine, The Future," *Houston Chronicle*, June 2, 1985.

—Blackstone, William, *Commentaries on the Laws of England*, Vol. 2 (Oxford 1766).

—Bloomberg, "US European Bank Write-downs and Losses," November 5, 2009.

—Boatright, Mody C., "E.P. Matteson, Pioneers in Texas Oil, An Oral History," *Dolph Briscoe Center for American History, The University of Texas at Austin* (Austin, Texas, July 22, 1953).

—Boone, Michael M., "Structuring and Documenting the Oil and Gas Loan," paper presented at the Third Annual Banking Law Institute, March 14, 1980).

—Brandenberger, B.J., "Transaction Activity vs. Nymex," *Oil and Gas Investor*, March 1, 2009.

—Brennan, Richard S., "Current Trends in Oil and Gas Financing," 25 *Rocky Mt. Min. L. Inst.* (1979).

—Bryant, Martin, "20 years ago today, the World Wide Web opened to the public," TNW, August 6, 2011, Thenextweb.com.

—Burrough, Bryan, *The Big Rich: The Rise and Fall of the Greatest Texas Oil Fortunes* (Penguin Books, 2009).

—Butler & Binion, *Environmental Law Simplified: A Practical Guide for Oil and Gas Operations* (Pennwell Corp., February 1993).

—Campbell, Eloise, "La Sal Del Rey," *Handbook of Texas Online*, Texas State Historical Association.

—Capehart, Mary Ann, "Drought Diminishes Hydropower Capacity in Western U.S.," *Water Resources Research Center*, Wrrc.arizona.edu.

—Chang, Ellen, "Term B Loans," *Here's the Money: Capital Formation 2007, Special Supplement to Oil and Gas Investor*, May 2007.

—Chargeable Acreage by Lessee Summary, Department of Oil and Gas, State of Alaska.

—Christian, C. Stephen, "Introduction to Commercial Bank and Non-Bank Institutional Financing In The Minerals Industry," *Mineral Financing* (1982), Section 2-18.

—Churchill, Winston, speech before the House of Commons, November 11, 1947.

—Clark, B.F., Jr., "Convergence of Capital," *Oil & Gas Financial Journal*, March 2006.

—Clark, James A. and Michel T. Halbouty, *Spindletop* (Random House, 1952).

—Clark, Scott, "Banks Made Oil Bash Possible, Now Share Hangover," *Houston Chronicle*, June 2, 1985.

—*Clarks' Security Transactions Monthly* (Matthew Bender & Company, Inc., Vol. 25, June 2009).

—Clouser, Gary, "Banker's Roundtable," *Here's the Money: Capital Formation 2009, Special Supplement to Oil and Gas Investor*, June 2009.

—Clouser, Gary, "Bankers' Buzz - Plenty of bank capital available for growth-hungry E&Ps," *Oil and Gas Investor*, August 2013.

—Clouser, Gary, "More than Plenty," *Here's the Money: Capital Formation 2007, Special Supplement to Oil and Gas Investor*, May 2007.

—Clouser, Gary, "Regional Credit No Problem," *Here's the Money: Capital Formation 2008, Special Supplement to Oil and Gas Investor*, May 2008.

—Cochran, F.B., "Financing with Oil and Gas Derivatives," *41 Rocky Mtn, Min. L. Inst.* (July 21, 1995).

—Cooper, Christopher, "Oil Patch Braces for Losses Amid Price Slump, Mergers," *The Wall Street Journal*, September 11, 1998.

—Cross, Terry I., "Oil and Gas Product Liens - Statutory Security Interests for Producers and Royalty Owners under the Statutes of Kansas, New Mexico, Oklahoma, Texas and Wyoming," *50 Consumer. Fin. L.Q. Rep.* 418 (1996).

—Cross, Terry I., "Statutory Contractor Liens Against Mineral Property," Dallas Bar Association – Energy Law Section, Review of Oil and Gas Law XXX, Dallas, Texas, August 27-28, 2015.

—Cross, Terry I., "Structuring and Documenting Oil and Gas Financing Transactions, Part Two," *Texas Oil and Gas Law Journal*, (Butterworth Legal Publishers, Austin Texas) Volume 6, No. 4 (1992).

—Crum, Lawrence L., "Banks and Banking," *Handbook of Texas Online*, Texas State Historical Association.

—Currriden, Mark and Natalie Posgate, "Capital Drying Up for Oil, Gas," *Dallas Morning News*, November 30, 2015.

—Daggett, Harriet Spiller, *Mineral rights in Louisiana* (Louisiana State University Press, 1949).

Sources

—Daintith, Terence, *Finders Keepers? How the Law of Capture Shaped the World Oil Industry* (Routledge, August 31, 2010).

—Darbonne, Nissa, "A Major E&P Capital Provider, Enron is Busy With Its Own Finances," *Oil and Gas Investor*, January 30, 2002.

—Darbonne, Nissa, "Capital Asset Envy," *Oil and Gas Investor*, April 1, 2009.

—Darbonne, Nissa, "Game-Changers, 1981-2011," *Oil and Gas Investor*, August 2011.

—Darbonne, Nissa, "Lessons Learned Offered From the 'Zone of Insolvency,'" *Oil and Gas Investor*, March 1, 2010.

—Darbonne, Nissa, "Where Art Thou Mezzanine Financier?," *Oil and Gas Investor*, June 4, 2002.

—Darbonne, Nissa, *The American Shales* (CreateSpace, April 30, 2014).

—Dartez, Frank, "Risk Analysis in Non Recourse Petroleum Lending," Graduate School of Credit and Financial Management, Stanford University, July 1969.

—Dash, Eric, "If It's Too Big to Fail, Is It Too Big to Exist?" *The New York Times*, June 20, 2009.

—David, Amiel and James Kipp, "Risk Factors in Oil and Gas Lending—New Alternatives," *Journal of Petroleum Technology* 1490 (December 1991).

—David, Amiel, PeTech Enterprises, IAEE/IELE Conference, Houston Texas December 11, 2003.

—Davis, Carolyn, "Domino Effect of Lower Oil/Gas E&P Capex Now Hitting Offshore, Midstream," *NGO Shale Daily*, January 9, 2015.

—DavisPolk, "Dodd-Frank Progress Report, Fourth Quarter 2015," Davispolk.com.

—Denbury Resources Press Release, October 8, 2008.

—Diamond, Stuart, "Setting Crude Prices in the Pits," *The New York Times*, December 9, 1984.

—Doan, Lynn and Dan Murtaugh, "U.S. Shale Fracklog Triples as Drillers Keep Oil From Market," *Bloomberg Business*, April 23, 2015.

—Eaton, Collin, "Bank loan standards bending for oil companies amid shale rush," FuelFix, May 22, 2014.

—Elliot, Katherine and Charles A. Gullick, et al., ed., *The papers of Mirabeau Buonaparte Lamar*, Vol. II (Austin, Tex., A.C. Baldwin, printers 1921-27).

—Ellis, Grover, Jr., "Production Payments and Other Trends in Petroleum Financing," Graduate School of Banking, Rutgers University, June 1955.

—Ely, Northcutt and Robert F. Pietrowski, Jr., "Changing Concepts in the World's Mineral Development Laws," paper presented at the IBA Seminar on World Energy Laws, Stavanger, Norway, May 1975 London: International Bar Association.

—Emergency Oil and Gas Guaranteed Loan Board, 13 CFR Chapter V. CFR Vol. 64, No. 207, October 27, 1999.

—Energy XXI Ltd, Form 10-Q, February 2, 2016.

—Fagan, Mary, "Sheikh Yamani predicts price crash as age of oil ends," *The Telegraph*, June 25, 2000.

—Fagin, K. Marshall and W.T. Drummond, "Life Insurance Company Loans On Oil & Gas Properties," 1 *Journal of the Society of Petroleum Evaluation Engineers* (1968-69).

—FDIC, OCC and FRS Joint News Release, "Regulators Announce Approval of Acquisition of Subsidiary Banks of First Republic Bank Corporation, Dallas, Texas, by NCNB Corporation, Charlotte, North Carolina," PR-148-88 (July 29, 1988).

—Federal Deposit Insurance Corporation. Division of Research and Statistics (FDIC), *History of the Eighties – Lessons for the Future* (Washington, DC: Federal Deposit Insurance Corporation, 1997).

—Federal Reserve Bank of St. Louis, Economic Research, Research.stlouisfed.org.

—Fehrenbach, T.R., *Lone Star: A History of Texas and the Texans* (Open Road Media: April 1, 2014).

—Ferris, Shauna, "How to Destabilize the Financial System: A Beginner's Guide," *Variance* 4:1, 2010.

—Financial Crisis Inquiry Commission (FCIC), *The Financial Crisis Inquiry Report, Authorized Edition: Final Report of the National Commission on the Causes of the Financial and Economic Crisis in the United States* (Public Affairs, January 2011).

—Fisher, Kevin and Elizabeth Muratet, "The Aftermath of Penn Square Bank: Protecting Loan Participants from Setoffs," 18 *Tulsa L.J.* 261 (1982).

—Fitzpatrick, J.C., "Land Ordinance of 1785, May 20, 1785," *Journals of Continental Congress*, Vol. 28 (Fitzpatrick ed., 1933).

—Fleming, Jeff and Barbara Ostdiek, *The Impact of Energy Derivatives on the Crude Oil Market* (The James A Baker III Institute for Public Policy of Rice University, April 7, 1998).

—Florence, Russ (ed.) "Banknotes: The Trailblazer," *BOK Financial Employee Weekly*, undated internal bank communication materials, Bank of Oklahoma.

—Foshee, Page S., "'Someone get the Governor an Aspirin:' Ross Sterling and Martial Law in East Texas," *East Texas Historical Journal*, Vol. 41, Issue 2 Article 5 October 2003.

—Foss, Michelle Michot, et al., "Sharp Cycles Ahead," *Oil and Gas Investor*, September 1, 2013.

—Frankel, P., *Essentials of Petroleum: A Key to Oil Economics* (Cass, 1969).

—Franks, Kenny A., "Hot Oil Controversy," *Encyclopedia of Oklahoma History and Culture*, Okhistory.org.

—Fratianni, Michele and Francesco Marchionne, "The Role of Banks in the Subprime Financial Crises," April 10, 2009. Papers.ssrn.com.

—Freidman, Nicole, "What Went Wrong in Oil-Price Forecasts?" *The Wall Street Journal*, December 10, 2015.

—Givens, Natalie and Han Zhao, "The Barnett Shale: Not so Simple After All," Republic Energy Inc., Republicenergy.com.

—Gold, Russell, *The Boom: How Fracking Ignited the American Energy Revolution and Changed the World* (Simon & Schuster, April 8, 2014).

Sources

—Goodman, Leah McGrath, *The Asylum: The Renegades Who Hijacked the World's Oil Market* (William Morrow, February 15, 2011).

—Gose, John A and Aleana W. Harris, "Deed of Trust, Its Origin, History and Development in the United States and in the State of Washington," *Real Property, Probate and Trust* (Summer 2005).

—Gramlich, Edward, "Loan Guarantee Programs," speech before the National Economists Club, Washington, D.C., April 24, 2003, Federalreserve.gov.

—Grant, Joseph M. Grant, *The Great Texas Banking Crash: An Insider's Account* (University of Texas Press, 1996).

—Gray, Richard M., "Debt Buybacks, Defaulting Lenders and Libor Market Disruption," *LSTA Loan Market Chronicle*, 2009.

—Grinstead, Cynthia, "The Effect of Texas U.C.C. Section 9.319 on Oil and Gas Secured Transactions," 63 *Tx. L. Rev.* 311, 322 (1984).

—Gueymard, A.G., "The Seventies-An Era of Transition For Petroleum & Minerals Financing," 17 *Rocky Mt. Min L. Inst.* 557 (1972).

—Haines, Leslie and William Pike, *America's Independents: From Black Gold to Diamond Jubilee, the 75th Anniversary of IPAA* (Hart Energy Publishing, LP, 2004).

—Haines, Leslie, "Banker Up," *Oil and Gas Investor*, April 29, 2004.

—Haines, Leslie, "Counterparty and Hedging Risks Grow," *Oil and Gas Investor*, July 29, 2008, Oilandgasinvestor.com.

—Hardwicke, Robert E., "Legal History of Conservation of Oil in Texas," *Legal History of Conservation of Oil and Gas: A Symposium* (Chicago: American Bar Association, 1938).

—Harrell, Ron, "Reserve Estimations for Business Decisions – Almost a Century of Progress in Creating Reserve Definitions," paper presented in Muscat, Oman, March 26-28, 2007.

—Harrison, Sylvia L., "Disposition of the Mineral Estate on United States Public Lands: A Historical Perspective," 10 *Pub. Land L. Rev.* 131 (1989).

—Hawkins, Wallace, *El Sal del Rey* (Texas State Historical Association, 1947).

—Hayes, Thomas C., "Abboud Out as Chief at Houston's First City," *The New York Times*, March 27, 1991.

—Hefner, Robert A., III, "The United States of Gas, Why the Shale Revolution Could Have Happened Only in America," *Foreign Affairs* 93(3) (May/June 2014).

—Heintz, J., "Production Payments and Other Energy Financing Alternatives," paper presented at the Rocky Mountain Mineral Law Foundation Institute "Oil and Gas Acquisition," November 1995).

—Helman, Christopher, "Inside The Semgroup Bust," *Forbes*, July 28, 2008.

—Helman, Christopher, "Who Will Get Caught When the Oil Debt Bubble Pops?" *Forbes*, December 19, 2014.

—Hertz, David B., "Risk Analysis in Capital Investments," *Harvard Business Review*, January/February 1964.

—Hicks, Doug, *Nearly Forgotten, The Amazing Story of the Glenn Pool, Oklahoma's First World-Class Oil Field* (Schnake Turnbo Frank, Inc., 2005).

—Hill, G.C., "Losses from Penn Square Bank Failures Total to $1.2 Billion and are Still Growing," *The Wall Street Journal*, April 12, 1984.

—Hinton, Diana D. and Roger M. Olien, *Oil in Texas: The Gusher Age, 1895-1945* (Clifton and Shirley Caldwell Texas Heritage, March 15, 2002).

—Hobson, Margaret Kriz, "Alaska Moves to Reclaim Part of ANWR from Federal Government," *E&E Energy Wire Newsletter*, October 20, 2014.

—Hunt, Russell F., "A Banker's Viewpoint on … Oil Loans," *The Independents' I.P.A. of A. Monthly*, January, 1953.

—Hurt, Harry, III, "The Most Powerful Texans," *Texas Monthly*, April 1976.

—Hutchins, Jeffrey D., "What Exactly is a Loan Participation?" 9 *Rutgers-Camden L.J.* 447 (1978).

—Isaac, William M., *Senseless Panic, How Washington Failed America* (Wiley, 2010), 145.

—Jickling, Mark, Coordinator Specialist in Public Finance, Government and Finance Division, "The Enron Collapse: An Overview of Financial Issues," *Congressional Research Service, The Library of Congress* (March 28, 2002).

—Johnson, Hubert Dee, "Legal Aspects of Oil and Gas Financing," *Institute on Oil and Gas Law* (1958).

—Jon Hughes, "Mile High Capital," *Oil and Gas Investor*, July 1, 2008.

—Kaplan, David A., "Unique Feature in Oil and Gas Reserve-Based Lending Facilities Can Increase Companies' Default Risk," *Standard & Poor's Ratings Services*, May 1, 2012.

—Kaplan, David A., et al., "Despite Risks, We Expect Excellent Recovery on Most Reserve-Based Lending Facilities of E&P Companies," *Standard & Poor's Ratings Services* 2 (January 18, 2013).

—Kearns, Jeff, "The Fed Eases Off," Bloomberg QuickTake, September 16, 2015.

—Kemp, John, "How Saudi Arabia successfully defended its U.S. oil market share: Kemp," Reuters, February 1, 2016.

—Kent, Sarah and Daniel Fitzpatrick, "J.P. Morgan to sell Commodities Business for $3.5 Billion," *The Wall Street Journal*, March 19, 2014.

—Khodadad, Nabil, "Trends in Financing Mining and Oil and Gas Projects," International Mining and Oil and Gas Law, Development and Investment, April 2009.

—King, Pamela, "Workforce: Not all oil industry segments suffer equally as prices slide," *Energywire*, January 26, 2015.

—Kingswell-Smith, Charles, presentation to IPAA Private Capital Conference, January 16, 2008.

—Kirgis, Frederic L., "Financing an Oil Venture," 1959 *U. Ill. F.* 459 (1959).

—Krauss, Clifford and James C. McKinley, Jr., "Hurricane Damage Extensive in Texas," *The New York Times*, September 13, 2008.

—Kutchin, Joseph W., *How Mitchell Energy & Development Corp. Got its Start and How it Grew: An Oral History and Narrative Overview* (Universal Publishers, 1998).

—Lacy, John C., "The Historic Origins of the U.S. Mining Laws and Proposals for Change," 10 *Nat. Resources & Env't* 13 (Summer 1995).

—Land, Paul E., "Cal Canal Gas Field," *California Department of Conservation, Division of Oil & Gas, Publication no. T26S* (Division of Oil & Gas 1983).

Sources

—Landers, Jim, "Economy Drains Small Texas Oil Firms," *Dallas Morning News*, March 31, 1982

—Leavenworth, Geoffrey, "Big Texas Banks Vie for Energy Loans," *Texas Business*, December, 1979.

—Leverett, Dr. Flynt testimony before U.S. Senate Committee on Energy and Natural Resources, January 10, 2007.

—Lewis, George R., *The stannaries: a Study of the Medieval Tin Miners of Cornwall and Devon* (D. Bradford Barton Ltd., 1965; reprint of 1908 publication).

—Loan Syndications & Trading Association, Primary Market Committee Model Credit Agreement Provisions 2011, August 2011.

—Lorusso, Mike, "Lending in a Boom Market," *Oil & Gas Financial Journal*, August 11, 2014.

—Love, Ben, *My Life in Texas Commerce* (Texas A&M University Press: 2005).

—Lowe, John and Owen Anderson, Ernest Smith and Christopher Kulander, *Cases and Material on Oil and Gas Law*, 6th Ed. (West, 2013).

—Macquarie Tristone Energy Lender Price Survey, Q3, 2014.

—Maginnis, John T., "Financing Oil and Gas Development," 15, *The Business Lawyer* 693 (April 1960).

—Malavis, Nicholas, *Bless the Pure & Humble: Texas Lawyers and Oil Regulation, 1919-1936* (Texas A&M University Press; 1st edition, 1996).

—Mallon Resources Corp. 8-K for June 15, 1995, Ex. 1.

—Mannino, Edward F., *Lender Liability and Banking Litigation* (ALM Properties, Inc., Law Journal Press, 1989).

—Marcosson, Isaac F., *Black Golconda, Romance of Petroleum* (Harper & Brothers, 1924).

—Markham, Jerry W., *A Financial History of the United States: From Christopher Columbus to the Robber Barons (1492-1900)* (M.E. Sharpe, 2002).

—Martin, Douglas, "Michel Halbouty, Oilman of Legend, Dies at 95," *The New York Times*, November 14, 2004.

—Martin, Patrick and J. Lanier Yeates, "Louisiana and Texas Oil & Gas Law: An Overview of the Differences," 52 *La. L. Rev.* 769 (March 1992).

—Masterson, Carlos B., "Severance of the Mineral Estate by Grant of Land and by the Sovereign and Adverse Possession," 30 *Tex. L. Rev.* 323 (1952).

—Maultsby, Vance K., Jr., "Overview of Mineral Financing, Conference on Mineral Financing," paper presented at the Rocky Mountain Mineral Law Foundation, November 1982.

—McElvaney, Eugene, "Some Aspects of Financing Oil and Gas Transactions," *Fifth Annual Institute on Oil and Gas Law and Taxation as it Affects the Oil and Gas Industry, Southwestern Legal Foundation* (1954).

—McElvaney, Eugene, letter to W.A. Kirkland, August 14, 1934.

—McElvaney, Eugene, letter to W.A. Kirkland, August 22, 1935.

—McKellar, James W., "Oil and Gas Financing, 'How It Works,'" paper presented at the 32nd Annual E.E. Smith Oil, Gas & Mineral Law Institute, March 31, 2006.

—Mecoy, Don, "Crusader Energy Group Inc. defaults on loan, files for bankruptcy," NewsOK.com, March 31, 2009.

—Miller, Thomas Lloyd, *The Public Lands of Texas, 1519-1970* (Norman: University of Oklahoma Press, 1972).

—Mitchell Energy & Development Corp., "Mitchell Completes Work Force Reduction, Sets Capital Budget," PR Newswire, Feb. 22, 1999.

—Mont, Joe, "Three Years In, Dodd-Frank Deadlines Missed As Page Count Rises," *Compliance Week*, July 22, 2013.

—Monteith, Edward E., Jr., "Financial Criteria Of Oil And Gas Lending, Institute," *Oil and Gas Law* (1966).

—Moody's Investors Service Inc., "Recoveries More Certain for Senior Debt Holders in Oil and Gas," January 17, 2013.

—Moon, Chris, "Kansas Oil Producers to Recoup Millions with SemGroup Plan," *Wichita Business Journal*, September 27, 2009.

—Morris, John, "Banks of Mid-America Treads Water, Waits for Cheap Oil to Subside," *American Banker* (April 30, 1986).

—Mullen, J. Thomas, "The Future of Bank Financing of the Oil and Gas Industry," paper presented at Eastern Mineral Law Foundation, 9th Institute, May, 1988.

—Mullen, Thomas, et al., "An Introduction to Legal Documentation Used in Bank Financings for the Oil and Gas Industry," paper presented at the Rocky Mountain Mineral Law Foundation, November 1982).

—Murray, Tim, "The Ins and Outs of Mezzanine," *Here's the Money: Capital Formation 2007, Special Supplement to Oil and Gas Investor*, May 2007, 31.

—Murray, Tim, presentation at 2005 IPAA OGIS Private Capital Conference, April 18, 2005.

—National Conference of State Legislatures Fiscal Affairs Program, September, 2012.

—Nelson, Grant S. and Dale A. Whitman, *Real Estate Finance Law* (5th ed.), § 1.6 (Thompson West: 2010).

—Newman, Kara, *The Secret Financial Life of Food: From Commodities Markets to Supermarkets* (Columbia University Press, December 4, 2012).

—Nichols, Jeff and Kim Mai, "The Regulation of Swaps and Derivatives and its Impact on Business after Dodd-Frank," paper presented at State Bar of Texas 11th Annual Advanced Business Law Course, November 7-8, 2013.

—Niles, Hezekiah, et al., *Niles Weekly Register, Volume 50* (The University of Chicago Libraries, April 9, 1836).

—Nolan, John M., et al. "Texas Annotated Promissory Note," Advanced Real Estate Law Course 2001, Dallas, June 20-22, 2001.

—Nordin, D. Sven, *Rich Harvest: A History of the Grange, 1867–1900* (University Press of Mississippi: 1974).

—O'Keefe, John, "The Texas Banking Crisis Causes and Consequences 1980-1989," FDIC Division of Research and Statistics, July 1990.

—OCC Bulletin 2016-9.

Sources

—Office of the Comptroller of the Currency, "Oil and Gas Production Lending," Comptroller's Handbook (April 2014).

—Olien, Roger M. and Diana Davids Hinton, *Wildcatters: Texas Independent Oilmen* (Texas A&M University Press, May 24, 2007). (Original, 1984 edition identifies Hinton as Diana Davids Olien.)

—Olien, Roger M., "Oil and Gas Industry," *Handbook of Texas Online*, Texas State Historical Association.

—Ottinger, Patrick, "From the Courts to the Code: the Origin and Development of the Law of Louisiana on Mineral Rights," 1 *LSU J. of Energy L. & Resources* 6 (2012).

—Owens, W.A., "Pioneers In Texas Oil," *Dolph Briscoe Center for American History, The University of Texas at Austin* (Austin, Texas, July 22, 1953).

—Palmer, Jerrell Dean and John G. Johnson, "Big Inch and Little Big Inch," *Handbook of Texas Online*, Texas State Historical Association.

—Payne, Stephen, "Edge Hires Parkman Whaling To Assist In Paying Credit Facility Deficit," *Oil and Gas Investor*, January 16, 2009.

—Pierobon, Jim, "George P. Mitchell: Founder of Shale Gas Here's How He and His Team Did It," *The Energy Fix*, August 5, 2013.

—Pirog, Robert, *The Role of National Oil Companies in the International Oil Market*, CRS Report for Congress (August 21, 2007).

—Pizzo, Stephen, et al., *Inside Job: The Looting of America's Savings and Loans* (McGraw-Hill, 1989).

—Plummber, F.B. and E.C. Sargent, "Underground Waters and Subsurface Temperatures of the Woodbine Sand in Northeast Texas," The University of Texas Bulletin, No. 3138, October 8, 1931.

—Price, K., D. Gonsoulin and Jason Fox, "Reserve Based Finance: A Tale of Two Markets – Part 2," *Oil & Gas Financial Journal*, February 2014.

—Price, Kevin, et al., "Reserve Based Lending Markets: From Projects to Borrowing Bases," *Oil & Gas Financial Journal*, August 1, 2006.

—Prindle, David F., *Petroleum Politics and the Texas Railroad Commission* (University of Texas Press, Austin, 1981).

—Quillen, Kimberly, "Energy Partners files Chapter 11 bankruptcy," *The Times-Picayune*, May 1, 2009.

—Quinion, Michael, "Wild Strike," *World Wide Words, Investigating the English Language Across the Globe*, quoting the *Rutland Herald*, March 20, 1838.

—Randazzo, Sara, "Oil Downturn Sends Texas Law Firm Packing," *The Wall Street Journal*, November 27, 2015.

—Reddy, Sumathi, "The 20% Who Spread the Most Disease," *The Wall Street Journal*, December 15, 2014.

—Reifenberg, Anne, "Crude Oil Futures to Hold New Options," *Dallas Morning News*, November 9, 1986.

—Reinhold, Robert, "U.S. Helps Texas Survive Death of Bank," *The New York Times*, October 14, 1984.

—Renewal Promissory Note dated March 10, 1982, from Murchison Brothers to First National Bank in Dallas.

—Richards, William R., Thomas A. Mitchell and Michael S. Johnson, *"Oil and Gas Conservation in Utah After* Cowling: *The Law of Capture Receives a New Lease on Life,"* 14 J. Energy Nat. Resources & Envtl. L. 1, 1994, (quoting Symposium, *"Legal History of Conservation of Oil and Gas,"* Min. L. Section of the A.B.A. 233 (1938))).

—Richardson, Scott, "Volatility Presents Opportunity," presentation to Houston Energy Finance Group, February 17, 2016.

—Rintoul, William, *Drilling Through Time, 75 years with California's Division of Oil and Gas* (California Division of Oil and Gas, 1990).

—Rippy, Merrill, *Oil and the Mexican Revolution* (Leiden, Netherlands, E. J. Brill, 1972).

—Rivas, Claudia Perez, "Tekoil Files For Bankruptcy," *Upstream,* June 11, 2008.

—Robinson, William Wilcox, *Land In California: The Story of Mission Lands, Ranchos, Squatters, Mining Claims, Railroad Grants, Land Scrip, Homesteads* (University of California Press, 1979).

—Romanov, Jane Fleck and James L. Irish, "An Overview Of Sources Of Capital And Structuring Investments In Oil And Gas," 34 *Rocky Mt. Min. L. Inst.* (1988): Section 13.26.

—Rowan, R., "The Swinger Who Broke Penn Square Bank," *Fortune,* August 23, 1982.

—Sachse, Harry S., "A Comparison of the Landowner's Rights to Petroleum in France and Louisiana," 23 *La. L. Rev.* 722 (1963).

—Sawers, Brian, "The Right to Exclude From Unimproved Land," 83 *Temple Law Review* 665 (2011).

—Schafer, E.W., "Computer Time-Sharing and the Petroleum Evaluation Engineer," 3 *Journal Of the Society Of Petroleum Evaluation Engineers* (January 1970).

—Scheid, Brian, et al., "US crude production to rise to 9.3 million b/d in 2015: EIA," Platts, March 10, 2015.

—Schumpeter, Joseph, *Capitalism, Socialism, and Democracy* (1942).

—Scott, John R., "Some Aspects of Oil and Gas Financing," *Fifth Annual Institute on Oil and Gas Law and Taxation as it Affects the Oil and Gas Industry, Southwestern Legal Foundation* (1954).

—Sellers, Steven M., "Lawyers go Green," *American Association for Justice,* 2013 Westlaw 49-Jan JTLA TRIALA 22 (Reuters).

—Shamel, Charles H., "Mining, Mineral and Geological Law," *The Making of the Modern Law: Legal Treatises* (Gale, Making of Modern Law, December 17, 2010), (quoting 1383 Law of Don Alonzo XI).

—Shearer, Robert, "Oil and Gas Lending – the Borrower's Perspective," paper presented at 26th Annual E.E. Smith Oil, Gas & Mineral Law Institute, March 31, 2000.

—Sheehan, Chris, "Margins Pressure Energy Uplift," *Oil and Gas Investor,* February 2014.

—Sheehan, Chris, "Mezzanine Moves," *Oil and Gas Investor,* February 1, 2013.

—Shell Oil Co. lease, Dan Harrison III, DrillingInfo.com.

Sources

—Sherman, Josh and Sean Clements, Opportune LLP, "Capital Availability for E&Ps," *Oil & Gas Financial Journal,* June 9, 2015.

—Sherrod, Gerald E., "What Makes Those Bank Engineers So Conservative," 1 *Journal of the Society of Petroleum Evaluation Engineers* (1968-69).

—Singer, Mark, *Funny Money* (Knopf: May 12, 1985), 146.

—Smith, Cameron, "Plenty of Private Capital Available- to the Right Type Companies," *Oil and Gas Investor,* September 4, 2002.

—Smith, Griffin, Jr., "Empires of Paper," *Texas Monthly,* November 1973.

—Smith, Julia Cauble, "Panhandle Field," *Handbook of Texas Online,* Texas State Historical Association.

—Smith, Julia Cauble, "Santa Rita Oil Well," *Handbook of Texas Online,* Texas State Historical Association.

—Snow, Nick, "The VPP Option - It's Back," *Here's the Money: Capital Formation 2004, Oil and Gas Investor,* May 2004.

—Sorkin, Andrew Ross, "As Credit Crisis Spiraled, Alarm Led to Action," *The New York Times,* October 1, 2008.

—Standard & Poor's Ratings Services, "Despite Risks, We Expect Excellent Recovery on Most Reserve-Based Lending Facilities of E&P Companies," January 18, 2013.

—Standard & Poor's Ratings Services, "Utilities & Perspectives, Global Utilities Rating Service," Vol. 11, No. 43 (October 28, 2002).

—Standard & Poor's, "S&P's Default And Recovery Analysis Of U.S. Oil And Gas E&P Sector Provides Implications For The Future," March 26, 2006.

—Steinberg, Julie, "Falling Oil Prices Worry Regional-Bank Investors," *The Wall Street Journal,* January 21, 2016.

—Stell, Jeannie, "Banking Up," *Oil and Gas Investor,* September 6, 2007.

—Stell, Jeannie, "Distressed Finance," *Oil and Gas Investor,* March 1, 2009.

—Stephens, Bret, "The Marvel of American Resilience," *The Wall Street Journal,* December 22, 2012.

—Stevens, Thomas G., "Current Developments in Petroleum Financing," 23 *Journal of Petroleum Technology* 202, (1971).

—Steward, Dan, "The Shale Gas Miracle: A Tribute to George P. Mitchell," presented at the Academy of Medicine, Engineering and Science of Texas, January 12, 2012 Annual Conference "Energy for Life," Houston, Texas.

—Steward, Dan, *The Barnett Shale Play: Phoenix of the Fort Worth Basin: A History* (The Fort Worth Geological Society, 2007).

—Stockwell, Oliver, "The Boundaries of the State of Louisiana," 42 *La. L. Rev.* 1043 (Spring 1982).

—Strohl, Paul E., "Gas Into Gold: The New Alchemy of Financing Oil and Gas Acquisitions in the 1990s," 39 *Rocky Mt. Min. L. Inst.* 16-1 (1993).

—Sturngold, James, "Merc Leaves Potatoes Behind," *The New York Times,* February 10, 1986.

—Summers, W.L., "Property in Oil and Gas," 29 *Yale Law Journal* 174 (1919).

—Talbot, Kurt A., presentation to IPAA Private Capital Conference.

—Taylor, Bertie, "Capital Markets Outlook: The Road Ahead," *Oil and Gas Investor*, August 1, 2010.

—Taylor, Bertie, "Mitigating Risk," *Oil and Gas Investor*, April 1, 2010.

—Terry, Lyon F. and Kenneth E. Hill, "Valuation of Oil and Gas Producing Properties for Loan Purposes," paper presented at Annual Meeting of Petroleum Branch, American Institute of Mining and Metallurgical Engineers, 1953.

—Terry, Lyon F., "Bankers Like to Do Business with Oil Men," *The Oil and Gas Journal* (November 21, 1955).

—Texas State Library and Archives Commission, "Introduction," Tsl.texas.gov.

—The American Law Institute, Past and Present ALI Projects, Ali.org.

—The American Oil & Gas Historical Society, "End of Oil Exchanges," Aoghs.org.

—The Avalon Project, Documents in Law, History and Diplomacy. "The First Charter of Virginia; April 10, 1610." Yale Law School, Lillian Goldman Law Library.

—*The Big Inch and the Little Inch Pipelines, The Most Amazing Government-Industry Cooperation Ever Achieved*, Texas Eastern Transmission Corporation (Tetco), (May 2000).

—The Meridian Resource Corp., Form 8-K, April 13, 2009.

—*The Oil Bank for Oil Men*, Bank of Oklahoma, internal publication, c.1990.

—*The Pittsburgh Press*, November 21, 1931.

—Thompson, Elmo, letter to W.A. Kirkland, August 25, 1934.

—Thompson, Ernest O., "Flare Gas Wastage in Texas: Steps Taken to Utilize," speech to the American Gas Association, May 1, 1947, Texas State Archives, Railroad Commission Collection.

—Thompson, R. Elmo, "Legal And Other Aspects of Financing The Oil Industry," 3 *Rocky Mt. Min. L. Inst.* (1957).

—Toal, Brian A., "Big Deals," *Here's the Money: Capital Formation 2004, Special Supplement to Oil and Gas Investor*, May 2004.

—Toal, Brian A., "Capital Malls," *Oil and Gas Investor*, April 29, 2000.

—Toal, Brian A., "Credit Where Credit Is Due," *Oil and Gas Investor*, April 1988.

—Toal, Brian A., "Focused On Yield," *Oil and Gas Investor*, April 29, 2005.

—Toal, Brian A., "Lending Trends," *Oil and Gas Investor*, January 1, 2008.

—Toal, Brian A., "Regional Bankers Court Borrowers," *Oil and Gas Investor*, November 4, 2002.

—Toal, Brian A., "Rising Credit Tide," *Here's the Money: Capital Formation 2007, Special Supplement to Oil and Gas Investor*, May 2007.

—Toon, Steve, "Who Put Out The Fire? Banks Soften On Killer Borrowing-Base Redeterminations For E&Ps," May 4, 2009.

—TXCO Resources Inc., Form 8-K, May 13, 2009.

—U.S. Energy Information Administration, Independent Statistics & Analysis.

—U.S. General Accounting Office, *Financial Audit: Resolution Trust Corporation's 1995 and 1994 Financial Statements*, Report to the Congress, July 1996.

Sources

—U.S. Senate, Seventy-Ninth Congress, Second Session, *Hearings before a Special Committee Investigating Petroleum Resources* (Washington D.C.; U.S. Government Printing Office, 1946).

—United States Dept. of State, *State Papers and Correspondence Bearing upon the Purchase of the Territory of Louisiana* (Washington, Govt. Print Office, 1903)

—Vaughan, Vicki, "TXCO nearing bankruptcy," *Express-News* (San Antonio), May 13, 2009.

—Vollaro, Daniel, "Lincoln, Stowe, and the 'Little Woman/Great War' Story: the Making and Breaking, of a Great American Anecdote," *Journal of the Abraham Lincoln Association* (2009), Vol. 30.

—Voorhees, James D., "Financing Oil and Gas Operations on Credit Mortgages and Liens," 5 *Rocky Mt. Min. L. Inst.* (1960).

—Wagner, Bob and David Johnson, "Debt Wars," *Oil and Gas Investor*, May 1, 2009.

—Walker, A.W., "Fee Simple Ownership of Oil and Gas in Texas," 6 *Tex. L. Rev.* 125 (1928).

—Wallace, Wilson, Continental Illinois National Bank & Trust Company of Chicago, "Bank Financing of Oil and Gas Production Payments," paper presented to the Faculty of the Southwestern Graduate School of Banking, Dallas, Texas, July 1962).

—Warner, C.A., "Texas and the Oil Industry," *The Southwestern Historical Quarterly*, 50, No. 1 (July 1946).

—Weidner, William, "Mezzanine Capital Flows Appear to be Changing," *Oil and Gas Investor*, June 4, 2002.

—Weidner, William, "Private Capital Flow," *Oil and Gas Investor*, March 14, 2008.

—Williams, Howard R. and Charles J. Meyers, et al., *Williams and Meyers, Manual of Oil and Gas Terms, Fourth (4th) Edition* (Matthew Bender, 1976).

—Williams, Howard R. and Charles J. Meyers, *Oil and Gas Law*, 1 Sections 203.1 and 204.4 (1988).

—Williams, James L., WTRG Economics, "Oil Price History and Analysis," Wtrg.com.

—Williamson, Harold F., *The American Petroleum Industry: The age of energy, 1899-1959* (Northwestern University Press, 1963).

—Wilson, Wallace, "Determination of Loan Value," internal bank memoranda, Continental Illinois Bank and Trust, June 1967.

—Wolfson, Martin H., *Financial Crises: Understanding the Postwar U.S. Experience* (M E Sharpe Inc, June 30, 1986).

—Wolters, General Brigadier Jacob F. to Governor R.S. Sterling, 14 October, 1931, Records of Ross S. Sterling, Texas Office of the Governor, Archives and Information Services Division, Texas State Library and Archives.

—Yale, Gregory, *Legal Titles to Mining Claims & Water Rights in California under the Mining Law of Congress of July, 1866* (1867).

—Yergin, Daniel, *The Prize: The Epic Quest for Oil, Money & Power* (Simon & Schuster, January 15, 1991).

—Yergin, Daniel, *The Quest: Energy, Security, and the Remaking of the Modern World* (Penguin Books: September 20, 2011).

—Zuckerman, Gregory, *The Frackers: The Outrageous Inside Story of the New Billionaires* (Portfolio, November 5, 2013).

—Zweig, Phillip L., *Belly Up: The Collapse of the Penn Square Bank* (Ballantine Books, August 12, 1986).

INDEX

413

Index

Index

Index

Index

Index

Index

Relinquishment Act of 1919 (Texas), 24
Republic Bank (Midland), 255
Republic National (Dallas), 96, 102, 108, 122, 137, 143, 196, 230, 238, 281, 297
Res communes, 8
Res extra patrimonium, 8
Res nullius, 8, 33
Res publicae, 8
Reserves, *proved*, 133-134, 169, 173, 179, 205, 213, 224, 284-285, 287, 295, 305, 331, 352-353, 364, 366, 373; *probable*, 134, 168, 366; *possible*, 134, 287, 366
Resource Conservation and Recovery Act of 1976, 209
Rhabdomancy, 46
Richards, Brad, 256
Richardson Oils Inc., 147, 149
Richardson, Sid, 101, 103, 148-149
Richbell Information Services, Inc. v. Jupiter Partners, L.P., 182
Ricker, Rupert, 47
Rig loans, 235
Rimco/Resource Investors Management Co., 280, 282
Robinson, W.W., 29
Rockefeller, Andrews & Flagler, 264
Rockefeller, John D., 42-43, 264
Rocky Mountain Mineral Law Foundation, 260
Rogan, Charles, 23
Roosevelt, President Franklin, 82, 84
Royal Bank of Scotland (RBS), 318, 360, 363
RPI Institutional Services, 282
Rubin, Robert, 304
Rucks, Billy, 276
Rule 37, 73-74, 87-88
Rule of capture, 56, 58-60, 66-67, 69, 83, 94
Ryder Scott Co. LP, 127

S.H. Griffin No. 4, 325-326
Sachse, Harry S., 33, 37
Safe Drinking Water Act of 1974, 209
Sales and Leasing Act of 1931, 24
Salomon Smith Barney, 301
Salt dome trap, 53-54
Sanders, Judge Barefoot, 251-252
Santa Rita No. 1, 47-49, 325
Sanwa Bank, 256
Saratoga Resources Inc., 351
Saudi Arabia, 193, 219-220, 236, 268, 319, 371, 385
Savings & Loans (S&Ls), 201, 240-245, 251, 340, 366, 384
Sawers, Brian, 59
Schafer, E.W., 185-186
Schroeder, Scott, 294
Schumpeter, Joseph, 311, 386
Scotia Bank/Scotiabank, 257, 367
Scott, John, 102, 122
Seagrams Distillers, 112
Sealy, John, 72
Seattle-First National Bank (SeaFirst), 228-229, 297
Second National Bank, 139
Section 29 federal income-tax credits, 290
Security Pacific, 297
Seeligson Field, 93
Seidman, Bill, 251-252
Selectric, 187
SemGroup LP, 208, 334-336
Seminole Field, 80
September 11, 2001, 312, 318-319
Seven Sisters, 306
Seven Year War, 31
Seward's Folly, 18
Shale, 2, 3, 38, 172, 205, 290, 321, 324, 326-327, 329, 332-333, 341, 345-346, 351, 353, 356-359, 363-364, 366, 368, 370-371, 373, 377, 385-388; *Bakken*, 358-359, 370, 387; *Barnett*, 321, 324-328, 346, 351, 359, 387; *Eagle Ford*,

Index

427

Index

ABOUT THE AUTHOR

Bernard F. (Buddy) Clark, Jr. grew up in Houston, Texas, well aware of the needs producers face for capital. As chief financial officer for Mitchell Energy & Development Corp. for 45 years, his father was often flying to New York and Chicago to meet with commercial and investment bankers for funds to finance Mitchell Energy's constant need of capital.

Following graduation from University of Texas Law School in 1982, Clark joined the established Houston oil and gas firm of Butler & Binion LLP as a member of its energy-finance group, working with producers and bankers, principally Allied Bank of Texas and its successors, First Interstate and Wells Fargo, as well as with the FSLIC in the late 1980s in its takeover of Dallas-based S&Ls. Clark was also special counsel to the **Emergency Oil and Gas Guaranteed Loan Board** in 1999-2000.

In 1999, he joined the Houston office of national law firm Haynes and Boone LLP where he chairs the firm's energy practice.

Praise for *Oil Capital*

"Mr. Clark's book **should be required reading** for finance professionals in the energy business. He **explains a century of evolution** that allowed U.S. independents in the past decade to scale up tight oil and gas production and transform the global energy market."
—Bill White, Senior Advisor, Lazard Ltd.;
Formerly U.S. Deputy Secretary of Energy and
Mayor of Houston

"*Oil Capital* is a **well told and thoroughly researched** history of the evolving relationship between American oil and gas producers and their lenders. Mr. Clark's legal training and 30 years of experience in petroleum finance give him a unique ability to crystallize this only-in-America story. This book is **a must read** and will remain an authoritative reference for serious students of oil and gas finance."
—Owen L. Anderson, Professor and Distinguished
Oil and Gas Scholar, The University of Texas School of Law, and
Kuntz Chair Emeritus and Cross Research Professor Emeritus,
The University of Oklahoma College of Law

"Mr. Clark **comprehensively explores** the symbiotic relationship between petroleum independents and their critically needed bankers **with a fascinating look** from the oil industry's earliest days through to today's transformational shale revolution."
—Tom Petrie, Chairman, Petrie Partners LLC, and
Author, *Following Oil: Four Decades of Cycle-Testing Experiences and What They Foretell about U.S. Energy Independence*

"Mr. Clark's **fast-paced, keenly interesting** *Oil Capital* is the first book to tell the whole story of the intrepid wildcatters and the methodical bankers to whom they turn to satisfy their insatiable need for capital. It gets to the heart of a leading reason why America continues to be among the largest suppliers of oil and gas in the world: energy finance. Told with a deep understanding of financial markets, corporate law and the oil business, *Oil Capital* **belongs in the collection of anyone interested in American energy.**"
—Chris Kulander, Ph.D., Director, Oil & Gas Law Institute,
South Texas College of Law

"**In colorful prose**, Mr. Clark aptly chronicles the love/hate relationship among energy bankers and their E&P clients … who are always ready to '**inhale capital**.'"

—Arthur L. Smith, President, Triple Double Advisors LLC;
Retired Chairman and CEO, John S. Herold Inc.; and
Author, *Something from Nothing: Joe B. Foster and the People Who Built Newfield Exploration Company*

"Understanding how the American oil and gas industry has evolved and thrived provides **rich and essential understanding** of how and why it will continue to redefine what is possible toward fueling a new century of quality of life. *Oil Capital* contains the secrets of generations of U.S. wildcatters' financial success and is *the* **capital playbook** for this and future generations of explorers."

—Nissa Darbonne, Author, *The American Shales*, and
Editor-at-Large, *Oil and Gas Investor*

"*Oil Capital* is the definitive book on the history and evolution of financing the oil and gas industry by one of the foremost experts active in the business. This book **should be read** by anyone involved **in the industry**."

—Tim Murray, Managing Director and
Head of Energy Origination,
Benefit Street Partners LLC

CPSIA information can be obtained at www.ICGtesting.com
Printed in the USA
LVOW08*2139230516

489599LV00003B/3/P